YOUTH, CRIME, AND JUSTICE

LEARNING THROUGH CASES

ERIKA GEBO
SUFFOLK UNIVERSITY

CAROLYN BOYES-WATSON
SUFFOLK UNIVERSITY

ROWMAN & LITTLEFIELD

LANHAM · BOULDER · NEW YORK · LONDON

Senior Editor: Sarah Stanton
Assistant Editor: Carli Hansen
Senior Marketing Manager: Kim Lyons
Interior Designer: Kathy Mrozek
Cover Designer: Sally Rinehart

Published by Rowman & Littlefield
A wholly owned subsidiary of The Rowman & Littlefield Publishing Group, Inc.
4501 Forbes Boulevard, Suite 200, Lanham, Maryland 20706
www.rowman.com

Unit A, Whitacre Mews, 26-34 Stannary Street, London SE11 4AB, United Kingdom

British Library Cataloguing in Publication Information Available

Library of Congress Cataloging-in-Publication Data
Names: Gebo, Erika, author. | Boyes-Watson, Carolyn, author.
Title: Youth, crime, and justice : learning through cases / Erika Gebo, Suffolk
    University, Carolyn Boyes-Watson, Suffolk University.
Description: Lanham : Rowman & Littlefield, [2018] | Includes bibliographical
    references and index.
Identifiers: LCCN 2017024055 (print) | LCCN 2017037368 (ebook) |
    ISBN 9781442237469 (electronic) | ISBN 9781442237445 (cloth : alk. paper) |
    ISBN 9781442237452 (pbk. : alk. paper)
Subjects: LCSH: Juvenile delinquency—Case studies. | Problem youth—
    Case studies. | Juvenile justice, Administration of—Case studies.
Classification: LCC HV9069 (ebook) | LCC HV9069 .G395 2018 (print) |
    DDC 364.36—dc23
LC record available at https://lccn.loc.gov/2017024055

∞™ The paper used in this publication meets the minimum requirements of American National Standard for Information Sciences—Permanence of Paper for Printed Library Materials, ANSI/NISO Z39.48-1992.

Printed in the United States of America

CONTENTS

Youth, Crime, and Justice: Learning Through Cases is an innovative textbook designed to serve as a primary text for courses in juvenile delinquency / juvenile justice; youth crime / gangs; youth and society; childhood / adolescent development; youth violence prevention; and youth in conflict with the law. This comprehensive textbook adopts a youth-development perspective that unifies the content and provides a holistic way to think about juvenile justice and delinquency grounded in what we know about youth in American society.

Youth, Crime, and Justice: Learning Through Cases covers the historical evolution of the juvenile justice system along with the core developmental institutions in modern society charged with the socialization, nurturance, guidance, and regulation of children and youth, including child welfare, schools, and the juvenile system. Adopting a life course perspective, the textbook examines the changing legal, social, regulatory, and political landscape of childhood and adolescence in American society, with consistent focus on dynamics of race, class, ethnicity, gender, power, and privilege. The lens of intersectionality reinforces the dynamic interactions of situated social positions and multiple marginalities that shape the life experiences of youth as they navigate toward adulthood.

A primary focus of the textbook is to examine what we know about "what works" (and what doesn't work) to prevent and intervene in delinquency. Scientific advancement, especially with regard to adolescent brain development, has reasserted the basic premise that youth are indeed different from adults. Yet we know that positive youth development is not applied for all youth: Race, ethnicity, class, gender, geography, power, and privilege shape the reality of juvenile justice and our treatment of youth within American society.

The textbook is divided into three sections encompassing the major areas of study for youth, crime, and justice. **Part I: Foundations of Youth, Crime, and Justice** examines the historical landscape of societal development of the concept of "childhood" and how that evolved into systems of care for youth who were perceived as being maltreated or behaving poorly. **Part II: Pathways to Crime** examines the nature of delinquent activity and victimization of youth, as well as explanations for that behavior for boys and for girls, with additional focus provided on what we know about gangs and serious offenders. Schools as a critical developmental institution with profound influence on positive youth development and delinquency is given special attention. **Part III: The Contemporary Juvenile Justice System** provides an understanding of the historical and current landscape of our juvenile justice system, including chapters dedicated to police, courts, and corrections. We end the book with a discussion devoted to what works and what does not, and how that is shaped by science, intersectionality, and positive youth development. The future of juvenile justice is explored in relation to what we currently know and questions how far we are willing to go to ensure that all our children are well. Given the importance of developmental institutions that shape our responses to youth deviance, throughout this book we ask our readers to consider a critical, thought-provoking question: *How well are* all *of our children?*

THE LEARNING THROUGH CASES MODEL

This innovative textbook is part of the *Learning Through Cases* series. Each chapter begins with a compelling case that illustrates the core concepts, real-life stories, and dilemmas that frame the ongoing challenges of the societal institutions charged with meeting the needs of children and youth. Each case is then followed by chapter content that presents key explanatory concepts, theories, research, and debates on the issues raised in the case.

Learning Through Cases is a popular teaching style for students. The case model offers students and instructors the pedagogical power of the narrative to frame the complex dynamics of the lives of diverse youth within families, communities, schools, child welfare, and juvenile justice systems. The casebook approach creates a lively interactive classroom environment based on discussion and dialogue among students and instructors. Students remain focused and interested in the drama of the cases; are better able to apply the concepts; become active participants in the learning process; and have a deeper understanding of the issues presented in lectures and the text. The case-study method allows students to apply what they are learning to a real-life case, making the material even more "real" to them. Students become *invested* in a case designed to raise critical questions for discussion and investigation. Cases empower students to think independently and to actively utilize the concepts presented in the chapter.

OVERVIEW OF CHAPTERS

Chapter 1 begins with *Judging Gina*, the story of Gina Grant, a young woman whose past history of juvenile delinquency was leaked to the media, resulting in a denial of admission to several of the top universities in the country. This case raises key tensions in the philosophy of the juvenile justice system and core questions about the purpose of the system in responding to juvenile crime. Our second case, *Saving or Exploiting Children?*, examines the orphan train movement of the nineteenth century to investigate the historical origins of both child welfare and the juvenile justice system, and their relationship to changes taking place within the structure of American society. This is followed in chapter 3 by the contemporary case, *A Tragedy or a Crime?*, about Cristian Fernandez, a twelve-year-old charged with homicide as an adult in the state of Florida. This chapter illustrates the changing paradigms of juvenile justice over its one-hundred-year history, and raises key questions about where juvenile justice has been and where it is headed.

Cases in Part II explore what we know about youth misbehavior and juvenile crime in modern American society. *Learning the Code* in chapter 4 tells the story of Geoffrey Canada, a young boy growing up in the South Bronx before the widespread availability of guns. This chapter looks at theories of delinquency and explanations of patterns in youth crime among boys in American society. Chapter 5 focuses on what we know about patterns of delinquency and crime among girls in American society, utilizing the case study *Addicted to Love: Growing Up on the Track*, a story about commercial sexual exploitation of young girls. Chapter 6, *Confessions of a Former Latin King*, presents the story of a former violent gang member telling of his journey into the life of gangs, as well as his exit, to illustrate key themes in a study of gangs and serious offenders. Chapter 7 opens with the events at Columbine, in *Understanding the Horror at Columbine High School.* The chapter looks at the developmental institution of public school and its backdrop for juvenile crime, as well as for effective intervention and prevention.

Part III cases examine our modern juvenile justice system. *Victor Rios—Changing What Police See*, the case study in chapter 8, explores the role of police in the dynamics of juvenile crime and justice processing by introducing the story of Victor Rios, a Latino youth from the inner city who grows up to become a sociologist dedicated to changing the mind-set of police and their relationship to inner-city youth of color. Chapter 9 looks at the contemporary juvenile court in *Judging Our Youth*, the story of a powerful judge who systematically ignores the constitutional rights of juveniles in his courtroom. In chapter 10, *From Punishment to Rehabilitation* chronicles the transformation of the juvenile prison system from a vermin-infested nightmare to a model of positive youth development as an illustration of what could be in juvenile correctional treatment. The final case, *A Matter of Degrees*, tells the story of Dwayne Betts, a juvenile who served adult time and, against the odds, reformed his life. Through his story Betts offers key guideposts for effective intervention and prevention for the juvenile justice system of the future.

FEATURES OF *YOUTH, CRIME, AND JUSTICE*

This text is well suited to lecture, seminar, and online course formats. The combination of cases and chapter content makes it easy to generate in-class, at-home, online assignments and discussion assignments. Each chapter includes several elements to facilitate student comprehension, including:

1. Learning objectives
2. Critical thinking questions
3. Key terms and definitions
4. Review and study questions
5. Check It Out resources for students

A companion Instructor's Manual (including chapter outlines and sample class exercises) and Test Bank (including multiple-choice, true/false, and essay questions) are available. E-mail textbooks@rowman.com for more information about these materials.

FOUNDATIONS OF YOUTH, CRIME, AND JUSTICE

Youth, Society, and the Law

LEARNING OBJECTIVES

By the end of the chapter, you should be able to do the following:

- Articulate the core challenges of the juvenile justice system.
- Describe the significance of age within a life course perspective.
- Define childhood and adolescence as social and legal constructions.
- Define delinquency as social and legal constructions.
- Identify the role of the moral entrepreneur.
- Discuss the difference between folkways, mores, and laws.
- Define intersectionality and its importance for the study of juvenile justice.
- Articulate the perspective of positive youth development.

Case Study 1: Judging Gina

The *Boston Globe Sunday Magazine* article was called "Beating the Odds." The reporter's assignment was to write about children who overcame the worst of personal circumstances to achieve personal success. By all accounts, seventeen-year-old Gina Grant fit the profile perfectly.

Gina's father succumbed to lung cancer when she was eleven years old; three years later her mother died. Living on her own since her sixteenth birthday, Gina was a straight-A student; co-captain of the tennis team; and tutor to poor children. Her friends described her as a "wonderful person," her teachers and school administrators said she was "caring, loving, giving of herself at all times." The article praised her positive attitude: "You can acknowledge that bad things happen, but to feel I'm a victim, that's just not good."

Gina Grant had achieved a dream cherished from childhood: early admission to Harvard University, the most prestigious university in the world. One strong memory from her childhood was that her father wanted her to go to Harvard. Says Gina's uncle, "He always wanted her to go there because he thought Gina was the best."

But Gina never entered the ivy-covered halls of Harvard University. By the time the glowing *Globe* article hit the newsstand, an anonymous tipster had mailed a thick packet containing dozens of newspaper clippings dated four and half years earlier both to Harvard and to the *Boston Globe*. These clippings revealed what Gina Grant had not told the reporter when she referred to her mother's death: that she herself, at age fourteen, had killed her mother, brutally and violently, in her home in Lexington, South Carolina.

By Monday morning, Gina received a call from her guidance counselor informing her that Harvard was recalling its offer of admission. The morning paper carried details of Gina Grant's dark past. Within days, Columbia University and Barnard College also withdrew offers of admission.

Secrets and Rages

Practically everyone in Lexington, South Carolina, described Gina as a golden child. Born in 1976 to Charles Grant, civil engineer, and mother Dorothy Mayfield, who worked as an executive secretary in a bank, Gina and her sister grew up in an affluent, conservative suburban community. In her quiet neighborhood, people described Gina as just about the nicest teenager you could ever meet. According to Eileen, her closest friend since nursery school, "Gina was . . . the best-hearted person I ever knew."

But there were secrets even her best friend did not know. After Gina's father's yearlong battle with cancer, her mother's drinking went from bad to worse. She was able to hold down a job, but most nights she drank herself into oblivion. Gina's sister worked as a nurse and tried not to leave Gina alone with her mother. Mostly Gina spent as much time as possible at school or at Eileen's house. Gina shared little about what was going on at home. Both sisters worked to hide their mother's alcoholism from friends and neighbors, pretending all was fine and normal. Even to her closest friend, Gina denied anything was wrong at home.

That is, until ten days before the murder. On Labor Day weekend, Gina confided to Eileen that her mother was "out of control, going into rages," getting angry over little things, such as when someone finished all the milk in the house, and even crazier, blaming Gina for her father's death. Gina confessed her fear that her mother might do her harm. She told Eileen she had found a handgun hidden under her mother's mattress that she removed, "just in case." When the girls told this to Eileen's mother, she immediately phoned the sheriff's office, only to be told there was nothing they could do about these fears until something "actually happened."

A Whole Lot of Lying

There were others in South Carolina who would later come to a different conclusion about why Gina chose that weekend to confess her fears to her best friend. Most of these skeptics were law enforcement officials involved in the interrogations of Gina after the crime. In their view, it was entirely plausible that those secrets were really a part of Gina's cold-blooded, premeditated plan to murder her mother.

On the night of September 13, 1990, Dana Grant, Gina's older sister, arrived home to find the front and side doors locked. When she tried to use her key, something prevented her from entering the door. Alarmed, Dana went next door and made a 911 call. Approaching the house with the sheriff, Dana and the neighbor found Gina standing outside, distraught. Gina told her sister that she and Momma had gotten into a fight, and that Momma was hurt—maybe dead.

Inside the house, the sheriff found a gruesome scene: Dorothy Mayfield's head was battered, a knife stuck in her throat, and blood was everywhere. Gina gave her first statement at two a.m. at the police station, where she described how her drunk mother had grabbed her, hit her, slapped her, and then fallen down the stairs. Somehow, her mother had a knife. For a while they struggled, but then her mother committed suicide by stabbing herself in the throat.

The story was not convincing to the detectives. Even before the forensics investigation, it was clear to these seasoned officers that the head injuries were not caused by a fall down a set of carpeted stairs; nor was it likely that death was caused by the knife wound that they believed happened after Dorothy was deceased.

They challenged Gina with these facts, but she stuck to her story. Meanwhile, investigators found a plastic bag in Gina's bedroom closet full of bloody towels, along with her mother's jacket, soaked in blood. The bag also contained a lead-crystal candlestick encrusted in dried blood. Confronted with this evidence, Gina told a new version of her story, which included the candlestick and her effort to clean up, claiming she was afraid they would think she had killed her mother. Everything else, she insisted, had happened just as she said.

Yet, the autopsy told a different story. Dorothy had been killed in the kitchen, hit from behind with the candlestick, with a great deal of force. She was struck at least thirteen times. The knife was inserted in her throat after she was dead, with her hand placed on the handle to make it seem as if she had inflicted the wound upon herself. The candlestick had been carefully wiped clean of fingerprints.

Police investigators quickly focused on Gina's relationship with her boyfriend, Jack, as the real source of conflict between Gina and her mother. They believed that, rather than being afraid of Dorothy, Gina was furious with her for trying to prevent her from dating Jack. Although both Gina and her boyfriend swore that he was not present there on the night of the murder, his fingerprints were found on the knife. On the suspicion that Gina had called him to help her dispose of the body, Jack was arrested and charged as an accessory to murder.

Three weeks later, Gina told police she wanted to make a new statement about what really happened that night. This time she said it was her boyfriend who killed her mother. According to her statement, he arrived during a fight in which her mother had threatened her with a knife. In her defense, Jack picked up the candlestick and hit her mother in the head. In a phone conversation with Jack's mother, Gina admitted she was trying to avoid going to jail by placing blame on Jack. She told his mother that Jack was innocent and had not been there that night at all.

Gina, following the advice of her lawyer, agreed to plead no contest to voluntary manslaughter in return for the prosecution's willingness to drop the murder charge. Gina and her boyfriend were sentenced to be detained in a youth correctional facility for a time not to exceed their twenty-first birthdays. After Gina spent nine months in the South Carolina juvenile system, a juvenile judge agreed to allow her to be transferred to a residential school for children in Massachusetts, under the supervision of her aunt and uncle, who agreed to pay for her care and to provide support. The South Carolina Parole Board opposed this decision, but the judge ruled that it was in the best interests of Gina to move away from South Carolina to be near family.

After six months in the Massachusetts facility, Gina was allowed to move home with her aunt and uncle and to attend public school. Within a few months, she had moved out on her own, supported by a modest trust fund from her parents' estate. Gina Grant had begun a new life.

A Sealed Record Broken

According to the juvenile code of South Carolina, juvenile records are sealed from the public and can only be reopened if the individual becomes involved in another violent crime. The actual juvenile court proceedings are closed to the public, and reporters and editors are expected to withhold the names of juveniles in their reporting about the crime.

The rationale for these statutes goes to the heart of the mission of the juvenile justice system. The purpose of the sealed record is to avoid burdening the juveniles with negative judgments for the rest of their lives. Once the public knows the facts, the idea of a fresh start becomes very difficult. Because the mission of the juvenile justice system is to act in the best interests of the child, sealed records are key to allowing juveniles to move forward in building new lives.

Yet in Gina's case, the sheriff's office released Gina's full name to the press, and the local newspaper decided to print her name in the story that ran the next day. According to the reporter for the local paper, the sheriff of Lexington County knowingly ignored the law that protects the identity of youth offenders because he believed that "the juvenile justice system makes a mockery of justice." The editors of the paper also decided to reveal Gina Grant's identity. They knew the public would lose interest if they did not have a name and face to go with the gruesome story. The story was covered in dozens of newspaper articles in South Carolina, avidly followed by a readership that knew nothing about Gina except what they read in the papers about the crime.

When Gina agreed to be interviewed by the *Globe* reporter for the positive piece, she omitted telling the reporter about how her mother died. Was she being deceitful when she said that the circumstances of her mother's death were "too painful to discuss"? Was she entitled to keep that part of her past in the past?

Confronting the Past

Gina had already told the truth about what happened to those closest to her in Massachusetts. After six months of dating, Gina confessed to her boyfriend the truth about how her mother died, and together they told his parents. Said the boyfriend's mother, "We all cried over it for three days."

Later Gina sought their advice about how to answer questions on her college applications. Was she obliged to tell? How should she answer the question on the Common Application that asks, "Have you ever incurred serious or repeated disciplinary action, or have you ever been suspended?" Should she talk about it in her college essay?

Her boyfriend's parents counseled her to keep these facts to herself. Her juvenile record was sealed, which meant legally she was not obligated to reveal this information. On the Common Application she answered "no" about her record of disciplinary and school misconduct. When it came to the Harvard interview, she told them her mother died in an accident.

Once the *Globe* article put Gina back in the media spotlight, dredging up the grim truth of her past, Gina needed to tell a wider circle of friends, coworkers, and teachers about her past. Most of the people who knew Gina remain steadfast in their support of her character. All those who knew Gina believe she had been driven to an extreme reaction because of equally extreme conditions of abuse and stress.

Did Harvard Do the Right Thing?

After receiving the anonymous courier delivery, the admissions committee held a special meeting on the day the story about Gina Grant's crime appeared in the *Boston Globe*. By that evening, Harvard had issued a press statement rescinding her offer of admission, claiming that "misrepresentations" on Gina's application raised questions about her moral character.

The prestige of Harvard, combined with the sensational nature of the crime, led to a firestorm of national and international media coverage. Angry students held demonstrations on Gina's behalf, arguing that she had paid her debt to society and deserved to be treated like everyone else. The *Harvard Crimson*, the campus newspaper, was inundated with letters of support.

The *New York Times* issued an editorial, as did the *Boston Globe*. Articles appeared in *The New Yorker*, *The Nation*, the *Chicago Tribune*, the *LA Times*, the *Washington Post*, and, of course, in the South Carolina press. College newspapers across the country debated the question of whether or not a murderer should be admitted to a freshman class. Television coverage included *Nightline*, *Meet the Press*, and *60 Minutes*. The sensational quality of the news was irresistible; Gina's past was a secret no more.

According to many lawyers that came to her defense, Gina Grant was following the law in how she answered these questions about her past. Every state and the federal government have statutes providing for the sealing, expungement, or limited access to juvenile records. The details of these statutes vary from jurisdiction to jurisdiction. Some provide specific criteria for sealing; others exclude certain offenses. At least half of the states explicitly allow juveniles to deny that a record exists, while others offer no guidance about how a person is to respond to questions about his or her past. Many statutes have a waiting period after which the record is sealed—usually after the individual has served time in a juvenile facility, or after probation—and many rescind the seal if another offense is committed.

Lawyer Margaret Burnham pointed out that Massachusetts law prohibits educational institutions from asking applicants about any criminal behavior that did not result in a criminal conviction. In the juvenile system, juveniles are adjudicated "delinquent," which is different than a criminal conviction. Other lawyers pointed out that the law creates a legal fiction of a "clean slate"; Gina was following the law when she denied any involvement in the juvenile justice system. Gina's lawyer in juvenile court in South Carolina said, "This girl has paid her debt. That chapter in her life should have been closed, and she should have been able to start over."

Gina herself said little other than issuing a brief statement: "I deal with this tragedy every day on a personal level. It serves no good purpose for anyone else to dredge up the pain of my childhood. In addition, I have no wish to defame my mother's memory by detailing any abuse." Both Burnham and Jack Swerling, one of her South Carolina attorneys, point out that Gina turned down lucrative deals from television and movie studios clamoring for rights to her story. She could have become very wealthy, but all she wanted was to be left alone to live her life.

The Right to Start Over?

The debate in the media continued. On the one hand, many argued that attending Harvard was a privilege, not a right. While Gina Grant had the opportunity to start over, this did not include attending the most prestigious university in the country—or any other university, for that matter. There were many who did not feel Gina had the right to be free of a past that included something as shocking and heinous as matricide. Furthermore, Harvard had an obligation to other members of the community. How could they be sure that Gina Grant would not be a threat to others?

On the other hand are the basic ideals of the juvenile justice system; the reality of a twenty-four-hour news cycle; and the sad truth of an unforgiving American public when it comes to crime. Closed hearings, confidentiality, judicial discretion, and sealed records exist for a reason. Juveniles are adjudicated "delinquent," not convicted as "criminals," because of the diminished responsibility associated with acts committed by children. A veil of secrecy is set over these proceedings to protect the child from the harsh judgments of the community who may only know what they read in the press. The procedural protections around the juvenile court exist in recognition that the public will condemn the individual, youth or adult, and judge them accordingly. There is no public forgiveness. In the eyes of many, an offender is always an offender.

Tufts University was the single university to uphold an offer of acceptance. According to the president of Tufts, "Our admissions people advised me that there was no apparent fraudulent statement, nothing deceitful, in her application. She paid her penalty. That's supposed to be enough under our system. I like to think that this university is caring and forgiving. Any other choice would have been antithetical to our beliefs, so I don't think we even had a choice about what to do."

Yet Gina's arrival on the campus of Tufts was not exactly warm and fuzzy. The day before she was to arrive, a conservative student group blanketed the campus with flyers protesting her presence on campus. Although the administration worked hard to pull them down, hundreds remained on bulletin boards and campus light poles.

Nineteen-year-old Gina Grant began her freshman year on a campus deeply divided about her right to be there. Four years later, Gina Grant graduated from Tufts. This, too, was reported in the press, and on websites and blogs that track the lives of the infamous within our society. Yet again, they told the story of her past.

THINKING CRITICALLY ABOUT THIS CASE

1. Should juvenile justice records remain sealed, or does the public have the right to know about someone's youthful past? Do you think it depends on the type of offense committed? What should have been done in Gina's case?

2. How might Gina's troubled family history, her school record, and her general demeanor have played a role in the juvenile judge's decision? In your view, should those factors be taken into account?

3. What was the impact of the decision by the South Carolina sheriff to release Gina's name to the press? Do you agree or disagree with this decision? Explain your answer.

4. Did Harvard and other colleges who rescinded their offers of admission do the right thing; or did Tufts do the right thing by admitting her? Explain the rationale for your position.

5. Do you think Gina may have been treated differently by the juvenile justice system or the press had she been poor and/or a youth of color? Why or why not?

REFERENCES

This case is based on the following sources:

"An Offer Grant Should Have Refused," *Washington Post*, August 20, 1999.

"For Student Who Killed Her Mother, Acceptance," *New York Times*, June 11, 1995, Sunday, Late Edition.

"2d University Admits Student Who Killed," *New York Times*, May 11, 1995, Thursday, Late Edition.

"After Rejection by Harvard, Questions in Mother's Death," *New York Times*, April 25, 1995, Tuesday, Late Edition.

"Harvard Slams Door on Teen Who Beat her Mom to Death," *Hamilton Spectator* (Ontario, Canada), April 25, 1995.

"It's Justice by Degrees," *Daily News* (UK), April 23, 1995.

"Truth Holds Key to Harvard Rejection Case," *New York Times*, April 19, 1995.

"Poisoned Ivy; Harvard and Yale Make Embarrassing Admissions," *New York Times*, April 16, 1995.

"A Rude Welcome Back: Tempests Greet President," *Washington Post*, April 16, 1995, Sunday, Final Edition.

"Straight A's—And I Killed My Mother," News Review, *Sydney Morning Herald*, Australia, April 15, 1995, Saturday.

"Her Mother Slain, Her Life's the Issue," *USA TODAY*, April 14, 1995.

"Student Who Killed Mother Loses Offer From Harvard; Early Admission Revoked After Reports Emerge," *Washington Post*, April 8, 1995.

INTRODUCTION

THIS BOOK EXAMINES THE JUVENILE JUSTICE system—ITS origin and transformation over the more than one hundred years of its existence. We begin our study of the juvenile justice system by examining the response of the authorities to Gina Grant. As a minor, Gina was not "tried and convicted of a crime"; instead, she was "adjudicated delinquent" by the juvenile court. These words are different for a reason. The legal meaning of *delinquency* is different from the legal meaning of *crime*. The concept of delinquency reflects the legal notion that fourteen-year-old Gina was too young to possess the "criminal mind" of an adult. Authorities therefore needed to respond to her illegal behavior differently than if she had been an adult. This is the core rationale for the existence of a juvenile justice system separate from the adult criminal justice system: Children are different from adults, and therefore not legally responsible for their actions in the same way adults are.[1]

In the juvenile system, the overarching goal is to act "in the best interests" of the child, and to provide rehabilitation and care, also called *child welfare*. In the adult criminal justice system, the dominant goal is to protect public safety and to impose punishment for criminal conduct. Gina's case was heard in the juvenile system, where the goal is to ensure that a single act does not destroy a youth's entire future. For this reason, the law required that the details of the case be shielded from the public to allow her the chance to start over free from the stigma associated with youthful misdeeds. We see from the case that once the information was made public, it was impossible for Gina to be free of that stigma.

We see too that there were many other voices that expressed different opinions about the appropriate response to Gina Grant. By the time Gina committed her offense, the juvenile justice system was no longer operating exclusively on the principles of rehabilitation and child welfare. By the middle of the twentieth century, defense lawyers and juvenile prosecutors joined social workers, probation officers, and judges as key decision-makers in the fate of any young person brought before the juvenile court. In the 1960s most of the due process protections required by the US Constitution in adult criminal proceedings, such as the right to an attorney and the right to remain silent, also applied to juvenile court proceedings. Then, in the 1990s, legislatures across the country enacted legal changes to allow for the vigorous prosecution and adult-size punishment for juveniles, like Gina Grant, who committed acts of violence. By the twenty-first century, the goals of public safety and punishment were added to the goals of rehabilitation and child welfare as competing social objectives for the juvenile justice system.[2]

Today many observers wonder: Do we really need a juvenile justice system at all? What is the purpose of having an entirely separate legal system for handling the illegal behavior of youth? If we do have a separate system, in what ways is the juvenile justice system different from the adult criminal justice system? Why is it different?

JUVENILE JUSTICE SYSTEM CORE CHALLENGES

Pondering the purpose of the juvenile system raises a deeper layer of questions we explore in this textbook: At what age is an individual mature enough to be held legally accountable for their conduct? What does it mean to be an adult or a juvenile in our society? When does childhood end and adulthood begin? Are adolescents different from children? Are they different from adults?

Probing deeper is yet another set of challenges. After the death of her husband, Gina's mother was an inadequate parent for her daughter. Who is responsible for the care, guidance, and protection of children and youth when parents and guardians fail to uphold their responsibility? What if society does not approve of the manner in which parents are raising their child? Does society have the right to take a child from parents who are not providing proper care and guidance? Whose decision is it to determine what is proper adult care and guidance?

And finally we must ask: Who is responsible when a child without adequate adult care or guidance commits a criminal act? How should we judge the actions of children who have been hurt, abused, or neglected by adults? Are children to blame for the conditions in which they grow up? Are they responsible for the choices they make under those circumstances? What is the fair and just response?

These are profound questions any society must address. These are the very challenges that led to the invention of the juvenile court back in 1899, and are the concerns that continue to shape its structure, process, and philosophy. To properly study the juvenile justice system, we must widen our lens and look at structures and institutions for the care, regulation, and guidance of children and youth within our society. This includes families, schools, and neighborhoods—not just the juvenile justice system and its associated institutions of child welfare, courts, police, and residential or correctional facilities meant to punish and, at the same time, rehabilitate youth in their care.

The Question of Age in the Law

Within the Anglo-American tradition, children have never been held to the same legal standard of responsibility as adults. Yet, the actual age of legal criminal responsibility has changed dramatically over the past hundred years. Before the invention of the juvenile court, the age of seven was a bright line between childhood and adulthood. Below the age of seven, children were categorically incapable of committing crime. Between ages seven and fourteen, judges and juries were instructed to take age into consideration in order to excuse or lighten the punishment for each case brought before the court. By age fourteen, a person was considered a fully formed adult.[3]

This legal status changed in the nineteenth century when a series of reforms led to the creation of the original juvenile court in the state of Illinois. The age of adulthood was raised to age sixteen—much closer to the modern standard. Today, each state has the legal authority to set the age of majority for a variety of different purposes. Over the last hundred years states have raised, lowered, and raised again the legal age of adulthood as attitudes and beliefs about the meaning of childhood, adolescence, youth, and adulthood have changed within the wider society. In 2015, for the purpose of **criminal liability**—which is the age at which a person is held responsible in adult court—forty-two states set the upper age of jurisdiction of the juvenile system at age seventeen; seven states set it at sixteen; and two states set it at the younger age of fifteen (see table 1.1).[4]

CRIMINAL LIABILITY
The age at which a person is held responsible for illegal acts or omissions in adult court.

TABLE 1.1	Upper Age of Original Juvenile Court Jurisdiction, 2015		
State	**Age 15**	**Age 16**	**Age 17**
Number of States	2	7	42
Alabama			X
Alaska			X
Arizona			X
Arkansas			X
California			X
Colorado			X
Connecticut			X
Delaware			X
District of Columbia			X
Florida			X
Georgia		X	
Hawaii			X
Idaho			X
Illinois			X
Indiana			X
Iowa			X
Kansas			X
Kentucky			X

(continued)

TABLE 1.1 | *(Continued)*

State			
Louisiana		X	
Maine			X
Maryland			X
Massachusetts			X
Michigan		X	
Minnesota			X
Mississippi			X
Missouri		X	
Montana			X
Nebraska			X
Nevada			X
New Hampshire			X
New Jersey			X
New Mexico			X
New York	X		
North Carolina	X		
North Dakota			X
Ohio			X
Oklahoma			X
Oregon			X

(continued)

TABLE 1.1	*(Continued)*	
Pennsylvania		X
Rhode Island		X
South Carolina	X	
South Dakota		X
Tennessee		X
Texas	X	
Utah		X
Vermont		X
Virginia		X
Washington		X
West Virginia		X
Wisconsin	X	
Wyoming		X

(OJJDP: Upper Age Limit of Juvenile Court Jurisdiction. Available at www.ojjdp.gov/ojstatbb/ structure_process/qa04101.asp.)

According to the laws of South Carolina, Gina was below the legal age of criminal responsibility, and because of her age, her case fell under the original jurisdiction of the juvenile authorities within the state. Under South Carolina law, a judge had the authority to decide to legally treat Gina as a juvenile or to transfer her to the adult criminal justice system to be tried as an adult. In all states, youth can be tried in adult court under certain circumstances. In some states, such as Florida and Idaho, there is no minimum age for transferring juveniles to adult court. Many people in South Carolina believe that Gina's case should have been tried in the adult criminal justice system.

States also set the legal age of majority for a variety of other adult privileges and responsibilities, such as the right to drive a motor vehicle, to work, or to rent an apartment. Most states set the age at which a person can decide to leave school without parental consent at sixteen. Youth may be legally old enough to get a full-time job and rent an apartment, but they are not old enough to buy alcohol until they are twenty-one. One of the rationales for lowering the voting age in the United States from twenty-one to eighteen in 1971 was the discrepancy between the age at which youth were drafted into the military and when they were afforded the adult privilege to vote in national and state elections.[5] Critics argued that it was fundamentally unfair to believe that youth were old enough to die for their country, but not old enough to help choose the leaders making the decisions about going to war.

The question of whether or not it is fair to treat a youth as an adult for one purpose and not another is the same in Gina's case. Fourteen-year-old Gina could have been legally tried as an adult and given an adult sentence for the crime under South Carolina law. At the same time, given her age, she would not have been old enough by law to drive, vote, drink, buy cigarettes, leave school, or even buy a ticket to an R-rated movie.

SOCIO-ECOLOGY: AGE IN A LIFE CONTEXT

Establishing the age of adulthood is both a legal question and a sociological one. At what age is a person ready to make the transition to adult roles and responsibilities within our society? A **life course perspective** recognizes that human beings grow up within a social context that shapes the stages and processes of that development. The **ecological context**, or socio-ecological context, within the field of sociology looks at the changing nature of a society, and how those changes shape the process of human development.[6] Urie Bronfenbrenner defines the life course perspective as the systematic study of the processes through which the properties of the person and the environment interact to produce continuity and change in the characteristics of the person over the life course. This means that how we grow and develop depends on the interplay between our biology and the context in which we grow to be fully fledged adult members of our particular social group.

Most of us know the story of Romeo and Juliet in which two ill-fated young lovers secretly marry despite the vicious feud between their powerful families. In the end, both families bear the loss of a beloved child when the lovers take their own lives rather than face separation from one another. What most of us today do not realize about this familiar story is that the likely ages of the two lovers is around twelve or thirteen years old. In Shakespeare's time, the sixteenth century, persons of that age were viewed as entering adulthood—young and passionate, not yet wise and experienced—but certainly ready to accept the roles and responsibilities of adulthood.

Today the idea of thirteen-year-olds joining together in matrimony is both culturally unacceptable and legally prohibited, even with the approval and consent of their parents. All US states, except one, require a couple be eighteen years old in order to marry without parental permission.[7] In Nebraska, the age is set at nineteen years old. Parental consent alone is not sufficient to allow youth below the age of legal majority to marry in many states; courts must also authorize that decision.

What has changed between the time of William Shakespeare and the society we live in today to help us understand these different societal attitudes and laws about the age of marriage? The answer is not to be found simply in the physical development of human beings, but in the changes related to the ecological context of roles and responsibilities throughout the life course.

LIFE COURSE PERSPECTIVE
View of individuals that takes into account experiences over time that influence individual development and action.

ECOLOGICAL CONTEXT
An individual's behavior is affected by relationships, the community, and the society; also called socio-ecological context.

In chapter 2, we will see that the idea of "childhood" as a separate, important, and significant stage of the life course emerges gradually throughout time, reflecting important changes in the structure of the family and the wider society. The term *adolescence* came into use around the beginning of the twentieth century to refer to a distinct phase of human development in the life course.[8] The word *teenager* was not used until the 1940s.[9] We will look at what was changing in American society at the time that accounted for the invention of new concepts to describe this stage of life. Today, we hear more about the phase of "emerging adulthood" or "young adulthood," reflecting the societal shift of viewing the transition to full adult roles as extending well into a person's twenties.[10] We are also learning that, from a biological standpoint, the human brain is not fully mature, with adult decision-making skills and a fully formed personality, until a person's mid- or even late twenties.[11] This knowledge is influencing both the legal understanding of youth culpability and our social expectations about the age of full adulthood.

SOCIAL AND LEGAL CONSTRUCTIONS

Childhood and Adolescence

Although the ideas of childhood, adolescence, and adulthood seem to us to be shaped by our physical development, these stages of life are termed **social constructions**. That means they are shaped and defined by the norms, values, roles, and societal institutions in the society, rather than identified by some clearly demarcated differences that cut across societies. In some cultures, children as young as six or seven are given responsibilities for doing tasks such as gathering wood or carrying water that take them miles away from direct adult supervision. During the nineteenth century, it was not uncommon for a twelve- or thirteen-year-old to be sent unaccompanied to journey thousands of miles to find work in the New World. Today, in the United States, most parents would not dream of allowing a six-year-old to walk unaccompanied to the store or to the park; and many people would criticize, judge, and even charge a parent with negligence who did so.

Norms are rules of a society or group that carry expectations of how people must, should, or may or may not behave under specific circumstances. Norms will vary from one culture to another and from one era to another, but every society has powerful, often unwritten, rules that regulate conduct. Norms can be broken down into three types: folkways, mores, and laws. **Folkways** refer to a wide and extremely important range of unwritten rules for everyday behaviors, from what we wear, to manners of speech, body language, etiquette, and social manners.

There are some norms that are of greater importance to the group, called **mores**.[12] These are behaviors the group considers to be morally right or wrong; sacred or taboo. Violating these rules elicits much more powerful reactions from members of the group than mere gossip or social disapproval. In many cultures, it is socially permissible, and even expected, for a parent to strike his or her own child. The reverse, however, is generally not acceptable; unless a child is very young, a child striking a parent is often considered taboo.

A **law** is the third type of social norm. Laws are norms that have been codified to be written into statutes and enforced through the use of coercion backed

SOCIAL CONSTRUCTION
Created ideas about individuals and ideas based on a shared sense of reality.

NORMS
Societal or group expectations of how people must, should, may, or may not, behave under specific circumstances.

FOLKWAYS
Group expectations about everyday behaviors of its members.

MORES
Norms of great importance to the group.

LAW
Written norm enforced through state authority.

by the authority of the state. The key element in defining "law," according to Max Weber, is that laws are norms enforced by specialized institutions—like the police, courts, and correctional systems—that have been granted the power to use force to obtain compliance.[13] In modern societies with highly developed political structures, most of our mores have been written into law.

We learn norms through the process known as **socialization**, by which we are taught to conform to the "code" of our particular group. Each individual must learn the right way to behave in order to be accepted and successful within the group. In some cultures, children are taught to be "seen and not heard," while in others they are taught to articulate their thoughts and express opinions in conversations with adults. In some cultures, such as some Asian cultures, it is considered rude if children make eye contact when listening to adults, while in other cultures, such as Anglo-American cultures, children will be scolded for averting their eyes: "Look at me when I am talking to you!" When we fail to follow the norms of the group, the reactions of others tell us right away that we have broken the "code" of how to appropriately behave. The societal responses, from shaming to being arrested, motivate us to conform to those expectations.

The law is a basic institution in American society that shapes the relationships between adults and children, defining what it means to be a family, as well as how people are allowed to and expected to treat one another within the family.[14] The law shapes the relationships we call "family" by defining who can marry; who is a legal parent; what the obligations of parenthood are; and what parents are prohibited from doing to their children. The law also defines how the state may interfere within that family, even to the point of dissolving those legal ties altogether. Thus, the state plays a powerful role in human relationships, which we will consider throughout these chapters on youth, crime, and justice.

Delinquency

Sociologists use the term **deviance** to refer to conduct that is contrary to the norms of conduct or social expectations of the group. Sociologists have long argued that there is nothing inherently deviant about any form of conduct.[15] A behavior is deviant if it is viewed and reacted to as such by others within the society. The concept of delinquency is a social construction rooted in what society responds to as deviant conduct by youth and children.

The legal concept of **delinquency** arose with the invention of the juvenile justice system to refer to illegal acts committed by legal minors. As we will see in the next chapter, the nineteenth-century reformers who created the concept of delinquency believed it was necessary to invent a new set of institutions to respond to youth who were violating what they saw as the norms of society. This deviance included a wide range of behaviors, most of which were not crimes, such as staying out late at night, drinking alcohol in saloons, or hanging out at dance halls and smoking cigarettes—actions that violated the mores of these middle-class reformers. To them, these were serious transgressions that required a strong response, so they passed laws that defined a range of offenses that applied only to children, and called it delinquency.

Harold Becker coined the term "**moral entrepreneurs**" to refer to people who seek to impose a particular view of morality on others within society.[16]

SOCIALIZATION
The process by which we are taught to conform to the code of our particular group.

DEVIANCE
Any conduct which is contrary to the norms of a group.

DELINQUENCY
Illegal acts committed by legal minors.

MORAL ENTREPRENEURS
Individuals who attempt to change behavior by mobilizing the group against the behavior or for making sure that a law is written against a behavior.

Moral entrepreneurs, he believed, are those people who identify certain forms of conduct as particularly dangerous and in need of social control by others within the group. These moral entrepreneurs are often responsible for mobilizing the group against the behavior or for making sure that a law is written against a certain form of conduct by engaging in **moral crusades**, or social action to demand change. These activists are also able to construct a sense of **moral panic**, or fear, about the threat of this behavior to the well-being of the entire society.

What upset reformers in the nineteenth century is different from what upset adults about the behavior of youth in the 1920s; teenagers in the 1950s; or gang members in the 1990s. But there were moral crusades in each of these eras. What they all have in common is the use of the term *delinquency* to refer to behavior deemed socially dangerous or inappropriate that needed to be controlled. As we study the one-hundred-plus-year history of the juvenile justice system, we will see many different moral crusades in response to deep anxiety and worry about the behavior of youth.

INTERSECTIONALITY

In a diverse society, social norms are always a source of conflict. Not every subculture in society embraces, practices, and believes in the same norms. The power associated with class, wealth, and privilege enables some groups to impose their norms on other less-dominant groups. For all of its history, the juvenile justice system has focused on the regulation of behavior of those who are poor and marginalized in society. The system has treated youth differently depending on a host of factors, including wealth, status, race, ethnicity, sexual orientation, and gender. Today the concept of **disproportionate minority contact (DMC)** refers to the fact that black and brown youth are more likely to be arrested, sent to court, and placed in correctional facilities than white youth.[17] These youth are overrepresented in the justice system when compared with their numbers in the general population in society.

Throughout this text we will continually address the issue of youth and justice through the lens of **intersectionality**. The term *intersectionality* refers to the study of how physical and social context and social statuses like gender, class, race, and ethnicity can privilege and discriminate against individuals in society.[18] Socio-ecological context shapes the life experience of individuals within society. Race, class, and gender shape the context in which youth mature. These also shape societal reactions and responses to youthful behavior in complex, overlapping, and interdependent ways.

Let us consider again the fate of Gina Grant. As a white female from a middle-class family, we need to ask, to what extent did her social position and privileged status shape the court's decision to legally respond to Gina as a juvenile? Would her fate have been similar if she had been poor, or male, or African-American, Latino, or Native American? In chapter 3 we look at a different case involving a poor youth of color, Cristian Fernandez, who also committed a serious act of violence at a young age. Cristian's case, however, was handled quite differently. How did his social status—his race, class, and gender—affect his fate within the juvenile justice system? These are hard but essential questions to address.

MORAL CRUSADES
Actions taken by those who seek to impose a particular view of morality on others within a group.

MORAL PANIC
Imposition of fear about the threat of a behavior to the well-being of the group.

DISPROPORTIONATE MINORITY CONTACT (DMC)
Overrepresentation of black and brown youth in the justice system compared with the general population of black and brown youth in society.

INTERSECTIONALITY
The study of how social statuses associated with gender, class, race, and ethnicity influence the opportunities, privileges, choices, and discrimination within the society.

Throughout this book we will explore the impact of intersectionality on reactions to delinquency and juvenile justice system treatment.

POSITIVE YOUTH DEVELOPMENT LENS

The Masai, an African tribe, uses a standard greeting among adults when they meet each other in the community. Instead of our customary "How are you?," to which we usually respond, "I'm fine, thanks. How are you?," they ask each other: "How are the children?," to which the customary response is, "The children are well." Notice they ask this of all adults, whether they are parents or not, and the question is not about any particular child but about the general health and well-being of *all* children. As a society, when we look at rates of youth suicide, depression, obesity, drug and alcohol abuse, teen pregnancy, school dropout, and violence, we must ask ourselves: How well are *our* children?

The juvenile justice system, including the child welfare system, is designed to care for maltreated and abandoned children, and schools are part of a network of institutions our society has created to care for and to educate our youth. Sociologists call these establishments **developmental institutions**, providing nurture, guidance, and socialization that extends beyond families. The family is the principal institution in our society for raising children; this is true in all societies. But from an ecological context, families are nested within a larger set of institutions—such as schools and churches—that help to raise and care for youth. The juvenile justice system is among the developmental institutions we have created to care for children when families are struggling to do so. At their core, these systems are about how we address the well-being of *all* our children.

To answer questions about the purpose, goals, and future of the juvenile justice system, we need to look broadly at the ecological context in which young people develop into mature and responsible adults within our society. This textbook utilizes the lens of **positive youth development (PYD)**. This perspective recognizes that children and youth develop into mature adults within the context of relationships with parents, teachers, friends, neighbors, and relatives, along with the influence of community norms and societal laws and policies.[19] Rather than focus on the deficits and problems associated with youth, PYD focuses on the inherent strengths and capacities within youth. PYD states that given the right mix of opportunities and supportive positive relationships, youth will thrive and transition into healthy adulthood.[20]

While the focus of this book is on the specialized institution of the juvenile justice system, to understand that system, we must examine its relationship to the structure of American society. In this book we look at how intersectionality shapes the trajectory of growing up in American society. We look at this from a socio-ecological context, in which the individual is also affected by relationships, the community, and society. How do these systems interact for youth in our society? Positive youth development provides a platform for understanding how to encourage and support healthy development for all youth. How well are *all* our children? This is the most important question to ask when considering the purpose and future of the juvenile justice system.

DEVELOPMENTAL INSTITUTIONS
Organizations and systems beyond the family that nurture, care for, and socialize youth.

POSITIVE YOUTH DEVELOPMENT (PYD)
Focuses on youth strengths and abilities, rather than deficits, that lead to healthy development.

KEY TERMS

criminal liability The age at which a person is held responsible for illegal acts or omissions in adult court.

delinquency Illegal acts committed by legal minors.

developmental institutions Organizations and systems beyond the family that nurture, care for, and socialize youth.

deviance Any conduct which is contrary to the norms of a group.

disproportionate minority contact (DMC) Over-representation of black and brown youth in the justice system compared with the general population of black and brown youth in society.

ecological context An individual's behavior is affected by relationships, the community, and the society; also called socio-ecological context.

folkways Group expectations about everyday behaviors of its members.

intersectionality The study of how social statuses associated with gender, class, race, and ethnicity influence the opportunities, privileges, choices, and discrimination within the society.

law Written norm enforced through state authority.

life course perspective View of individuals that takes into account experiences over time that influence individual development and action.

moral crusades Actions taken by those who seek to impose a particular view of morality on others within a group.

moral entrepreneurs Individuals who attempt to change behavior by mobilizing the group against the behavior or for making sure that a law is written against a behavior.

moral panic Imposition of fear about the threat of a behavior to the well-being of the group.

mores Norms of great importance to the group.

norms Societal or group expectations of how people must, should, may, or may not, behave under specific circumstances.

positive youth development (PYD) Focuses on youth strengths and abilities, rather than deficits, that lead to healthy development.

social construction Created ideas about individuals and ideas based on a shared sense of reality.

socialization The process by which we are taught to conform to the code of our particular group.

REVIEW AND STUDY QUESTIONS

1. Why is it important to look at society as a whole to understand the development and changes in the legal responses to behaviors of youth?

2. How do laws differ from folkways or mores? Does everyone agree on what should be a law? Why or why not?

3. Describe the development of delinquency as a social construction.

4. Explain the concept of "age" as a social construction.

5. What is meant by intersectionality, and how does that play a role in the juvenile justice system?

6. How might the positive youth development perspective be different from the current focus of the juvenile justice system?

7. Identify the areas of an ecological context to youth development. What are some key individuals and/or developmental institutions in each area?

8. Explain the concept of a "moral entrepreneur." Give an example of a moral panic and moral crusade related to youth within our society.

9. Explain the concept of socialization. Who are the socializing agents within our society? What are the ways we learn proper norms for social behavior?

10. What is the life course perspective? What are some key developmental experiences that influence and shape a person's life?

CHECK IT OUT

Read

Bonn, S. A. *Moral Panic: Who Benefits from Public Fear?*:

www.psychologytoday.com/blog/wicked-deeds/201507/moral-panic-who-benefits-public-fear

Watch

Positive Youth Development Examples—Peter Benson-Sparks:

www.youtube.com/watch?v=TqzUHcW58Us

Men of Boys Town (1941)

NOTES

[1] Mack, J. (1909). The Juvenile Court. *Harvard Law Review, 23,* 104–22.

[2] Zimring, F. E. (2005). *American Juvenile Justice.* New York: Oxford.

[3] Grossberg, M. (2002). Changing Conceptions of Child Welfare in the United States, 1820–1935. In M. K. Rosenheim, F. E. Zimring, D. S. Tanenhaus, and B. Dohrn (eds.), *A Century of Juvenile Justice,* 3–41. Chicago: University of Chicago Press.

[4] Available at www.ojjdp.gov/ojstatbb/structure_process/qu041Q1.asp.

[5] Engdahl, S. (2009). *Constitutional Amendments: Beyond the Bill of Rights: Amendment XXVI—Lowering the Voting Age.* New York: Greenhaven Press.

[6] Bronfenbrenner, U. (1979). *The Ecology of Human Development: Experiments by Nature and Design.* Cambridge, MA: Harvard University Press.

[7] Data available at www.law.cornell.edu/wex/table_marriage.

[8] Elder, G. H., Johnson, M. K., and Crosnoe, R. (2003). The Emergence and Development of Life Course Theory. In J. T. Mortimer and M. J. Shanahan (eds.)., *Handbook of the Life Course,* 3–19. New York: Springer.

[9] Côté, J. E., and Allahar, A. L. (1994). *Generation on Hold: Coming of Age in the Late Twentieth Century.* New York: New York University Press.

[10] Arnett, J. J. (2000). Emerging Adulthood: A Theory of Development from Late Teens to Early Twenties. *American Psychologist, 55,* 469–80.

[11] Blakemore, S., and Choudhury, S. (2006). Development of the Adolescent Brain: Implications for Executive Function and Social Cognition. *Journal of Child Psychology and Psychiatry, 47,* 296–312.

[12] Sumner, W. S. (2007). *Folkways: A Study of Mores, Manners, Customs, and Morals.* New York: Cosimos.

[13] Mommsen, W. J. (1989). *The Political and Social Theory of Max Weber: Collected Essays.* Chicago: University of Chicago Press.

[14] Huntingdon, C. (2014) *Failure to Flourish: How Law Undermines Families.* New York: Oxford University Press.

[15] Goode, E., and Ben-Yehuda, N. (2009). *Moral Panics: The Social Construction of Deviance.* West Sussex, UK: Wiley-Blackwell.

[16] Becker, H. S. (1995). Moral Entrepreneurs: The Creation and Enforcement of Deviant Categories. In N. J. Herman (ed.), *Deviance: A Symbolic Interactionist Approach,* 169–78. Lanham, MD: Rowman & Littlefield.

[17] Piquero, A. R. (2008). Disproportionate Minority Contact. *The Future of Children, 18,* 59–79.

[18] Choo, H. Y., and Ferree, M. M. (2010). Practicing Intersectionality in Sociological Research: A Critical Analysis of Inclusions, Interactions, and Institutions in the Study of Inequalities. *Sociological Theory, 28,* 129–49.

[19] Lerner, R., Almerigi, J. B., Theokas, C., and Lerner, J. V. (2005). Positive Youth Development: A View of the Issues. *Journal of Early Adolescence, 25,* 10–16.

[20] Catalano, R. F., Berglund, M. L., Ryan, J. A. M., Lonczak, H. S., and Hawkins, J. D. (2004). Positive Youth Development in the United States: Research Findings on Evaluations of Positive Youth Development. *The ANNALS of the American Academy of Political and Social Science, 591,* 98–124.

Youth and Developmental Institutions

LEARNING OBJECTIVES

By the end of this chapter, you should be able to do the following:

- Describe the "child savers" and their mission.
- Describe the system of family-based social control.
- Explain how urbanization, immigration, and industrialization impact family-based social control.
- Contrast the social meaning of "childhood" in different eras.
- Identify the reasons for the emergence of "adolescence."
- Identify the origins of the legal concept of *parens patriae*.
- Describe the evolution of *parens patriae*.
- Describe the origins of the child welfare system in the juvenile court.
- Apply the concept of intersectionality to the treatment of immigrants; youth of color; and girls in the early era of the juvenile justice system.

Case Study 2: Saving or Exploiting Children?

Alton was eight years old when he was bundled onto a train with his two little brothers, Gerald and Leo. The girls boarding the train wore new dresses with white pinafores while the boys wore white dress shirts, neckties, and suit coats. Alton had never seen such fine clothing. He figured he and the other ten children from the orphanage must be going to meet someone very important. Then the stern matron turned to Alton and told him he was "lucky" to be getting on the "orphan train." Alton bristled. He hated the word *orphan*. No matter what anyone said, he and his brothers were not orphans; their father was alive and well, and had promised to come back for them. He did not need or want a new family; he already had a family that he missed desperately.

A Ward of the State

For young Alton life had gone from bad to worse in the last two years. He was born to a large family living on a small farm. His mother died after delivering the last of seven children. Alton was in the middle, with three older and three younger siblings, including the newborn. Grief-stricken, Alton's father found himself unable to care for his large, young family. He told the three eldest to fend for themselves and sent them out into the world. Next, he found homes with neighbors for the newborn and one-year-old Gerald. Last, he took Alton, then age seven, and his four-year-old

brother Leo to the Jefferson County Orphanage in Watertown, New York, where he arranged to pay three dollars a week until he could figure out how to care for his family. When the payments stopped, the boys became legal wards of the state.

As an adult, Alton vividly remembered what it felt like to live in the orphanage. His family may have been poor, but as a child he had been happy. Life in the orphanage was terrible. "We went from being part of a close family to feeling like outcasts. Nobody visited us, nobody wanted us, nobody loved us. We were just two more homeless kids in a country that already had too many."

Hunger is what he remembers most about the orphanage: There was never enough food, and fighting was what they did to survive, physically and emotionally. As an adult, Alton still bore a scar on his arm where he was stabbed by a fork when reaching across the table for a biscuit. The children from the orphanage attended local schools where other children mercilessly teased them for being unwanted or having raggedy clothing. Alton fought back every time: "I think my temper saved me. I struck back at the world with my fists when I was being put down. I refused to believe I was worthless."

The punishment from the matrons for misbehavior was always the same: no food, and solitary confinement. Young Alton spent hours in a tiny room with nothing but an empty stomach and his fierce fury to keep him company. But what he remembers most about the orphanage was the lack of any kindness or affection: "We were always being ordered around, told to stand here, to line up there. We had to march in line wherever we went. We lived off charity, wearing castoff clothing people gave us. Our only gift at Christmas was an apple or orange. We had no future. It would have been easy to give in to hopelessness."

But Alton had a reason to cling to hope. He had his younger brother; and he had the dream of being reunited with his father and larger family. He thought of nothing else. So when the matron informed him that this train was to take him to a new family, Alton went into high alert. All he wanted was to be back with his own family: He was not an orphan, and had no desire to be part of a "new family."

The Pink Envelope

Standing on the platform in his starchy new clothes, Alton heard someone calling his name. He turned to see a man frantically running down the tracks carrying a small child. After all this time, at last, it was his father! Alton threw himself into his father's arms, but soon realized that his father had not come to take him home. Instead he had brought with him the youngest child, Gerald, now three years old. He put the chubby hand of the toddler into Alton's hand and hurriedly explained that all the younger brothers would now be together.

Eight-year-old Alton begged his father not to leave, but with tears streaming down his face, his father pushed them onto the train, frantically instructing Alton to keep his brothers together and to write as soon as they got to their new home. With trembling hands his father thrust a pink envelope pre-stamped and pre-addressed into Alton's hand. Write, his father repeated, and tell me where you are. Alton begged to stay with his father, but the matron pushed them onto the train. Alton ran to the window and pressed his face against the glass, hoping to see his father one more time, but it was too late.

On the train, the pink envelope was all Alton had to connect him to his father and his hope of a reunited family. He clung to it with a vow that he would one day find a way to get himself and his brothers back to his father. As the train clattered on, Alton touched the envelope again and again, like it was a talisman that would save him and his brothers from the grim fate that lay ahead. Alton now had proof that his father was alive and intended to bring the family back together.

The matron ordered Alton to remove his suit coat so she could stow it where it would not get wrinkled. Alton told her about the precious envelope inside his pocket, and she left him alone. For the first time since his mother had died, Alton felt happy when he lay down to sleep that night. He now knew that his father had not abandoned them; the pink envelope was proof he was going to bring them all together again one day. Alton swore to himself that he was going to help make that happen.

When he woke in the morning, the first thing he did was reach for the pink envelope in his coat pocket. It was gone. Frantically he searched the car and called for the matron. When he saw her face he knew she had taken it. "Where you are going you won't be needing that. You need to forget about it" was all she said.

As an adult, Alton remembers, "That pink envelope had given me back some hope. I can't explain how defeated I felt with it gone. It just took the life out of me. I wouldn't let anybody see me cry, but nights on that train I'd lie there with tears rolling down my cheeks and my heart breaking all over again. First my mother, then my other brothers and my sister, and now my father again. How could I have lost so much?"

The Selection

After several days on the train, the matron informed the children that they would be arriving in a town where people would come to "select" them. Alton had no idea what that meant. They were taken to a church in a small town in Texas and "put up" to stand on a stage. A crowd of people looked at them and asked them questions. Some people touched them: One man felt Alton's muscles; another opened his mouth and inspected his teeth. Alton remembers feeling so mad he wanted to bite down on that hand.

That day no one "selected" Alton or his two younger brothers, but Alton watched with dread as another pair of brothers screamed when one was chosen and the other left behind. The next stop was another small town in Texas. The children followed the usual routine, and before Alton knew what had happened, a couple had scooped up Gerald and walked away with him to sign papers. Alton stood there helpless as Gerald wailed when he realized he was being taken from his brothers. Two minutes later Leo was chosen by an elderly couple. Suddenly, Alton was truly alone. Leo begged the couple to take his brother as well, and reluctantly they agreed. But a week later they changed their minds: They only wanted Leo, and the matron returned for Alton. The following placement lasted less than a week before the couple sent Alton back.

A New Family

The third placement did not start well either. Alton was full of rage and rude to his new "family." On his first night when asked to chop wood, he refused and was roundly swatted by his new "father" for being disrespectful to his family. But in the end, despite the raw start, the couple was fundamentally kind and truly wanted Alton as their son. They spent the first week introducing him to all their neighbors as their new "son." Over time they legally adopted him and renamed him Lee. They kept in touch with the families that had taken in Alton's brothers to make sure all three brothers could stay in contact with one another.

Alton's journey on the orphan train had a happy ending. He never saw his father or sister again, but he grew up loved and cared for by his adoptive parents.

He married, had children of his own, and maintained close ties to his two younger brothers. Later in life, when an article about the orphan trains was published, Alton reunited with his older brothers who had tried for years to reconnect with their lost siblings. None of them knew the fate of their father, but to Alton the pink envelope was proof that his father had loved his family and wanted to be reunited with them one day.

The Not-So-Lucky Ones

Alton was one of the lucky ones. For others the experience was far worse. Historians estimate that around 15 percent of the children were put into abusive situations, but no one really knows how many because no records were kept that followed the fate of the children in their new homes. Although agencies claimed to be vetting the homes, in reality, anyone who showed up at the selection could walk away with a child. Many knew of cases where children were brought to farms and never seen or heard from again. The children were never brought to town or sent to school. In some cases the children may have run away, but no one ever learned what had happened to them.

For many children of the orphan trains, placement with strangers was little better than being a farmhand or a servant. Families with eight or nine children were not looking for a new son or daughter. As one orphan rider said, "They didn't want a child; they wanted a slave." For many of the children, their experience was always that of being an outsider, a servant who was unloved. Unlike Alton, they were never made to feel part of the family.

The Myth: Nostalgia for the Rural Life

Between 1853 and 1929, an estimated quarter of a million children were put on trains and transported from the cities of New York and Boston to small towns across the Midwest where they were literally "put up" on a platform for local families to inspect and choose among them. The term "putting up" referred to the opportunity for townspeople to inspect the children before making their choices. Eventually that term came to refer to the process of legal adoption in this country.

Charles Loring Brace was the founder of the orphan train movement. The son of a history teacher, he was educated at Yale and ordained as a minister. Brace was very critical of the orphanages, like the one that Alton had lived in, that provided care for orphans and poor children. He thought these orphanages and similar reformatories were brutal and unhealthy

environments. He believed the best solution was to place children in a family in the countryside far from the corruption of the city.

In 1872 Brace published an account of life on the streets of Manhattan called *The Dangerous Classes of New York and Twenty Years of Work among Them*. In this book, he described the alcoholism, gangs, disease, and crime on the Manhattan streets known as Misery Row. In his mind, the best chance for children to prosper was to remove them from the city and place them in rural settings. He believed in the inherent healthfulness of the rural setting and extolled the virtues of the American farmer as the most "solid and intelligent class" in American society. Brace founded the Children's Aid Society, a private charity dedicated to helping the impoverished children on the streets of New York, upon this belief. The Children's Aid Society alone put over one hundred thousand children onto orphan trains headed west.

Child or Slave?

Historians point out that despite the glowing rhetoric, few of the orphan children ever came to be adopted by their new "families." In fact, historians have discovered that most of the children who rode the trains were not orphans at all. Some had been abandoned by their parents and left in orphanages, but many more were just poor immigrant children who were roaming the streets in search of food, money, or a place to play. Sometimes children were turned over to the agency because their mothers were unmarried. Reformers argued that by transporting them out west, these children could start "afresh," free of the shame of their origins.

Many of the children were, like Alton, forcibly or deceptively taken away from their families. The agents of the Children's Aid Society worked hard to convince parents to give up their children for better lives. Many were told the arrangements would be temporary, or that their children would send money back to their families. Just as the stern matron intervened to destroy the pink envelope as the sole connection between Alton and his biological father, these child savers believed it was an act of charity to sever ties between children and the parents they judged as unfit, depraved, and immoral. Reformers deeply believed they were saving innocent children from a life of misery and poverty by placing them in more-wholesome environments in the countryside and taking them from parents who were unable to properly care for them.

Orphan Train Economics

The driving forces behind the orphan trains were twofold: First was the need to remove troublesome children from the streets of cities like New York and Boston. It was estimated that about thirty thousand poor children were living under the grates and in the coal cellars, parks, and alleyways of New York City. These children committed petty crimes and were often locked up in jails with adult criminals. The children both generated fear and pulled on the heartstrings of wealthier citizens, who feared that the "dangerous classes" were threatening to undermine the foundation of American society. They believed that the parents—mostly immigrants—were to blame for their own economic destitution. The children, however, were morally "innocent" and could still be set on a better path if only they could be "saved" from the corrupting influence of their surroundings.

The other necessity behind the Orphan Train was the demand for labor in the vast farmlands of the West. The Homestead Act of 1862 offered 160 acres to any settler willing to work the land. More than anything else, settlers needed extra hands, strong and able, to help out on family farms. Only poor white immigrant children were allowed on orphan trains, not black children. Organizers knew that many white families would be unwilling to adopt black youth and treat them as one of their own. They also feared that if they included black children, the process of "putting up"—parading children on a stage for onlookers to examine and choose—would resemble a slave auction and make this whole system appear uncomfortably close to slavery.

Why It Ended

The last orphan train ran in 1929, just before the start of the Great Depression. A number of factors led to the demise of the movement. Probably the biggest reason was the drop in demand for labor in the Midwest. Once the land was settled, there was less of a need for young boys to chop wood, haul water, and tend the animals, or for young girls to help out with household chores. Meanwhile, Midwestern cities had their own poor children to deal with and passed laws prohibiting the shipment of dependent children from other states. Further, a shift in the philosophy of family assistance child welfare within the United States brought an end to the orphan train movement. The new profession of social work focused on how to provide assistance to families with dependent children so that they could

better care for their own children, and a system of foster care developed to provide temporary child care for families, like Alton's, with the hope that parents could reunite with their children.

THINKING CRITICALLY ABOUT THIS CASE

1. The "child savers" acted to protect the well-being of children like Alton. Do you believe that the matron made the right decision by taking the pink envelope from young Alton? Why or why not?

2. Do you believe that Alton's father, who admitted that he was unable to care for his three youngest sons, should still have had legal parental rights? Why or why not?

3. The biggest fear that Alton had was to be separated from his two youngest brothers; luckily for him, his adoptive family made efforts to keep the three brothers in contact with one another. In your opinion, should the state separate siblings, or should they be required to keep them together? Explain.

4. Do you believe that this program was a form of exploitation or a sincere effort to find children a better life with caring adults? Explain.

5. Based on Alton's experience, do you believe the system did the right thing in finding him a new home? Explain.

6. How, if at all, has the societal view of the role of children changed since Alton's time?

REFERENCES

This case is based on the following sources:

Cook, J. F. (1995). A History of Placing Out: The Orphan Trains. *Child Welfare*, 74, 181–97.

Frost, J. L. (2005). Lessons from Disasters: Play, Work, and the Creative Arts. *Childhood Education*, 82, 2–9.

Jalongo, M. R. (2010). From Urban Homelessness to Rural Work: International Origins of the Orphan Trains. *Early Childhood Education Journal*, 38, 165–70.

Kahan, M. (2006). Put Up on Platforms: A History of Twentieth-Century Adoption Policy in the United States. *Journal of Sociology and Social Welfare*, 33, 51–72.

Trammell, R. S. (2009). Orphan Train Myths and Legal Reality. *Modern America*, 5, 3–13.

Warren, A. (1996). *Orphan Train Rider: One Boy's True Story*. New York: Houghton Mifflin.

INTRODUCTION

IN THIS CHAPTER WE TRACE THE history of the juvenile justice system from its origins in the nineteenth century. Charles Loring Brace dedicated his life to saving children from what he believed would be a future of misery, crime, and corruption. Brace was one of many **child savers**, who headed a reform movement that led to the founding of the juvenile justice system.[1] During this time, there was an effort on the part of the wealthy and elite within society to address the problem of poverty and disorder on the streets of the city. Women, in particular, were highly active in a series of moral crusades, including the temperance (antialcohol) movement that focused on a need to establish moral order in a rapidly changing society.[2] Like all moral entrepreneurs, reformers were motivated by a sense of urgency or moral panic that the social order was in serious danger of collapse. The structure of society was changing, and the pattern of familial supervision, care, and control of children and youth, traditionally in rural villages and small towns, fell apart in cities bursting with hordes of new immigrants. There was intense concern over the problem of pauperism, or poverty, and even greater concern for the troublesome behavior in city streets by youth of the impoverished classes.

The establishment of the juvenile and family court along with child labor laws, foster care, public education, and reform schools were efforts by moral entrepreneurs to respond to social disorder in these growing urban centers. Reformers invented the term *delinquency* to refer to the illegal acts committed by children, but their concern was not really about crime. The term *juvenile delinquency* had, and continues to have, a broader social meaning than the legal concept. It refers to youthful behavior that powerful adults see as deviant, dangerous, problematic, and disturbing. These behaviors violate a sense of moral order. New immigrants brought norms and behaviors that were socially unacceptable to the existing culture of the established elite—white, Anglo-Saxon Protestants. Some believe that even more than "caring" for other people's children, was the stronger desire to "control" these children, to mold them in ways that reformers found socially acceptable.[3]

This was the context in which the institution of the juvenile justice system was born. Underlying the creation of new developmental institutions to socialize and supervise youth was the societal recognition of both childhood and adolescence as important phases of human development. The ideals of this movement were shaped by a view of childhood familiar to us today: the belief that children are born innocent but highly vulnerable to the negative influences of adults within their environments.[4]

The societal elite were working to establish new systems for caring for children based on new attitudes toward the special responsibility of adults to provide children with a structured and protected upbringing during childhood. There was a recognized need to create institutions to care for the children who were neglected or abused by their families, and an equally intense need to create new laws and institutions to regulate the moral and social behavior of unruly adolescents in order to socialize them to become respectable and productive citizens.

CHILD SAVERS
Privileged individuals who sought to protect children from the ills of society, often by removing lower-class and immigrant youth from their environments.

DECLINE OF FAMILY-BASED SYSTEMS OF SOCIAL CONTROL

Before the massive changes brought by industrialization, most people lived in small rural communities where family was society's main economic and social unit. Children were widely viewed as economic assets expected to labor for the benefit of the family and subject to the absolute authority of the father. In his own home, the father was king. The church and the community reinforced the authority of the father in disciplining members of his household, including children, women, and servants.[5]

All family members lived and worked together in family-based industries. As soon as they were able, children were assigned tasks such as weeding, gathering kindling, tending to animals, and caring for younger siblings. The rhythms of daily life were common for family members of all ages: They woke together; slept in the same room; ate the same foods; enjoyed the same entertainments; and went to bed at the same time.

If a family had too many mouths to feed, children were "**placed out**," sent to relatives to serve in their household; or hired out as apprentices for a fee.[6] Among the early settlers to America, many children arrived as indentured servants or apprentices required by law to serve and obey their masters until the age of majority. These servants and apprentices were also subject to the absolute authority of the master, whose will was enforced through the local magistrates.

Among the privileged classes, marriage arrangements were made, ensuring that power and prestige would stay intact.[7] Infants born to those in the privileged classes were sent off at birth to be cared for by distant wet nurses in the country. Privileged young male children, aged eight or nine, would be assigned to a squire (or knight), in a kind of apprenticeship for an adult role, while young girls were placed in households to acquire the necessary skills for marriage in maintaining a household. By the early teen years, as we saw with the fictional characters of Romeo and Juliet, individuals assumed adult roles and responsibilities.

EMERGENCE OF CHILDHOOD

According to Phillip Ariès, one of the first historians to research the topic, the modern conception of childhood began to develop between the thirteenth and the sixteenth centuries.[8] In the Middle Ages (700–1500 CE), what we now recognize as the period of life called "childhood" simply did not exist. Aries argued that high rates of infant mortality typical of the pre-modern era dampened the emotional attachment between parents and infants. Because so few infants survived into childhood, parents did not invest in them emotionally until the child was older.

> **PLACED OUT**
> Youth sent to relatives to serve as household servants or hired out as apprentices for a fee.

Ariès noted that in medieval paintings, infants and small children appear as "miniature adults" draped in tiny versions of adult dress, with adult-like faces. This began to change in the fifteenth and sixteenth centuries, as artists began to portray the dimpled features of children and babies dressed in clothing especially designed for them. Toys, games, songs, and rhymes composed specifically for children began to appear. The first pediatric textbook was written in the sixteenth century, reflecting an awareness that children's physical needs were distinct from adults. The idea of romantic love also began to change the institution of marriage, from a purely economic transaction between two families, to an emotional union between two people, as portrayed in *Romeo and Juliet*. This also influenced how children were valued and treated, increasing their emotional importance over their economic contribution in the family unit.

Changes in the structure of households and society help to explain this shift in attitude toward childhood. As the towns and cities grew, more and more merchants, tradespeople, and craftsmen were able to build larger houses with first floors that afforded separate space on the upper floors for parents and children. The idea of the "nursery" as a specific room designed for the care of children appeared among the wealthy. Increasingly, educational systems, particularly for the aristocratic and middle classes, provided a more-formalized period of instruction for the young outside the home. Books and pamphlets were written to guide parents in how to educate and instruct their children. Gradually the period we now call "childhood" emerged as a special stage of life with the idea that adults had a responsibility to provide a physical and social environment for children that was suited to their needs, sheltered from the adult world.

Stubborn Child Laws

By the seventeenth century, the attitude of adults shifted from one in which children were either used or ignored to one in which children needed to be controlled, educated, shaped, and disciplined.[9] New England colonists embraced a view of children shaped by the biblical idea of original sin: Children required obedience, discipline, and respect for authority in order to overcome the inherent sinfulness of the human soul. **Patriarchy** was also the foundation for the family-based social control within the colonial society. The authority of the male was upheld by religious and social norms of the community, which had been codified into legal norms.

Drawing from the Old Testament, the colony of Massachusetts passed the first "Stubborn Child Law" in 1646, making it a criminal offense for children to disobey their parents. This law gave power to the public authorities to intervene against children who failed to comply with parental authority. If children disobeyed the will of their parents, they could be publicly whipped by local authorities, or even put to death. Soon after the establishment of this law in New England, other colonies followed with similar statutes. These statutes also recognized the possibility that parents might abuse their own children. They established the child's legal right to claim self-defense if parental discipline was so extreme as to threaten the life of the child.

Legal authorities in the community enforced social norms about the proper way to raise and discipline children. Central to the moral and religious code was the importance of the work ethic for children as well as adults. Idleness was viewed as a moral failing. Families that permitted their children over the age of seven the "sin" of idleness were seen as "negligent and indulgent," and risked having their

PATRIARCHY
Social or family system in which the male is the head and governs all within the society or the household.

children removed from their home by town authorities and sent to live and work for other families. Parents were also required by law to teach their children to read and write primarily so they could read and study the Bible for themselves.

Although norms changed over time, laws granting the state the power to regulate and control how families care for and treat their own children began as early as the seventeenth century. The Puritan use of the law to enforce social norms on the families set the pattern for the relationship between families and the government that we have today.

INDUSTRIALIZATION, URBANIZATION, AND IMMIGRATION

Massive changes associated with industrialization brought dramatic changes to patterns of social life that undermined the small-town system of family-based social control. What began as a trickle became a flood as families left the fields and farms and flocked to the cities to find work in the factories in urban centers. Throughout the 1800s, successive tides of immigrant families from Europe swelled the populations of US cities. In 1790, New York City had the largest population, with 33,000 inhabitants. By 1830, only forty years later, New York had mushroomed to over 200,000 inhabitants; by 1850, the United States was in the midst of the first Industrial Revolution, and New York had over a half-million inhabitants. By 1880, New York would become the first US city to have more than one million residents.[10]

The traditional system of family-based social control could not be sustained in a city full of strangers. Poor families relied on the earnings of their children to augment their own meager wages as wave after wave of rural poor flocked to the cities to find work. Factory production relied on the inexpensive labor provided by children. Small hands could slip between the spindles of the looms in the textile mills and small bodies could easily fit down a chimney or coal chute for cleaning. It was often easier for poor children to find work than their fathers, who might only find occasional employment digging or carrying.

In crowded urban conditions with ten or twelve family members to a room, the children spilled out into the streets where they foraged, played, stole, and begged for food and money from passersby. European families often had only enough money to send one child to America; this child was expected to live with others, and return a portion of their earnings to their impoverished families back home. This was known as the "padrone system" in Southern Italy.[11]

Back in their European villages, children had always worked alongside adults. In the New World, children did the same. Poor children did all kinds of work: peddling flowers, selling cigarettes and newspapers, shining shoes, sweeping floors in the saloons, and running messages and packages from one business to another. The so-called "organ grinder children" were a common sight on the street corner, performing and begging passersby for a coin or two. Along the way they also committed petty crime with small hands and swift feet: filching food from street vendors, shoplifting, and pickpocketing for wallets.

George W. Matsell, New York City's first chief of police, provided a description of these "idle and vicious children . . . who infest our public thoroughfares, hotels, docks" in his 1849 semiannual report on *The Problem of Vagrant and Delinquent Children*. He saw these children as doomed to a life of misery. Matsell points out that "a large proportion of these juvenile vagrants are in the daily practice of pilfering wherever opportunity offers, and begging when they cannot steal." Police at the time referred to these children as "street rats."[12]

Many of these immigrants were Catholic families from Ireland, Italy, and Eastern Europe. American-born Protestants viewed Catholicism as an inferior form of Christianity, full of ignorant ritual. To the established middle- and upper-class Protestants, these new immigrants were an inferior and degraded race. They viewed the cultural habits of the new immigrants as uneducated, immoral, and dangerous. Primary among these habits was the use of alcohol—wine, whiskey, and beer—viewed by sober, middle-class Protestants as a source of sin and misery. The poverty of these immigrants and the foul living conditions within the urban tenements was, in their opinion, the result of these sinful habits and attitudes.

To the respectable middle-class citizen, the saloons and dance halls of the urban immigrant neighborhood were both a sign and source of corruption. If immigrants were miserably poor it was because they brought it upon themselves with lax moral standards, poor work ethics, and indulgence in the sins of liquor and fornication. They were to blame for the squalid conditions of their lives. Their children, however, were innocent and could be saved.

Reformers came to the conclusion that the only way to prevent the overwhelming problem of poverty was to prevent it from happening in the next generation by removing the young from their parents and indoctrinating them with the moral education their parents failed to provide. These reformers believed that children of the poor required an environment with strict discipline and supervision to avoid succumbing to the temptations of immoral behavior. The solution was the creation of institutions that would indoctrinate poor youth with good work habits and solid moral character.

INSTITUTION-BUILDING ERA

The combination of poverty and diminished family control set the stage for a sense among the elite of a threat to the social stability of American society. They believed that new institutions were needed to manage the behavior of poor youth. These wealthy and civic-minded citizens built a variety of different institutions, including orphanages, houses of refuge, reform schools, and workhouses to rescue the children of the poor from poverty and the corrupting influence of the city.

A report published in 1818 on the problem of pauperism (or poverty) coined the term *juvenile delinquency* to refer to the crimes committed by youth and to the growing problem of vagrancy and idleness among the young.[13] In 1820, the Society for the Prevention of Pauperism conducted a survey of US prisons and found many children convicted of petty crimes housed among the inmates. By 1823, the group had renamed itself the Society for the Reformation of Juvenile Delinquents in the City of New York. In 1824, the New York legislature passed a bill to create the first reform institution for children in the United States aimed at resocializing these children.

The first publicly funded institutions for the care of juvenile delinquents were established in the 1820s.[14] The New York House of Refuge was created in 1824, while in Philadelphia and Boston such houses were created in 1826. Baltimore followed suit in 1830. The Houses of Refuge movement embraced three core features that were foundational to the modern juvenile justice system.[15] The first was the recognition that juveniles were different from adults and should be kept separate from adults. The second was the idea that a young person within the House of Refuge was there to be reformed, not to serve a criminal sentence. Therefore, an **indeterminate placement** occurred, where the length of stay was determined by the judge, or until the young person reached the age of adult majority. The last innovation was to focus on the child not as a lawbreaker, but as either incorrigible (which means uncontrollable) or neglected by the parents, and for the institution to take the legal role of the parent in disciplining and controlling that child.

Reformatories and Houses of Refuge

The internal structure of these institutions reflected the belief in the power of hard work, rigid discipline, and religious education. Financially, institutions relied on philanthropy, public funding, and contracting out the labor of the children to local businesses as a source of revenue. Historian David Rothman provides the following description of the daily routine in the New York House of Refuge:[16]

> The first bells rang at sunrise to wake the youngsters, the second came fifteen minutes later to signal the guards to unlock the individual cells. The inmates stepped into the hallways and . . . marched in order to the washroom. . . . From the washroom they are called to parade in the open air and undergo a critical inspection as to cleanliness and dress. Inmates next went in formation to chapel for prayer, and afterwards [spent] one hour in school. At seven a.m. the bells announced breakfast, and then a half-hour later, the time to begin work. The boys spent till noon in the shops, usually making brass nails or cane seats, while the girls washed, cooked, and made and mended the clothes. At twelve o'clock, a bell rings to call all from work, and one hour [was] allowed for washing and dinner. At one o'clock, a signal is given for recommencing work, which continues till five in the afternoon, when the bell rings for termination of the labor of the day. There followed thirty minutes to wash and to eat, two and one half hours of evening classes, and finally, to end the day, evening prayers. The children are then marched to the sleeping halls, where each takes possession of his separate apartment, the cells are locked, and silence is enforced for the night.

Just as young Alton experienced the orphanage as a harsh place devoid of kindness and any affection, these institutions quickly became prison-like environments relying on punishment and deprivation to control youth. When Charles Loring Brace created the orphan train, his aim was to save children both from their own immoral families and from the imposed misery of institutions like the New York House of Refuge.

EMERGENCE AND REGULATION OF ADOLESCENCE

The concept of "adolescence" as a stage between childhood and adulthood began to develop in the United States toward the end of the nineteenth century, with the decline of the farming economy and rise of formal education. All children,

INDETERMINATE PLACEMENT
Juvenile facility stay for an unspecified amount of time determined by the judge, or until legal age of majority.

as we will see in chapter 7, were to be educated to some extent. In the classic one-room schoolhouse of the 1800s, all children were educated together, just as they would be if they were learning around the fire at home. At Harvard College, for example, one of the early educational institutions for upper-class males, the freshman class had youth ranging in age from twelve to twenty. By the end of the nineteenth century, with the establishment of free secondary public education funded by local taxes, at least some education was accessible to all social classes. Society placed more importance on being literate and obtaining an education. It was then that schools separated youth into classes based on age using written examinations to regulate the passage from one "grade" to the next.

Such **age segregation** in schools and in factory and office workplaces increased the importance of the **peer group** as an influence on a young person. In the farm household, youth would spend most of their daily lives in the company of their kin and neighbors of different ages. But life in cities and towns was different. Adults worked in a different part of the factory than children and youth; in schools, children and youth were segregated into age groupings, creating peer groups. This spilled over onto the city streets, where youth began to congregate in age-based groups. The phenomenon of "gangs" began to emerge on these streets in the nineteenth century.

Under these new conditions of urban life, parents faced difficulties in disciplining and controlling older youth. The father of the household lost his position of authority over his sons, who were more literate, able to speak English, and able to earn as much or more in the factory than their father. Youth came under the influence of their peers more than their family elders. Adolescent girls refused to follow the customary traditions of courtship from the Old Country that restricted involvement with boys until marriage. Both girls and boys resisted arranged marriages. Conflicts between parents and youth often erupted in physical fights and beatings, sometimes fueled by alcohol, which shocked the genteel middle classes.[17]

CONTROLLING ADOLESCENT GIRLS

For girls, child saving focused on regulating the sexual behavior of poor, young females in the attempt to enforce the norms of middle-class morality. Elite educated women of the nineteenth century found an outlet for involvement in public life by focusing on the needs of vulnerable children and adolescent girls. Women reformers, for example, led an aggressive campaign to raise the legal age of sexual consent—in some states, as low as age ten or twelve—to the age of sixteen, and advocated for the enforcement of statutory rape charges, even for girls who willingly engaged in sexual activity. Reformers used the new juvenile system to confine girls who engaged in premarital sex, especially with multiple partners, or were at risk of engaging in sex, until they were of marriageable age. During the nineteenth century and early twentieth century, girls spent five times longer than males in the early juvenile institutions.[18]

The first reform school for girls was the State Industrial School for Girls established in 1856 in Lancaster, Massachusetts.[19] According to historian Barbara Brenzel, over two-thirds of the girls confined in that institution were accused of committing moral rather than criminal offenses: vagrancy, beggary, stubbornness, deceitfulness, idle and vicious behavior, wanton and lewd conduct, and

AGE SEGREGATION
Separation of individuals based on age.

PEER GROUP
A group of individuals who spend time together.

running away. Most of those committed were immigrants, many of them Irish, who were apprehended and convicted for immorality and waywardness because they were out with men frequenting dance halls, saloons, and vaudeville shows. A detailed study of the Cook County Juvenile Court of Illinois between 1906 and 1927 found that the two most common charges against girls were immorality and incorrigibility.[20]

The institutional regime for girls' reformatories focused on the reformation of "loose women" into paragons of propriety and chastity.[21] The girls were taught domestic skills and then typically sent into the care of families to work as domestic servants or detained until they were married. While the institutions boasted a family-like home atmosphere, in reality they relied heavily on coercive and punitive control. A statement issued by the Ladies Committee of the New York House of Refuge describes the changes that occurred within the reformatory: "[S]he enters a rude, careless, untrained child, caring nothing for cleanliness and order; when she leaves the House, she can sew, mend, darn, wash, iron, arrange a table neatly, and cook a healthy meal."[22]

RACIAL SEGREGATION

The reformers who created the modern juvenile justice system almost exclusively focused on "saving" and reforming white immigrant boys and girls. Just as white child savers did not place African Americans onto the orphan trains, so too did white reformers deny the status and benefits of childhood to youth of color who committed delinquent offenses.[23] White elites generally rejected the idea of mixed-race institutions, especially in the South. A 1923 federal census of children in institutions found nearly half of all black delinquents were housed in adult prisons and jails rather than in juvenile institutions.[24]

In the early part of the twentieth century, middle-class African Americans began to advocate for the state to create separate juvenile institutions for black youth. These segregated institutions were poorly funded and suffered from the same shortcomings as the juvenile institutions for poor whites. While the rhetoric suggested that these were home-like institutions offering education, religious instruction, and loving support, the reality was that most juvenile institutions quickly came to resemble prisons with heavy reliance on isolation, physical punishment, and harsh treatment.

PARENS PATRIAE LEGAL DOCTRINE

When challenged to explain the legality of these new institutions that removed children from their families, the courts relied on the ancient principle of **parens patriae** as legal justification for state power over natural families. This legal doctrine is rooted in patriarchy, in which the father holds sole authority within the household to wield complete control over children, as well as their wives, subordinates, and servants. The Latin phrase *parens patriae* was used to describe the legal status in which the king served as "father" and protector of his subjects.

During the Middle Ages, the king established specialized courts known as chancery courts to settle property disputes.[25] As the "father of the country," under this legal doctrine the king was able to take control of the property of

> **PARENS PATRIAE**
> Doctrine that allows the juvenile court to act as a father figure to all children.

wealthy orphaned children, allowing the monarch to consolidate and extend his own power. Hundreds of years later, nineteenth-century reformers revived the doctrine of *parens patriae* as the source of legal authority for taking poor children—who were not orphans and may have committed no crime—away from their biological families into the custody of the state.

A significant legal ruling in 1838 demonstrated this new legal interpretation of the doctrine of *parens patriae*. The case involved the regulation of adolescent girls.[26] Mary Ann Crouse was a fifteen-year-old who had been committed by a justice of the peace to the Philadelphia House of Refuge at the request of her mother, who said she was "incorrigible" because she refused to obey her. Mary Ann Crouse was typical of the girls who were committed to the House of Refuge for defying parental rules in their desire to be out at night.

Mary Ann's father found out his daughter was being detained after the girl had been legally committed to the institution. He filed a **writ of habeas corpus**, which is a legal claim to the court arguing that a person is being imprisoned or detained illegally. He hired a lawyer to argue that his daughter had been imprisoned without a jury trial or due process, and that this was a violation of the US Constitution.

The decision of the court upheld the legality of her incarceration, relying on the doctrine of *parens patriae*. In this decision, the court explained that the state was intervening, not to punish her, but to save her from a life of misery and crime. The judge stated that commitment to the House of Refuge was an act of charity that would provide her with habits of industry, reshape her mind through religion and morality, and, above all, separate her from the "corrupting influence of improper associates." Since it was clear from her immodest behavior that Mary Ann's own parents were unable to provide proper parental supervision, the court stated it was the right and duty of the state to do so. With this ruling the court established that the state could declare itself the guardian or parent if they found the natural parents unfit or unable. Even though Mary Ann Crouse had a biological parent willing and able to care for her, the court established its power to judge the parenting skills of natural parents and its right to supplant parental values with the court's values, literally taking the child from its natural parents.

ORIGINS OF CHILD WELFARE

The juvenile justice system is the foundation for our child welfare system: The two systems are intertwined in their origins. Today researchers recognize the high degree of overlap between children and youth who are involved in the foster care system and those who are involved in the juvenile justice system. The term **dual-system youth**, or **multi-system youth**, refers to the interconnections between dependency, neglect, abuse, and delinquency. As we will see in chapter 3, these systems separated only in the latter half of the twentieth century. In the original juvenile court, all three legal categories were within its jurisdiction.

In 1874, the first Society for the Prevention of Cruelty to Children was established.[27] By 1900, there were over three hundred such societies across the United States. Modeled after the Society for the Prevention of Cruelty to Animals, these organizations focused on lobbying state legislatures to pass laws criminalizing negligent parents and allowing for the legal removal of children from the home. Agents of the Society were given the legal power to remove children from their

WRIT OF HABEAS CORPUS
A legal claim to the court arguing that a person is imprisoned or detained illegally.

DUAL-SYSTEM YOUTH
Youth who are, or who have been, involved in both delinquency and the child welfare systems; also called multi-system youth.

homes. They also were given the power to arrest anyone who interfered with their work. In New York City alone, by 1890, the Society was making placement decisions for fifteen thousand poor and neglected children every year.[28]

As we see with the orphan train movement, the practice of child removal became the hallmark of the future child welfare system.[29] Families struggling with the burdens of poverty, discrimination, and hardship, and desperately in need of social assistance, were instead criminalized, stigmatized, and wrenched apart by a system that was more punitive than supportive. It is not surprising that historian Linda Gordon discovered that poor immigrant families called the Society for the Prevention of Cruelty to Children "the Cruelty."[30] Many poor families lived in fear of losing custody of their children when they could not meet the standards set by the middle-class agents of society.

Young Alton's experience in the orphanage was a common one for youth removed from their homes and placed in institutional care. Alton was removed from a home that was poor, but where he experienced a sense of love and belonging, and was put in an institution that lacked kindness, affection, and basic compassion for its young charges. As we will see in later chapters, attempts to create a home-like atmosphere in juvenile facilities have repeated this pattern of failure. The invention of the foster care system was a response to this dismal pattern, and an attempt to provide temporary care in a real home for children who needed to be removed from their parents.

In 1870, another case, quite similar to Mary Ann Crouse's, concerned a sixteen-year-old boy committed to a reformatory. This case also challenged the legal authority of the state to take custody of children and incarcerate them for their own good. In *O'Connell v. Turner*, the Illinois Supreme Court ruled that the state could only interfere with parental custody upon proof of "gross misconduct" or total unfitness on the part of the parent(s).[31] The state legislature then repealed the power of private aid societies like the Society for the Prevention of Cruelty to Children and the Children's Aid Society to take custody of children based on noncriminal conduct.

JUVENILE COURT CREATION

The response of reformers to this legal setback was to lobby the legislature to create a specific law to establish a juvenile court and grant the juvenile court original legal jurisdiction over all three populations: children and youth who are orphaned, and therefore considered **dependent youth**; children and youth who are deemed to be neglected or abused by their parents; and children and youth whose behavior is troublesome or illegal, otherwise known as delinquent youth. The culmination of nearly a century of experimentation was the establishment of the first specialized juvenile court in 1899 in the state of Illinois to deal with all children in need of care. The legislation that established the court was titled "An Act to Regulate the Treatment and Control of Dependent, Neglected, and Delinquent Children."

The explicit aim of the juvenile court was to function as a social welfare agency, not as a criminal court. The juvenile court held original jurisdiction for all cases removing those younger than sixteen who had committed a crime from the jurisdiction of the criminal court entirely. The intention of the juvenile court was never to operate as a criminal justice system, but to operate as a child welfare system with paternalistic control over the upbringing of the children if

DEPENDENT YOUTH
Youth who are orphaned, who are deemed inadequately cared for, or who are harmed by parents are placed under state control.

the parents were deemed inadequate. Under the *parens patriae* doctrine, the core justification and guiding principle was to act "in the best interests of the child."

The juvenile court would also determine the "fitness" or "amenability" to reform of individual children by determining whether they belonged in juvenile court, or if they should be brought before the criminal courts. The juvenile probation officer emerged as a crucial occupation within the juvenile system, responsible for supplying the judge with information about the child's home life, and with providing community-based supervision for those adjudicated delinquent by the court. The jurisdiction of the court included judging the quality of the parenting these children received. The new profession of social work emerged to fulfill the court's mandate to protect children from criminally abusive and/or neglectful parents.

The institution of the juvenile court spread rapidly across the nation. By 1905, ten states had enacted a juvenile court law; by 1915, forty-six states and the District of Columbia had a juvenile court; and by 1930, all states had an established juvenile court and juvenile justice system.[32]

Status offenses are a very clear outgrowth of the *parens patriae* doctrine. These are offenses that would not be a crime if committed by an adult, and may not even be considered delinquent offenses. They include running away, truancy, curfew violations, and failure to obey parents/guardians, otherwise known as incorrigibility, or ungovernability. This allows the court to take control of the youth and provide services. Today states vary in how they handle youth who have committed status offenses. Some states, such as Iowa, address truants as delinquents, where punishment can be imprisonment, and parents can be prosecuted for their child's being late for and/or failure to attend school; whereas in Georgia, truants are considered as needing services, and subject to juvenile court jurisdiction, but not to punishments such as fines and imprisonment.[33]

COMPARING RHETORIC WITH REALITY

At every point in our examination of the juvenile justice system—from changes in the past to those transformations taking place today—we explore both the hopes and aspirations for the system and the actual practices and daily realities of the system. The "talk," or rhetoric, about the juvenile justice system is not always in alignment with the "walk," or actual practice. There is often a contradiction between what reformers say is happening in the system they create and what actually occurs.

We can see this gap between the "talk" and the "walk" in the case of the orphan train movement. Despite the rhetoric, most of the children placed on the trains were not, in fact, orphans. They were poor, but most had families who were struggling to provide for them. We see too that the motivation of rural families who came to the churches and town halls was not to adopt a child as their own, but to find laborers to work on the farm. Furthermore, despite the idealized image of rural life, not all farmers were as "kind and intelligent" as Brace believed, and at least some were cruel, abusive, and/or neglectful in their treatment of the youth.

In this chapter we also continue to see how intersectionality—in this case, the dynamics of place, class, race, and gender—shapes differential treatment of children within the system. Not all poor children were invited to board the orphan trains: African Americans, along with Native Americans, Chinese, and Hispanic children were not considered worthy of being "saved." Well into the twentieth

STATUS OFFENSES
Actions that are deemed illegal only for youth.

century, African-American youth and other youth of color continued to be sent to the adult criminal system. We see too that in the nineteenth century, girls were more likely to be detained and incarcerated for violating moral codes of sexuality that applied only to females, a pattern that persists today.

Finally, we see in the history of the juvenile justice system that the power associated with class, wealth, and privilege allows some groups to impose their norms on other groups. In a diverse society, social norms are always a source of conflict. Specifically, middle- and upper-class reformers used the power of the state to respond to and to regulate the conduct of poor families and their children. Although the intentions were often altruistic, the institutions created were designed for "other people's children" rather than their own.

In the next chapter we turn to the important transformations that took place within the juvenile justice system in the twentieth century. As always, a key question for us to consider is: How well are *all* the children within our society?

KEY TERMS

age segregation Separation of individuals based on age.

child savers Privileged individuals who sought to protect children from the ills of society, often by removing lower-class and immigrant youth from their environments.

dependent youth Youth who are orphaned, who are deemed inadequately cared for, or who are harmed by parents are placed under state control.

dual-system youth Youth who are, or who have been, involved in both delinquency and the child welfare systems; also called multi-system youth.

indeterminate placement Juvenile facility stay for an unspecified amount of time determined by the judge, or until legal age of majority.

parens patriae Doctrine that allows the juvenile court to act as a father figure to all children.

patriarchy Social or family system in which the male is the head and governs all within the society or the household.

peer group A group of individuals who spend time together.

placed out Youth sent to relatives to serve as household servants or hired out as apprentices for a fee.

status offenses Actions that are deemed illegal only for youth.

writ of habeas corpus A legal claim to the court arguing that a person is imprisoned or detained illegally.

REVIEW AND STUDY QUESTIONS

1. What were the moral and social goals of the child savers? What were the positive and negative effects of their actions?

2. How did societal changes, such as industrialization, urbanization, and immigration, affect how children were viewed by society?

3. How were these systems developed to socialize youth different for immigrants? For lower-class youth? For girls?

4. When did the stage of "adolescence" emerge within the life course? What social factors led to the emergence of this stage of development?

5. What were the consequences of age segregation in schools and in the workplace? How does this practice contribute to the emergence of gangs and other age-related peer groups?

6. What are the origins of the *parens patriae* doctrine in English law?

7. What does *parens patriae* mean in the context of addressing youthful misbehavior? What institutions resulted as an outgrowth of that philosophy?

8. Describe the origins of the child welfare system within the juvenile justice context.

9. Apply the concept of intersectionality to the behavior of the child savers. How did the treatment of youth vary by race, class, gender, and ethnicity?

10. How did the rhetoric or "talk" of the early juvenile reforms compare to the reality or the "walk" of the actual institutions created for children and youth?

CHECK IT OUT

Watch

Century of Childhood:

www.youtube.com/watch?v=P-TDIBDg9V8

San Francisco Industrial School: www.youtube.com/watch?list=UUUbtUu9G11TDQzIrxiXR3HQ&v=rn0TIGn3BUM

Web

Dual System / Status Youth Reform:

http://rfknrcjj.org/our-work/dual-status-youth-reform/

NOTES

[1] Platt, A. M. (2009). *The Child Savers: The Invention of Delinquency* (40th anniversary ed.). New Brunswick, NJ: Rutgers University Press.

[2] Rothman, D. (1971). *The Discovery of the Asylum: Social Order and Disorder in the New Republic*. Boston, MA: Little, Brown and Co.

[3] Platt, *The Child Savers: The Invention of Delinquency*.

[4] Costin, L. B. (1985). The Historical Context of Child Welfare. In J. Laird and A. Hartman (eds.), *A Handbook of Child Welfare*, 34–60. New York: Free Press.

[5] Coontz, S. (1988). *The Social Origins of Private Life: A History of American Families 1600–1900*. New York: Verso.

[6] Ariès, P. (1962). *Centuries of Childhood: A Social History of Family Life*. (Baldick, R., Trans.). New York: Random House.

[7] Ibid.

[8] Ibid.

[9] Sutton, J. (1988). *Stubborn Children: Controlling Delinquency in the United States, 1640–1981*. Berkeley: University of California Press.

[10] Rank by Population of the 100 Largest Urban Places, Listed Alphabetically by State: 1790–1990. Source: US Bureau of the Census, Internet Release Date: June 15, 1998.

[11] Gordon, L. (1988). *Heroes in Their Own Lives*. New York: Viking.

[12] Matsell, G. W. (1850). *Semi-Annual Report of the Chief of Police from May 1, to October 31, 1849*. New York: City of New York.

[13] Mennel, R. M. (1973). *Thorns and Thistles: Juvenile Delinquents in the United States: 1825–1940*. Lebanon, NH: University Press of New England.

[14] Fox, S. (1996). The Early History of the Court. *The Juvenile Court, 6*, 29–38.

[15] Sutton, *Stubborn Children: Controlling Delinquency in the United States, 1640–1981*.

[16] Rothman, D. (1971). *The Discovery of the Asylum: Social Order and Disorder in the New Republic*. Boston: Little Brown and Co.

[17] Golden, R. (1997) *Disposable Children: America's Welfare System*. Belmont, CA: Wadsworth.

[18] Knupfer, A. M. (2001). *Reform and Resistance: Gender, Delinquency, and America's First Juvenile Court*. New York: Routledge.

[19] Brenzel, B. (1975). Lancaster Industrial School for Girls: A Social Portrait of a 19th Century Reform School for Girls. *Feminist Studies, 3*, 40–53.

[20] Chesney-Lind, M., and Sheldon, R. (2014). *Girls, Delinquency and Juvenile Justice*. (4th ed.). New York: John Wiley & Sons.

[21] Brenzel, B. (1983). *Daughters of the State*. Cambridge, MA: MIT Press.

[22] Chesney-Lind and Sheldon, *Girls, Delinquency and Juvenile Justice*.

[23] Pisciotta, A. W. (1983). Race, Sex, and Rehabilitation: A Study of Differential Treatment in the Juvenile Reformatory. *Crime and Delinquency, 29*, 254–68.

[24] Bush, W. (2010). *Who Gets a Childhood? Race and Juvenile Justice in 20th Century Texas*. Athens, GA: University of Georgia Press.

[25] Sutton, *Stubborn Children: Controlling Delinquency in the United States, 1640–1981*.

[26] Pisciotta, A. W. (1982). Saving the Children: The Promise and Practice of *Parens Patriae*. *Crime and Delinquency, 29*, 254–68.

[27] Olson-Raymer, G. (1983). The Role of the Federal Government in Juvenile Delinquency Prevention: Historical and Contemporary Perspectives. *Journal of Criminal Law & Criminology, 74*, 578–600.

[28] Fox, The Early History of the Court, 29–38.

[29] Golden, *Disposable Children: America's Welfare System*.

[30] Gordon, *Heroes in Their Own Lives*. New York: Viking.

[31] Fox, The Early History of the Court, 29–38.

[32] Ibid.

[33] Office of Juvenile Justice and Delinquency Prevention Statistical Briefing Book. Online. Available at: www.ojjdp.gov/ojstatbb/structure_process/qa04121.asp?qaDate=2013; Iowa Compulsory Education Code, http://coolice.legis.iowa.gov/Cool-ICE/default.asp?category=billinfo&service=IowaCode&ga=83&input=299.

Paradigms of Youth Justice

LEARNING OBJECTIVES

By the end of the chapter, you should be able to do the following:

- Articulate the "cycle of reform" thesis.
- Identify the four different paradigms in juvenile justice.
- Explain significant concepts under the four juvenile justice paradigms.
- Identify major policies and programs under the four juvenile justice paradigms.
- Describe community/restorative justice.
- Describe positive youth development.
- Explain what is meant by evidence-based practices.

Case Study 3: A Tragedy or a Crime?

On Thursday June 2, 2011, a grand jury issued an indictment against twelve-year-old Cristian Fernandez, making him the youngest person to be charged with first-degree murder in the history of Jacksonville, Florida. No longer a juvenile in the eyes of the law, the indictment required a transfer from juvenile hall to the adult jail, where Cristian was placed in an isolation cell for inmates in need of protection. On Saturday, June 4, Cristian Fernandez, along with eighty fellow inmates, were transported to court in orange jumpsuits bound by shackles around their wrists and ankles. To most observers it was a strange sight to see a sixth grader shuffle into court amid a crowd of grown men.

A Toddler Dies

Three months earlier Susana Fernandez had carried her two-year-old son, David, limp and unresponsive, into the emergency room. Cristian had been babysitting his younger siblings while his mother went to the bank. Susana rushed home after a panicked Cristian called to say David was unconscious after a fall from the top of the bunk bed.

Investigators later found that Susana did not immediately bring the unconscious baby to the emergency room; instead, she cleaned his face, changed his diaper, put his blue pajamas on, put ice on his head and some alcohol on a tissue, which she waved under his nose, hoping it would revive him. Records show she searched the Internet for what to do when someone has a concussion; how to wake someone who is unconscious; and how to treat head trauma. After many hours, when David still had not regained consciousness, she put the toddler in the car and, after dropping the other children at school, took him to the hospital for treatment. Once there, there was little the doctors could do; the toddler died two days later.

This was not the first time Susana had brought little David to an emergency room with injuries. Only two months earlier, he had come in with a broken leg. This time she had waited two days before turning to medical authorities. Later, she would explain that she turned to the hospital only as a last resort, trying her own home remedies first, because she feared her children would be taken from her.

Susana had good reason to be afraid social services would take her children. The hospital authorities had already opened an investigation, suspecting someone in the household had harmed the baby. Both times Cristian had been home alone with the baby. After David died, authorities moved quickly to arrest Susana on charges of aggravated manslaughter by culpable negligence, for waiting so long to seek medical attention. Then they took Cristian into custody for questioning.

The Interrogation

Police investigators focused their attention on Cristian's claim that David's injuries were caused by a fall from the bunk bed. Before they could interrogate Cristian about what had happened, they had to issue Miranda rights to him. Miranda rights are a mandatory police procedure prior to any questioning that informs a suspect of his constitutional right not to answer the questions posed by the police, and to request legal representation during questioning. In 1967, the Supreme Court ruled that juveniles must knowingly and voluntarily agree to waive their right to an attorney before they can lawfully participate in a police interrogation. The Court requires police to inform suspects in plain language that they have the right to remain silent; that anything they say will be used against them in court; that they have the right to have an attorney present; and that the court will appoint one for them if they cannot afford to hire one. If a suspect is informed of these rights and agrees to waive them, only then will the court consider any confessions made during an interrogation to be legally admissible as evidence.

A videotape of the interview between twelve-year-old Cristian and a female Jacksonville police detective shows the exchange before Cristian signs the waiver, allowing the police to question him without legal representation. Cristian sits alone in a small, windowless room, handcuffed and shackled. The female detective kindly greets him and removes the handcuffs, telling him she wants him to be comfortable. The detective explains she is going to ask him questions, but first she has to discuss something else with him. Cristian nods and listens attentively. She repeats the familiar lines: You have the right to remain silent; you have the right to an attorney, and anything you say here may be used against you in court. Cristian asks her what they are going to talk about, and she says she can't tell him that right now. Then she asks him to read aloud the preamble on the form, which he does promptly, straightening his back and reciting the words as any good student would do when asked by the teacher. Then she asks him to sign the waiver, which he also does dutifully, hunching over the paper as he painstakingly signs his name in cursive letters.

After signing away his right to an attorney, other police officers come to interrogate Cristian many times about what took place the morning he was caring for his younger brother. They tape-record his admission that the toddler did not fall from the bed. Instead, Cristian tells police that his little brother made him angry, so he pushed him into a bookshelf and hit him hard, again and again.

A Twelve-Year-Old Adult?

The decision to keep Cristian in juvenile court or to indict him in criminal court lay in the hands of state prosecutor, Angela Corey. Under Florida criminal code at the time, prosecutors could choose to charge a child of any age either as an adult or a juvenile, for any criminal offense. With his taped confession as evidence, Angela Corey makes the decision to file a charge of first-degree murder. The police had the statement in which Cristian admitted he was angry when he pushed his younger brother into the bookcase; that he carried him, unresponsive and bleeding, to the bed; and that he then called his mother and told her a lie.

The public defender assigned to represent Cristian vigorously argued that Cristian should stay in the juvenile justice system. The public defender twice had Cristian examined by psychologists, and both times those experts determined that he was "amenable" to treatment and a good candidate for rehabilitation. In addition to documenting the sordid details of his life,

defense attorneys argued that Cristian had had no plan or intent to kill his brother. He had lost his temper—in fact, he had even told police that he was thinking about his bitter feelings toward his stepfather at the time.

But the prosecutor took a different set of issues into account in deciding whether or not to charge Cristian as an adult. Prosecutors often prioritize the concern about public safety above the best interests of the child. While prosecutors might have agreed that Cristian was amenable to treatment, they refused to take the chance that Cristian might one day again threaten public safety. According to Angela Corey, her concern was that Cristian was just too damaged to ever be free within the community. In a revealing—and some felt, heartless—statement, Corey said, "In the end . . . one of the key factors was this: Juvenile jurisdiction ends at age twenty-one. . . . My fear is that whatever has happened to this young man in his short time on Earth cannot be solved in eight years."

The charge of first-degree murder in the state of Florida carries with it a mandatory sentence of life without parole. If convicted, Cristian would live his entire life in prison.

A Child without a Childhood

Within days of the indictment, accounts of Cristian's home life began to appear in the newspapers. Cristian's mother, Susana, was eleven years old when she became pregnant with Cristian. Her early childhood had been happy in the care of her grandmother in the Dominican Republic, but at age eight, a mother she barely knew moved her to Miami. Susana's mother, a drug addict, often left her alone. A police report when she was eleven showed her abandoned at school, unable to tell anyone the name of the motel where she lived with her mother. One of the few people she knew was a neighbor who had an eighteen-year-old brother. When Susana became pregnant, Jose Antonio Fernandez, the eighteen-year-old neighbor, was convicted of statutory rape and placed on probation for ten years.

Social service records show a continued pattern of neglect of both the child-mother and her baby. At fifteen months, Cristian was hospitalized for pneumonia, and hospital records show this was the first time the baby had been seen by a pediatrician since he was two months old. Social services intervened when two-year-old Cristian was found wandering the streets, dirty and naked, at four a.m. outside a motel where his thirty-four-year-old grandmother was getting high. Susana, then fourteen, had left the toddler with her mother to sleep over at a friend's house. The state charged the grandmother with neglect, and she was given a case plan to follow. The family then moved to a trailer with no electricity or water. There, Susana and Cristian stayed alone all day while the grandmother went out to get high. Finally, a neighbor alerted social services, and this time they removed the toddler, now three years old. Fourteen-year-old Susana insisted on going with her baby. Both were placed into foster care.

Foster care proved not much better, or safer, especially for Cristian. While there, he was sexually molested by an older child, and shortly thereafter, at age four, watched his foster mother die of a heart attack. Susana meanwhile found a new boyfriend, married him, and after two years took six-year-old Cristian to live in a new home with his stepfather and two additional stepbrothers, ages two and four.

From Bad to Worse

Instead of a life of stability and love, Cristian now endured yet another source of trauma: physical and emotional abuse by his stepfather. A large and violent man, the stepfather developed an immediate and intense dislike for his young wife's eldest son. Cristian was sexually molested by his twelve-year-old cousin, but his stepfather blamed Cristian, accusing him of being gay. Cristian was then sent to live with relatives he had never met in the Dominican Republic, to be "cured."

A year later, when Cristian was allowed to return home, the physical violence and emotional abuse intensified. Neighbors reported that they often saw Cristian doing laundry for the family, carrying groceries, and caring for younger children. They described him as polite but quiet, always in a hurry, as if fearful he would be in trouble if he took too long getting home. Neighbors tried to reach out to Susana, but she too kept her distance, staying behind closed doors with her children.

One day Cristian showed up at middle school with a swollen left eye and a broken rib. Cristian told the school nurse that his father had punched him that morning because he thought the boy had gotten dressed in front of his three-year-old half-sister. The injury to his eye was so severe that the school sent him to the hospital, where doctors immediately notified the police. The school called both parents, but the father refused to come to the school, and only Susana showed up. The police went to the home to arrest the stepfather.

When the police arrived at the home, a little girl opened the door. She turned and ran toward a rear bedroom, clearly frightened. Police noticed tiny bloody footprints as she ran away. They followed to find the stepfather dead from a gunshot wound to his head, a 9mm handgun clutched in his right hand.

The day after the suicide, neighbors watched in stunned silence as young Cristian carried bag after bag of clothing, kitchen equipment, and other personal items out of the apartment and into the car. They offered to help, but his mother refused to let anyone else assist. At age twenty-four, Susana had no one but Cristian to help her care for the three younger children, all under the age of six. In desperation and in hope of a fresh start, Cristian's mother took her four children to the city of Jacksonville to be near her only living relative, a stepsister she barely knew.

Two Mothers Intervene

Alicia Torres was a feisty kindhearted bartender whose son Anthony was a classmate of Cristian Fernandez at the Kernan Middle School in Jacksonville at the time of his arrest. What Anthony told his mother was very different from what she read in the newspapers. The headlines portrayed a violent juvenile charged with murder; her son described an honor student, shy and quiet, who passionately loved school. "He was not one of the troublemakers," her son said. "He was a person you would never have believed would do anything wrong."

Torres had never been involved in any public cause; never contacted officials or advocated for the rights of those who were in need. But something about this case got under her skin. Her first step was to reach out to the stepsister, the only known legal relative, to get permission to visit Cristian inside the county jail. Other than lawyers, social workers, and jail officials, Alicia was the first visitor to come to see Cristian. She found a boy, sad, lost, and alone.

They visited for two hours. Torres explained to him that while he didn't know her, he knew her son Anthony, who went to the same school. When she reminded him of a school field trip she had chaperoned, his face lit up, and they began to talk about school. He was full of questions: Did she think he would be able to go back to sixth grade even if he was twenty-one? What about his homework and the schoolwork he was missing? What about the afterschool program he loved; could he go back there one day? Cristian also asked about his mother and his younger siblings. Who was looking after them? When would he see them again? He knew his mother was being held in the same jail, but he was not allowed to see her. He asked Alicia if she would bring his mother some extra lotion he had that he thought she might like. He told Torres, "I always wanted to make my mom proud of me and take the stress off her because there are so many of us, and so many things to be done around the house."

At the end of the visit, Torres told him that she might not be back to see him for a while, but that didn't mean he had been forgotten. "The last thing I said to him was, 'Just remember, beyond this point, even if you don't see me again, or for a long time, I'm going to be fighting for you.' " Torres left that meeting vowing to do what she could for this boy, who had had so little help from adults in his young life.

Torres began by giving an interview to a Spanish-language publication, sharing the details behind the case where a poor child of color in need of treatment and support was being treated like an adult. "What's putting him in jail going to do? Cause him to suffer more abuse? He's already been there, done that," said Torres. Other media outlets picked up the story, and Torres was bombarded with requests for interviews.

Over a thousand miles away, in New Hampshire, Melissa Higginson, a freelance writer and mother of two, read the story and called Torres to offer her help. Together they started a website and a petition to have Cristian returned to juvenile court, where he would have a chance to get help and one day have a decent life. On the website, the mothers stated their belief that this was a case where the system had failed a child, time and time again. To punish him as an adult was an outrage. The partnership blossomed into a friendship, where the two spoke several times a day, rallying the public to express their outrage at the adult prosecution of a young boy.

Torres organized a community meeting and staged a rally outside the Duval County Courthouse on the day of Cristian's court hearing. On the day of the rally, Torres brought a bouquet of thirteen orange balloons, one for each year of his life. Surrounded by cameras, Torres delivered a box tied with a bow, full of petitions, with a total of 170,000 signatures from the community, demanding that the state prosecutor withdraw the murder charge and return Cristian to juvenile court jurisdiction.

The publicity surrounding the case drew the attention of a prestigious group of private attorneys who offered to work pro bono (without charge) to save Cristian from adult prosecution. A new set of lawyers—a total of eight powerful attorneys from five prominent Jacksonville law firms—now took up the fight on Cristian's behalf, with the vocal support of the Latino community, organized by the two mothers who had vowed to never give up on this young boy.

Waiving a Constitutional Right as a Juvenile

The defense attorneys turned their attention to the police interrogations held within the first few weeks of the case. That was when the state got a signed confession from Cristian admitting to pushing his brother into the bookshelf. They focused on the key question of whether or not Cristian really understood what he was doing when he signed the document, waiving his constitutional right to an attorney.

Judge Miranda Cooper reviewed the videotape of Cristian's interrogation and the transcript of the proceedings. In her ruling she found many aspects of the process troubling. At no time did the interrogating police officer actually ask Cristian if he understood what these rights meant, or if he even understood the meaning of the word "waive." Cristian simply nodded or said "yes" to her questions, but she did not check to see if he really understood.

Judge Cooper ruled in favor of the defense declaring the confession obtained during the interrogations inadmissible at trial. "While the defendant may have appeared responsive and intelligent during the interrogation, the court cannot ignore the fact that the defendant was a twelve-year-old child with no knowledge of the legal system," Cooper wrote. "Moreover, this court cannot ignore expert testimony that the defendant was unable to fully comprehend the Miranda warnings or appreciate the consequences of waiving his rights."

The Plea Agreements

Without the evidence needed for a conviction, both sides were ready to negotiate a plea agreement. First and foremost was the defense's demand that the case be heard in the juvenile court. In juvenile court, Cristian pleaded guilty to manslaughter and aggravated battery and received a disposition that would keep him in a secure juvenile facility until he turned nineteen in January 2018, to be followed by eight years of probation.

Susana also pleaded guilty to aggravated manslaughter for neglecting David by not getting him to the hospital sooner, and for trying to cover up the past violence committed by Cristian. A judge sentenced her to ten years in prison, but credited her with the two and half years she had already served, and suspended the remainder of her sentence to probation, requiring her to spend ninety days at a domestic violence shelter, and two more years at a halfway house for counseling and other services.

Too Little, Too Late?

After she was jailed for the death of her toddler, Susana wrote a letter published in the local newspaper. In that letter Susana said that she and her children desperately needed help. She pointed out that social services in the state of Florida knew about the struggles of her family and yet had offered very little assistance to her and her family. Even after the violent suicide of her husband, all the system did was place her family on a waiting list for counseling.

Other observers looked even further back in Susana's life and asked: Where was the system when Susana was an eleven-year-old pregnant rape victim living with a cocaine-addicted mother? Or a fourteen-year-old child-mother trying to raise a toddler? When Cristian showed up at school with injuries; when David came to the hospital with broken bones; and when her husband shot himself in front of her three children—each time, the police, schools, health-care systems, and social services were officially involved, and yet no services or assistance were offered to a family in crisis.

Yet once Susana and Cristian were charged with crimes, the response of the system was condemnation and calls for punishment. Many wonder what would have happened to Cristian and Susana if the bighearted pair of mothers had not raised a public outcry that brought an expensive team of legal experts to their side. Would the system have quietly transferred yet another young boy of color into adult court and sentenced him to a life behind bars?

THINKING CRITICALLY ABOUT THIS CASE

1. How should the system of care have been different for Susana when she was growing up? What should have been different for Cristian?

2. Does that system of care, or any system, share the blame in what happened to the Fernandez family? Explain.

3. Do you agree that Cristian's case should have been heard in criminal court? Why or why not?

4. Do you believe that Cristian understood his constitutional right to remain silent? Why or why not?

5. How did the introduction of two moral entrepreneurs change the outcome of the case?

6. Why do you think the justice process and outcome was so different for Cristian Fernandez as compared to Gina Grant in Case Study 1?

REFERENCES

This case is based on the following sources:

Newspapers

"A Judge Shows How Justice Should Work," *Florida Times-Union*, September 8, 2013.

"No Prison for Mother of Cristian Fernandez," *Florida Times-Union*, August 15, 2013.

"A Young Mother Tries to Save Two Sons and Loses Everything," *Tampa Bay Times*, July 15, 2013.

"Prosecution Loses an Expert Witness: Psychologist Says Boy Unlikely to Have Understood Constitutional Rights," *Florida Times-Union*, June 28, 2013.

"Fernandez Defense: Rights Were Violated," *Florida Times-Union*, May 19, 2013.

"Fernandez Pleads Guilty; New Charge as Juvenile Averts Murder Trial," *Florida Times-Union*, February 9, 2013.

"Interrogation of Cristian Ruled Out," *Florida Times-Union*, August 8, 2012.

"Support for Cristian Links 2 Distant Women," *Florida Times-Union*, February 9, 2012.

"Will There Be Others Like Cristian?" *Florida Times-Union*, November 17, 2011.

"This Child Never Had a Childhood," *Florida Times-Union*, June 15, 2011.

"Upbringing May Have Caused Boy to Snap," *Florida Times-Union*, June 12, 2011.

"Baby-Faced and Facing Life with No Parole," *Florida Times-Union*, June 5, 2011.

Articles

Biaenella, S. "A Second Chance." Available at www.huffingtonpost.com/melissa-ross/biannela-susana-a-second-chance_b_3900367.html.

Nostro, A. (2013). The Importance of an Expansive Deference to *Miller v. Alabama. American University Journal of Gender, Social Policy & the Law*, 22, 167–92.

Taylor-Thompson, K. (2014). Minority Rule: Redefining the Age of Criminality. *New York University Review of Law and Social Change*, 38, 144–99.

INTRODUCTION

To state prosecutor Angela Corey, Cristian Fernandez was a dangerous person whose actions proved he was capable of committing murder. In her role as public prosecutor, Corey believed it was her responsibility to protect the public from a potentially dangerous predator. The defense counsel and the community voices organized by the two mothers saw Cristian as a child deserving of protection and in need of treatment due to the severe mistreatment and abuse he had suffered. In the classic **adversarial system**, each side stakes a position. Here the prosecution claimed that public safety was paramount, and that eight years in the juvenile justice system was not sufficient to reduce the risk he posed to others in the community. In

response, the defense vigorously presented evidence of Cristian's **amenability to treatment** to argue he should remain within the juvenile system.

The plea agreement was the result of an adversarial process. By successfully challenging the legality of the interrogation, the defense was able to suppress a key piece of evidence—the confession—that prosecutors needed to prove their case against Cristian. Cristian and Susana benefited from a skilled defense team providing an estimated three million dollars' worth of legal expertise. They "won" the case through successful plea negotiations, which returned Cristian to the juvenile system.

The contemporary juvenile justice process is very different from the classic juvenile justice process envisioned by the founders of the juvenile court. The original purpose of the juvenile system was for the state to act "in the best interests of the child," which means to act on behalf of the children, not against them. In the original juvenile court, there was no need for a defense attorney because the state was not engaging in a prosecution: The judge, social workers, and probation officers were all there to help, not punish, the child. The judge would act as a wise father, deciding what was best for the child.

But by the twenty-first century, the juvenile system was no longer completely different from the adult adversarial criminal justice system. Today, in juvenile court, both defense and prosecutors argue their respective sides. And no longer is the best interest of the child the only priority. The interest of public safety can outweigh what is best for the individual child. Acknowledging that adults had failed Cristian, the state prosecutor nonetheless argued that Cristian posed a danger to the community, and therefore should be tried and punished as an adult.

This chapter compares and contrasts four complex paradigms of the juvenile justice system. A **paradigm** is a cognitive framework containing basic assumptions, ways of thinking, and methodologies that are commonly accepted by members of a discipline or group. In the previous chapter, we reviewed the gradual development of the **classical juvenile justice paradigm**, a core set of

ADVERSARIAL SYSTEM
System of justice where two parties argue their sides in front of an impartial judge who makes a decision on which side wins the case.

AMENABILITY TO TREATMENT
Ability of offender to respond to actions taken to improve his/her behavior.

PARADIGM
A cognitive framework containing basic assumptions, ways of thinking, and methodologies that are commonly accepted by members of a discipline or group.

CLASSICAL JUVENILE JUSTICE PARADIGM
Initial period of juvenile justice that removed youthful offenders from community settings to treat them in residential facilities.

understandings about children and adolescence that led to the creation of the original juvenile court in 1899. In this chapter, we provide an overview of how that original paradigm changed during the twentieth century, as well as the ideas and assumptions that shape the paradigm of juvenile justice emerging in the twenty-first century. In later chapters, we take a closer look at how each of these paradigms has shaped and is shaping the policies and procedures of the juvenile justice system.

We begin with the original vision that developed in the nineteenth century and remained more or less dominant for the first six decades of the twentieth century. We then turn to the ideas that emerged in the 1960s and 1970s, when many of the core assumptions of the original court were challenged, leading to dramatic changes to the system. During this time the introduction of **due process rights** in the juvenile court laid the foundation for more constitutional criminal procedures in the juvenile system.[1] At the same time, this paradigm emphasized community-based diversion programs, especially for youth who committed status offenses, that removed youth from all or some of the juvenile justice process.

Next we examine another set of reforms associated with the "get tough" on crime movement that emerged in the 1990s, which yet again revised and reformed both the understanding of the juvenile system and the legal machinery designed to handle youth crime. During this period, there was broad disillusionment with the ideal of rehabilitation and heightened concern over the danger of predatory youth violence, especially in urban centers. These concerns led to more adult-like juvenile proceedings and more mechanisms to process youth, like Cristian, in criminal court, leading to the reform of juvenile statutes to also include punishment as a purpose.

The final paradigm we examine in this chapter is the set of assumptions and ideas that have been emerging in the last twenty years based on new developments in different fields, including neuroscience, evidence-based treatment, the philosophy of positive youth development, and principles of community / restorative justice. Today, there is renewed focus on the community as the primary location for prevention and intervention; the impact of trauma on the behaviors of youth; and interest in keeping juvenile offenders connected to families, schools, and neighborhoods through community-based programming. There is also emphasis on both monitoring youth and reducing racial and gender disparities in the juvenile justice system. We call this emerging paradigm "positive youth development and community / restorative justice," and cover these developments in detail throughout the later chapters of the text.

DUE PROCESS RIGHTS
Protect individual's rights to fair and constitutional judicial proceedings.

CYCLE OF REFORM
Pendulum of rehabilitation and punishment for juvenile offenders that swings back and forth across juvenile justice eras.

JUVENILE JUSTICE CYCLES OR SHIFTS?

Some scholars, like Thomas J. Bernard, argue that we can look at juvenile justice as an enduring pattern in which a **cycle of reform** swings back and forth from rehabilitation to punishment for juvenile offenders.[2] Each reform period is shaped by shifts in social attitudes toward children and concerns of moral crusaders, who demand action to change the current system. In some eras, moral crusaders believe that youth are dangerous and the system is too lenient, while in other eras, reformers believe the system is too harsh and that it transforms minor delinquents into serious criminals. At all times, what remains common among reformers is the belief that (at least some) children are different than adults; that (at least some) children should be treated with a less-punitive approach than adults; and that by changing the juvenile justice system, we will reduce the problematic behaviors of youth, especially male youth, within our society.

Alternatively, other scholars believe that there are relatively distinct periods in juvenile justice that reflect the prevailing notions about youth and society at the time.[3] In each period, some previous juvenile justice practices are replaced or reformed in ways that are sincerely believed, at least by some, to improve the system of justice for youth. These shifts are believed to be different in key ways from previous reform efforts, and they generally build on lessons learned from previous efforts. For example, there continue to be those who argue against the need for a separate juvenile justice system, believing that youth will be more justly treated if there is a single justice system to address criminal conduct. Today, however, many of those proponents recognize that youth are developmentally immature and not as culpable as adults, which was not the case in previous reform eras.[4]

Perhaps it is most accurate to see the current juvenile justice system as a product of all these periods—a repository of our society's ongoing efforts to create institutions to care for children and youth. These institutions are created and revised according to youth's perceived place in society, and how society perceives its obligation to care for all its children—indeed, all vulnerable members of any age in our society. Today, as in previous paradigmatic eras, there is a need to critically examine both the "talk" (rhetoric) of juvenile justice reform and the "walk" (reality)—how the policies and procedures are actually implemented day to day. Looking back over a century of juvenile justice reform shows the need to use the lens of intersectionality to examine how things like race, gender, ethnicity, sexual orientation, class, and religious background impact how youth and children are treated within the juvenile justice system.

The juvenile justice system is still very much a work in progress as our society continues to examine and reexamine the systems we have created to respond to the needs and misdeeds of our youth. Key points in each juvenile justice paradigm are briefly identified in table 3.1 and detailed in the sections that follow. We encourage you to think about the juvenile system in your own generation, and what you believe is important to change, abolish, or create in order to support children and youth in our society.

THE CLASSICAL JUVENILE JUSTICE PARADIGM

In the previous chapter we learned that progressive reformers articulated a new social construction of childhood and adolescence that reflected significant changes in society. They passed new laws that reshaped the relationship between the family and the state, granting power to the government to intervene in the lives of parents and children in new ways. They also created new institutions such as reform schools, the juvenile court, public schools, and child welfare systems, with new roles and new responsibilities in caring for youth.

We learned too that these institutions were shaped by both the dreams and fears of those in positions of privilege and power. The child savers cared deeply about the plight of poor, immigrant children and were dedicated to alleviating the misery that was so disturbingly evident on the streets of cities. They believed in the innocence of children and the vulnerability of youth to bad influences. But

TABLE 3.1	Paradigms of Juvenile Justice	
Dominant Paradigm (Era)	**Key Concepts**	**Program and Policy Outcomes**
Classical Juvenile Justice Paradigm (1900s–1950s)	Rehabilitation In the best interests of child Positivism and faith in medical science "Child Saving" *parens patriae*	Houses of Refuge Training schools Juvenile courts Child guidance / court clinics Therapeutic interventions
Juvenile Rights (1960s–1970s)	Due process Decriminalization of status offending Deinstitutionalization Diversion Principle of least-restrictive alternative Principle of radical intervention	Legal safeguards (i.e., right to attorney, right to confront accusers) Creation of separate processes for status offenders Diversion Community-based programs
Get Tough (1980s–2000s)	Public safety Deterrence Retribution Serious and violent juvenile offending Super-predators Status offenders as pre-delinquents	Changes to state juvenile codes to include punishment Adult prosecution through transfers/waivers Increased penalties for juvenile crime Lower age of adulthood Zero-tolerance policies in schools
Emerging Paradigm: Positive Youth Development and Community / Restorative Justice (2000s–Present)	Evidence-based treatment Accountability Adolescent brain development Intersectionality	Evidence-based programs and practices Gender-specific and culturally responsive programming Reduction of DMC Dismantling school-to-prison pipeline Restorative practices Transition to adulthood for vulnerable populations Youth leadership programming

they also feared the disorder and chaos of the so-called dangerous classes. They disapproved of their morals and habits; this, they believed, was the cause of their impoverished misery. They saw the lower classes as a threat to a way of life they valued and cherished, and created institutions that used the coercive power of the state to control and punish those who violated what they saw as the behavioral standards of decent American society.

As a result, the institutions they created reflect this mixed agenda of trying to care for children and using the coercive power of the law to shape and mold youth in accordance with their view of proper conduct and behavior. With the exception of public schools, most of the systems and institutions created during the classical era focused on addressing the needs and behavior of children and youth from poor families. Reforms were couched in the rhetoric of family, charity, and love, but in reality relied also on coercion, exploitation, and punishment of children, and also of parents who were neglectful or abusive.

Positivism and Faith in Rehabilitation

The use of scientific evidence to understand crime and rehabilitate offenders is a key foundation for both the juvenile and adult justice systems. **Positivism** is a broad philosophical approach that relies on objective scientific proof to understand and shape both the natural and social world. The social sciences of psychology, psychiatry, and sociology offered the hope that with scientific understanding of juvenile crime, it was possible to devise treatment regimens to successfully alter delinquent behavior.[5] Along with the juvenile court came the profession of probation. Gradually, volunteers and aid workers for youth involved in systems of care gave way to college-educated professionals with advanced degrees in sociology, social work, psychology, and criminal justice.[6]

The **medical model** impacted the way youth were addressed in the juvenile justice system, especially during the 1940s and 1950s. Deviant youth were considered sick and in need of "curing" through modern medicine. Diagnosis and treatment by medical and social work professionals using the mantle of science included making moral judgments about the quality of parenting and predictions about the moral character of the child. The child guidance movement and juvenile clinics attached to the court were an outgrowth of this classical era, in which children who were believed to be prone to delinquency were diagnosed with mental illness and treated at facilities for maladjusted behavior.[7]

With the authority of the juvenile court, the judge, along with other professionals, possessed the legal power to remove a child from a family deemed unsuitable and to forcibly detain that child for treatment within the juvenile system until he or she reached the legal age of majority. Poor immigrant youth and youth of color were often the targets of their intervention. The rhetoric of acting in the best interests of the child was in reality a system of social control, particularly for poor immigrants and youth of color. Treatment was often a euphemism for punishment, with facilities that more closely resembled a prison than a school or family environment. Youth were often "cured" through their removal from their home environment and placed into these institutions that provided medical and behavioral therapies to "fix" them.

THE JUVENILE RIGHTS PARADIGM

By the 1960s there was growing concern about the unbridled power of the juvenile court, leading to the start of the **juvenile rights paradigm**. After six decades, the basic premise of the juvenile court as a benevolent institution was called into question by a new set of moral crusaders focused on the due process rights of youth. Youth did not have all the procedural safeguards, such as the right to an attorney, that adults had, and yet they could be severely punished even for seemingly minor acts. The US Supreme Court, under the leadership of Chief Justice Earl Warren, ruled on a number of cases which radically transformed the legal procedures of the juvenile court by increasing the due process rights of juveniles.

Many of these cases are detailed in chapter 9, but one stands out as a landmark court decision. *In re Gault* concerns a fifteen-year-old boy arrested by police on the complaint from a neighbor that he had made harassing phone calls.[8] Gault received jail time without consultation with his parents or an attorney. The judge

POSITIVISM
Broad philosophical approach that relies on science to understand the social world.

MEDICAL MODEL
Addressing troublesome youth as sick and in need of medical treatment to be cured.

JUVENILE RIGHTS PARADIGM
Era that provided increased procedural safeguards to juveniles involved in the juvenile justice system.

adjudicated, or sentenced, Gault as a delinquent, committing him to a locked juvenile justice facility until the age of twenty-one. The US Supreme Court ruled that Gault was unconstitutionally denied his due process rights, which included a right to a defense attorney and the right to remain silent. In its decision, Justice Fortas famously stated that the condition of being a boy did not justify a kangaroo court.

The term *kangaroo court* is an expression that refers to the idea of a sham or mockery of fair procedure. Instead of a fair hearing of the facts by an impartial judge, the person in charge is in the "pocket" of those with money to buy a predetermined outcome. Supreme Court justices observed that youth who were brought before the juvenile court were getting the "worst of both worlds." Often they were either sent to adult court or were confined within the juvenile system for many years, without the basic procedural fairness the Constitution guarantees for all adults.

Over the next decade, a series of rulings radically transformed the judicial proceedings of the juvenile court. Most importantly, the Court ruled that states could not incarcerate juveniles unless it could prove they had committed acts of delinquency—that is, acts that would be crimes if committed by adults. And, like adults accused of crimes, juveniles were now entitled to defense counsel who could confront and cross-examine witnesses, and the state had to present evidence that would prove its case beyond a reasonable doubt.

Some critics believed that the due process reforms represented an erroneous step backward for the whole existence of the juvenile court. The dissenting opinion in the Gault case pointed out that the very mission of the juvenile court was to act on behalf of the child, not to prosecute him/her as a criminal.[9] To make the proceedings in the juvenile court more adult-like undermined the very purpose for which the court had been created under the *parens patriae* doctrine. They argued that this was a step toward the eventual demise of a separate juvenile court with special protections for youth. Indeed, Barry Feld, a juvenile court scholar, often refers to this period as creating a "scaled-down criminal court" in which youth were not offered full protection from adversarial proceedings under the guise of the best interest of the child.[10]

Noninterventionist Philosophy

The idea that intervention could do more harm than good was the driving force behind the noninterventionist reforms to remove youth from the control of the juvenile justice system. In 1974, the US Congress passed the federal **Juvenile Justice and Delinquency Prevention Act (JJDPA)** to address a widespread concern about the problem of juvenile delinquency and the abuses of the juvenile system. The act created the Office of Juvenile Justice and Delinquency Prevention to conduct research on delinquency causes and prevention, and it also set firm guidelines for juvenile systems across the United States, with the provision that state juvenile justice systems would only receive federal funds if they followed the mandates of the JJDPA and its subsequent reauthorizations.

The mandates of the original 1974 JJDPA focused on four key reforms to the original juvenile justice system.[11] These can be summarized as the "Four D's." The first was the **decriminalization** of status offenders. Neglected youth and those in need of services were to be treated differently from youth who committed acts that were criminal offenses. The original meaning of the term

JUVENILE JUSTICE AND DELINQUENCY PREVENTION ACT (JJDPA)
Act that decriminalized status offenses, promoted diversion of minor offenders, and deinstitutionalized most juvenile offenders.

DECRIMINALIZATION
Removing behaviors from the juvenile (or adult criminal) justice legal code.

delinquency did not distinguish between crimes and other behaviors that were not illegal but were problematic for youth, such as running away, underage drinking, and breaking curfew, as well as defying home and school rules. These behaviors clearly signaled that a young person was in need of adult supervision and guidance. The JJDPA sought to ensure that this distinction was made clear in implementation, with lesser penalties for youth who were status offenders.

The new federal rules along with the court rulings directed juvenile courts to **divest** themselves of jurisdiction for these status offenders, meaning they would create separate procedures and institutions for handling them. The JJDPA required that status offenders no longer be confined with youth who had committed crimes, and no longer held in secure facilities/lockups against their will. Status offenders could be detained for up to twenty-four hours, but legally it was no longer possible to commit youth to a locked facility based on status offenses alone.

The rationale for **deinstitutionalization** came from the idea that locking up youth in prison-like settings isolated from home and community was doing more harm than good. The JJDPA required states to seek the "least-restrictive alternative" for all youth adjudicated delinquent. This meant that **diversion**, including non-institutional alternatives to juvenile justice facilities, had to be exhausted first before out-of-home placements could be considered. Diversion to community-based programs for counseling, mentoring, education, job training, or drug treatment was designated the preferred option to confinement for less-serious delinquent offenders.

States were directed to create alternative programs for youth that would provide rehabilitative services without the stigma, isolation, and coercion associated with the classical juvenile justice paradigm's reformatories and industrial schools. The recognition that institutionalization could cause more harm than good was at the forefront of the JJDPA and the noninterventionist movement.[12] Additionally, the idea was gaining traction that labeling youth as delinquent may in fact cause a social reaction in which people would treat them negatively, possibly leading the youth to commit even more delinquent acts and continue down the path of delinquency and deviance.[13]

For youth who had committed delinquent acts, the JJDPA required that they no longer be held in adult jails and lockups. In cases where no juvenile cells or facilities existed, youth were to be fully separated from incarcerated adults both in "sight and sound." Juveniles were not to see or hear adults in their cells, recreational spaces, common areas, or dining halls.

THE GET TOUGH PARADIGM

By the 1980s, and throughout the next two decades, a new series of juvenile justice reforms swept across many states, ushering in the **get tough paradigm**. Reforms were made in response to a juvenile crime spike and the public perception that juveniles were committing more dangerous and violent crimes. Critics of the juvenile justice system argued that system leniency was contributing to a crisis in public safety in communities. An upcoming demographic increase in the number of preteen youth fueled the fear of "super-predators"—youth who would commit terrible acts of violence and overrun the juvenile justice system. This fear was further promulgated by some academics and moral entrepreneurs,

DIVEST
Removing interest in specific behaviors (such as status offenses) from the purview of the juvenile justice system.

DEINSTITUTIONALIZATION
Removing individuals from residential or locked facilities.

DIVERSION
Keeping individuals out of the juvenile justice system, or juvenile placements through alternative programs.

GET TOUGH PARADIGM
Punitive policies that increased the penalties for juvenile offenses and facilitated the transfer and waiver of juvenile cases into adult courts.

resulting in a moral panic.[14] Media fanned the flames by splashing the front pages of newspapers with atypical, violent crimes committed by juveniles. Pundits and politicians gave voice to the outrage felt by the public. The spike in violent street crime; the moral panic regarding the violent lawlessness of youth; and a disillusionment with the ideal of rehabilitation and treatment resulted in quickly passed legislation to "get tough" with juveniles, particularly those who committed violent acts.

The idea that "nothing works" in efforts to rehabilitate offenders was popularized in the early 1970s when an article published by Robert Martinson claimed that the evidence of high rates of recidivism proved the failure of all current approaches to rehabilitation.[15] Though he later revised his position and others pointed to rehabilitative successes, those studies were largely ignored.[16] The voices of critics who thought that the system was harming children rather than "curing" them now were joined by even louder voices who argued that treatment did not prevent violent juvenile offenders from committing more crimes after leaving the system. These attitudes paved the way for moral crusaders advocating for more punishment and less treatment for violent juvenile offenders, to achieve their goal of more punishment for youthful offenders.

The legislative changes of this era focused on punitive juvenile justice policies; increasing the ability of adult courts to hear juvenile cases for serious offenses; and mandating that punishment be an expressed purpose in juvenile justice statutes. States already had laws that allowed courts to treat juvenile offenders as adults under certain circumstances, but now legislatures passed laws ensuring that more juvenile cases would be heard in adult court by lowering the minimum age for adult court waivers, or by transferring discretion over court venue from the judge to the prosecutor, as in Cristian's case.[17] These changes are discussed in more depth in chapter 9.

In addition, this era saw an increase in the length and harshness of sentencing for juveniles. The motto of "adult time for adult crime" led states to pass provisions that allowed juveniles to serve adult-length sentences.[18] Even if youth were adjudicated in juvenile court, they could be transferred to adult prisons when they reached the age of majority to serve time, if they were serious, chronic, or violent offenders. Primary and secondary schools were not immune to this punitive shift. Instead of addressing fighting and stealing in the school itself, police were called to arrest and prosecute. This led to the concept of the school-to-prison pipeline, because, for some youth, schools were the initial point of contact to enter the juvenile justice system.[19] We will return to the idea of the school-to-prison pipeline in chapter 7.

Some argue that the due process reforms of the 1960s set the stage for the get tough paradigm that followed in later decades. By asserting that children and adults shared the same rights, it was a small step to argue that they also should be subject to the same sanctions when they violated the law.[20] The reality of get tough policies was that punitive sanctions fell primarily on the shoulders of lower-class male youth of color, who were, and continue to be, prosecuted, transferred, and incarcerated at much higher rates than their white counterparts, and more so than in previous paradigm eras.[21] The result is that these youth have been further segregated from society with the belief that they are a more violent subset of the "dangerous" lower class.

THE POSITIVE YOUTH DEVELOPMENT AND COMMUNITY / RESTORATIVE JUSTICE PARADIGM

The first decade of the twenty-first century has brought with it new understandings and new reform movements that reenvision the purpose and goals of the juvenile justice system. Over the course of this textbook, we will examine emerging ideas that are shaping current reform efforts in juvenile justice systems across the nation. As always, many of these efforts by reformers and crusaders are a response to the perceived failures and harms of the current juvenile justice system. We term this emerging paradigm the **positive youth development and community / restorative justice paradigm**.

Impetus for New Paradigm

Two issues stand out as motivations for a new paradigm: mass incarceration and advancements in neuroscience. Foremost among the perceived failures and harms of the current juvenile (and also adult) justice system is the awareness that mass incarceration has had tremendous negative impacts—and associated costs—on communities of color. Many argue that the punitive justice system has contributed to generations of family and neighborhood dysfunction, where adult black and brown males are systematically incarcerated. These policies are viewed as a profound injustice, contributing to a lack of faith in the legitimacy of the law, especially among youth in communities of color.[22] The issue of disproportionate minority contact (DMC) in the justice system through racial profiling, overpolicing, and punitive sentencing has become the new rallying cry of the contemporary civil rights movement.

The federal government, as well as activist citizens, is demanding that schools, juvenile justice agencies, and adult criminal justice systems not only monitor racial disparities, but also find strategies to reduce them.[23] The downturn of the world economy has necessitated scrutiny into publicly funded programs, organizations, and institutions. As a result, the US Congress has attempted to rein in spending on corrections through the promotion of alternatives to incarceration and reductions in incarceration sentences and sentence lengths.[24] More public awareness of the problem of DMC, as well as proposals and programs to remedy those problems, is discussed in Part III of this book, The Contemporary Juvenile Justice System.

The second factor behind current reforms arises from advances in the modern scientific understanding of brain development during adolescence. To some extent, the 2000s have seen a return to the original assumption of the juvenile court—namely, that juveniles are deserving of special treatment by virtue of their immature status as youth. Neuroscientific development in our understanding of the human brain has challenged the current conception that the judgment and reasoning skills of adolescents are equal to that of adults. Youth simply are not "miniature adults," and thus require a separate and distinct justice system to respond to their misbehaviors.[25]

With technological advances in brain imaging, scientists have been able to monitor in real time how the brain works when a person is reacting to a situation or trying to make a decision. Researchers also are able to compare the cognitive processing at different stages of the life course, including childhood, adolescence, and adulthood. The evidence is clear that between the ages of roughly twelve to twenty-five, the normal human brain undergoes dramatic growth and

POSITIVE YOUTH DEVELOPMENT AND COMMUNITY / RESTORATIVE JUSTICE PARADIGM
Emerging era focusing on using prosocial, community-based treatment for justice-involved youth.

development.[26] Although it does not grow in size beyond age six or so, the brain remodels itself in extremely important ways during this period of the life course.

The normal teenage brain is significantly different than the normal adult brain. Teens are more impulsive than adults; they are more attracted to risk-taking and thrill-seeking; they are less able to anticipate negative consequences; and they are more responsive to immediate rewards, especially the social rewards that come from peers.[27] This new evidence helps to explain why teens are more likely to engage in risky behavior, especially in the company of peers. We examine these new findings in detail in chapter 4, as well as how the impact of drugs, trauma, loss, and other adverse experiences affect the development of youth.

The growing evidence about the developmental immaturity of the adolescent brain, in turn, has influenced the US Supreme Court in its rulings on the constitutionality of certain kinds of punishments for crimes committed during childhood and adolescence. In 2005, in the case of *Roper v. Simmons*, the US Supreme Court declared the imposition of the death penalty for acts committed while a person was a juvenile was a violation of the Eighth Amendment prohibition on cruel and unusual punishment.[28] Evidence from neuroscience led the justices to the decision that juveniles are less responsible for their actions than adults, and less deserving of the harshest punishment. In several additional rulings, the Court used similar arguments to prohibit the sentence of life without parole for noncapital (murder) offenses. The Court also struck down state statutes of mandatory life without parole for crimes committed as juveniles. These and other significant juvenile justice legal cases are discussed in chapter 9.

Evidence-Based Policies, Practices, and Programs

Just as brain science has guided reforms in thinking about the culpability of youth, evidence from rigorous scientific studies has shown that there are both processes and programs that are successful in addressing youthful misbehavior; **evidence-based** is the term used to describe them. We know that *how* justice professionals go about the business of identifying and processing youth for system involvement is important. The right kinds of interventions, delivered in the right way and tailored to the individual needs of the youth, do make a positive difference. Youth and their families who feel as though they were listened to and as though they were treated fairly, even if they receive punishments, are more likely to have faith in the system and less likely to reoffend.[29] Delinquency prevention and intervention programs that address the cognitive-behavioral aspects of thinking patterns also show success in reducing delinquency.[30] Interventions are discussed more fully in chapter 11.

There is also a growing recognition that to have lasting positive impact, the needs of girls and those from different cultures must be reflected in gender-specific and culturally sensitive programming.[31] We discuss cultural differences and devote separate chapters later in the book to understanding the psychosocial developmental needs of males and females in order to fully appreciate the discussion of interventions that address gender and cultural needs.

Positive Youth Development

Today, the term **emerging adulthood** is used to describe youth in their twenties who might not yet be fully independent from their parents.[32] A growing body of research shows that over half of youth in their twenties live at their relatives'

EVIDENCE-BASED
Practices, programs, and policies that have been shown through scientific evaluation to work to prevent and intervene with juvenile justice system youth.

EMERGING ADULTHOOD
Youth in their early to mid-twenties who have not fully taken on adult responsibilities independent of relatives, especially parents.

home, typically a parent's, for some period of time while they become economically and socially independent.[33] This is far different from two generations ago, when twenty-somethings had full-time jobs and children. Yet, how this conception plays out in the system put into place for youth who have committed wrongdoing is another story. There is a two-track system in which young, middle-class youth are provided a safety net of returning to the nest, to save money and figure out their next move, while lower-class twenty-somethings without economic and social support are on their own, with only a punitive welfare or criminal justice system as interventions when they make mistakes.

By adopting the lens of positive youth development (PYD) discussed in chapter 1, we see that the juvenile justice system cannot be considered separately from the larger ecological context in which it resides. In some ways, there is a renewed attention to the concerns raised in the 1960s and 1970s that focused on the communities in which youth live. Instead of seeing youth as a source of the problem in need of "fixing," this perspective shifts focus to the context in which they are developing by asking, "How healthy are our communities?" Can we reinvest some of the funds earmarked for incarceration into more community-based programs that provide more opportunities for youth to have positive developmental experiences during adolescence? Recognizing the assets of youth, including talents, drive, intelligence, leadership, and creativity, is critical to this perspective.[34]

PYD is discussed in the next two sections, and chapter 11 concludes with a discussion of how evidence-based practices and PYD may be the future of juvenile justice.

Community / Restorative Justice

One element of the latest reform agenda has been an effort to balance the rehabilitation needs of youth with community-safety and victim-justice needs, in a community setting. **Restorative justice** has a broad purpose in both the adult and juvenile justice systems, seeking to replace the punishment emphasis with one focused on repairing the harms done by crime by creating an active role for victims within the justice process. Community / restorative justice emphasizes the belief that these interactions should be community-based.

In the 1990s, the US Office of Juvenile Justice and Delinquency Prevention promoted Balanced and Restorative Justice (BARJ), which encourages state juvenile justice systems to focus attention on the needs of victims and to promote youths' accountability in repairing the damage done both to the victim and to the community.[35] Supporters of this approach have instituted programs in communities and detention centers that seek to bring young offenders face-to-face with their victims, including those in their own families, who have been negatively affected by their behavior.

Youth are given an opportunity to learn firsthand how their behaviors impact others, which, in turn, helps them to develop empathy and positive maturation. More commonly known as *restorative practices*, this philosophy has also been highly influential in schools, in helping to dismantle the school-to-prison pipeline.[36] The emphasis in this approach is consistent with positive youth development, as youth learn how to take responsibility and repair the harm they have done as part of their own process of growth and development. We take a careful look at this philosophy and its implementation in subsequent chapters on schools and the justice system.

Many of the youth involved in juvenile justice also have been involved with the child welfare systems.[37] As discussed in chapter 2, youth involved with both

RESTORATIVE JUSTICE
Addressing the needs of the offender, victim, and community when an offense has been committed.

systems at some point in time are called dual-system youth. The juvenile justice and child welfare systems must work together in the best interests of the child for dual-system youth.

How well do our systems function to protect vulnerable children? If we look at the experience of Cristian, we see that there were repeated systems failures of protection and care, not just for Cristian and his siblings, but also for his mother Susana when she was a minor. Unfortunately, this may be far too common. Research shows that there is often a lack of communication between the two systems.[38] Current practice emphasizes the prevention of youth from "crossing over" from one system to the other, and to promoting positive youth development principles in both systems.[39] As in both Cristian and Susana's cases, youth attract the attention of the child welfare system long before engagement in the juvenile justice system. A long-term focus on healthy youth development involves investing in the families through an effective child welfare system that supports the homes, schools, and neighborhoods in which these youth are raised.

We close this chapter by considering how the case of Cristian Fernandez would be handled if the juvenile justice system was operating with ideas arising from the emerging paradigm. At age twelve, Cristian had suffered numerous adversities that would have impacted his emotional and cognitive development. Cristian was a victim of childhood trauma. Susana too is likely to be in need of intervention given her own troubled childhood and adolescence. As a young female subject to statutory rape, Susana was in need of programming and supports tailored to her gender-specific needs. Based on our understanding of adolescent brain development, we could assume that Cristian would benefit from treatment and positive inputs from a healthy environment within the context of supportive relationships with adults.

In this emerging paradigm it is important for the community to be involved as part of the solution by examining its own resources and systems. How could a family in such need have repeatedly fallen through the cracks? Why were there no supports available to this struggling family? What needs to change within the neighborhoods, schools, social services, and juvenile justice system so that future tragedies do not occur? There are no easy answers, but it has always been the challenge of the juvenile justice system to try to answer these questions in order to take care of all children in all communities.

KEY TERMS

adversarial system System of justice where two parties argue their sides in front of an impartial judge who makes a decision on which side wins the case.

amenability to treatment Ability of offender to respond to actions taken to improve his/her behavior.

classical juvenile justice paradigm Initial period of juvenile justice that removed youthful offenders from community settings to treat them in residential facilities.

cycle of reform Pendulum of rehabilitation and punishment for juvenile offenders that swings back and forth across juvenile justice eras.

decriminalization Removing behaviors from the juvenile (or adult criminal) justice legal code.

deinstitutionalization Removing individuals from residential or locked facilities.

diversion Keeping individuals out of the juvenile justice system, or juvenile placements through alternative programs.

divest Removing interest in specific behaviors (such as status offenses) from the purview of the juvenile justice system.

due process rights Protect individual's rights to fair and constitutional judicial proceedings.

emerging adulthood Youth in their early to mid-twenties who have not fully taken on adult responsibilities independent of relatives, especially parents.

evidence-based Practices, programs, and policies that have been shown through scientific evaluation to work to prevent and intervene with juvenile justice system youth.

get tough paradigm Punitive policies that increased the penalties for juvenile offenses and facilitated the transfer and waiver of juvenile cases into adult courts.

Juvenile Justice and Delinquency Prevention Act (JJDPA) Act that decriminalized status offenses, promoted diversion of minor offenders, and deinstitutionalized most juvenile offenders.

juvenile rights paradigm Era that provided increased procedural safeguards to juveniles involved in the juvenile justice system.

medical model Addressing troublesome youth as sick and in need of medical treatment to be cured.

paradigm A cognitive framework containing basic assumptions, ways of thinking, and methodologies that are commonly accepted by members of a discipline or group.

positive youth development and community / restorative justice paradigm Emerging era focusing on using prosocial, community-based treatment for justice-involved youth.

positivism Broad philosophical approach that relies on science to understand the social world.

restorative justice Addressing the needs of the offender, victim, and community when an offense has been committed.

REVIEW AND STUDY QUESTIONS

1. What is the cycle of reform? After reading the chapter, do you believe that the juvenile justice system operates in a cyclical reform fashion?

2. What is the meaning of the word *paradigm*? Describe the key assumptions and beliefs for each of the four paradigms discussed in this chapter. What are the distinctive features of each juvenile justice paradigm?

3. What happened in the legal case *In re Gault*? What was the significance of this Supreme Court ruling for the juvenile rights paradigm?

4. Identify and describe the Four D's—decriminalize, divest, deinstitutionalize, and divert—of the 1974 Juvenile Justice and Delinquency Prevention Act.

5. Explain the difference between status and delinquency offenses. Why did reformers believe it was necessary to treat these offense categories differently?

6. How has emerging research on brain science changed the juvenile justice system? How have neuroscience and evidence-based practices shifted how we think about youth who commit delinquent acts?

7. Explain the meaning of a new phase of youth development called "emerging adulthood."

8. What is the significance of evidence-based practice? What are some important key insights that have emerged from rigorous scientific research on "what works"?

9. What are the key features of community / restorative justice? What does restorative justice mean for youthful offenders?

10. Having read this case study and the chapter, what things do you think need to be reinforced, revised, or created to support positive youth development in our society?

CHECK IT OUT

Listen/Watch

America's Juvenile Injustice System | Marsha Levick | TEDxPhiladelphia:

www.youtube.com/watch?v=8cPRB9XxOlI

NOTES

[1] Feld, B. (1999). *Bad Kids: Race and the Transformation of the Juvenile Court.* New York: Oxford.

[2] Bernard, T. J., and Kurlychek, M. (2010). *The Cycle of Juvenile Justice* (2nd ed.). New York: Oxford.

[3] Butts, J. A., and Mears, D. P. (2001). Reviving Juvenile Justice in a Get-Tough Era. *Youth & Society, 33,* 169–98.

[4] Zimring, F. E. (1998). *American Youth Violence.* New York: Oxford.

[5] Coser, L. A. (1977). Auguste Comte: The Law of Human Progress. In *Masters of Sociological Thought.* Long Grove, IL: Waveland.

[6] Grossberg, M. (2001). Changing Conceptions of Child Welfare in the United States, 1820–1935. In M. Rosenheim, F. Zimring, D. S. Tannenhaus, and B. Dohrn (eds.), *A Century of Juvenile Justice,* 3–41. Chicago: University of Chicago Press.

[7] Lerner, P. (2002). Twentieth-Century Developments in America's Institutional Systems for Youth in Trouble. In Rosenheim et al., *A Century of Juvenile Justice,* 74–110.

[8] See www.uscourts.gov/educational-resources/educational-activities/facts-and-case-summary-re-gault.

[9] Ibid.

[10] Feld, B. C. (1997). Abolish the Juvenile Court: Youthfulness, Criminal Responsibility, and Sentencing Policy. *Journal of Criminal Law and Criminology, 88,* 68–136.

[11] See http://www.ojjdp.gov/compliance/jjdpchronology.pdf.

[12] Cohen, S. (1985). *Visions of Social Control: Crime, Punishment, and Classification.* New York: Basil Blackwell.

[13] Adams, M. S., Robertson, C. T., Gray-Ray, P., and Ray, M. C. (2003). Labeling and Delinquency. *Adolescence, 38,* 171–86.

[14] Dilulio, J. J. (1995). The Coming of the Super-Predators. *Weekly Standard,* November 27, 23–28.

[15] Martinson, R. (1974). What Works? Questions and Answers about Prison Reform. *The Public Interest, 35,* 22–54.

[16] Cullen, F. T., and Gilbert, K. E. (2013). *Reaffirming Rehabilitation.* New York: Taylor Francis.

[17] Torbet, P. (1999). *Getting Tough on Juvenile Crime: A Paradigm Shift for Juvenile Justice?* Washington, DC: Office of Juvenile Justice and Delinquency Prevention.

[18] Zimring, *American Youth Violence.*

[19] Available at www.aclu.org/fact-sheet/what-school-prison-pipeline.

[20] Feld, *Bad Kids: Race and the Transformation of the Juvenile Court.*

[21] Soler, M. (2007). *Disproportionate Minority Contact: Practical Applications and Implications.* Washington, DC: Center for Children's Law and Policy.

[22] Clear, T. (2007). *Imprisoning Communities: How Mass Incarceration Makes Disadvantaged Neighborhoods Worse.* New York: Oxford; Mauer, M. (2006). *Race to Incarcerate.* New York: The New Press.

[23] Available at www.nttac.org/index.cfm?event=dmc.modelResource.

[24] Kirchhoff, S. M. (2010). *Economic Impacts of Prison Growth.* Washington, DC: Congressional Research Services.

[25] Scott, E., and Steinberg, L. (2010). *Rethinking Juvenile Justice.* Cambridge, MA: Harvard University Press.

[26] Blakeman, S., and Choudhury, S. (2006). Development of the Adolescent Brain: Implications for Executive Function and Social Cognition. *Journal of Child Psychology and Psychiatry, 47,* 296–312.

[27] Scott, E., and Grisso, T. (2005). Developmental Incompetence, Due Process, and Juvenile Justice Policy. *North Carolina Law Review, 83,* 793–845.

[28] See Court opinion at www.supremecourt.gov/opinions/04pdf/03-633.pdf.

[29] Tyler, T. R. (2002). *Trust in the Law: Encouraging Public Cooperation with the Police and Courts.* New York: Russell Sage Foundation.

[30] Lipsey, M. W., Howell, J. C., Kelly, M. R., Chapman, G., and Carver, D. (2010). *Improving the Effectiveness of Juvenile Justice Programs: A New Perspective on Evidence-Based Practice.* Washington, DC: Georgetown University, Center for Juvenile Justice Reform.

[31] Hawkins, S. R., Graham, P. W., Williams, J., and Zahn, M. A. (2009). *Resilient Girls: Factors that Protect Against Delinquency.* Washington, DC: Office of Juvenile Justice and Delinquency Prevention, Girls Study Group; MacKinnon-Lewis, C., Kaufman, M. C., and Frabutt, J. M. (2002). Juvenile Justice and Mental Health: Youth and Families in the Middle. *Aggression and Violent Behavior, 7,* 353–63.

[32] Arnett, J. J. (2004). *Emerging Adulthood: The Winding Road from the Late Teens through the Twenties.* New York: Oxford.

[33] US Census Bureau. (2014). *America's Families and Living Arrangements: 2014.* Available at www.census.gov/hhes/families/data/cps2014.html.

[34] Lerner, R., Almerigi, J. B., Theokas, C., and Lerner, J.V. (2005). Positive Youth Development: A View of the Issues. *Journal of Early Adolescence, 25,* 10–16.

[35] Office of Juvenile Justice and Delinquency Prevention. (nd). *Balanced and Restorative Justice: Program Summary.* Washington, DC: Author.

[36] Schiff, M. (2013). *Dignity, Disparity, and Desistance: Effective Restorative Justice Strategies to Plug the "School-to-Prison Pipeline."* Available at http://civilrightsproject.ucla.edu/resources/projects/center-for-civil-rights-remedies/school-to-prison-folder/state-reports/dignity-disparity-and-desistance-effective-restorative-justice-strategies-to-plug-the-201cschool-to-prison-pipeline.

[37] Available at www.modelsforchange.net/publications/332.

[38] Herz, D., Lee, P., Lutz, L. . . . Kelley, E. (2012). *Addressing the Needs of Multi-System Youth: Strengthening the Connection between Child Welfare and Juvenile Justice.* Washington, DC: Georgetown University, Center for Juvenile Justice Reform and Robert F. Kennedy Children's Action Corps.

[39] Ibid.

PATHWAYS TO CRIME

PART —— I

PART —— II

PART —— III

Delinquency, Victimization, and Pathways to Offending for Boys

LEARNING OBJECTIVES

By the end of this chapter, you should be able to do the following:

- Understand how crime is officially and unofficially recorded.
- Identify key problems with official reporting.
- Identify general patterns of offending and victimization for boys.
- Discuss why theory is important in explaining and preventing crime.
- Broadly identify the differences between person-centered, society-centered, and critical theories.
- Articulate how integrated theories build on person-centered and society-centered theories.
- Discuss three prominent person-centered theories.
- Discuss three prominent society-centered theories.

Case Study 4: Learning the Code

Michelle Obama considers him one of her personal heroes. Born and raised in the South Bronx, Geoffrey Canada came of age learning how to survive on the streets. At age fifteen his mother sent him to live with his grandparents so he would have access to better public schools. An avid student, Canada earned a full scholarship to Bowdoin College, an elite school, followed by a degree from Harvard University School of Education. He came back to his old neighborhood to found the Harlem Children's Zone, an innovative set of coordinated programs that offer tutoring, recreational programming, parenting skills, drug counseling, and community outreach to youth and their families.

Canada made it in the world outside the neighborhood of his youth and returned as an adult with a fierce commitment to create change for the next generation of youth growing up in urban poverty. But Canada still remembers what it felt like to be a young boy learning to navigate the streets of a poor, inner-city community.

Life in the South Bronx

The social world of a child is physically very small. There is home—for Canada, an apartment with two bedrooms, a living room and kitchen, and the hallway beyond his front door. Outside was a busy sidewalk that led to stores, playgrounds, and schools. To Canada and his three older brothers, Union Avenue was the world where the drama of life took place.

This drama was high stakes for a young boy needing to prove himself among his peers. In his autobiography, *Fist, Stick, Knife, Gun*, Canada recounts how

he learned to be a man. It began with an early tutorial when he was four years old. This lesson didn't happen to him personally, but to his older brothers, ages five and six. The brothers had been at the playground and came home without the younger boy's jacket, which had been taken by an older boy. They ran home expecting their mama to get it back from the bully. She refused. Instead she sent them back to the playground to fight for that jacket, with the stern warning about the beating they would get if they dared come home without it.

As an adult, Canada reflects on the "lessons" learned that day: Never let someone take something that is yours without fighting back. Stand up for yourself; no one will be able to keep you safe from those who will prey on you. And whatever you do, never let yourself be a victim. There were other lessons as well, including always protect your brothers. His mother was most angry at the six-year-old for failing to watch out for his younger sibling. He learned to never let someone victimize the weaker members of your family, and to always stick together. And he learned the deeper lesson that shaped the psyche of Canada and all the boys on Union Avenue as they struggled toward manhood: Never give in to fear or let what you feel show on your face.

Canada's mother knew her boys were afraid of the bigger boys on Union Avenue. She also knew there was little she could do to keep them safe from the bullying and aggression they would face every day in the concrete spaces of the streets, neighborhood, and schools where they gathered and played. Her sons would need to learn to master their fears and to act brave despite the terror they felt. They could not run home to their mama and survive on the streets. To teach her boys this lesson, she threatened them with an even worse beating than they would ever receive on the street if they came back home without that jacket.

Years later, Geoffrey Canada also reflected on the plight of his mother with profound empathy. As a single mother raising four young black boys on a meager salary, she couldn't afford to move her family to a safer neighborhood. She did everything in her power to change where her children grew up and how they were educated. Yet, in the South Bronx where they lived, the street code was much stronger than their own family. Like many other parents, his mother felt she needed to teach her sons the attitudes they needed to survive: "Don't cry. Don't act afraid. Don't tell your mother. Take it like a man. Don't let no one take your manhood." As a parent himself, Canada found he needed to do the same for his own child—in a different time and place, but still a poor, inner-city neighborhood where the norms of everyday life include a status system regulated by a willingness to resort to violence.

A Subculture of Violence

Who made these rules? How were they enforced, and who were the enforcers? Canada describes a status system that operated on his block—one that he came to realize operated in just the same way on many other blocks across the vast grid of the inner city. At the top of the pecking order were the older boys in their late teens and early twenties who literally "owned the block." Rarely around, these boys were involved in gangs and the drug business, and cycled in and out of jail. Below them were the fifteen- and sixteen-year-olds. These were the boys who enforced the code on the block that shaped the lives of the younger cohort, the middle school boys, ages ten, eleven, and twelve, who, in turn, dominated the little ones.

The core street lessons were about violence, respect, and masculinity. It was necessary to be willing to use violence to establish your status. Respect came with displays of skill and heart: You had to prove yourself as both willing and able to fight. Even if you lost, the fierceness with which you fought earned you a badge of honor. Each new arrival on the block would be challenged to fight an opponent of roughly his same age and size. Your status was determined by the outcome of the fight.

Age and physical prowess helped to determine the social order of the block. Those at the top got the most money and the best-looking girls. They were the ones to settle disputes and enforce order on the newcomers. If challenged, they defended their positions, but the order worked to keep the violence in check: Those who had proven their toughness were treated with deference and respect. Everyone banded together to defend the block against challenges from other blocks in the city. The lowest status and worst violence was reserved for those who did not fight at all. There was no choice to opt out of the system. Boys who refused to fight were severely beaten to send the message to everyone else. Faced with his first challenge at age seven, Canada knew whatever happened could not be as bad as what would happen if he tried to avoid it.

As Canada grew older, the challenges posed by this subculture of violence grew more intense. Getting to and from school required passage through other blocks governed by different sets of gangs and groups of youth. Inside school, the need to fight and to show no signs of weakness or fear increased exponentially. Public school gathered children across many different blocks of the city, each with its own pecking order. One's reputation needed to be established among a whole new set of boys from other neighborhoods. Passing from elementary school to middle school meant making a place in a new pecking order with far older, bigger, and meaner boys.

For Canada, his strong interest in school and books made him vulnerable to others who assumed he was weak. All the "eggheads," or kids in the smarter tracks in school, were targets for aggression. There was another emotion fueling that aggression: resentment. The smart boys posed a threat to the code of the street that valued toughness and physical prowess above the intellectual prowess of the educational system and dominant society. Because they were good with books and numbers, these youth did not suffer the daily humiliation felt by so many children, especially boys, whose only experiences at school were of repeated failure and rejection. The need to put eggheads at the bottom of the pecking order were made more urgent by the nagging suspicion that one day they would be the ones with the real power.

Canada learned early on that adults were powerless to keep youth safe from this subculture of violence. Even the installation of metal detectors in the school designed to protect classrooms and hallways from knives and guns only communicated to the youth that the violence would take place on the way to and from school. Metal detectors told youth that adults were terrified and powerless to stop the violence. As Canada's mother had taught him, adults offered no real protection to boys being threatened by other boys: If you could not stand up for yourself, you would be branded a victim. The norms were absolute. In Canada's words, "We didn't tolerate cowards."

From Fists to Knives to Guns

In sixth grade, Canada acquired his first knife. By then his world had widened. He traveled from Union Avenue, often in the company of older boys from the block, making him feel powerful, but sometimes he traveled on his own, or with one or two boys his own age. There were times he suffered the humiliation of being jumped or robbed of a baseball glove or basketball at the park. Having a knife in his pocket changed the equation. It was his "passport" to a wider world. With the knife in his pocket, twelve-year-old Canada felt bold, secure, and empowered. Canada's mother never knew he had this weapon; the world of the street and what he needed to do to survive among his peers was not something he ever discussed with her.

When Canada was growing up, guns were rare. Fists were the primary weapon, but would be augmented by an array of weapons if needed. The rules of Union Avenue that limited violence to fists gave way to the presence of weapons: sometimes broken bottles, car antennae, and sticks, but mainly knives and, later, guns. The subculture of violence became more chaotic, less orderly, and much more dangerous over time. Once guns were prevalent, and as easy to acquire as a pack of gum or can of soda, they would forever alter the code of the street in the inner-city neighborhood.

By the time he was in college, there was an explosion of handguns available on the street. By now Canada was attending Bowdoin, an elite, nearly all-white college on the coast of Maine. He had spent his late teens living with his grandparents in a middle-class community. Once in college, daily life was as far from Union Avenue as one could imagine, with its bucolic tree-lined streets and bobbing boats in the harbor. Home from college, walking from his new apartment on 183rd Street to his old neighborhood of Union Avenue, Canada felt afraid of these fourteen- and fifteen-year-olds who swaggered down the street, giddy with the sense of power that came from the guns tucked in the waistbands or pockets of their pants. At nineteen Canada was far removed from the daily life of the teenagers on his old block. Gangs and drugs dominated the street life and transformed the rituals of violence that took place in inner-city neighborhoods. Like most everyone else, Canada felt he needed to buy a gun for his own "protection."

He bought the gun legally in Maine but never thought to use it or carry it there. When he went back home to the Bronx for winter break, he slipped it in his luggage, and once home, kept it in his pocket just like everybody else. Canada noticed how the gun in his pocket changed his attitude and stance on the street. The "rules" of conduct he had so painstakingly learned as a boy involved a delicate dance of deference and respect. Violence through fighting was the currency through which a boy earned status and respect among the subculture of men. Canada had learned to show no fear even when he was terrified; to saunter, not run; to know when to look someone in the eye with great calm and when to avoid eye contact at all costs. This code of conduct was subtle but powerful in its regulation of a status order that meant everything to the young men desperate to earn their way into manhood.

A gun in his pocket changed Canada from the inside out. It began with a shift in how he felt when he walked down the street. Before when he walked down the street, his goal was to minimize confrontation by managing it, not running from it. Now, with a gun in his pocket, he felt emboldened, even arrogant: Why should he cross the street? Why shouldn't he look that group of young men blocking his path to the grocery story right in the eye? Why not insist they move out of his way? The gun made him feel powerful. It was intoxicating. The gun, he suddenly realized, made him reckless. Canada knew that sooner or later if he continued to carry, he would pull the trigger. The stakes were high and he had a lot to lose if that happened. He put the gun down once and for all.

The New Code of the Street

After decades of working with boys growing up on the same streets as he did, but in a new subculture of violence shaped by the presence of guns, Canada despairs over the harsh new lessons each young man must learn in a community where everyone is armed. The means to achieve respect and power have been replaced by a more lethal weapon. No longer is it just one's reputation on the line, but one's life. The young boys explain to Canada they would rather be "judged by twelve than carried by six," meaning they would rather use the gun and be locked up or sentenced to death than die on the street and have their casket be carried by six pallbearers.

When everyone carries guns for protection, no one feels safe. Canada's Harlem Children's Zone (HCZ), however, is one massive, holistic effort to provide a buffer against the subculture of violence. It is a safe space to learn for children living on some of the most violent streets in America. HCZ not only provides education and college preparation, but also other services to youth and their families, including health care and employment training in order to rebuild communities from the inside out.

THINKING CRITICALLY ABOUT THIS CASE

1. Discuss the subculture of violence described by Canada and its relationship to the ideal of masculinity. What did it mean to "be a man" in the world that Canada grew up in? What messages about masculinity did you learn growing up in your family and neighborhood?

2. Discuss how Canada's mother played a critical role in shaping her sons' values and creating opportunities for her children. How did your own parents and guardians shape your values and priorities?

3. What were the key turning points for Canada that enabled him to create the Harlem Children's Zone? What does this say about the effect of the social environment on individuals?

4. How have guns transformed individuals and violence in neighborhoods? Do you think there should be more limitations on guns and gun ownership as a result? Would your opinion be altered if you lived in a neighborhood with high gun violence? Explain.

5. What needs to change in order to create a less-violent subculture in these neighborhoods? What kinds of interventions would make a difference?

REFERENCES

This case is based on the following sources:

Bryant, A. "To Stay Great, Never Forget Your Basics." New York Times, December 18, 2011.

Canada, J. (1995). *Fist, Stick, Knife, Gun*. Boston: Beacon Press.

————. (1998). *Reaching Up for Manhood*. Boston: Beacon Press.

Duncan, A. "Geoffrey Canada: School Reformer." *Time*, April 21, 2011.

Harlem Children's Zone website, www.hcz.org.

INTRODUCTION

Geoffrey Canada's story opens a window into the socialization of boys growing up in the inner city. For Canada and his peers, the challenge of growing up required achieving, proving, and maintaining a gendered identity. Among the boys on Union Avenue, being and acting male carried with it a set of requirements about how to act, think, look, and feel in order to achieve "masculinity" in the eyes of their peers. Masculinity, and femininity, are both social constructions, consisting of norms about expected behavior, attitudes, and beliefs based on sex that are shared and enforced by a social group. Canada's narrative about his experience demonstrates his belief that violence is learned behavior.

When the public reads about yet another drive-by shooting, the image they carry is of a cold-blooded predator. What Canada's story helps us to understand is that what appears to be an absence of emotion may be learned behavior and a conditioned mask designed to hide the feelings of vulnerability, fear, and love that boys feel. Like soldiers in war, they have learned to act "cold"—to dominate their own fear, to project indifference, to never show weakness. Canada helps us to understand that this psychology is created within a subculture separate from but also shaped by the dominant society.

This chapter starts with a discussion of the patterns of offending and victimization behavior for boys. The major theories of juvenile delinquency dominant within the literature today are then reviewed. Most of the theories covered in this chapter were developed to understand the behavior and experience of male youth. Age and gender are two characteristics most associated with both criminal offending and victimization. Girls, who constitute about one-quarter of those in the juvenile justice system, have different patterns of offending, victimization, and pathways to delinquency. We examine girls' patterns in chapter 5.

MEASURING DELINQUENCY

UNIFORM CRIME REPORTING (UCR)
Arrest report compiled yearly by the Federal Bureau of Investigation from information provided by US law enforcement agencies across the country; supplanted by NIBRS.

NATIONAL INCIDENT-BASED REPORTING SYSTEM (NIBRS)
Official reporting that provides arrest details.

INDEX CRIMES
More-serious crimes, including murder, non-negligent manslaughter, forcible rape, robbery, aggravated assault, burglary, larceny, arson, and motor vehicle theft.

There are three methods for measuring delinquency and crime. Together, these measures provide a comprehensive picture of delinquency. Originally, crime was measured officially through the **Uniform Crime Reporting (UCR)** Program, compiled yearly by the Federal Bureau of Investigation from information provided by law enforcement agencies across the country, giving information on offenses and characteristics of offenders. Today, the UCR has been replaced by the **National Incident-Based Reporting System (NIBRS)**, which provides offense details, including descriptions of the incidents and arrestees.

There are two types of crime recorded for NIBRS: Group A offenses, which include twenty-two crime categories and some detail about the incident, and Group B offenses, which are more minor and include ten crimes for which only arrest data are reported.[1] More-serious crimes are often called **index crimes**, and they include murder, non-negligent manslaughter, forcible rape, robbery, aggravated assault, burglary, larceny, arson, and motor vehicle theft. Non-index crimes include all other crimes, except traffic violations.

There are significant limitations with using official reports of crime. First, not all crime is reported to police. The number of unreported crimes is referred to as the **dark figure of crime**. Crimes go unreported for many reasons. Sexual assault crimes, offenses that occur within households, and crimes in poor neighborhoods are significantly underreported in official statistics.[2] Another limitation of official data is that not all police departments interpret and record offenses the same way, so there is a lack of uniformity which can lead to difficulties when trying to compare statistics across different locations.

To address lack of reporting, the federal government developed the **National Crime Victimization Survey (NCVS)** that asks people about their experience with criminal victimization. The NCVS is conducted every year using a sampling technique that ensures fair representation of the US population. The NCVS reports on the dark figure of crime. This method, too, has its limitations. There may be underreporting, meaning respondents do not speak up about their victimization; or overreporting, meaning respondents perceived the victimization happened more than it actually did. The NCVS protocol is to interview only those individuals age twelve and older in the household, so victimization by younger children is underreported.[3] Finally, given that it is a sample of households, it is subject to sampling error, meaning that the victimization of those interviewed may not be accurately generalized to the US population as a whole. Taken together, however, UCR and NCVS provide a good empirical picture of certain kinds of crime in the United States.[4]

The third measure of crime is through a method called **self-report surveys**. Self-report surveys allow individuals to reveal information about law violations without legal repercussions. Importantly, self-report surveys have shown that delinquency is normative across racial and ethnic boundaries, although young males of color are more likely to be in the juvenile justice system.

Two nationwide youth self-report surveys conducted at regularly scheduled intervals are key sources of knowledge about adolescent drug use, delinquency, and weapon use: the Youth Risk Behavior Surveillance System (YRBSS), administered by the US Centers for Disease Control and Prevention, which asks questions about risky behavior in and out of school, including drug and alcohol use, dating practices, fighting, and weapon carrying; and the Monitoring the Future Survey, which asks students to self-report their drug, alcohol, and tobacco use. These surveys help to give us an overall picture of adolescent risk-taking and delinquent behavior and, over time, provide trends on drug use and delinquency.

Self-reports have their limitations as well. Individuals may lie, forget, make mistakes, or exaggerate their involvement in delinquency. Analysis of self-reported delinquency surveys, however, generally shows that they are accurate and reliable.[5] Taken all together, official sources of data and self-report data help us to understand what types of crimes are being committed, by whom. They also shed light on the characteristics of victims of crime.

Intersectionality and Delinquency

Comparisons between official and self-report delinquency measures show that minor offending, including trespassing, vandalism, and petty theft, are common among youth from all backgrounds, regardless of race, ethnicity, class, or gender.

DARK FIGURE OF CRIME
The number of unreported crimes.

NATIONAL CRIME VICTIMIZATION SURVEY (NCVS)
Official survey that asks people about their own criminal victimization.

SELF-REPORT SURVEYS
Surveys that allow individuals to reveal information about their own law violations without legal repercussions.

Youth of color, however, particularly black youth, are more likely to be arrested for delinquency offenses.[6] In fact, the arrest rate for black youth in 2013 was more than four times the arrest rate for white youth.[7] While girls' self-reported delinquency patterns have remained stable over a thirty-year period, arrests of girls, particularly for simple assault, have increased significantly over that same time frame.[8]

These discrepancies point to differential patterns of delinquency detection by authorities and official treatment. Youth of color are policed more heavily in poor, urban communities where tactics such as zero-tolerance policies for any law violations and hot-spot policing mean that delinquent behaviors are more likely to be detected by authorities. As we will see in chapter 5, girls' behaviors were traditionally addressed outside of the juvenile justice system. That practice has changed, resulting in a myriad of negative consequences, including girls being removed from their homes more quickly than boys.[9]

Self-report measures show that white youth participate in drug use more than black youth, yet the arrest rate for drug violations by black youth was 1.5 times higher than for whites.[10] The reasons for this disparity are, in part, due to the locations in which many black youth live. Again, poor communities are more likely to be policed more heavily. Additionally, punitive criminal justice responses to drug use, rather than treatment-oriented public health responses, are more likely to be employed in economically disadvantaged communities.[11] Furthermore, while drug rates in the most impoverished communities are no different than many other communities, drug availability and selling is significantly higher in lower-income communities.[12] These communities have few resources to muster in which to address systemic problems, leaving the justice system to be the first stop, rather than the last, in addressing social problems.[13] Overall, official and self-report measures of crime tell us that race, ethnicity, and gender intersect in ways that reinforce detection and system sanctions for those in the most distressed communities.

A SNAPSHOT OF JUVENILE CRIME AND VICTIMIZATION

Delinquency Offending

Juveniles aged ten through seventeen constituted 10.8 percent of the population and 9.2 percent of all arrests in the United States in 2014, demonstrating that juvenile arrests were slightly lower than the population of juveniles in society.[14] In the past, juveniles have been slightly disproportionately represented in the justice system, meaning that they committed more crime than their numbers in the population, though adults commit the majority of all crimes. Most arrests of youth are for nonserious criminal offenses, such as theft, simple assault, and drug abuse violations.[15] That said, juveniles constituted 10.4 percent of all violent crime arrests in 2014, and 68 percent of juvenile offenders used a firearm.[16] The media and public perception that juveniles make up the majority of offenders and are violent offenders, however, is unfounded.

Juveniles most often commit crime in concert with other youth.[17] This group context, or **co-offending**, can be explained in part through neuroscience. As discussed in chapter 3, adolescents' brains are not fully developed, making them more

CO-OFFENDING
Youth who commit crimes in concert with other youth.

susceptible to risk-taking and to peer influence than are adults.[18] Opportunity also plays a role in the peer context of offending. Juveniles have more free time with peers than do working adults, providing more opportunity to offend. Indeed, data show that juvenile crimes are most likely to take place in the afterschool hours, when there is a lack of adult supervision.[19]

Importantly, both official statistics and self-report surveys show that there is a pattern to delinquency for most youth in which delinquency begins after age ten, peaks during the late teen years, and rapidly declines and disappears by the mid-twenties (see figure 4.1).[20] While not all youth are arrested, minor offending is a normative part of the life course across different racial, ethnic, gender, and class backgrounds.[21]

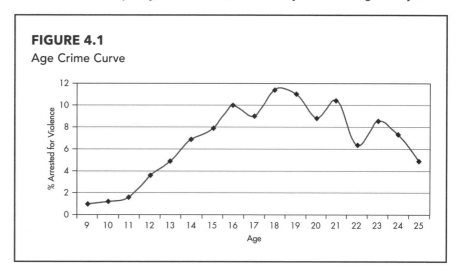

FIGURE 4.1
Age Crime Curve

Across different societies, research has consistently found that approximately 6 percent of youth commit over half of the crime in locations, and they generally do not "specialize" in any one type of crime, such as drug offending or vandalism.[22] These high-offending youth are termed **chronic offenders**. Generally, this means that they have committed five or more offenses, whether or not they have been caught.[23] Thus, if we compare these youth to other youth who are not high-rate, or chronic, offenders, we may be able to learn more about what causes crime, as well as how to prevent it. Several scholars have attempted to do so. Terrie Moffitt developed a classification system, or taxonomy, to help explain different offending patterns. Other scholars have since added to the stock of knowledge about offender types.

Evidence shows that there are at least two types of offenders: adolescent-limited and life course–persistent.[24] **Adolescent-limited offenders** engage in delinquent and criminal activity during peak crime-prone years (ages sixteen to twenty-four) and are like their peers in many other ways, but have more risk factors. They stop, or desist, from crime as they move into adulthood. **Life course–persistent offenders**, in contrast, start offending in adolescence and continue into adulthood, and are more likely to be chronic offenders.

The Rise and Fall of Juvenile Crime

Arrests have gone down since their peak in the late 1980s and early 1990s. Some of this is due to the decriminalization of drug offenses, as well as the general downward shift in offending.[25] Similarly, while there are over one million juvenile delinquency cases in courts, that number has declined since its peak in the 1990s (see figure 4.2). The general decline in juvenile crime, arrests, and court cases, however, does not obscure the fact that youth of color continue to be disproportionately processed into the juvenile justice system, and that girls are a growing minority of system-involved youth.

CHRONIC OFFENDERS
Individuals who have committed five or more offenses.

ADOLESCENT-LIMITED OFFENDERS
Individuals who engage in delinquent activity during peak crime-prone years and desist in adulthood.

LIFE COURSE-PERSISTENT OFFENDERS
Individuals who begin offending in adolescence and continue into adulthood.

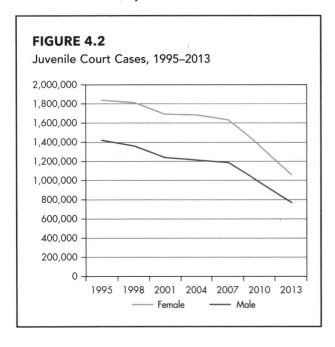

FIGURE 4.2

Juvenile Court Cases, 1995–2013

Intersectionality and Delinquency Patterns

Male youth are more likely to be arrested and prosecuted for crime, particularly violent crime, than are females. In 2014, males accounted for 71 percent of all juveniles arrested, and 82 percent of juvenile violent crime arrests.[26] Males constitute the majority of offenders in almost every category, with the exception of prostitution. That said, females make up a larger percentage of all arrests and juvenile court caseloads today than they have at any other point in time, although self-report measures show no large increase in offending. Female court cases constituted approximately 28 percent of a court's caseload in 2013, compared with approximately 18 percent in 1985.[27] The large jump in female court cases is due in part to how society views girls today, and how the justice system views the offenses they are likely to commit. In many ways, these "bad girls" of today are likely not all that different from girls thirty years ago.

Again, we will explore the reasons for female involvement in offending as well as the disparities in juvenile justice processing in depth in chapter 5.

We know from self-report measures that delinquency is common among all racial and ethnic groups; yet, research shows that disproportionate minority contact (DMC) is a reality. As previously discussed, black youth are four times more likely to be arrested than whites, and funneled into the system; and 74 percent of black youths' cases are petitioned to juvenile court compared to only 27 percent of white youths' cases.[28] Black youth also are more likely than white youth to be waived or transferred to adult court for serious offenses and criminal court processing.

Several hypotheses exist for why there are ethnic differences in juvenile justice trends. One hypothesis is **differential involvement**, in which youth of color are more likely to be involved in crime, especially serious crime. The second hypothesis is **differential treatment**, in which the justice system treats youth of color more harshly than white youth. More recently, refined self-report studies and advanced statistical techniques have been used to study the issue.[29] The relationship between offending, race/ethnicity, patterns of arrest, and juvenile justice system processing is further complicated by geographical and community differences. Again, however, the results of more heavily policed poor neighborhoods and the greater availability of drugs and guns in those communities, combined with the lack of resources, must be understood as part of the context when examining official patterns of delinquency.

Intersectionality and Status-Offending Patterns

Because of the differences in how states classify status offenses, it is difficult to compare status offenses across states. The FBI does not report statistics for truancy, incorrigibility, and running away, but NIBRS data show that liquor law violations, as well as curfew and loitering charges, constituted approximately

DIFFERENTIAL INVOLVEMENT HYPOTHESIS
Explanation for DMC is that youth of color are disproportionately involved in serious crime.

DIFFERENTIAL TREATMENT HYPOTHESIS
Explanation for DMC is that youth of color are given more punitive treatment in all stages of juvenile justice processing.

5.2 percent each of all arrests of juveniles in 2014.[30] The most common status offense that reaches the juvenile court is truancy.[31]

Males and females show similar patterns in status offenses heard in the juvenile court. There were 109,000 status offense petitions in 2013, with males making up 58 percent of those petitions.[32] While males are more likely to be taken to court for delinquency offenses, females are more likely to be taken into custody by police and sent to court for a status offense than they are for a delinquency offense. Further, females are more likely to be taken in for status offenses than are males who commit those same offenses.[33] Again, a paternalistic view that girls need the care and protection of the court is consistent with our discussion of the evolution of the juvenile court and the different expectations for girls and boys.

With regard to race and ethnicity, white youth are more likely to be sent to court for status offenses, followed by black youth. The pattern in petitioned offenses shows that status-offense cases of white youth are upward of 9,000 per year, while status-offense cases for black youth are upward of 2,000.[34] Meanwhile, Native American youth have the highest rate of status offense cases petitioned to court, and Asian youth have the lowest. For all youth, truancy is the most common status offense, and for all but black youth, liquor law violations are the second most serious status offense.[35] The second most common status offense for black youth is ungovernability.

There have been few examinations of how gender, race, and ethnicity intersect to affect youth who are petitioned to court for status offenses. Existing evidence shows that gender, race, and ethnicity all affect how status offenders are handled. Geography and social class also are factors. Although there are no national-level data on these intersections, one study in urban Arizona found that there was no difference in treatment of white and black males by the court system, but Native American and Hispanic males were treated more harshly. Black and Hispanic females also were treated more harshly by the court when compared with white females.[36] Disentangling the effects of juvenile justice system treatment is difficult and nuanced, as it varies by location, but it is clear that the pattern of unequal treatment must be addressed.

VICTIMIZATION AND CRIME

A specific set of risk factors known as **adverse childhood experiences (ACEs)** make individuals particularly vulnerable to poor health and can affect behavior. ACEs are early negative life events that can have lasting impacts on individuals. They include emotional, physical, or sexual abuse; emotional or physical neglect; domestic violence; substance abuse; mental illness; divorce or separation; and crime.[37] ACEs cut across ecological domains influencing the way individuals process information to the extent that they lead to poor outcomes later in life, including higher rates of victimization and delinquency. Recent research has shown that individuals with higher numbers of ACEs are at greater risk of experiencing alcoholism, domestic violence, and unemployment in adulthood.[38] Research aimed at better understanding the role ACEs play in the life course is rapidly expanding. Of the ACEs, victimization has received a fair amount of attention in the youth and justice literature.

Youth who have been victimized by child maltreatment are more likely to end up in the juvenile justice system as delinquents and status offenders than those

ADVERSE CHILDHOOD EXPERIENCES (ACES)
A specific set of risk factors that make individuals vulnerable to poor well-being.

who have not.[39] These youth are also more likely to experience physical and mental health problems. Approximately one out of twenty-five children is abused or neglected each year in the United States.[40] This includes physical abuse, emotional abuse, sexual abuse, or neglect. Often, children can experience more than one type of maltreatment. Most children who fall into the child maltreatment category are neglected; this means that parents or legal guardians have failed to: provide adequate food/clothing/shelter; protect them from domestic violence; get them into schools / provide education.

Exposure to violence, even as a bystander, negatively affects child development and well-being.[41] Exposure includes experiencing violence firsthand; experiencing vicarious (secondhand) violence; and growing up in neighborhoods with high levels of community violence where violence may be witnessed.[42] Consequences of exposure to violence include depression, post-traumatic stress (PTS), anxiety, domestic violence perpetration, and aggression.[43]

Intersectionality and Victimization Patterns

Laws in all states prohibit labeling a family neglectful if neglect is solely due to poverty, yet most maltreated children identified by courts are poor. According to official statistics, black and Hispanic youth are more likely to be maltreated than white youth. For every 1,000 black children in the population, 50 are maltreated. For every 1,000 Hispanic children in the population, 30 are maltreated; and for every 1,000 white children in the population, 29 are maltreated.[44] Females are slightly more likely to be victims of abuse and neglect; and long-term negative consequences of maltreatment may be more detrimental for females.[45] Further, female victimization is more likely to occur in the home than male victimization.[46] Girls are more likely to be assaulted by family members, while boys are more likely to be assaulted by nonrelated acquaintances.

In contrast, males and youth of color are disproportionately more likely to be victims of crime. Place also matters with regard to victimization. Those most at risk for violence and exposure to violence are males of color living in urban areas.[47] Again, this shows the very powerful effect that community conditions can have on individuals. Victimization, both at the hands of others and by exposure to violence, is not equally distributed across location or across ethnic and gender lines.

THEORIES OF DELINQUENCY

Understanding why some youth violate rules while others do not has always been a feature of human societies. We strive to understand in part so we know how to respond to the behavior. Those responses are shaped by a set of ideas about *why* that behavior occurs. Historically, the religious belief that the forces of good arise from the will of God in battle with forces of evil arising from the Devil was a dominant explanation for criminal behavior in the seventeenth century. Individuals who strayed from the will of God were susceptible to dark forces that tempted them or possessed them, causing them to do bad acts. At the time of the Salem witch trials, this belief led to the execution of individuals who refused to confess and renounce their allegiance to the Devil.

The eighteenth and nineteenth centuries brought a different set of explanations for criminal behavior. The classical school of criminology has its origins in the Age of Enlightenment, which replaced the idea that divine forces shape human conduct with the idea of free will. Instead of being compelled by the Devil, those who commit crime were understood to be making a choice to do so for conscious, rational reasons, such as getting rich or seeking pleasure. Consequences were a set of swift and certain punishments that would deter the rational person from choosing crime in the first place.[48] Rational persons will choose to obey the rules if the costs of being "bad" outweigh the benefits.

In the nineteenth century, the idea of free will was challenged by the positivist school of criminology. Social sciences studies in sociology and psychology asserted that a person's motivations, feelings, and beliefs are shaped by a variety of factors, both internal and external. Humans still make choices, but they are constrained by forces beyond their control. Biological factors, such as diet, nutrition, hormones, genes, neurological development; psychological factors, such as trauma, family structure, and mental illness; and social and environmental factors, such as poverty, education, socialization, discrimination, culture, and inequality, all shape one's choices and opportunities.

The juvenile justice system emerged with the belief that youth were incapable of forming rational decisions like adults, and that they were highly vulnerable to negative influences by family members, peers, and the neighborhood. The classical paradigm, discussed in chapter 3, embraced the possibility that scientific study of human behavior would provide the knowledge that would help to create interventions that would prevent, rehabilitate, and reform.

Theories help us to understand possible causes of delinquency, and by doing so, we can act to intervene and prevent further delinquency. If we do not pay attention to theory, then we do not really know what truly works in eliminating and/or reducing delinquency. Consider Cristian Fernandez, from Case Study 3. If we believe that he is simply a bad kid who repeatedly hit his little brother because he was in a bad mood, then we might feel morally justified in punishing him with life in prison. If, however, we believe that his physical aggression was shaped by an unconscious reaction to his own abuse at the hands of his stepfather, then we would feel morally justified in offering him treatment and a chance at rehabilitation.

Scientific Study of Juvenile Delinquency

A theory is more than a set of assumptions or hypotheses about what motivates human behavior. It is a series of interconnected statements that explains a phenomenon. Scientific methodology demands that the validity, or accuracy, of any theory is tested through observable evidence by continually asking how well a theory predicts real-world behavior. The earliest academic studies of delinquency occurred in the 1800s, prior to the establishment of the juvenile court. Since that time, theory development has been expanded and initial theories have been refined.

Delinquency theories can be grouped into broad categories: sociological theories, or macro perspectives; and sociopsychological theories, or micro perspectives. The reality is, however, that *both* sociological and psychological characteristics cause delinquency. In the case of Geoffrey Canada, his childhood environment—including the "lessons" he learned from his mother—played a role in shaping his reactions to people and situations, but so did his college experiences outside the South Bronx that led him to put down his gun. Integrated perspectives, taking into account both macro and micro forces, may most accurately represent why delinquency occurs and why it stops.

Our theoretical discussion is organized under three headings: a) person-centered theories; b) society-centered theories; and c) critical theories. Critical theories address the inequalities in society's treatment of groups and the forces that shape and maintain the structure of inequality within the society.

PERSON-CENTERED THEORIES

Rational Choice Theory

The idea of the rational actor emerged in the Age of Enlightenment, in opposition to the dominance of religious explanations for human behavior. Contemporary theories within criminology continue to explore how rational decision-making influences criminal behavior, and the term *deterrence theory* is often used as an equivalent or subtype of **rational choice theory** (RCT). RCT is rooted in the economic theory of cost-benefit analysis: If the benefits of the activity (i.e., pleasure of using drugs) outweigh the costs (i.e., pain of imprisonment), then individuals will engage in the activity. This is also known as a *hedonistic calculus*. Individuals conduct a cost-benefit analysis before engaging in deviance. Indeed, in Canada's case, it was a rational decision to carry a gun for protection, as well as a rational one to set it aside in fear of what he would lose should he use it. As Canada points out, many youth in the inner city are making a rational choice when they calculate that they would rather be "judged by twelve than carried by six." They choose the calculated risk of being arrested and going to prison over the risk of being shot dead by a rival gang.

This theory has many limitations in its application to adolescents. It is difficult to apply rational choice theory to juvenile delinquency because we know from research that the adolescent brain does not process information the same way an adult brain does. Juvenile decision-making is rooted in the emotional centers of the brain, and it is highly sensitive to the influence of peer pressure and impulsivity. A more-mature Geoffrey Canada was able to reason through the future consequences that might happen should he continue to carry a weapon; that is much more difficult to do at a younger age.

Individuals often have erroneous perceptions about the likelihood of getting caught and the punishments for a crime.[49] Drug and alcohol use further undermines the rational basis for making decisions. Yet, deterrence-based initiatives may in fact work for some younger people under some circumstances. Research shows that identifying high-rate offenders, usually older teens or young adults, placing them on notice that they will be prosecuted to the fullest extent of the law if they are in violation, and at the same time directing them to other positive opportunities, effectively reduces criminality in high-crime areas of cities.[50]

Biosocial Theories

Biological theories emerged to explain criminal offending in the nineteenth century. Some of these strike us today as fairly outlandish, such as William Sheldon's popular theory that human body types are associated with different temperaments, or the field of phrenology that used the shape of a person's forehead to predict criminal tendencies. The idea that criminal behavior is genetic or

RATIONAL CHOICE THEORY (RCT)
Individuals will engage in crime if the benefits outweigh the costs.

inherited was often used to justify policies such as forced sterilization of women and men who were believed to be "feebleminded" or mentally deficient. The so-called science of eugenics, which posited that criminality passed within families through genetic transmission, was highly discredited once it was discovered that it was widely used by Adolf Hitler's scientists to intellectually justify genocidal programs of mass extermination.[51]

Contemporary theories are more sophisticated in the understanding of the interplay between genetic factors and environmental factors. The debate between nature, the influence of inborn characteristics, and nurture, the influence of external factors such as diet, parenting, and neighborhood, is not all one or the other. Biosocial theories emphasize the complex interaction between both biological factors and social/environmental forces.

Brain development and functioning is influenced by the inputs from the environment, such as the quality of parental nurturing, adequate nutrition, and exposure to ACEs. The concept of *neuroplasticity* states that the human brain during childhood and adolescence is responsive to inputs from the environment, and is shaped and adapts to those influences more dramatically than it does during adulthood.[52] The brain is more sensitive to external influences, both positive and negative, during this time. This helps to explain why juveniles are more amenable to treatment than adults: Their brains are more sensitive to the environment.

Some individuals are also more sensitive to environmental influences than others. Those whose brain chemistry is most susceptible to negative external influences are also more responsive to rehabilitation. For example, researchers have found that individuals with certain genes that produce high levels of MAOA, or monoamine oxidase, are less likely to become aggressive later in life when exposed to early childhood abuse than those with genes that produce lower levels of this brain chemical.[53] This means that the effects of an abusive childhood environment influence individuals differently depending on their genetic makeup.

The study of ACEs on the incidences of mental and physical health in later life illuminates the interplay between biological and social forces.[54] Modern science is only just beginning to understand the complex ways that social influences interact with biology throughout the life course to shape individual behavior. We will return to the impact of ACEs in our discussion of interventions in chapter 11.

Psychological Theories

Psychological theories examine personality differences among people. Sheldon and Eleanor Glueck were among the first researchers to study personality differences between youth who engage in juvenile delinquency and those who do not. In the 1940s, they compared a sample of five hundred incarcerated delinquent boys with a group of five hundred nondelinquent boys enrolled in public school, finding personality differences between the two groups.[55] The delinquent group was more extroverted, impulsive, fearless, hostile, and suspicious toward authority, and had lower self-esteem as compared to the nondelinquent group. Not all the differences between these groups were negative: Delinquent youth also were highly likable and social.

Sigmund Freud is considered the father of psychoanalytic theories that focus on early childhood experiences in the formation of adult personality. Freudian theory posits that all human beings have three interacting parts to personality: an *id*, an unconscious life force that seeks to maximize pleasure and avoid pain; the *superego*, or conscience, which is an unconscious internalization of society's norms and values; and an *ego*, or rational consciousness, which mediates between the drives and desires of the id and the demands and guilt of the superego. Freud believed that healthy personality formation was dependent on the formation of all three components of the personality in balance with one another during the first five years of life. If development does not occur in appropriate ways, the resulting neurosis can be manifested in criminal behavior. It is difficult to test this theory, which relies on subjective interpretation of thoughts. There is little empirical basis to support the idea that delinquency is a result of unresolved childhood issues, but the theory has been used as a basis for cognitive theory refinement.[56]

Cognitive theory is concerned with how individuals form thoughts, which are the basis for our behaviors. Those who do not fully develop moral reasoning are likely to engage in deviance. These individuals, especially youth, may believe that deviance is not necessarily wrong. Using violence is considered "appropriate" and justified in places like Union Avenue in the South Bronx, where Canada grew up. This theory has often been combined with behavioral theory, described in the next section. Studies show that there is some support for cognitive theory. In particular, treating justice system–involved youth with cognitive behavioral therapies is one of the most effective interventions to reduce recidivism.[57] We will expand further on that finding in chapter 11.

Influenced by Freud, Erik Erikson posited that personality formation occurs through eight stages of human development, from birth to old age. At each stage, a key dilemma must be successfully resolved in order for the individual to retain a psychologically healthy personality.[58] The key stages relevant for involvement in juvenile delinquency occur in early childhood and adolescence. During infancy, the relationship between the caregiver and infant establishes a basic sense of trust and security in human relationships. Youth who have been maltreated in early childhood may develop attachment disorders and have difficulties in establishing healthy relationships later in life. Early success or failure in school, and the degree to which that is reinforced by parents, will affect how youth feel about their own sense of competence.

In adolescence, the key dilemma is to establish a sense of identity, interpersonally and sexually. As youth struggle to define themselves apart from their family of origin, there is a sense of confusion about identity that increases the importance of friends outside the home and experimentation with different behaviors. Peer associations become highly influential during this stage because of the uncertainty youth have about who they really are. This explains why delinquency is likely to occur in a group context and in opposition to parental values.

Psychological theories lay out a framework in which healthy personality development occurs. Personality is influenced through interactions within the family, at school, and with peers. Intersectionality plays a role as well. Since the early twentieth century many researchers have studied the relationship between intelligence and criminal behavior. They have found a consistent relationship between low IQ and delinquency. Importantly, that relationship is affected by school performance and neighborhood factors.[59] Studies find that engagement in delinquency is a function of negative peer associations and school failure, especially for youth of color living in high-crime neighborhoods.

We now turn to those society-centered theories where the main cause of delinquency is the environment.

SOCIETY-CENTERED THEORIES

Society-centered theories shift our attention from the individual to groups and structures within society. We begin with social learning theories that emphasize processes whereby individuals learn, adopt, and rationalize norms, values, and behaviors; and then we focus on theories that emphasize social structures and institutions.

Learning/behavioral theories focus on the process through which humans learn norms, beliefs, and values from others. The main idea is that all behavior, both positive and negative, is learned from those we come in contact with most often. Behavioral theory adds a variation. Behavioral psychologists, like Albert Bandura, emphasize reinforcement mechanisms.[60] If a behavior is reinforced by a positive event or reaction, that behavior will continue. Geoffrey Canada, for example, received positive reinforcement from both his mother and his peers by adhering to the street code that approved of physical fighting. If such behavior is punished, the behavior is likely to be extinguished. By moving to a middle-class neighborhood, Canada acquired a different set of behavioral norms which were positively reinforced that helped to prepare him for college success.

Social learning theory predicts that those with whom we are in contact most frequently will have the greatest impact. When delinquent youth are segregated from prosocial peers and placed with other delinquent youth, the likelihood of delinquency is increased. This is one of the reasons why reformers have urged that status offenders be separated from delinquent youth, and one of the reasons why delinquent youth should be kept separate from adult offenders. There is a question of whether or not youth are delinquent first and seek out deviant peers, or if youth truly learn that deviance from peers. Regardless of that ordering, we do know that association with deviant peers is one of the strongest predictors of delinquency.[61]

Differential Association

Edwin Sutherland developed the most influential social learning theory, known as **differential association**. He argued that all criminal behavior, like all human behavior, is learned through interactions with others in intimate group settings.[62] The level of learning increases with the frequency, duration, intensity, and priority of the group within the life of the individual. Through interaction with the group, individuals adopt favorable or unfavorable attitudes toward the law, depending on group norms. This theory applies equally to youth learning the attitudes toward street crime from their friends as it does to the executive in the corner office learning the attitudes and techniques necessary to commit white-collar crime.

Ronald Akers and Robert Burgess built upon differential association by including principles of behaviorism and operant conditioning.[63] According to their version, people learn through imitation of others with whom they most closely associate, and those people provide positive and negative reinforcement that maintains the behavior. The term *differential reinforcement* refers to the

SOCIAL LEARNING THEORY
Behavior is learned from those with whom we are in contact most frequently.

DIFFERENTIAL ASSOCIATION
Criminal behavior is learned through interaction with deviant peers.

rewards—approval, money, status, food, affection—that increase the behavior. The group also is the source of basic value judgments that allow the youth to feel positive about themselves and their actions.

Gresham Sykes and David Matza added the concept of **techniques of neutralization** to learning theory. Techniques of neutralization allow youth to rationalize their antisocial behavior even while they engage in activities that may be contrary to their values and norms.[64] Sykes and Matza argued that all individuals desire to see themselves in a positive light, and rationalizing minimizes their blame for deviant acts. Youth neutralize negative feelings from their misdeeds by doing things like denying responsibility ("He hit me first"); denying injury ("It was only shoplifting; it didn't hurt anyone"); denying a victim ("He had it coming"); accusing adults of hypocrisies ("You did that as a kid"); and justifying the act by appealing to a higher loyalty ("It was an order from the gang leader").

Social Disorganization Theory

Social disorganization theory derived from University of Chicago researchers Clifford Shaw and Henry McKay, who examined large-scale changes in society in the 1920s and 1930s. Unlike small, rural, close-knit communities, they observed that cities experienced rapid population growth, high population mobility, persistent poverty, and ethnic heterogeneity, leading to social instability. They believed this instability created a breeding ground for crime because traditional social controls in the community and family could no longer operate effectively.[65]

Robert Sampson and William Julius Wilson have built on these ideas to argue that patterns of racial and class segregation have created and reinforced zones of urban instability that experience high rates of crime and delinquency.[66] Poverty alone is not the driving force of crime rates; rather, it is the inability of the community and its institutions to enforce local norms and regulate the behavior. Because of high residential turnover, residents do not associate with one another and form bonds of trust and shared values. They isolate themselves, limiting their ability to act together to keep their community safe.

The term **collective efficacy** refers to the capacity of the community to work together on a shared set of tasks.[67] It begins with the willingness of residents to speak up and intervene when they witness something happening, such as youthful misconduct on the street. Sampson and his colleagues have argued that in order for citizens to feel empowered to hold youth accountable, they must feel a sense of trust and social cohesion with neighbors. Otherwise, everyone assumes it is "none of their business" and withdraws to the privacy of their own home.

Delinquency results from lack of positive values transmission in neighborhoods that experience high population mobility, poverty, economic decline, and fear of crime.[68] In order to reduce delinquency, communities need to come together to advocate for and obtain needed improvements to community infrastructure, including enticing businesses to set up shop and ensuring that schools have good teachers and administrators.[69] The African proverb "It takes a village" is relevant to this theory. Community members must see the children in the neighborhood as "their" children, and take on the task of caring for them to increase positive youth development and to decrease the odds of delinquency.

TECHNIQUES OF NEUTRALIZATION Rationalization of antisocial behavior that is contrary to individual values.

SOCIAL DISORGANIZATION THEORY Delinquency is the result of community instability and the inability of social institutions to transmit proper values to youth.

COLLECTIVE EFFICACY The capacity of the community to work together on a shared set of tasks.

Anomie and General Strain Theory

The term **anomie** refers to a state of normlessness where people experience confusion, anxiety, and alienation from the values of the group. Emile Durkheim, often called the father of sociology, coined the term as he observed a rapidly changing society. Robert K. Merton applied these ideas to crime.[70] He argued that all societies provide norms about life goals and the means to achieve them.

Merton argued that all Americans share the same goals in life of acquiring wealth, status, and power, often termed the "American Dream."[71] Many come to America in search of these very things, but not all have the same ability to achieve those goals. Individuals like Geoffrey Canada—brought up in poor neighborhoods with parents who are occupied with the survival tasks of providing food, clothing, and shelter, and who go to schools that cannot afford good teachers or provide access to current technology and books—must overcome barriers in order to achieve those goals. When there is a mismatch between the goals an individual is socialized to achieve and the means to achieve those goals, there is strain or tension.

Strain is resolved through innovation. When individuals are unable to achieve these goals through the traditional means of going to school and working at well-paid jobs with room for advancement, they get creative and resort to unconventional means to obtain these ends, which can include crime and delinquency.[72] Crime and delinquency provide an alternate means to achieving the dominant goals of wealth, status, and power.

General strain theory (GST) states that individuals experience strain not only from the disjuncture between goals and means, but also from many other negative events, such as loss of a job or victimization.[73] Humans find different ways to cope with such strain, filtered through their social environment. Delinquency is one adaptation. GST helps to explain why a child may resort to delinquency in order to cope with the loss of parental divorce if there is not a positive force in her environment to help her adjust to that change. Some studies show that this strain is a precursor to delinquency.[74] Importantly, GST can explain why some youth growing up in the same environments become delinquent and others do not, as we see in the case of Canada.

Social Control Theory

Social control theory shifts attention from the question of why people violate norms and rules to a more-fundamental question of why people conform in the first place. The theory attempts to explain the forces that produce adherence to the law, positing that those who maintain strong bonds with conventional groups, institutions, and individuals are less likely to become delinquent because they do not want to jeopardize their good standing in society.[75] Perhaps the reason Canada finally put down his gun was because he was doing well for himself in society, and by carrying a weapon, he knew he was placing his future at risk. Social control theory focuses on the development of internal controls—those values, norms, and habits that are internalized; and the operation of external controls—the structures of support, surveillance, monitoring, and supervision that keep behavior of individuals in check.

The most influential theorist within this tradition is Travis Hirschi, who emphasized social bonds. Hirschi argued that youth with strong bonds to

ANOMIE
A state of normlessness where people experience confusion, anxiety, conflict, and alienation.

GENERAL STRAIN THEORY
Stress due to the inability to achieve positive goals, the removal of positive stimuli, or the introduction of negative stimuli that can lead to delinquency.

SOCIAL CONTROL THEORY
Those who maintain strong bonds to conventional society are less likely to be delinquent.

conventional society will not engage in delinquency, while those with weak bonds are more likely to do so.[76] He identified four distinct dimensions of social bonds. The first is *attachment*, or the extent of emotional bonds with conventional values passed through parents, teachers, or close peers that help youth internalize their norms and values. The second dimension is *involvement*, or the extent to which the individual's time and daily life is engaged in activities. Youth who are busy with prosocial activities, like school, sports, and art, are unlikely to get involved in delinquent activities.

The level of *commitment* to activities is the third dimension of social bonds. Individuals who invest time and energy into activities that will reward them in some fashion are less likely to jeopardize that through rule violation. They have developed what is called a **stake in conformity**. The final element is *belief*. This refers to the internalized beliefs the individual holds about the basic fairness and morality of the system. When individuals believe a system is fair, they are more inclined to follow the rules; if they believe the system is rigged due to race, class, or other inequities, they are more likely to engage in delinquent behavior.

As a whole, the implications of social control theory are that youth should be involved in prosocial activities, such as schools, churches, and clubs, and be closely bonded with conventional individuals if we expect them to internalize conventional norms. Social control theory also suggests that opportunities to succeed must be provided for all youth. In order to have a stake in conformity, youth must believe that there is a genuine pathway to long-term success. When youth perceive that there is no legitimate place for them within the social structure, they will neither invest time nor believe in conventional norms. It is necessary to create meaningful avenues for youth to be involved in society, like those discussed in positive youth development, as important mechanisms to ensuring the formation of positive social bonds.

Subcultural Theory

Subcultural theory developed to explain patterns of gangs and boys' delinquency in the United States. In this chapter's case study, we see evidence of an alternative set of values and norms among males in the South Bronx: the **code of the street** that values toughness and violence as a means to achieve respect. Deviant subcultures provide individuals with support and nurturance that they do not receive from the dominant culture, especially in highly distressed neighborhoods. Subcultures emerge as a means to help youth deal with the status frustration they experience by their inability to measure up to the standards of middle-class American society.

Albert K. Cohen argued that the norms of youth gangs were nonutilitarian: They committed crime for excitement and fun rather than to provide an income. He also observed that they enjoyed expressing their anger and malice at the dominant society through being negative and hostile. The subculture of the gang was a set of oppositional values created in reaction to the dominant middle-class value system.[77] Mainstream middle-class values included ambition, individual responsibility, achievement, delayed gratification, courtesy, restraints on physical aggression, and respect for property. This theory helps to explain the strong resentment other boys felt toward Canada, who succeeded in school and loved learning.

STAKE IN CONFORMITY
The result of investment and commitment to conventional activities that buffers against delinquent activity.

SUBCULTURAL THEORY
A shared set of alternative values and norms distinct from the dominant culture developed by a subgroup.

CODE OF THE STREET
Thesis that under conditions of concentrated disadvantage, inner-city neighborhoods produce a violent subculture.

Richard Cloward and Lloyd Ohlin combined subcultural theory with Merton's general strain theory to argue that because lower-class boys cannot compete in the middle-class arena, they create an alternate or **differential opportunity structure** where they can succeed, such as entry into illegal drug dealing.[78] These subcultures also offer an alternative way to earn status and respect through displays of heart, skill, and nerve; and they also provide a place to just chill out and retreat through use of drugs and alcohol.

Marvin Wolfgang and Franco Ferracuti argued that violence in lower-class males is not oppositional to mainstream society, but a more-extreme version of a dominant set of cultural values around violence.[79] While the wider society relies on state agents of violence—military and police to uphold laws through force— people in poor communities, especially young males, must rely on their own use of violence to address conflicts. Elijah Anderson's work on the code of the street developed this thesis further by arguing that the extreme disadvantage and isolation of inner-city neighborhoods of color have produced a more-violent code of conduct for its residents.[80] Lack of responsiveness of the police means that everyone must take steps to protect themselves in a culture where "might makes right," and verbal and physical aggression is the means for achieving personal security. We explore these ideas in greater detail when we look at gangs in chapter 6.

Labeling Theory

Labeling theory is a social reaction theory that turns attention away from the activities and behavior of youth and focuses instead on the activities and behavior of institutions that respond to youth. As we learned in chapter 2, juvenile justice and the very idea of delinquency was created by upper-middle-class activists, who defined a social problem and created laws and institutions to address it. We must understand who within society defines the problem and how systems for responding to those problems shape the behavior of youth.

A key idea in labeling theory is the assertion that no behavior is inherently deviant or delinquent; rather, it is the societal reaction or response to the behavior that defines it as a "crime." Those in a position to create delinquency definitions and confer the designation onto individuals are those with the power in society. Those who receive the label, in contrast, as we have seen from chapters 1 and 2, are those without such power.

According to Edwin Lemert, a two-stage labeling process occurs.[81] **Primary deviance** refers to youth who have committed deviant acts but are not considered "delinquents" by others. The self-concept is not affected at this stage. An example of this would be teens who commit vandalism, petty crime, or underage drinking but still are viewed by others and by themselves as "good kids." As we have seen, research shows that nearly all youth commit multiple acts of delinquency at some point in their teen years, yet most do not acquire the label of delinquent.

Secondary deviance occurs when youth are stigmatized by society and labeled delinquents. At this point, they then begin to engage repetitively in highly visible "bad" acts. Individuals develop an identity around negative behavior that will further fuel delinquent activity in a self-fulfilling prophecy. In other words, they begin to develop a "delinquent career." For many youth, particularly black and brown youth from poor neighborhoods, negative experiences in schools as early as preschool translate to an early start to a deviant career. The labels

DIFFERENTIAL OPPORTUNITY STRUCTURE
Subculture that offers alternative means to earn status, respect, and other social rewards.

LABELING THEORY
Delinquency is in part the product of the activities of institutions and individuals that respond to youth behavior.

PRIMARY DEVIANCE
Youth commit acts of delinquency but are not treated or categorized as "delinquents" by others.

SECONDARY DEVIANCE
Youth are labeled delinquents and develop an identity around that label.

of being "stupid," "lazy," "difficult," or "troubled" affect children and those who interact with them.[82]

The clear policy implication that stems from this theory is to avoid labeling by preventing youth from entering the juvenile justice system. Edwin Schur expanded on this idea by espousing a policy of **radical nonintervention** by the system.[83] He argued that the best approach with the vast majority of youthful offenders is to officially ignore their behavior. By not treating their behavior as serious, most will outgrow these youthful indiscretions on their own and will not develop a self-concept that supports negative behavior. Many would argue that this is exactly what happens for many middle-class and privileged youth who engage in delinquent acts but are never processed and labeled as delinquents during their adolescent years.

INTEGRATED THEORIES

Integrated theories combine some theoretical tenets from at least two theories into a comprehensive, unified perspective of delinquency and crime. They have become popular in recent years as it has become clear that we need better explanations for crime and as advances in computer software have been able to model complex relationships among different delinquency factors. In some theory-testing research, integrated theories are better able to explain delinquency and crime than single theories.[84] There are some problems with theory integration, however, because not all theoretical perspectives start from the same premise. Some theories start from the premise that individuals have natural deviant tendencies (rational choice theory), while others start from the idea that individuals are socialized into deviant actions (social disorganization). Two of the more-popular integrated theories are life course theories and latent trait theories.

Life course theories hypothesize that factors influencing individual behaviors change as people mature, as does an individual's propensity to commit crimes. These theories model the developmental process, and are able to explain the age–crime relationship, which shows that most crime occurs between the ages of sixteen and twenty-four. Changing interpersonal and structural factors throughout life are emphasized. For example, drawing on social control theory using the Glueck data, *age-graded theory* finds that even those who have early-onset delinquency, a key risk factor for future criminality, can alter their criminal trajectory paths through turning points. Things like good jobs, marriage, military service, and having children can increase law-abiding behavior.[85] Certainly, in Canada's case, we see that his physical move from Union Avenue to his grandmother's house, and to a school that could provide a thriving learning environment, enabled him to do well and to attend a prestigious college. These were turning points in his life.

Importantly, at key life moments, involvement in delinquency can hamper future turning points. A juvenile record might prevent a youth from entering military service later in life, or gaining a steady job. Gang involvement may lead to incarceration, which in turn undermines marriage and future employment. There is a form of cumulative disadvantage that reduces the number of pathways open to youth who get involved in the juvenile system early in their lives. We must focus on pivotal junctures in the lives of youth to develop key support systems for these critical periods.

RADICAL NONINTERVENTION
Policy that ignores minor youthful misbehavior and allows youth to age out of delinquency.

LIFE COURSE THEORIES
The factors influencing behaviors change over time, as does propensity to commit.

Latent trait theories, in contrast to life course theories, define some conditions present at birth, such as the presence/absence of certain chemicals in the body, or occurring early in life, such as victimization, as accounting for the onset of criminality. A person's criminal disposition remains stable over time with social forces and opportunities influencing the likelihood of crime. *Self-control theory* is one latent trait theory developed from social control theory. Delinquency is the result of low self-control, which is developed through biological processes and improper socialization.[86] Delinquency is prevented through strong, prosocial bonding. Self-control theory is also called a *general theory of crime*, because it aims to explain delinquency, crime, and deviance throughout the life course.

Low self-control, often demonstrated through impulsivity, is a result of ineffective parenting. Impulsivity may translate to delinquency in teenage years, and then show up as lack of conformity later in life, where individuals have difficulty keeping jobs and maintaining relationships with significant others. This theory also explains the age–crime curve. Although the number of offenders in society remains constant, opportunities for committing delinquent activities vary over time, and that is why crime rates fluctuate. Self-control, while an individual trait, is largely developed from a sociological base of an individual's environment. Studies have shown support for this theory as a cause of deviant behavior, both in the United States and internationally.[87]

CRITICAL THEORIES

Inequality and power in the wider society are at the heart of critical theories aimed at understanding crime and delinquency. Justice systems are shaped by power and privilege and operate in ways that maintain the status quo. In American society, social class intersects with race and gender as the key structures of inequality. Throughout this textbook, we examine those intersections. Those who are processed by the system are overwhelmingly in the lower class, while middle- and upper-class misbehavior goes unpunished. Wealth, status, and power insulate those in higher social classes from the juvenile and adult justice systems.

Critical theorists take a macro view of understanding social problems. Karl Marx developed an analysis of modern capitalist societies that argued the conflict between workers and owners is the driving force within societies.[88] Those with economic power, the capitalists, are able to transfer that power to the political, educational, and cultural spheres of society. His analysis predicted that the relentless and intense exploitation of workers by the factory-owning class would eventually lead workers to overthrow that economic system and create a more just and equitable economic system based on shared economic ownership.

Critical theories in the Marxist tradition expanded and developed on these ideas to explain how they shape crime and the justice system. Laws are written by those in power to protect their own interests, and even when they do break the laws, the rich and powerful are generally able to avoid accountability for their misdeeds.[89] Corporate and white-collar crime, which cause a great deal of financial and physical harm in society, are rarely prosecuted or punished compared with the efforts to police and prosecute street crime. Other critical theorists point

LATENT TRAIT THEORIES
Define some conditions present at birth or occurring early in life as accounting for the onset of criminality.

out that most street crime is committed against those in the lower classes. These theorists argue that it is important to address the social conditions—including poverty, unemployment, inadequate housing, drug addiction, under-resourced schools, and community programming—in order to effectively reduce criminal offending and victimization in these communities.[90]

At the same time, critical race theorists point out that the criminal justice and juvenile justice systems are institutions that are oppressive to working-class communities, especially poor communities of color. As noted at the outset of this textbook, the disproportionate representation of immigrants, black and brown youth, and poor individuals in the juvenile system has been true since the origins of juvenile justice. Youth of color in highly distressed neighborhoods are more likely to be policed, arrested, detained, sentenced, and incarcerated.[91] This leads to labeling and the onset of delinquent careers that may lead to a lifetime of incarceration. The concept of "cradle-to-prison pipeline" refers to the complex process of labeling that begins at birth and leads lower-class youth of color into adult criminal roles.

A good theory should help us both understand and explain why things happen. Here we have looked at many of the most prominent delinquency theories. Most of them addressed boys' delinquency, sometimes without careful attention to separating out how such pathways may shift for boys from different racial, ethnic, and social classes.

The next chapter will look at how those pathways to delinquency are different for girls.

KEY TERMS

adolescent-limited offenders Individuals who engage in delinquent activity during peak crime-prone years and desist in adulthood.

adverse childhood experiences (ACEs) A specific set of risk factors that make individuals vulnerable to poor well-being.

anomie A state of normlessness where people experience confusion, anxiety, conflict, and alienation.

chronic offenders Individuals who have committed five or more offenses.

code of the street Thesis that under conditions of concentrated disadvantage, inner-city neighborhoods produce a violent subculture.

collective efficacy The capacity of the community to work together on a shared set of tasks.

co-offending Youth who commit crimes in concert with other youth.

dark figure of crime The number of unreported crimes.

differential association Criminal behavior is learned through interaction with deviant peers.

differential involvement hypothesis Explanation for DMC is that youth of color are disproportionately involved in serious crime.

differential opportunity structure Subculture that offers alternative means to earn status, respect, and other social rewards.

differential treatment hypothesis Explanation for DMC is that youth of color are given more punitive treatment in all stages of juvenile justice processing.

general strain theory Stress due to the inability to achieve positive goals, the removal of positive stimuli, or the introduction of negative stimuli that can lead to delinquency.

index crimes More-serious crimes, including murder, non-negligent manslaughter, forcible rape, robbery, aggravated assault, burglary, larceny, arson, and motor vehicle theft.

labeling theory Delinquency is in part the product of the activities of institutions and individuals that respond to youth behavior.

latent trait theories Define some conditions present at birth or occurring early in life as accounting for the onset of criminality.

life course–persistent offenders Individuals who begin offending in adolescence and continue into adulthood.

life course theories The factors influencing behaviors change over time, as does propensity to commit.

National Crime Victimization Survey (NCVS) Official survey that asks people about their own criminal victimization.

National Incident-Based Reporting System (NIBRS) Official reporting that provides arrest details.

primary deviance Youth commit acts of delinquency but are not treated or categorized as "delinquents" by others.

radical nonintervention Policy that ignores minor youthful misbehavior and allows youth to age out of delinquency.

rational choice theory (RCT) Individuals will engage in crime if the benefits outweigh the costs.

secondary deviance Youth are labeled delinquents and develop an identity around that label.

self-report surveys Surveys that allow individuals to reveal information about their own law violations without legal repercussions.

social control theory Those who maintain strong bonds to conventional society are less likely to be delinquent.

social disorganization theory Delinquency is the result of community instability and the inability of social institutions to transmit proper values to youth.

social learning theory Behavior is learned from those with whom we are in contact most frequently.

stake in conformity The result of investment and commitment to conventional activities that buffers against delinquent activity.

subcultural theory A shared set of alternative values and norms distinct from the dominant culture developed by a subgroup.

techniques of neutralization Rationalization of antisocial behavior that is contrary to individual values.

Uniform Crime Reporting (UCR) Arrest report compiled yearly by the Federal Bureau of Investigation from information provided by US law enforcement agencies across the country; supplanted by NIBRS.

REVIEW AND STUDY QUESTIONS

1. Explain the meaning of positivism. How does the scientific study of juvenile delinquency (and crime in general) differ from earlier explanations for this behavior?

2. Explain the rational choice theory of criminal behavior. Why is it difficult to apply to adolescent delinquent behavior?

3. Explain how the study of ACEs (adverse childhood experiences) is an example of a biosocial theory.

4. Use the concepts of differential association and differential reinforcement to explain the changes in behavior of Geoffrey Canada during his early adolescence and young adulthood.

5. Explain the concept of collective efficacy. What are the characteristics of communities with high levels of collective efficacy? How does collective efficacy reduce delinquency? Why do communities that are socially disorganized have less collective efficacy?

6. Explain Merton's theory of a mismatch or strain between goals and means in the pursuit of the American Dream. How does this theory help to explain delinquent behavior?

7. Define Sykes and Matza's "techniques of neutralization." What are some common examples of this type of rationalization?

8. Identify the four dimensions of social bonds. Explain how Travis Hirschi's theory of social bonds predicts delinquent behavior.

9. Explain the difference between primary and secondary deviance. What is the policy of radical nonintervention? Why did Schur believe this was an effective way to prevent delinquency?

10. Identify the key dynamics at the heart of critical theories of delinquency. In these theories, what are the central factors shaping lives of poor youth that result in juvenile justice system involvement?

CHECK IT OUT

Read

Cullen, F. T., Agnew, R., and Wilcox, P. (2014). *Criminological Theory: Past to Present: Essential Readings.* New York: Oxford.

Office of the Surgeon General. (2001). *Youth Violence: A Report of the Surgeon General.* Rockville, MD: Author. Available at www.ncbi. nlm.nih.gov/books/NBK44294/.

Watch

Risk and Protective Factors: www.youtube.com/watch?v=7MnalNpbQrg

American History X (1998)

The Breakfast Club (1985)

Thirteen (2003)

Web

Crime in the US: www2.fbi.gov/ucr/ucr_general.html#basics

Monitoring the Future Survey: www.monitoringthefuture.org/

Youth Risk Behavior Survey: www.cdc.gov/HealthyYouth/data/yrbs/index.htm

NOTES

[1] Federal Bureau of Investigation. (nd). *A Guide to Understanding NIBRS.* Available at www.fbi.gov/about-us/cjis/ucr/nibrs/2011/resources/a-guide-to-understanding-nibrs.

[2] Maxfield, M. G., Weiler, B. L., and Widom, C. S. (2000). Comparing Self-Reports and Official Records of Arrests. *Journal of Quantitative Criminology 16,* 87–110.

[3] Finkelhor, D., and Ormrod, R. (2000). *Characteristics of Crimes against Juveniles.* Washington, DC: Office of Juvenile Justice and Delinquency Prevention.

[4] See www2.fbi.gov/ucr/cius_04/appendices/appendix_04.html.

[5] Hindelang, M. J., Hirschi, T., and Weis, J. G. (1981). *Measuring Delinquency.* Thousand Oaks, CA: Sage.

[6] Piquero, A. (2008). Disproportionate Minority Contact. *Future of Children, 18,* 59–79.

[7] Puzzanchera, C., and Hockenberry, S. (2016). *National Disproportionate Minority Contact Databook.* Developed by the National Center for Juvenile Justice for the Office of Juvenile Justice and Delinquency Prevention. Available at www.ojjdp.gov/ojstatbb/dmcdb/.

[8] Zhan, M., Brumbaugh, S., Steffensmeier, D., . . . , and Kruttschnitt, C. (2008). *Violence by Teenage Girls:*

Trends and Context. Girls Study Group Bulletin. Washington, DC: Office of Juvenile Justice and Delinquency Prevention.

[9] Sherman, F. T., and Black, A. (2015). *Gender Injustice: System-Level Juvenile Justice Reforms for Girls.* Available at www.nationalcrittenton.org/wp-content/uploads/2015/09/Gender_Injustice_Report.pdf.

[10] Puzzanchera and Hockenberry, *National Disproportionate Minority Contact Databook.*

[11] Beckett, K. (2012). Race, Drugs, and Law Enforcement: Toward Equitable Policing. *Criminology & Public Policy, 11,* 641–53.

[12] Saxe, L., Kadushin, C., Beveridge, A., . . . , and Brodsky, A. (2001). The Visibility of Illicit Drugs: Implications for Community-Based Drug Control Strategies. *American Journal of Public Health, 91,* 1987–1994.

[13] Massey, D. S., and Denton, N. A. (1998). *American Apartheid: Segregation and the Making of the Underclass.* Cambridge, MA: Harvard University Press.

[14] Calculations from https://ucr.fbi.gov/crime-in-the-u.s/2014/crime-in-the-u.s.-2014/tables/table-32 and www.census.gov/topics/population/age-and-sex/data/tables.2014.html.

[15] Office of Juvenile Justice and Delinquency Prevention (OJJDP) Statistical Briefing Book. Available at www.ojjdp.gov/ojstatbb/crime/JAR_Display.asp?ID=qa05274.

[16] www.ojjdp.gov/ojstatbb/ezashr/asp/vic_display.asp.

[17] Zimring, F., and Laquer, H. (2015). Kids, Groups, and Crime: In Defense of Conventional Wisdom. *Journal of Research in Crime and Delinquency, 52,* 403–13.

[18] Steinberg, L. (2008). A Social Neuroscience Perspective on Adolescent Risk Taking. *Developmental Review, 28,* 78–106.

[19] See Office of Juvenile Justice and Delinquency Prevention (OJJDP) Statistical Briefing Book. Online. Available at www.ojjdp.gov/ojstatbb/offenders/qa03301.asp?qaDate=2010.

[20] National Institute of Justice. (2014). *From Delinquency to Young Adult Offending.* Available at www.nij.gov/topics/crime/Pages/delinquency-to-adult-offending.aspx#age.

[21] Shulman, E. D., Steinberg, L. D., and Piquero, A.R. (2013). The Age–Crime Curve in Adolescence and Early Adulthood Is Not Due to Age Differences in Economic Status. *Journal of Youth & Adolescence, 42,* 848–61.

[22] Wolfgang, M., Figlio, R., and Sellin, T. (1972). *Delinquency in a Birth Cohort.* Chicago: University of Chicago Press; D'Unger, A., Land, K., McCall, P., and Nagin, D. (1998). How Many Latent Classes of Delinquent/Criminal Careers? Results from Mixed Poisson Regression Analyses. *American Journal of Sociology, 103,* 1593–1631.

[23] Skardhamar. T. (2009). Reconsidering the Theory on Adolescent-Limited and Life-Course Persistent

Anti-Social Behavior. *British Journal of Criminology, 49,* 863–78.

[24] Moffitt, T. (1993). Adolescence-Limited and Life-Course Persistent Antisocial Behavior: A Developmental Taxonomy. *Psychological Review, 100,* 674–701.

[25] Puzzanchera, C., and Kang, W. (2014). Easy Access to FBI Arrest Statistics 1994–2012. Online. Available at www.ojjdp.gov/ojstatbb/ezaucr.

[26] www.ojjdp.gov/ojstatbb/crime/qa05104.asp?qaDate= 2014.

[27] Author's analysis of www.ojjdp.gov/ojstatbb/ezajcs/.

[28] Hockenberry, S., Puzzanchera, C. (2015). *Juvenile Court Statistics 2013.* National Center for Juvenile Justice, www.ojjdp.gov/ojstatbb/njcda/pdf/jcs2013.pdfbid.

[29] Thornberry, T. P., and Krohn, M.D. (2000). The Self-Report Method for Measuring Delinquency & Crime. *Measurement & Analysis of Crime & Justice,* Vol. 4. Washington, DC: US Department of Justice, Office of Justice Programs.

[30] See www.ojjdp.gov/ojstatbb/crime/qa05104.asp?qaDate=2014.

[31] Hockenberry and Puzzanchera, *Juvenile Court Statistics 2013.*

[32] Ibid.

[33] Chesney-Lind, M., and Pasko, L. (2013). *The Female Offender: Girls, Women and Crime* (3rd ed.). Thousand Oaks, CA: Sage.

[34] Sickmund, M., and Puzzanchera, C. (eds.). *Juvenile Offenders and Victims: 2014 National Report.* Pittsburgh, PA: National Center for Juvenile Justice.

[35] Ibid.

[36] Freiburger, T. L., and Burke, A. S. (2011). Status Offenders in the Juvenile Court: The Effects of Gender, Race, and Ethnicity on the Adjudication Decision. *Youth Violence and Juvenile Justice, 9,* 352–65.

[37] Edwards, V. J., Anda, R. F., Dube, S. R., Dong, M., Chapman, D. F., and Felitti, V. J. (2005). The Wide-Ranging Health Consequences of Adverse Childhood Experiences. In K. Kendall-Tackett and S. Giacomoni (eds.) *Victimization of Children and Youth: Patterns of Abuse, Response Strategies,* 8.1–8.12. Kingston, NJ: Civic Research Institute.

[38] Dube, S. R., Anda, R. F., Felitti, V. J., Edwards, V. J., and Croft, J. B. (2002). Adverse Childhood Experiences and Personal Alcohol Abuse as an Adult. *Addictive Behaviors, 27,* 713–25; Anda, R. F., Felitti, V. J., Brown, D. W., Chapman, D., Dong, M., Dube, S. R., . . . , and Giles, W. H. (2006). Insights into Intimate Partner Violence from the Adverse Childhood Experiences (ACEs) Study. In P. R. Salber and E. Taliaferro (eds.) *The Physician's Guide to Intimate Partner Violence and Abuse.* Volcano, CA: Volcano Press; Liu, Y., Croft, J., Chapman, D., Perry, G., Greenlund, K., Zhao, G., and Edwards, V. (2013). Rela-

tionship between Adverse Childhood Experiences and Unemployment among Adults from Five US States. *Social Psychiatry & Psychiatric Epidemiology, 48,* 357–69.

[39] Currie, J., and Tekin, E. (2012). Understanding the Cycle: Childhood Maltreatment and Future Crime. *Journal of Human Resource, 47,* 509–49.

[40] Sickmund and Puzzanchera, *Juvenile Offenders and Victims: 2014 National Report.*

[41] World Health Organization. (2014). World Report on Violence and Health. Geneva, Switzerland: Author.

[42] Voith, L., Gromoske, A., and Holmes, M. (2014). Effects of Cumulative Violence Exposure on Children's Trauma and Depression Symptoms: A Social Ecological Examination Using Fixed Effects Regression. *Journal of Child & Adolescent Trauma, 7,* 207–16.

[43] Buka, S. L., Stichick, T. L., Birdthistle, I., and Earls, F. J. (2001). Youth Exposure to Violence: Prevalence, Risks, and Consequences. *American Journal of Orthopsychiatry, 71,* 298–310.

[44] Ibid.

[45] Children's Bureau. *Child Maltreatment 2013.* Available at www.acf.hhs.gov/programs/cb/resource/child-maltreatment-2013; Gilbert, R., Widom, C. S., Browne, K., Fergusson, D., Webb, E., and Janson, S. (2009). Burden and Consequences of Child Maltreatment in High-Income Countries. *Lancet, 373,* 68–81.

[46] Zahn, M. A., Agnew, R., Fishbein, D., . . . , and Chesney-Lind, M. (2010). *Causes and Correlates of Girls' Delinquency.* Girls Study Group. Washington, DC: Office of Juvenile Justice and Delinquency Prevention.

[47] Finkelhor, D., Turner, H., Ormrod, R., Hamby, S., and Krackle, K. (2009). *National Survey of Children's Exposure to Violence.* Washington, DC: Office of Juvenile Justice and Delinquency Prevention.

[48] Bentham, J. (1988). *The Principles of Morals and Legislation.* Amherst, NY: Prometheus.

[49] Ariely, D. (2008). *Predictably Irrational: The Hidden Forces that Shape Our Decisions.* New York: HarperCollins.

[50] Braga, A. A., and Weisburd, D. (2012). The Effects of "Pulling Levers" Focused Deterrence Strategies on Crime. *Campbell Systematic Reviews, 6,* 1–90.

[51] Kühl, S. (1994). *The Nazi Connection.* Oxford, UK: Oxford.

[52] Davidson, R. J., and McEwen, B. S. (2012). Social Influences on Neuroplasticity: Stress and Interventions to Promote Well-Being. *Nature Neuroscience, 15,* 689–95.

[53] Fergusson, D. M., Boden, J. M., and Horwood, L. J. (2011). MAOA, Abuse Exposure, and Anti-Social Behaviour: 30-year Longitudinal Study. *British Journal of Psychiatry, 198,* 457–63.

[54] Reavis, J. A., Looman, J., Franco, K. A., and Rojas, B. (2013). Adverse Childhood Experiences and Adult Crim-

inality: How Long Must We Live Before We Possess Our Own Lives? *The Permanente Journal, 17,* 44–48.

55 Glueck, S., and Glueck, E. (1950). *Unraveling Juvenile Delinquency.* Cambridge, MA: Harvard.

56 Strachey, J. (ed.). (1999). *The Standard Edition of the Complete Psychological Works of Sigmund Freud.* (Reprint). New York: Vintage Books.

57 Lipsey, M. W., and Wilson, D. B. (1993). The Efficacy of Psychological, Educational, and Behavioral Treatment. *American Psychologist, 48,* 1181–1209.

58 Erikson, E. H. (1950). *Childhood and Society.* New York: W. W. Norton.

59 Lynam, D., Moffitt, T., and Southamer-Loeber, M. (1993). Explaining the Relation between IQ and Delinquency: Class, Race, Test Motivation, School Failure, or Self-Control? *Journal of Abnormal Psychology, 102,* 187–96.

60 Bandura, A. (1977). *Social Learning Theory.* Englewood Cliffs, NJ: Prentice Hall.

61 Haynie, D. L. (2001). Delinquent Peers Revisited: Does Network Structure Matter? *American Journal of Sociology, 106,* 1013–57.

62 Sutherland, E. H. (1947). *Principles of Criminology.* Chicago, IL: Lippincott.

63 Burgess, R. L., and Akers, R. L. (1966). A Differential Association–Reinforcement Theory of Criminal Behavior. *Social Problems, 14,* 128–47.

64 Sykes, G., and Matza, D. (1957). Techniques of Neutralization: A Theory of Delinquency. *American Sociological Review, 22,* 664–70.

65 Shaw, C. R., and McKay, H. D. (1972). *Juvenile Delinquency and Urban Areas* (rev. ed.). Chicago: University of Chicago Press.

66 Sampson, R. J., and Wilson, W. J. (1995). Toward a Theory of Race, Crime, and Urban Inequality. In J. Hagan and R. D. Peterson (eds.), *Crime and Inequality,* 37–56. Stanford, CA: Stanford University Press.

67 Sampson, R. J., Raudenbush, S. W., and Earls, F. E. (1997). Neighborhoods and Violent Crime: A Multi-Level Study of Collective Efficacy. *Science, 277,* 918–24.

68 Shaw and McKay, *Juvenile Delinquency and Urban Areas* (rev. ed.).

69 Bursik, R., and Grasmick, H. G. (1993). *Neighborhoods and Crime: The Dimensions of Effective Community Control.* New York: Lexington Books.

70 Adler, F., and Laufer, W. S. (1995). *The Legacy of Anomie Theory.* New York: Transaction.

71 Messner, S. F., and Rosenfeld, R. (2007). *Crime and the American Dream* (4th ed.). Belmont, CA: Thomson Wadsworth.

72 Merton, R. K. (1968). *Social Theory and Social Structure.* New York: Simon & Schuster.

73 Agnew, R. (1992). Foundation for a General Strain Theory of Crime and Delinquency. *Criminology, 30,* 47–87.

74 Ostrowsky, M., and Messner, S. (2005). Explaining Crime for a Young Adult Population: An Application of General Strain Theory. *Journal of Criminal Justice, 33,* 463–76; Broidy, L. (2001). A Test of General Strain Theory. *Criminology, 39,* 9–36; Slocum, L. A., Simpson, S., and Smith, D. (2005). Strained Lives and Crime: Examining Intra-Individual Variation in Strain and Offending in a Sample of Incarcerated Women. *Criminology, 43,* 1067–1110.

75 Hirschi, T. (2002). *Causes of Delinquency.* Piscataway, NJ: Transaction.

76 Hirschi, T. (1969). *Causes of Delinquency.* Berkeley: University of California Press.

77 Cohen, A. K. (1955). *Delinquent Boys: The Culture of the Gang.* Glencoe, IL: The Free Press.

78 Cloward, R. A., and Ohlin, L. E. (1960). *Delinquency and Opportunity: A Study of Delinquent Gangs.* New York: Routledge.

79 Ferracuti, F., and Wolfgang, M. E. (1967). *The Subculture of Violence.* New York: Routledge.

80 Anderson, E. (1999). *The Code of the Street.* New York: W. W. Norton.

81 Lemert, E. M. (1967). *Human Deviance, Social Problems, and Social Control.* Englewood Cliffs, NJ: Prentice Hall.

82 Loeber, R., and Farrington, D. P. (2001). *Serious and Violent Juvenile Offenders: Risk Factors and Successful Interventions.* Thousand Oaks, CA: Sage.

83 Schur, E. M. (1973). *Radical Non-Intervention: Rethinking the Delinquency Problem.* Englewood Cliffs, NJ: Prentice-Hall.

84 Pratt, T. C., and Godsey, T. W. (2003). Social Support, Inequality, and Homicide: A Cross-National Test of an Integrated Theoretical Model. *Criminology, 41,* 611–43.

85 Sampson, R., and Laub, J. (1993). *Crime in the Making: Pathways and Turning Points through Life.* Cambridge, MA: Harvard University Press.

86 Gottfredson, M. R., and Hirschi, T. (1990). *A General Theory of Crime.* Stanford, CA: Stanford University Press.

87 Pratt, T. C., and Cullen, F.T. (2000). The Empirical Status of Gottfredson and Hirschi's General Theory of Crime: A Meta-Analysis. *Criminology 38,* 931–64.

88 Marx, K. (1992 ed.). *Capital,* Vol. 1. London: Penguin.

89 Quinney, R. (1980). *Class, State, and Crime.* New York: Longman.

90 Lea, J., and Young, J. (1984). *What Is to Be Done about Law and Order?* New York: Penguin.

91 Sampson, R. J., and Laub, J. H. (1993). Structural Variations in Juvenile Court Processing: Inequality, the Underclass, and Social Control. *Law & Society Review, 27,* 285–312.

Delinquency, Victimization, and Pathways to Offending for Girls

LEARNING OBJECTIVES

By the end of the chapter, you should be able to do the following:

- Identify general patterns of offending and victimization for girls.
- Understand how gender ideals play a role in gender socialization and behavior.
- Articulate justice system gender biases.
- Explain why traditional delinquency theories do not adequately explain girls' involvement in delinquency.
- Discuss three prominent feminist theories that explain girls' delinquency.
- Define and identify delinquency risk, along with protective and promotive factors.

Case Study 5: Addicted to Love: Growing Up on the Track

The Fantasy

Tiffany leaves the group home located in Upstate New York, far from her neighborhood in the South Bronx, still wearing her pajama bottoms and fuzzy pink slippers beneath her winter coat. She boards the train to Grand Central and hops the subway to Port Authority. Beyond running away and going back to the city, she doesn't really have a plan. Her father is in jail, her mother somewhere in the city, probably getting high, but Tiffany has no idea where. All she knows is that she is fed up with foster care. In her third placement in less than three years, she has had enough. She wants to go "home," but she has no real destination in mind. She vaguely plans to walk around 42nd Street. As a cold rain begins to fall, everyone seems to be rushing somewhere but her. She is twelve years old.

A young man, neatly dressed, politely approaches her and asks if she is okay. They chat for a while and he invites her to get some food at a diner. Tiffany is impressed by the pretty tables and huge menu, and even more so by the attention from this man. Tiffany has never been taken out to dinner by anyone, much less a good-looking man who seems fascinated by her every word. He compliments her, tells her she is pretty, listens carefully to everything she says, and seems to really like her.

They sit for hours. She tells him all about her life—about her mother and father, and the three different foster homes she has lived in in the past three years; about losing her virginity at age nine to a boy in the foster home who broke her heart. She even shares with him her secret ambition to one day become a lawyer

and have three children. She confides that she actually has nowhere to go, and by the end of the meal, he invites her to live with him. He tells her he would like to be her boyfriend and then they will be a family. To twelve-year-old Tiffany, this seems like a dream come true. She has run away from all her troubles and, just like in the fairy tales, found her prince. Even his name is proof that dreams really can come true: He goes by the name "Charming."

The magic continues for several weeks, and later she recalls them as the best days of her life. Tiffany is living in an apartment with thirty-something Charming. He takes her shopping and buys her clothes and cheap jewelry. The outfits include jeans, a jacket, shirts, sneakers, and a grown-up sexy dress, along with a pair of high heels. During the day she cleans the apartment and cooks him dinner. Afterward they go to bed and have sex. Tiffany wants to please him: He teaches her how to dance and strip, just for him, in her sexy new dress and high heels. Tiffany believes they are in love, and that in a few years he will marry her. In her spare time she practices saying her married name over and over again in front of a mirror, and writing it out, again and again, with hearts and flowers. Everything is perfect.

Reality comes several weeks later when he tells her to dress up for a night out. Beforehand he plies her with drinks and then takes her to a bar. There he orders her to dance and then strip—as he has taught her to do privately for him—in front of a group of men. When she wakes up the next day her memory of the night before is fuzzy; she remembers taking off her clothes, she remembers sex with other men. She is confused and ashamed. On the bed next to her Charming is counting a pile of money. He shows her the money and explains that this is what her body has earned for "them." This is how they can afford rent and food. He tells her how much he loves her, and how happy he is that she is his girlfriend, but this is what she must do so they can live together as a "family."

For other girls the awakening to reality can be harsher. Sometimes a pimp arranges for the girl to be gang-raped by men who appear to be strangers but really are part of a plan to "break her in." Sometimes there is sheer coercion—guns and locked doors forcing a girl to do their bidding. But this is much less common than the sheer power of the seduction: Love is the lure that gets these girls into the trap with the pimp who they see as their lover, boyfriend, husband, or "daddy."

Life on the Track

This is the pattern, more or less, for most girls who "choose" to enter the commercial sex industry, where the average age of entry is thirteen. First there is the domestic violence: Mom, with an endless stream of boyfriends; the shouting, fighting, and bottles breaking late at night. This sets off a round of foster-care "placements" at age four, five, or six, where girls are handed off by strangers—police and social workers—to other strangers—foster-care workers and case managers. These placements are unfriendly, soulless, and often unsafe places that do not feel anything like home. The longing starts early: an unspoken craving for the love and safety of something called family.

Always, somewhere along the line, there is sexual abuse: It might be one of Mom's boyfriends, a male relative, or a "brother" in foster care. That's how it starts. No one cares, no one notices, no one intervenes. At age nine, ten, eleven, or twelve, the girl concludes that her body is not her own; her worth is in its usefulness to the men passing through her life; her value is in what they want her to do. It is all she has to depend on.

As she grows, so does her fury with the mother who is not acting like a mom, passed out, yet again, on the couch; and with the fathers, who are not acting like dads. The fights and arguments are endless; the foster-care placements, miserable and lonely. Now twelve, thirteen, or fourteen, she decides to take matters into her own hands. She packs a bag and walks out the door onto the street, in search of somewhere she can call home.

Within hours, sometimes minutes, he finds her: aimlessly walking the street, in a bus station, without a plan or a friend—too young to get a job, go to a bar, or even to buy a ticket to an R-rated movie. Sometimes he has been watching her, knowing that soon she would be ready for his move; sometimes he has already befriended her—chatting her up on the stoop, flirting, and flattering a girl-child desperate for someone to notice her. Other times he waits where he knows girls like her are likely to go when they have finally had enough. He can spot her a mile away.

This is how life on the track begins. The drug use comes later. When the endless nights of multiple men banging away at her body, punctuated by episodes of viciousness, threats, and humiliation, all become too much to bear—that is when drugs work their magic. The drugs come later to help her face yet another man, another beating, to manage the pain, and to get through the night. Drugs are powerfully addictive, and often that is what happens: twenty-something prostitutes addicted to drugs turning tricks to support their habits.

But that is not how it all began. Long before the girl became hooked on heroin or crack, she is in the throes of an even more powerful desire: an addiction to love. To the hope, the dream, the longing, and the fantasy of a family arising from the deep necessity to belong, to be loved, and to matter.

The "Family"

The next phase for someone like Tiffany is to be introduced to the "family." Pimps always run a stable of girls, sometimes called wives-in-laws or sisters, that earn them money. To make it work, they rely on the girls to collectively maintain the fantasy of a family in this sordid business of the sex trade.

Tiffany lives in a "house" with five other girls she calls her sisters, although none of them are related to her. At fifteen she is the "baby." Her pimp goes by the street name of "Dollars"; he is in his forties and has been living off the earnings of a circulating stable of women for over twenty years. Tiffany calls him "Daddy." The clothes on her back, the food on the table, and roof over her head all come from him. Every night the "family" eats dinner and then goes to "work." Each girl has to bring back a quota for the evening. None of the girls are allowed to handle any money; all of it goes to the pimp who provides all the necessities for his "family."

Violence in these so-called families is the norm, just as it was in the homes most of these girls grew up in. Like the drug use, the violence starts later when the girls start to talk back, complain, refuse to go out on the track, try to keep some of the money they have earned, or realize the trap of this life and set out to leave. The pimps use a divide-and-conquer strategy: One girl is designated the head girl and singled out for special privileges. She might be the "new girl" or mother of his child, or the one who earned the most that week. She is rewarded with small gifts or shows of affection until she makes a mistake or displeases him in some way. Then she is punished and demoted while he chooses another girl to assume the status of his favored "wife." The girls compete with each other for his attention and try to avoid displeasing him.

The worst punishment is reserved for any signs of independence. Pimps will cooperate in bringing back any girl who attempts to leave the life. Tiffany describes what happened to a girl who "talked back" to "Daddy." He stripped her naked, forced her onto the street, and then chased her down with his SUV while all his buddies looked on and laughed. He made sure the girls in his stable were there to watch, listen, and learn.

Exploited Child or Prostitute?

"John" is the term used to refer to the men who purchase sex from women. It is a generic expression that accurately captures the everyday quality of these men. They are husbands, fathers, brothers, and sons from every walk of life, including cops, judges, and prosecutors. One could also use the legally accurate term "statutory rapist" to describe these men. Even though the girls lie about their age, most are children well below the age of consent. Even with heavy makeup and high heels, a twelve-year-old does not look eighteen.

These men are not pedophiles seeking children. They simply don't see the girls they purchase as anything like their own daughters, nieces, or sisters. To them, they are "prostitutes" who choose to sell their bodies. Refusing to see them as human beings is part of the transaction: They are bodies to be used in the service of the male fantasy and desire. That is what men pay money for.

The law is complicit in treating these underage girls, who should be viewed as victims, as grown adults committing the crime of prostitution. Under most state laws, children under the age of seventeen are too young to consent to sex with adults, and therefore legal victims of statutory rape. But when money is exchanged, the legal perspective changes. The girl has now committed the crime of prostitution, and can be arrested and charged as a delinquent.

On the track, the girls are routinely arrested in sting operations by law enforcement. It is far less common for the men who buy and sell them to be arrested

for the crime of trafficking. Sting operations to arrest johns for soliciting sex result in sanctions that are little more than a slap on the wrist: a simple fine, or a morning session at the courthouse to dismiss the case. Law enforcement claims that girls are unwilling to testify in court against their pimps, which makes it difficult to build a case against them. For those who truly understand the commercial sex industry, this is hardly surprising. Girls are being held captive both psychologically and physically by their pimps. The idea that they would turn against their pimps in court when they have few alternatives and no real protection from retaliation is unrealistic.

While there are some law enforcement officers who view these girls as victims, there are many more who treat females of any age in the sex industry as deserving of the violence inflicted upon them. In one jurisdiction, police refer to the nightly work of going out and arresting prostitutes as "doing the trash run." Being viewed as human garbage by the arresting officers makes it hard for girls to trust that police really have their best interests at heart. Girls know from hard experience how the system fails to protect them when they are threatened or assaulted.

Violence from the men who buy their services is routine. The girls refer to it as a "bad date." What this means is that a john raped them, beat them, held a knife to them, or violated them in a sadistic form of torture. It happens all the time, and response from law enforcement is oftentimes indifference. Much of the system considers a vicious sexual assault to be a simple dispute over money—a "theft of services"—even when she is beaten so badly that she must be hospitalized, or when she is left for dead in an abandoned car by the highway after being gang-raped by a dozen men. Some do not see her as being worthy of protection because she "chooses" to sell her body.

Fighting for Change

Rachel Lloyd is a survivor of commercial sexual exploitation. She knows from the inside out the circumstances that drive girls into the life, and what challenges, both internal and external, keep them trapped there. She has learned the lessons from her own lived experience. She has also learned that each of these young girls has enormous potential and possibility.

Lloyd has a history no different from the girls she counsels at GEMS, an organization she created for these girls: an absent father, an alcoholic and suicidal mother, domestic violence, and despair at home. Thinking she could make it on her own while underage, Rachel left home for Germany and there fell into the life of teen prostitution. It's a familiar pattern: a boyfriend turned violent pimp; exploitation from the bars, brothels, and strip joints that profit from the sale of young female bodies; and indifference and thinly veiled disgust from law enforcement, who turn a blind eye to the brutality that traps young women who quite rightly realize that no one will come to their aid.

Rachel managed to break free, but not without the enormous struggle of someone who has suffered PTS from a life of trauma and physical abuse. The process of leaving is much more than a physical challenge; there are deep psychological barriers, as well. Just as it is hard for women to leave their abusive spouses, similar patterns emerge for girls trying to leave their abusive pimps who masquerade emotionally as daddies and lovers. What keeps the cycle of violence going are the apologies, the crying, the repentant kindnesses, more seductive than the capricious anger and violence. These men hold the power of life and death over the girls, who experience the same kind of twisted loyalty that captives give to their jailers.

To leave, the girls must face a world without the only source of love they believe is possible for them. They have been called bitches, whores, and sluts all their lives, and they have internalized this attitude against themselves. They feel the disapproval in their own families, communities, and the rest of society. The heavy weight of stigma drives them back to the underground nest where at least they have each other. They have come to believe that they are not worthy of any other kind of love—that this is all they are ever going to get—so when they are asked to walk away, the choice is excruciating. Pimps understand this; they know how to play on the girls' desires to belong and to be loved. They will always play the love card to try to lure the girls back. In the end, it is the addiction to "love" that is the hardest obstacle to overcome.

From Victim to Survivor to Leader

The good news is that love itself is not the problem but the solution. In 1998 Rachel Lloyd founded an organization called GEMS (Girls Educational and Mentoring Services) that provided the first program in the nation to offer services and safe housing for victims of commercial sexual exploitation. At first, it operated out of her own apartment, with girls sleeping on couches and wearing clothes from her own closet. Eventually, it grew to have its own space, with housing, communal kitchens, and offices. Girls are not locked up at GEMS; they are free to come and go. Many do return to their pimps, time and time again, as they struggle to trust the idea that a different life is possible for them.

Gradually, girls at GEMS begin to see themselves through another set of eyes. They begin to unlearn what they thought love was by witnessing what it means to be in healthy relationships. These girls have learned to associate love with all the wrong kinds of behaviors. The experience in their own families has set them up for life on the track. What they unlearn is the idea that violence is a form of love, and the idea that they are not worthy of being genuinely cared for.

At GEMS, girls are given the chance to stand up for themselves and to recast what has happened to them in a new light. GEMS urges girls to use the term "commercially exploited victim" rather than "prostitute" or "whore." As Lloyd says, "Prostitute is who you are—commercial exploitation is about what someone did to you." Through GEMS these young women become vocal proponents for changing the attitudes and laws that support the industry of selling young girls.

In 2010, the young women at GEMS were instrumental in helping to pass the first legislation in the nation to provide safe harbor for victims of commercial sex trafficking. Known as the Safe Harbor Act, the law shields sexually exploited youth from incarceration and juvenile delinquency proceedings. Just as women who are battered have not "engaged" in domestic violence, this bill attempts to establish that children in the sex trade are not engaged in prostitution: They are victims of sexual exploitation by adult men who buy and sell them. Under this law, children under the age of sixteen would be adjudicated in family court—regarded as crime victims rather than criminal perpetrators—and assigned as "persons in need of supervision" to safe houses from which they could access social services, including psychological counseling and medical care.

It's a first step in a good direction. For girls like Darlene, who testified before the New York State legislature and now holds a job, has her own apartment, and is looking forward to the rest of her life, several years at GEMS opened up a new path. But she remembers the time when she could not imagine this future for herself; she remembers how many times she went back to her "daddy," convinced that she literally belonged to him, body and soul. Darlene worries about the provision in the new law that states that if a girl leaves the Safe Harbor program even once, she is no longer eligible to avoid prosecution. Addictions are powerful; they take time to overcome. Relapses are inevitable. Like Rachel Lloyd, Darlene will also devote the rest of her life to helping other girls understand that they are not for sale, and that they are worthy of real love.

THINKING CRITICALLY ABOUT THIS CASE

1. In this case study, what do the girls learn about the social expectations and norms of femininity in our culture? Would you consider these norms an extreme version of the dominant norms for women in our society? Why or why not?

2. What do you believe would help young girls choose to leave the life of prostitution? What do they need? From whom?

3. How do institutions, including families, schools, and social services, play a role in sex trafficking? How do they also play a role in preventing it?

4. How are females who engage in sex acts treated differently by the justice system from males who engage in and/or run sex work?

5. A federal law addressing exploitation of children for sex work was not passed until 2010. How does this reflect societal values?

REFERENCES

This case is based on the following sources:

Federal Bureau of Investigation. (nd). Human Trafficking. Available at www.fbi.gov/about-us/investigate/civilrights/human_trafficking.

GEMS. Available at www.gems-girls.org/about/our-team/our-founder.

Lloyd, R. (2011). *Girls Like Us*. New York: HarperCollins.

———. (2012). Human Trafficking. TEDxUChicago. Available at http://tedxtalks.ted.com/video/TEDxUChicago-2012-Rachel-Lloyd.

INTRODUCTION

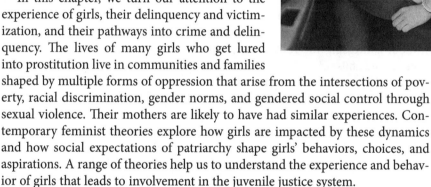

THE SOCIAL WORLD IS A HIGHLY GENDERED place. As we have seen in this case study, and the previous one (Case Study 4), gender shapes the socialization of boys and girls in the family, school, neighborhood, and in the juvenile justice system. Boys and girls have had different childhood experiences growing up in the same households. Their peer groups behave differently from one another. They face different challenges and expectations from teachers in school. As a result, boys and girls internalize different beliefs about themselves and about each other. It is not possible to isolate gender from an understanding of how our society, or the juvenile justice system, functions.

In this chapter, we turn our attention to the experience of girls, their delinquency and victimization, and their pathways into crime and delinquency. The lives of many girls who get lured into prostitution live in communities and families shaped by multiple forms of oppression that arise from the intersections of poverty, racial discrimination, gender norms, and gendered social control through sexual violence. Their mothers are likely to have had similar experiences. Contemporary feminist theories explore how girls are impacted by these dynamics and how social expectations of patriarchy shape girls' behaviors, choices, and aspirations. A range of theories help us to understand the experience and behavior of girls that leads to involvement in the juvenile justice system.

FEMALE PATTERNS OF OFFENDING AND VICTIMIZATION

Female Offending

Boys and girls travel different pathways to involvement in the juvenile justice system. As we saw in chapter 4, males are more likely to be in the juvenile justice system than girls, but most youth, regardless of gender, are in the system for minor offenses, such as simple assault and vandalism. Official statistics show that females typically constitute approximately 25 to 30 percent of all juvenile arrests.[1] Yet arrests of girls have increased significantly over the last fifteen years. For example, arrests for simple assault for girls increased 19 percent between 1997 and 2006, compared with a decrease of 4 percent for boys during that same time period.[2] Females, however, are much less likely to be involved in violent crime than are males.

The rise in arrests of girls over the last several years does not have a clear-cut explanation. While it may reflect actual changes in the behavior of girls, feminist scholars argue that these changes reflect different attitudes, policies, and practices toward girls than what was in place two decades ago.[3] Police are more likely to arrest girls today than they were in the past; and incidents that used to be informally handled, such as disputes between children and their family members, are more likely to result in arrest today. In contrast to boys, girls are more likely to be involved in disputes involving family or household members than they are in disputes with acquaintances or strangers. The increase in simple assault arrests for girls reflects the changing attitudes toward arrests between household members.

When it comes to violent offenses and serious property crimes, boys are over-represented in arrests for all categories, including homicide, rape, aggravated assault, and arson, at five times the rate of girls.[4] For both males and females, arrests for status offenses and minor delinquent offenses far outnumber arrests for more-serious and violent crimes. For both genders, larceny-theft, which includes shoplifting, is the most common criminal offense. Even here, males shoplift with more frequency than females. In fact, for every single offense category, males outnumber females with one exception: prostitution. As we saw in the case study, Tiffany, Rachel, and many others are commercially exploited because they have run away from victimization in the home, where they fall prey to older men as a means to survive. Incorrigibility is another response to victimization, but the juvenile justice system punishes girls for such actions, often without addressing the root causes, which further victimizes those who have experienced abuses.[5]

Official statistics are important, but they tell us only part of the story. When youth self-report on their own behavior, the discrepancy between male and female offending is not as great as what appears in the official statistics. Boys are more likely to report involvement in gangs, fighting, carrying weapons, and sexual assaults, and, with the exception of sexual assaults, the girls also report much more involvement in these crimes than what appears officially.[6]

Several important insights can be drawn from these data. First, males and females have a different relationship with serious delinquent activity. Violence is a male-dominated behavior, even if girls engage in violence more frequently than we might think. The gap between male and female arrests has narrowed significantly in recent decades, leading some to argue that girls are becoming more like males in terms of aggression.[7] Others disagree with this interpretation. We will consider the theoretical implications of that, and of girls' involvement in crime and delinquency, later in this chapter.

Female Victimization

As we saw from the last chapter, males are more likely to be victims of both violent and property crimes than females. The one area of victimization that females outnumber males is in the area of sexual assault. According to a recent UN World Report, the first sexual experience of 30 percent of women worldwide was a forced sexual assault.[8] This was especially true for girls under the age of fifteen. In the United States, girls experience rates of sexual abuse that are approximately four times higher than that of boys.[9] One in four girls in the United States will experience some form of sexual violence by the age of eighteen.

This chapter's case study shows that the hurt often begins at home. Childhood sexual abuse is usually committed by a trusted adult within the household, such as a father, stepfather, cousin, or mother's boyfriend. The mother, who is likely to have her own history of sexual abuse, does not protect her daughter. That failure of the mother to put her child's welfare before her loyalty to a man, or her addiction to alcohol or drugs, constitutes a deep sense of rejection and abandonment. Girls leave home to stop the hurt, and in search of family. They are vulnerable to manipulation by adult men who pose as fathers and boyfriends. Sexual abuse is an adverse childhood experience (ACE) that can have long-term consequences. Early sexual abuse is associated with chronic pain; mental health disorders, including depression and post-traumatic stress; truancy; school failure; and high-risk behaviors, such as early and unprotected sex and drug and alcohol use.[10]

Sexual abuse is but one form of violence against women, and it intersects with race and class in multiple ways. Jody Miller, for example, studied the experiences of African-American girls in an inner-city neighborhood in St. Louis. She found that girls must navigate a world full of constant sexual harassment and threats of sexual violence.[11] On the street, they are vulnerable to predatory behavior by adult men, and from boys their own age who constantly tease and harass them sexually. Girls discover that there are few protections for them from police or other authorities, so they rely on male friends and relatives to protect them on the street. Yet they are often victimized in the homes of the very friends and family on whom they rely.

Victimization itself is a precursor to delinquency.[12] Studies show that girls in the juvenile justice system have higher levels of child maltreatment and mental health issues than boys in the system. In one of the first comprehensive studies of ACEs, 45 percent of girls reported five or more ACEs compared to 24 percent of males.[13] Rates of PTS and other mental health disorders are also consistently higher in girls than among boys. National figures estimate that nearly 80 percent of females in the juvenile justice system meet the criteria for at least one mental health disorder compared to 67 percent of boys.[14] Offending cannot be disentangled from the lived experiences of youth.

We now take a closer look at what it means to view delinquency in relationship to the gendered nature of society.

FEMINISM AND INTERSECTIONALITY

There is no singular definition of feminism or a feminist perspective, but Kathleen Daly and Meda Chesney-Lind argue that there are five factors that distinguish feminist thought from other types of social and political thought.[15] First, gender is a social construction where biological differences are taken into account. Second, social life and social institutions are organized by gender. Third, men's dominance over women structures gender relationships. Fourth, our knowledge of the world reflects men's views. Finally, "Women should be at the center of intellectual inquiry."

Throughout the first section of this book, we have discussed the multiple ways in which girls have been viewed differently from boys, and how that translated into social institutions. It is for this reason that there is a separate chapter in this text to address girls. Here, we examine how socialization and knowledge is shaped by our society, rooted in patriarchy, and how feminist perspectives of delinquency differ from those in chapter 4.

As we see in the experiences of females in this case study, their lives were dominated by male figures and men's views of what it means to be female. We discussed the concept of patriarchy in chapter 2, where men are the heads of households, with all others subordinate to them. R. W. Connell extended this argument to say that in Western societies, the dominant ideal, which he termed **hegemonic masculinity**, is most closely associated with white middle-class males.[16] Hegemonic masculinity is a cultural ideal of manhood that helps males to maintain a position of dominance over women and children, as well as subordinate classes. The case study in chapter 4 illustrated how hegemonic masculinity is also shaped by race and class. A middle-class male may assert masculinity through intellectual achievement, sports, financial power, and professional expertise. In contrast, the avenues open for asserting masculinity for those in the lower class are through strength, daring, physical toughness, and displays of violence. For Geoffrey Canada, much of the code of the streets centered on the need to prove one's masculinity to a set of peers. Masculinity is a status that has to be created. Crime, especially violence, is one means for its creation that becomes especially relevant within highly distressed neighborhoods within society.

Rather than expressing anger and hostility toward males who dominate them and betray their loyalty, girls engage in conflict with each other. The concept of **horizontal violence** refers to the use of violence against those of equal status in a hierarchy. It is much more dangerous and difficult to act aggressively toward those in a higher social position than toward those who are equal in status. This concept helps to illuminate gang violence, for example, in which lower-class males of equal status fight with one another rather than attempting to use violence toward those in higher social positions. This concept has also been used to explain the pattern of girls' violence toward other girls and the competition for the attention of males.[17]

Gender Socialization

The concept of **differential socialization** refers to the gendered pattern of treatment of children by their parents, teachers, and other adults from infancy throughout adolescence.[18] Research shows parents continue to encourage male children to be more independent, inquisitive, competitive, and assertive, while female children are encouraged to stay close, behave nicely, and be dependent on adults.[19] As young children, parents promote and reward risk-taking among boys while girls are protected and taught to be careful.

Some believe this pattern of differential socialization helps to explain some of the observed differences in patterns of delinquency.[20] Girls tend to be more supervised and controlled by adults than boys, limiting their opportunities to engage in delinquency.[21] Girls also are socialized to avoid risks and follow the rules, thereby internalizing the directive for conformity. Consistent with differential socialization, research finds that delinquent behavior among girls is associated with lower levels of self-esteem, while for boys it is associated with higher levels of self-esteem.[22]

Children then create their own gendered peer cultures. For girls, the value of "being pretty" and the goal of being well liked by others starts at an early age. Popularity is an outgrowth of that culture. Popularity among girls is linked to attractiveness and socioeconomic status, while for boys, it is linked to athletic prowess and toughness.[23] This is problematic for both girls and boys. Research

HEGEMONIC MASCULINITY
Practices that promote the domination of men over women.

HORIZONTAL VIOLENCE
Violence directed toward one's peers.

DIFFERENTIAL SOCIALIZATION
Pattern of treatment that is different for girls and boys.

finds that girls, particularly white girls, may internalize negativity resulting in low self-esteem, poor body image, and depression.[24] For boys, internalizing cultural ideals of masculinity, reinforced through peer-group associations, translates into school behavioral problems and low educational achievement, with bleak employment options as a long-term outcome of the process.[25]

These gender socializations continue into adulthood and perpetuate what is called the **double standard**, where men and women are judged by different standards of behavior that also varies by race, ethnicity, and class. This is especially true for sexual behavior. Men are rewarded and women are punished for sexual encounters.[26] In adolescence, sexual activity negatively stigmatizes girls, while sexual activity increases the popularity of boys.[27] Yet, the double standard is enforced by both girls and boys. In Miller's research, discussed earlier, African-American girls are often in a no-win situation when it comes to resisting pressure from males to engage in sex. If they succumb they are often labeled as "whores" or "nasty" by other girls. If they resist, boys get angry and call them "stuck-up" or "bitches."[28]

Justice System Bias

The double standard has been used to explain the different treatment of boys and girls in the juvenile justice system. Scholars argue that girls' reactions to the high levels of trauma and abuse within their homes and neighborhoods are criminalized by the response of the juvenile justice and child protection systems, leading to a vicious cycle of abuse and imprisonment.[29] As discussed, females are disproportionately more likely to have victimization experiences at home that at least in part account for running away, yet these actions are defined and punished as delinquent behaviors.[30] These gendered pathways to crime are not considered relevant in the justice system.

Girls who run away also commit other offenses, such as petty theft, drug abuse, and prostitution, as survival strategies. Young girls find selling their bodies to be the one means available to them in a male-dominated world where the demand for young female bodies is high. Rachel Lloyd reminds us that it is important to use the term "victims of commercial exploitation" rather than "prostitutes," so that the link to gendered violence and oppression is not lost. The **Safe Harbor laws**, advocated by Lloyd, are a step toward recognizing the victimization of girls and the need for high-quality, **gender-specific programming** by the juvenile justice system. These laws, however, retain the legal authority to charge and detain girls as delinquents if they fail to comply with services.

To address the concerns of violence against females, the 1994 federal Violence Against Women Act (VAWA) encouraged states to implement mandatory arrest laws for domestic violence incidents. This meant that police were required to make an arrest when called to residences for domestic incidents. The unintended result of mandatory arrest policies was that girls who were involved in verbal or physical altercations with abusive parents or their mothers' boyfriends were more likely to be arrested than the adults involved when police were called to the house.[31] Arrest as a result of a domestic violence incident is another pathway into the juvenile justice system for girls. In general, police are more likely to believe the adult's version of the story, and police are reluctant to arrest a parent if there are other children who need to be cared for in the home.

DOUBLE STANDARD
Unequal application of a rule or principle to different peoples/groups.

SAFE HARBOR LAWS
Laws that protect and assist children that have been exploited for labor or sex.

GENDER-SPECIFIC PROGRAMMING
Interventions which are tailored to meet the specific developmental needs of girls.

As discussed, the recent uptick in girls' official delinquency, especially with regard to assault, has led some to argue that girls are becoming more like boys in their participation in violence, but self-report evidence shows that there are no significant differences in girls' behavior.[32] There has been some increase among reports of fighting by black girls and reports of injuring someone by black, white, and Hispanic girls, yet their involvement in violence remains low. Girls are still likely to act out against family members and people they know in contrast to the street aggression that characterizes boys' violence.

Changes in system practices have tracked more girls into the juvenile justice system, particularly for assault, causing a rise in the official statistics. Beyond domestic assaults, school altercations are now more likely than ever to be processed through the system rather than handled informally, and status offenses that once were labeled as "incorrigibility" have been relabeled as delinquent offenses.[33] The labels have changed, but the pattern of behavior is the same.

In later chapters, we will examine the features of the child welfare and juvenile justice systems that perpetuate a legacy of discrimination against girls that goes back to the start of the juvenile justice system in the nineteenth century. It fits in with a paternalistic view of the juvenile justice system in which females must be regulated more closely because they are more vulnerable to problems. As a result more girls are tracked into the system due to status offending, and status offending is a key factor in later delinquency involvement.[34] We also will look at the implementation of gender-responsive programming within the juvenile and child welfare systems that is designed to address the experiences and specific developmental needs of girls.

FEMALE PATHWAYS TO DELINQUENCY

Feminist scholars have long claimed an **androcentric bias** in the field of criminology. This means that most theories to explain crime and delinquency were written by men, about the behavior of males, and presented as the universal norm for the human experience. As we have seen, females' experiences are much different. The rise of feminist scholarship has contributed to significant developments in the understanding of female delinquency by increasing the number of women in academia who have conducted sustained, systematic research on the experience of girls and women. Researchers have studied the experiences of girls growing up in families, in schools, in neighborhoods, with peers, with boys, and in the juvenile justice system. Scholars have also focused attention on the dynamic of gender inequality within a male-dominated society using qualitative methods as a cornerstone to a deep understanding of a phenomenon.

Traditional Delinquency Theories

Early theories of crime and delinquency either ignored the question of female criminality or explained the low participation of females by reference to biological or psychological attributes believed to be intrinsic to females.[35] Feminists argue that the dominant delinquency theories of today (reviewed in chapter 4) are inadequate for understanding why and how girls get involved in delinquent behavior.[36] General strain theory, for example, states that class inequality denies poor youth the means to achieve the dominant cultural goals of success, status,

ANDROCENTRIC BIAS
Male-centered view of society.

and achievement. Crime is the result of the mismatch—or, in Merton's terms, "lack of fit"—between the strong cultural goal of success and the structural means to achieve that.[37] Those means are available to some within society and not others. Given that opportunities are blocked more for girls than for boys, we should see many more girls involved in crime than boys, which is clearly not the case.

There is a strong focus on masculinity and meeting the needs of achievement and competence in many traditional theories; yet, these do not explain the role of girls.[38] The experience of girls as part of delinquent peer groups, including gangs, is invisible. Even conflict theories focused on the issue of class inequality ignore both race and gender as equally powerful realities shaping lives of youth. Labeling theory is an exception.[39]

Labeling theorists in the 1970s focused on societal reaction to behavior deemed "wrong" by moral crusaders who had the power to create and enforce moral codes within society. Prostitution was studied through the application of the concepts of primary and secondary deviance. An initial experience with selling sex in exchange for money, food, or shelter—what some call **survival sex**—can develop into a deviant identity and career in which a girl adopts the label, internalizes the identity of whore or prostitute, and enters into this occupation as a lifestyle. The reaction of others, including men and those in power, then had powerful effects on how girls viewed themselves and, in turn, influenced their behavior. Since that time, however, feminist theories have rapidly developed.

Theories

Feminist theorists agree that women are oppressed and that this leads to victimization, delinquency, and crime. They disagree on the extent of oppression and on how it can be eradicated. We briefly review liberal feminism, postmodern feminism and feminist pathway theory, Marxism and socialist feminism, radical feminism, and multiracial feminism.

One of the first feminist theories was liberal *feminism*. The hypothesis was that as females became "liberated" from the traditional roles of daughter, wife, and mother to join men in the workplace as equals, females would behave more like males and therefore would begin to participate equally in crime and delinquency.[40] As we have discussed, this has not been the case. Even with the slight rise in girls' delinquency, compared to boys, there is no convergence in criminal patterns of behavior.

Like labeling theorists, *postmodern feminism* emphasizes the role of social constructions in how we view "delinquency," "justice," and "feminism."[41] **Feminist pathway theory** identifies the forces of abuse and economic exploitation that lead girls to engage in delinquent acts such as substance abuse or running away. The juvenile justice system interprets and reacts to these behaviors in a patriarchal way that labels girls as deviant, defiant, and/or promiscuous. Going further, feminist pathway theorists argue that we need to challenge those labels and the power of those who create them. Rachel Lloyd is well aware of these power dynamics as she tirelessly advocates the use of the term *commercial sexual exploitation* to help change the mind-set of the public and the females who have been victims of it.

Marxist and socialist feminism takes the view that class inequality is the dominant form of oppression, giving rise to other forms of oppression, such as

SURVIVAL SEX
Selling sex in exchange for money, food, or shelter.

FEMINIST PATHWAY THEORY
Exploitation of females leads to delinquency that is reacted to paternalistically by the juvenile justice system.

sexism. Women engage in commercial sex trafficking as a result of both economic exploitation and gender inequality. Patriarchy and capitalism reduce the options of poor women, who are forced to turn to the commercial sex trade to survive.

In contrast to Marxist and socialist feminism, the basis of *radical feminism* is sexism. Gender, as opposed to other forms of oppression, is the key point through which social structure is organized.[42] The victimization of girls and women, particularly through violent crimes such as sexual assault and rape, are methods used to continue patriarchal domination.

Multiracial feminism, in contrast, examines delinquency through an intersectionality approach informed by multiple forms of inequality.[43] Multiracial feminists argue that sensitivity to multiple forms of oppression and the complex ways in which they interact is central to understanding girls' delinquency. It is this intersectionality perspective that most informs this textbook. Feminist criminologists using the lens of intersectionality and multiple marginalities remind us that there is no unitary female experience. Experiences of girls are also shaped by other key statuses of class, race, ethnicity, sexual orientation, religion, region, and age. Further research is needed to explore how these different identities interact and intersect with one another in specific contexts to develop comprehensive theories of female delinquency.

RISK AND PROTECTIVE FACTOR FRAMEWORK

We end this chapter with a way to organize our knowledge of factors that increase the chances of delinquency (risk factors) and factors that buffer against delinquency (protective factors), paying close attention to intersectionality. This risk and protective framework can be used in a positive youth development approach to help shape our thinking about the juvenile system and appropriate actions the juvenile justice system can take to ensure that all children are well. Much needs to be done to understand how these factors interact with gender, race, ethnicity, and class, but there is a healthy dose of research insight into what helps youth to thrive and what harms them.

Factors that can influence youth to engage in high-risk behavior and delinquency are called **risk factors**. There are also certain elements that can buffer against high-risk behavior and delinquency, such as a good school system. These are called **protective factors**. A separate set of factors that enhance well-being are called **promotive factors**, such as positive social connections. Combined, these factors provide an avenue toward understanding delinquency, and have been used as a basis for theoretical development of an integrated life course model of delinquency prevention called the *social development model*.[44] These factors are often organized along the major dimensions, or domains, of youths' lives: individual factors, family factors, peer factors, school factors, and community factors.

Most research in the area of youth violence and antisocial behavior has primarily examined risk factors. Protective factors are not well understood, and we know even less about promotive factors. Risk and protective factors differ depending on adolescent development of the life course. For very young children (age four and under), school is not a risk or protective factor until they enter

RISK FACTOR
Something that increases the chances of a negative well-being outcome.

PROTECTIVE FACTOR
Something that buffers against the chances of a negative well-being outcome.

PROMOTIVE FACTOR
Something that increases the chances of positive well-being.

kindergarten or first grade. Alternatively, peers become increasingly important as a risk or protective factor as youth enter the preteen and teenage years, when youth are out of the home more often.

These factors interact such that they may be compounded in positive and negative ways. For example, poor performance in school may lead to a youth being placed in a classroom for low-performing students, some of whom may be involved in antisocial and delinquent behaviors. The youth then may adopt those behaviors as a consequence of these new peer relations. The US Surgeon General's Office compiled research in the risk and protective factor arena.[45] Youth who have more risk factors and fewer protective factors across more developmental domains are more likely to be delinquent, and this is true across gender lines.[46] Peer group is a key factor that cuts across intersectionality: Those who associate with deviant peers are more likely to be delinquent, while youth who associate with prosocial peers are less likely to be delinquent and more likely to succeed.[47]

Risk and protective factor studies point to the fact that intersectionality, including gender, ethnicity, and class, must be examined over adolescent time periods, as risk and protective factors change.[48] The Girls Study Group, a national panel of experts convened by the federal government, compiled delinquency risk and protective factors related to girls.[49] Family conflict and attachment to mothers may have more of an effect on girls than on boys, underscoring the importance of family for all youth, but particularly for girls.[50]

Early motherhood is a major risk factor for poor life outcomes.[51] Just as some boys join gangs in order to meet their needs for achievement, respect, identity, and companionship, girls—especially those in lower-income areas—may turn to early motherhood to fulfill their unmet needs. Motherhood satisfies strong developmental needs for identity, achievement, love, and security in a context in which there are few options available to girls.[52] Early motherhood is linked to poverty, school dropout, under- and unemployment, and criminal justice system involvement.[53] Pregnancy and early motherhood is compounded by girls' social location and their lived experiences, as feminist theories tell us.

This chapter has explored the very real gender differences for girls in society. Yet, within our examination of the gendered pathways for delinquency, we see that most youth do not become delinquent, even though intersections among gender, race, ethnicity, and class, in particular, limit opportunities for some. **Resiliency** is one key. Resiliency is based on the notion that people, institutions, and communities have the ability to overcome adversity. The reality is that most girls and most youth living in highly distressed communities do not become delinquent, which has yet to be adequately explained. In a later chapter, we will see that focusing on protective factors leads to more-positive outcomes than focusing on risks or deficits.

There is a strong connection between resiliency and positive youth development (PYD), although precise connections between them, and which comes first (resiliency or positive youth development) is contested.[54] Resiliency is part of PYD, and the notion that adversity typically does not equate with negative outcomes is a crucial concept. Understanding more of what makes individuals (and institutions and communities) resilient is important to furthering the protective factors that promote healthy development in young people. We return to these ideas in our discussion of "what works" in chapter 11.

RESILIENCY
The ability to recover from / withstand adversity.

KEY TERMS

androcentric bias Male-centered view of society.

differential socialization Pattern of treatment that is different for girls and boys.

double standard Unequal application of a rule or principle to different peoples/groups.

feminist pathway theory Exploitation of females leads to delinquency that is reacted to paternalistically by the juvenile justice system.

gender-specific programming Interventions which are tailored to meet the specific developmental needs of girls.

hegemonic masculinity Practices that promote the domination of men over women.

horizontal violence Violence directed toward one's peers.

promotive factor Something that increases the chances of positive well-being.

protective factor Something that buffers against the chances of a negative well-being outcome.

resiliency The ability to recover from / withstand adversity.

risk factor Something that increases the chances of a negative well-being outcome.

Safe Harbor laws Laws that protect and assist children that have been exploited for labor or sex.

survival sex Selling sex in exchange for money, food, or shelter.

REVIEW AND STUDY QUESTIONS

1. How are girls similar and different from boys in terms of their offending and victimization? Describe some typical pathways to delinquency for young women.

2. Explain the meaning of *androcentric bias* and give examples of this phenomenon in the study of delinquency.

3. Why do most traditional delinquency theories inadequately explain girls' delinquency?

4. Explain the meaning of the term *double standard* and show how the double standard affects male and female involvement in the juvenile justice system.

5. Explain the concept of *differential socialization* and provide several examples from your own life that illustrate this phenomenon.

6. What does it mean to examine delinquency from a feminist perspective?

7. What are some of the key feminist arguments for female involvement in delinquency and crime?

8. How do the insights of labeling theory help to explain the importance of calling young girls "victims of commercial exploitation" instead of "prostitutes"? What changes when we use a different label for this activity?

9. What are risk, protective, and promotive factors?

10. What is the meaning of *resilience*, and what do you believe helps to promote resilience in the lives of girls?

CHECK IT OUT

Watch

Very Young Girls (2007). Showtime.

NOTES

[1] National Center for Juvenile Justice. (2014). *Juvenile Arrest Rates by Offense, Sex, and Race.* Available at http://www.ojjdp.gov/ojstatbb/crime/excel/JAR_2011.xls.

[2] Zhan, M., Agnew, R., Fishbein, D., . . . , and Chesney-Lind, M. (2010). *Causes & Correlates of Girls' Delinquency.* Washington, DC: Office of Juvenile Justice and Delinquency Prevention, Girls Study Group.

[3] Schwartz, J., and Steffensmeier, D. (2014). Can the Gender Gap in Crime Be Explained? In F. Cullen, P. Wilcox, J. L. Lux, and C. L. Jonson (eds.), *Sisters in Crime Revisited: Bringing Gender into Criminology*, 229–59. New York: Oxford.

[4] National Center for Juvenile Justice. (2014). *Juvenile Arrest Rates by Offense, Sex, and Race.* Available at www.ojjdp.gov/ojstatbb/crime/excel/JAR_2011.xls.

[5] Ibid.

[6] Goodkind, S., Wallace, J. M., Shook, J. J., Bachman, J., and O'Malley, P. (2010). Are Girls *Really* Becoming More Delinquent? *Child and Youth Services Review, 31,* 885–95.

[7] Prothrow-Stith, G. (2006). *Sugar and Spice and No Longer Nice: How We Can Stop Girls' Violence.* New York: Wiley.

[8] World Health Organization. (2013). *Global and Regional Estimates of Violence Against Women.* Available at www.unwomen.org/en/what-we-do/ending-violence-against-women/facts-and-figures#sthash.oGOT3Vj1.dpuf.

[9] Children's Bureau. (2016). *Child Maltreatment 2014.* Available at www.acf.hhs.gov/sites/default/files/cb/cm2014.pdf.

[10] Springer, K. W., Sheridan, J., Kuo, D., and Carnes, M. (2003). The Long-Term Health Outcomes of Childhood Abuse. *Journal of General Internal Medicine, 18,* 864–70; Boden, J. M., Horwood, L. J., and Fergusson, D. M. (2007). Exposure to Childhood Sexual and Physical Abuse and Subsequent Educational Achievement Outcomes. *Child Abuse & Neglect, 31,* 1101–14.

[11] Miller, J. (2008). *Getting Played.* New York: New York University Press.

[12] DeHart, D. D., and Moran, R. (2015). Poly-victimization among Girls in the Justice System: Trajectories of Risk and Associations to Juvenile Offending. *Violence Against Women, 31,* 291–312.

[13] Baglivio, M. T., Swartz, K., Huq, M. S., Sheer, A., and Hardt, N. S. (2014). The Prevalence of Adverse Childhood Experiences (ACEs) in the Lives of Juvenile Offenders. *Journal of Juvenile Justice, 3,* 1–23.

[14] Ford, J. D., Chapman, J. F., Hawke, J., and Albert, D. (2007). *Trauma among Youth in the Juvenile Justice System.* Delmar, NY: National Center for Mental Health and Juvenile Justice.

[15] Daly, K., and Chesney-Lind, M. (1988). Feminism and Criminology. *Justice Quarterly, 5,* 497–538.

[16] Connell, R. W. (2013). *The Men and the Boys.* New York: Wiley.

[17] Chesney-Lind, M., and Shelden, R. G. (2014) *Girls, Delinquency, and Juvenile Justice.* New York: Wiley.

[18] Ruble, D. N., Martin, C. L., and Berenbaum, S. (2006). Gender Development. In N. Eisenberg, (ed.), *Handbook of Child Psychology, vol. 3,* 858–932. New York: Wiley.

[19] Zimmerman, T. S. (2013). *Integrating Gender and Culture in Parenting.* New York: Routledge.

[20] Block, J. H. (1983). Differential Premises Arising from Differential Socialization of the Sexes: Some Conjectures. *Child Development, 54,* 1335–54.

[21] Zahn, M., Agnew, R., Fishbein, D., . . . Chesney-Lind, M. (2010). *Causes and Correlates of Girls' Delinquency.* Washington, DC: Office of Juvenile Justice and Delinquency Prevention.

[22] Morash, M. (1986). Gender, Peer Group Experiences, and Seriousness of Delinquency. *Journal of Research in Crime and Delinquency, 23,* 43–67.

[23] Adler, P. A., Kless, S. J., and Adler, P. (200). Socialization to Gender Roles: Popularity among Elementary School Boys and Girls. *Sociology of Education, 65,* 169–87.

[24] Zurbriggen, E. L., Collins, R. L., Lamb, S., . . . Blake, J. (2010). *Report of the APA Task Force on the Sexualization of Girls.* Available at www.apa.org/pi/women/programs/girls/report-full.pdf.

[25] Whitehead, J. (2003). Masculinity, Motivation, and Academic Success: A Paradox. *Teacher Development, 7,* 287–309.

[26] Crawford, M., and Popp, D. (2003). Sexual Double Standards: A Review and Methodological Critique of Two Decades of Research. *The Journal of Sex Research, 40,* 13–26.

[27] Kreager, D. A., and Staff, J. (2009). The Sexual Double Standard and Adolescent Peer Acceptance. *Social Psychology Quarterly, 72,* 143–64.

[28] Miller, *Getting Played.*

[29] Chesney-Lind, M. (1989). Girls' Crime and Woman's Place: Toward a Feminist Model of Female Delinquency. *Crime & Delinquency, 35,* 5–29.

[30] Cauffman, E. (2008). Understanding the Female Offender. *The Future of Children, 18,* 119–42.

[31] Gebo, E. (2007). A Family Affair: The Juvenile Court and Family Violence Cases. *Journal of Family Violence, 22,* 501–9.

[32] Goodkind et al., Are Girls *Really* Becoming More Delinquent?, 885–95.

[33] Zahn, M. A., Hawkins, S. R., Chiancone, J., and Whitworth, A. (2008). *Violence by Teenage Girls: Trends and Context.* Washington, DC: Office of Juvenile Justice and Delinquency Prevention.

[34] Chesney-Lind, M., and Pasko, L. (2013). *The Female Offender.* Thousand Oaks, CA: Sage.

[35] Lombroso, C., and Ferrero, W. (1898). *The Female Offender.* New York: D. Appleton and Co.

[36] Chesney-Lind, M. (1989). Girls' Crime and Woman's Place: Toward a Feminist Model of Female Delinquency. *Crime & Delinquency, 35,* 5–29.

[37] Merton, R. K. (1938). Social Structure and Anomie. *American Sociological Review, 3,* 672–82.

[38] Miller, J. (2001). *One of the Guys: Girls, Gangs, and Gender.* New York: Oxford.

[39] Schur, E. M. (1984). *Labeling Women Deviant: Gender, Stigma, and Social Control.* Philadelphia, PA: Temple University Press.

[40] Adler, F. (1975). *Sisters in Crime.* New York: McGraw-Hill.

[41] Wonders, N. A. (1999). Postmodern Feminist Criminology and Social Justice. In B. A. Arrigo, (ed.)., *Social Justice, Criminal Justice: The Maturation of Critical Theory in Law, Crime, and Deviance,* 109–28. Belmont, CA: Wadsworth.

[42] Walby, S. (1990). *Theorizing Patriarchy.* Cambridge, UK: Basil Blackwell.

[43] Burgess-Proctor, A. (2006). Intersections of Race, Class, Gender, and Crime: Future Directions for Feminist Criminology. *Feminist Criminology, 1,* 27–47.

[44] Hawkins, J. D., and Weis, J. G. (1985). The Social Development Model: An Integrated Approach to Delinquency Prevention. *Journal of Primary Prevention, 6,* 73–97.

[45] Office of the Surgeon General. (2001). *Youth Violence: A Report of the Surgeon General*. Rockville, MD: Author.

[46] Herrenkohl, T. I., Maguin, E., Hill, K. G., . . . Catalano, R. (2000). Developmental Risk Factors for Youth Violence. *Journal of Adolescent Health, 26*, 176–86.

[47] Lösel, F., and Farrington, D. P. (2012). Direct Protective and Buffering Protective Factors in the Development of Youth Violence. *American Journal of Preventive Medicine, 43*, S8–S23.

[48] Fagan, A. A., Van Horn, M. L., Antaramian, A., and Hawkins, J. D. (2011). How Do Families Matter? Age and Gender Differences in Family Influences on Delinquency and Drug Use. *Youth Violence and Juvenile Justice, 9*, 150–70.

[49] Zahn, *Causes and Correlates of Girls' Delinquency.*

[50] Ge, X., Conger, R. D., Lorenz, F. O., and Simons, R. L. (1994). Parents' Stressful Life Events and Adolescent Depressed Mood. *Journal of Health and Social Behavior 35*, 28–44; Fagan, A. A., Van Horn, M. L., Hawkins, J. D., and Arthur, M. W. (2011). Gender Similarities and Differences in the Association between Risk and Protective Factors and Self-Reported Serious Delinquency. *Prevention Science, 8*, 115–24.

[51] Hawkins, J. D., Herrenkohl, T. I., Farrington, D. P., . . . Cothern, L. (2000). *Predictors of Youth Violence*. Washington, DC: Office of Juvenile Justice and Delinquency Prevention.

[52] Akella, D., and Jordan, M. (2011). Impact of Social and Cultural Factors on Teen Pregnancy. *Journal of Health Disparities Research and Practice, 8*, 41–62.

[53] Hawkins et al., *Predictors of Youth Violence.*

[54] Lee, T. Y., Cheung, C. K., and Kwong, W. M. (2012). Resilience as a Positive Youth Development Construct: A Conceptual Review. *Scientific World Journal,* doi:10.1100/2012/390450.

Gangs and Serious, Violent, Chronic Offenders

LEARNING OBJECTIVES

By the end of the chapter, you should be able to do the following:

- Discuss the roles guns, drugs, and peers play in offending.
- Define what is meant by serious, violent, and chronic (SVC) offenders.
- Discuss reasons why gangs form.
- Discuss reasons why youth join gangs.
- Discuss the definitional issues with gangs.
- Articulate the relationship between gangs and crime.
- Identify strategies to address gangs and SVC offenders.

Case Study 6: Confessions of a Former Latin King

Reymundo Sanchez is not his real name. The name is on the cover of two books—one that describes a journey toward becoming one of the most violent members of one of the nation's most violent gangs; and a second book about the struggle to step away from that life and learn how to be a different kind of man. Revealing the truth about the Latin Kings is a dangerous thing to do. The author of these books has to worry about gang members seeking retaliation, and the reaction of the criminal justice system for the many crimes he got away with. Writing under a pseudonym is a necessity.

Acting Without Hesitation

When Reymundo was fourteen years old, he jumped out the side door of a van and fired a sawed-off shotgun into a crowd standing on a corner. Minutes before he had been instructed by the driver of the van to pump and shoot, pump and shoot. After he leapt out and pulled the trigger, he heard screams, saw bodies on the ground, and the backs of those who were fleeing from his fire. He pointed the gun at one of them and watched him go down as the bullets hit him in the head and back. Seconds later, he was on the floor of a van as it peeled away.

It was a turning point in his career as a gang member, and future member of the Latin Kings. The other occupants of the van thumped him on his back; the girls kissed and hugged him; they handed him more wine, and another joint. Back on the street, word

spread and people he didn't know congratulated him. People offered him bags of weed, and someone even handed him a bike, saying, "Keep it brother, it's yours." There was no turning back now: He had passed a test—killing strangers on command, without hesitation, restraint, or remorse. He was on his way to becoming a King.

The Shame of Being a Punk

Just six months earlier, his reputation on the street could not have been worse. Like so many thirteen-year-olds, Reymundo had been hanging around the edges of gang life, half scared and half thrilled to be smoking and drinking with older boys and the sexy girls that surrounded them. The Spanish Lords, another Latino gang, had a "clubhouse"—a basement apartment in the building owned by someone's uncle. At the clubhouse, the gang gathered to get high and socialize. One day an argument broke out when Reymundo insulted the girlfriend of another boy. Challenged to a fight by an aggressive punch in the face, Reymundo proved himself a fierce fighter, letting loose an anger born in the humiliation of beatings in his own home. Others in the clubhouse were impressed.

The Spanish Lords invited him to join them as they headed to a restaurant near the school. On the way, they encountered a rival gang of whites who went by the name Chi-West. The Chi-West yelled out their gang name and ordered the "spics" to "go back to the island and take your roaches with you." Switchblades appeared and suddenly a brawl was under way. One of the Lords took off his sweater with gang colors and handed it to Reymundo for safekeeping as he set off on the chase. Unsure what to do, Reymundo tentatively followed down the street, but was jumped by two white guys in their twenties who shoved him to the ground and snatched the sweater. When the Lords returned Reymundo was empty-handed, having lost the all-important "colors" to a rival gang.

Reymundo did not understand what had just happened. The boy who had given him the sweater was in serious trouble for entrusting the gang "colors" to a non–gang member. As another boy explained, he was most likely going to be punished by having to undergo a "violation": generally a three-minute beating by two or three chosen members. For Reymundo, the situation was much more serious. He had to get the sweater back or face the consequences.

This was Reymundo's first lesson in the all-important matter of "colors." Gang colors mean everything to a gang. Members are willing to kill, maim, and die for them. People lose their lives over the color of their clothes. Reymundo was warned: Get it back from the Chi-West or become a target yourself. They gave him instructions: Bide your time, catch them off guard, but don't think that it's possible for you to forget about it.

Reymundo worried all winter; he tried to avoid going anywhere near the clubhouse, or even outside. When the warmer months arrived, the Lords grew impatient. They were ready to retaliate, and it was Reymundo's responsibility to get the sweater back. The Lords handed him and three others—a girl and two boys—a gun and warned them not to come back without the colors.

Around midnight they headed to the deserted schoolyard where the Chi-West were partying. The sweater was there on the back of the boy who took it, now defaced with colors from the rival gang. Reymundo pointed his gun and demanded it back, but in the moment could do nothing but tremble with fear. Others urged him to shoot, but he couldn't. One of the girls snatched the gun from his hand and began to shoot. Reymundo watched in horror as bullets hit the boy and then shattered the face of a girl next to him. Blood was everywhere. Suddenly they heard sirens. Someone grabbed the wide-eyed Reymundo and pushed him into a car.

Much to his eternal shame, tears flowed uncontrollably down his cheeks. He stayed indoors for days, pacing the room, obsessed by the image of the girl's face and chest spurting blood. When he ventured outside, he found the news had spread. Reymundo had failed. He didn't shoot, and he had to have a girl do it for him. The sweater was back, but Reymundo was in disgrace. Cold stares and curled lips met him everywhere he went. Even his girlfriend closed a door in his face, explaining she could not possibly have a punk for a boyfriend. Everywhere he heard people mutter *pendejo* ("punk"), "coward," "pussy," or *maricón* ("faggot") as he passed by.

The next time he was handed a gun and invited into the van, Reymundo knew what was at stake. Fortified with large quantities of alcohol, Reymundo knew that this time he had to pull the trigger or face a life without the protection and affiliation of a gang. Whatever he felt, he had to overcome it and kill another human being, up close and personal. The alcohol and drugs helped; but mainly it was the fear of being rejected and abandoned by the only people he thought of as his own.

Growing Up in Terror

Born in Puerto Rico, one of Reymundo's earliest memories was being left in the care of an aunt in a remote hilltop village with his sisters. Reymundo was four years old when he was anally raped by his eighteen-year-old cousin, who warned Reymundo that he would be killed if he told anyone. At age six, the family moved to Chicago, his mother with a new marriage and the promise of a better life in the States.

At first, his mother's marriage to Pedro was a good thing for the family. Pedro ran an illegal betting business and provided for his new family. Soon Reymundo's mother became pregnant and gave birth to a daughter, and later, a son. With the birth of his own children, Pedro's affection for his stepchildren faded. He developed a particularly strong aversion to his stepson Reymundo, who defied his orders to remain indoors during the spring and summer. The girls wisely avoided angering him, but Reymundo desperately wanted to go out and play baseball, his one true passion. He and his stepfather fought bitterly about it.

As life at home became his own personal hell, school was his one refuge and joy. In elementary school, Reymundo was an honor student who loved to read, draw, and write poetry. As he grew, he developed an affinity for sports—especially baseball. His desire to join the boys in the park made him risk the wrath of his stepfather time and time again. By middle school, the violence at home affected his behavior at school. Reymundo had become the class clown, angling for attention from adults, even if it was negative. His closest friends were other boys who defied school rules. Soon, they became the peers that meant the most to him.

The beatings began when he was about nine or ten. The worst part about it was that his mother not only refused to protect him, she often joined in, picking up an extension cord and whipping him along with Pedro. Once the beatings started, Reymundo sought refuge in the only place his parents would have trouble reaching him: deep under the bed, cowering against the wall where Pedro, large and fat, could not reach. They screamed at him, but Reymundo pressed his body to that wall to avoid those beatings. Sometimes his mother fetched a broom and continued to prod and poke him until her anger was spent. Reymundo spent most nights during his childhood under that bed, pressed against the wall: terrified, humiliated, angry, and above all, deeply bewildered and hurt that his own mother would treat him this way.

At age eleven, Reymundo was sent to live with his twenty-year-old stepbrother, Hector, whose business was selling heroin to junkies. His mother moved back to Puerto Rico with his stepfather Pedro, along with four sisters and a younger brother. Reymundo went with them at first but was sent back when the conflict between him and Pedro became too much for his mother to bear. To Reymundo, the decision to send him back to Chicago in the "care" of a drug dealer was only the latest in many acts of abandonment by his mother.

Too Scared to Say "No"

By age fourteen, Reymundo had shown that he was willing to shoot and kill. This made him an attractive recruit for the most powerful gang—the Latin Kings. In the 1940s, the Latin Kings gang was founded by migrants from the island of Puerto Rico in response to the harassment and discrimination by white and black gangs in Chicago. By the 1980s, the Latin Kings were a well-organized drug and gun enterprise largely run by adults from inside the state penitentiary. The Latin Kings provided Reymundo with the love, loyalty, and support that he was missing from his own family.

The Latin Kings offered membership to Reymundo through an initiation ritual of a three-minute beating without any blows to the head or groin. It was an offer he could not refuse. He accepted because he was too scared to say no. Reymundo did not immediately realize that the world of gangs is actually held together by fear, not love. Early in his career as a gangster, though, Reymundo saw that despite all the talk of brotherhood, there was no trust among gang members. Everyone lived in fear of betrayal, even by those closest to them.

In his memoir, Reymundo confesses that during those years the emotion he felt most was fear. He was afraid of getting hurt, afraid of the pain of beatings, and afraid of getting shot. He was also afraid of being alone; of being without friends; of being rejected, humiliated, and excluded. Above all, he was afraid of people finding out how scared he was. That was the biggest fear of all. To manage his terror and help him put on the act, he relied on alcohol, drugs, and an obsession with sex.

The Rise of Lil Loco

Reymundo continued to build a reputation for violence that eventually earned him his tag name, Lil Loco. After pulling the trigger that first time, the next incident to build his rep was a victimization by a rival gang. Reymundo was beaten so badly that he was hospitalized, in a coma for nine days. Once recovered, all Reymundo could think about was revenge. Older gang members assured him they had it covered. Even though he was not yet an official member, they saw him as one of their own, and had already taken steps to even the score.

But Reymundo came back to the street with a burning desire to strike back. Even when he was warned by the Latin Kings not to act without permission, he insisted on his need for personal vengeance. Reymundo began a spree of violence that included attacks on rival gangs and vicious fights with anyone who insulted or challenged him. Reymundo again showed himself to be a fierce fighter, willing to be lethal with his fists, feet, iron bars, and guns.

Later, as an adult, Reymundo realized that inside his adolescent self was a rage triggered by the childhood beatings from his mother and stepfather. Once the fighting started, he got lost in violent fury, fueled by copious amounts of alcohol. When he emerged from the trance, the response of others to his violence was intoxicating. The guys smiled at him; the girls admired him. He was elevated and important. Violence won him status, admiration, and respect.

A Business Affair

At fifteen, Reymundo was leader of the Peewee Latin Kings, the thirteen- to fifteen-year-olds who were below the Juniors, the sixteen- to nineteen-year-olds. The gang had strict rules about selling and using drugs: Alcohol and marijuana use was fine, but indulging in the use of heroin and cocaine was forbidden. Members found to use "product" instead of selling it; those who traded product for sexual favors; and those who skimmed profits into their own pockets, were severely punished through the method of "violations," or hits. The higher Reymundo rose in the gang hierarchy, the more he realized that the gang operated as a drug and gun business managed by adults far from the "action" out on the street.

Slowly, he realized that teenagers were merely the "foot soldiers" of the gang. The real heads were grown men, many of them serving long sentences in state prison. Occasionally, he caught a glimpse of high-level players in the operation, as well as police officers who kept them informed of raids; accountants who managed the money; and lawyers who sprang into action when brothers were arrested.

It Was Really Rape

As an adult, Reymundo looked back at his sexual behavior toward women and realized that on many occasions, when girls resisted, he forced himself on them. He didn't think of it at the time, but in retrospect he realizes what he really did was rape women. His attitude then was that girls were sexual objects to be used for that purpose. Some girls sold their bodies; others gave it away, especially to boys in gangs. Reymundo found that the more violent he was, and the higher he went in the gang hierarchy, the more girls were sexually available to him. He felt no remorse when he slapped a girl or forced her. He felt entitled to use her to express his anger or to get his needs met. The nearly constant intoxication from drugs and alcohol suppressed any feelings of guilt or remorse. Later, as an adult, Reymundo found he needed to unlearn many of the behaviors he took for granted in his relationships with women in order to form a genuine intimate attachment.

Gang membership for girls had its own rules in Reymundo's gang: Girls used violence to discipline each other and to regulate acceptable behavior toward males. Girls who violated these codes were severely punished, including being beaten or possibly killed by other girls. Female leaders were respected but subordinate to males. Girl gang members served as mules for drug selling by sneaking in drugs during prison visits. They also served as decoys for missions to set up an ambush, and acted as sexual rewards for males who had status within the gang.

No Friendly Officer

Reymundo remembered the presentation made by a police officer to small children gathered on the classroom rug. The officer told the children that it is the job of police to keep them and their families safe from harm. At first, Reymundo thought that the constant visits by police to his family apartment where his stepfather ran the illegal gambling business was about protecting his family. He still remembers when he learned a different lesson about the police. After witnessing a shooting, the police left the body on the street for hours, preventing relatives from embracing the body, threatening instead to arrest them. Rather than offering the family any solace or assistance, the police were aggressive and mean. Quickly, young Reymundo came to see the police as everyone else in the neighborhood did—as an enemy, never to be trusted.

Once he became involved in the gang life, the police were a force to be constantly dodged and avoided. Reymundo saw law enforcement as a blunt force: They rarely differentiated between those who were heavily involved in gangbanging and those who were on the periphery. When a crime occurred, arrests were made. Many gang members were serving time for crimes committed by other gang members. The code of loyalty required people to never snitch. The threat of violence to oneself and one's family kept the silence golden.

Reflection and Remorse

In his memoirs, Reymundo discusses images from his own acts of violence plaguing his dreams at night. He is particularly haunted by the death of a young boy—only twelve or thirteen—who admired him, followed him around like a puppy, and desired to be like him. The boy died from a bullet meant for him, the established sixteen-year-old gangster. The boy died in Reymundo's arms, and when the boy's grieving parents arrived on the scene, it was Reymundo they blamed for what happened to their son. These are the thoughts that kept Reymundo awake. He particularly remembered the father expressing disgust for gangsters and forbidding violence to be committed in his son's name.

The criminal justice system never apprehended Reymundo for his violent crimes. The system is complicit in this situation: Law enforcement will arrest any suspected gang member for a crime and are not too troubled by whether or not that particular individual was the guilty party. The result is that inexperienced and less-violent gang members routinely do time for crimes committed by the experienced and more-violent gang members. Lil Loco killed several times, and usually someone else—the last to run away, or the least-important or -protected member—was the one apprehended and convicted for the crime. When Reymundo was finally sent to prison at age twenty-one for two to four years, it was not for a violent offense, but for selling cocaine—a drug bust set up by a rival dealer.

Conviction as a Blessing

For a respected member of the Latin Kings, prison is a relatively safe and a predictable environment. Life on the inside mirrors life on the outside: Ethnic gangs dominate portions of the yard; certain areas of the cafeteria and gym are designated for different gangs. Violence is the currency to establish status and privilege. Individuals must affiliate or be perpetually victimized by the most deranged and vicious inmates. Drugs flow freely in the prison, brought in by girlfriends, guards, and lawyers, and the money from the drug business greases the wheels inside the prison just as it does on the outside.

Reymundo had no need to assert himself in prison; his reputation and status were well known by those inside, and he was left alone to do his time. For Reymundo, this was the first time he was able to focus on anything other than survival and the gang life. As a child, he had loved school, but had dropped out and never graduated from high school. In prison, he earned his GED and took advantage of all computer vocational training available to him

through the prison system. It was a new journey for Reymundo as he began to think about a different life for himself.

As a model prisoner serving time for a nonviolent drug offense, Reymundo worked his way up to a work-release program, where he found employment with his newfound computer skills. Once on probation in the community, his probation officer was pleased with his transformation from a baggy-pants gangster to a neatly dressed nine-to-five working man. The probation officer recommended an early termination of probation for Reymundo.

Getting Out

The first challenge for Reymundo in the new chapter of his life was to get out of the Latin Kings once and for all. No one wanted him to do this. The leadership urged him to stay, and offered him semiretirement, to be called into action only in case of emergency. Reymundo didn't want that, and wasn't worried about the pain of the violation for leaving—a three- to five-minute beating that could end in hospitalization, or even death. On the day that Reymundo endured the three-minute beating that officially terminated his life as a Latin King, an old affiliate called out "Once a King, always a King" as he walked by. Official or not, not everyone approves of someone walking away from the gang. Seconds later shots rang out, aimed at Reymundo, from rival gangsters. The bullets missed their target and instead hit a bystander, this time, a three-year-old boy.

As Reymundo sat on a bus covered in the blood of a small child, he vowed to find another way to live his life. The change did not happen overnight. For a while Reymundo still used and sold drugs, but eventually he landed a stable job at a university, where he met an educated woman. Through this intimate relationship, Reymundo learned about the larger structures of oppression and inequality that shape the lives of gang members on the streets of Chicago. He reflected on the reality of poor men of color killing one another, and wondered about who actually profits from the deadly arsenal of weaponry that floods the streets.

Reymundo also struggled with the gender codes he was taught about how to treat women. When he felt sexually rejected by his new girlfriend, he lost his temper and became violent. She was shocked by this behavior. He apologized, but there was nothing he could say to repair the damage. This time, Reymundo was forced to realize the truth about his own oppressive behavior toward women, and that he must change if he was ever to create a lasting intimate relationship with a woman.

His love affair with this woman evolved into a friendship that helped him move on with his life. In the closing chapters of his memoirs, Reymundo describes his current life—far from the streets of Chicago, now with a wife and children. He has earned his way into a steady job that provides for his family. He continues to work on his education and to build a respectable career for himself.

Reymundo reflects on the many forces that perpetuate the vicious life of gangs. Prisons, police, and courts do little to stop the carnage, and indeed, they are often part of the profitable flow of drugs, guns, and money involved. Reymundo thinks about his early days in school and is grateful that he had good experiences to draw upon later, when he learned that education and poetry were avenues toward a better life. He thinks a great deal about his mother—about her own rage that she turned toward her son—and realizes that while he cannot forgive her actions toward a defenseless child, he can forgive the woman herself. The book ends with a plea to everyone in this country to look at the racism and inequality that fuels gangs.

THINKING CRITICALLY ABOUT THIS CASE

1. How did Reymundo's early childhood experiences play a role in his later gang joining and deviant behavior? How does this fit with theories discussed in chapter 4?

2. How is racism exhibited in Reymundo's life through the social institutions through which he interacts?

3. Youth often join gangs for the chance of a better life. Do you think this happened with Reymundo?

4. Discuss how the code of the street perpetuates violence. Can the street code be changed? Explain.

5. What brought Reymundo to change his ways? What were the challenges he faced in doing so?

REFERENCES

This case is based on the following sources:

Brotherton, D. C., and Barrios, L. (2004). *The Almighty Latin King and Queen Nation.* New York: Columbia University Press.

Sanchez, R. (2000). *My Bloody Life: The Making of a Latin King.* Chicago: Chicago Review Press.

————. (2004). *Once a King, Always a King: The Unmaking of a Latin King.* Chicago: Chicago Review Press.

INTRODUCTION

Fʀᴏᴍ ᴡʜᴀᴛ ᴏɴᴇ ʜᴇᴀʀs ᴀɴᴅ sᴇᴇs ɪɴ ᴛʜᴇ media, dangerous and violent gangs permeate the daily life of most urban communities. Through his memoirs, Reymundo Sanchez provides a powerful and accurate description of the extreme end of the spectrum of gang activity. While the violence and drug dealing of the Latin Kings is our stereotypical view of gangs, it is far from reality for many youth gang members and those living in under-resourced urban communities. Nor is Reymundo a typical gang member. Quite the opposite: Reymundo rises to the top of the gang hierarchy because his behavior was exceptionally violent. As noted earlier, most youth engage in minor delinquent behavior at some point during adolescence. Some persist throughout adolescence and into adulthood, and about 6 percent of youth become persistent (chronic) offenders who also engage in serious offending, such as arson, and violent offending, or armed robbery.

This chapter focuses on the dynamics of youth gangs and on the **serious, violent, and chronic (SVC) offender**. Gangs are one dominant avenue for SVC offending, but not all gangs are violent, nor are all gangs equally engaged in crime. Furthermore, not all gang members are personally as violent as Reymundo came to be. Violent offenders, whether in gangs or not, make up a relatively small percentage of the overall youthful population, yet they typically account for a large proportion of crime in any given area.[1] It is difficult to predict who will become violent or chronic offenders, yet we do know that youth who have their first juvenile court referral before the age of thirteen are more likely to become violent offenders than if their first court referral was at age thirteen or older.[2] We examine here what we know about serious violent offending, about gangs, and about patterns associated with chronic violent offending. We close the chapter with research on promising innovations to address both gangs and serious violent offending.

CORRELATES

Guns

Several factors are highly linked, or correlated, with offending—and serious violent offending, in particular: they are access to guns, involvement with drugs, and delinquent peer association. An estimate of the number of guns in circulation in the United States is 300 million.[3] There are more guns in circulation in the United States than in any other nation, and there are more homicides and gun fatalities by a firearm in the United States than in any other nation. Firearms-related non-fatal injuries in 2013 totaled 84,258, while there were at least 8,124 gun-related homicides in 2014.[4] Put another way, there are about 30,000 gun deaths in the United States each year, which is about the same number of deaths that result from motor vehicle accidents.[5] Those who use guns often obtain them informally through family, friends, petty criminals, and thefts.[6] Firearms injuries and fatalities are distributed unequally across racial and ethnic lines. Blacks account for 55 percent of homicide victims, though they make up only 13 percent of the US population.[7] Whites, meanwhile, are more likely to commit suicide by firearms than any other ethnic group.

SERIOUS, VIOLENT, CHRONIC (SVC) OFFENDERS
Term used to describe the small portion of youth who repetitively engage in crime, and serious and violent crime in particular.

Homicide by firearm is consistently among the top three leading causes of death among young people; and homicide by firearm is *the leading* cause of death among black males ages fifteen to thirty-four, and the second-leading cause of death among Latinos.[8] The use of guns to commit violence, and mass shootings where many people are injured or die as a result of a single incident, is uniquely an American phenomenon among developed nations. These stark realities about guns in the United States have led the American Medical Association to declare firearms violence a public health crisis.[9]

Figure 6.1 illustrates the racial disparity in homicides of young males (ages fifteen to twenty-four). The figure displays homicide deaths per 100,000 males.[10] Of males ages fifteen to twenty-four in 1990, there were approximately 7 to 8 homicide victims per every 100,000 white youth, compared with 137 homicide victims per every 100,000 black youth. On a personal level, we see in the experience of Geoffrey Canada and in the life history of Reymundo Sanchez that access to guns changes the culture of violence among males by increasing volatility, along with increasing lethality. Addressing gun violence is an important step toward reducing crime and victimization in the United States, especially for black and brown males.

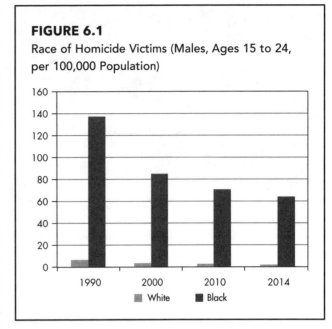

FIGURE 6.1

Race of Homicide Victims (Males, Ages 15 to 24, per 100,000 Population)

Drugs

Illicit and illegal drug use—which includes alcohol, marijuana, prescription pills, and "hard drugs," like cocaine, LSD, and methamphetamines—have been linked to high-risk and deviant behaviors. With the exception of marijuana use, which has remained stable over time, all other types of drug and alcohol use have declined over the last two decades; this includes heroin. The Monitoring the Future Survey examines drug (including alcohol) use and attitudes toward drug use among students in grades eight, ten, and twelve in the United States. This anonymous survey is administered to students in schools asking them to self-report their drug use. Parents and teachers are not provided with their responses in order to prompt more-honest answers from the youths themselves. In 2014, students reported that drug use for all grades combined was 27.2 percent, compared to the peak of 34.1 percent in 1997.[11] A video link at the end of the chapter to an interview with the director of the National Institute on Drug Abuse gives more detailed information about trends in youth drug use.

When broken down by ethnicity, the data show that white youth are most likely to be the consumers of alcohol, and Asians have the lowest rate of alcohol use.[12] Males are more likely to use and abuse substances than females, both in and outside of the juvenile justice system.[13] Yet, with the exception of alcohol and marijuana use, it is youth of color who are more likely than whites to be arrested for drugs. Drug use itself has been linked to delinquency, poor school performance, and risk-taking behaviors, such as engaging in unprotected sex.[14]

Research shows that youth who both use and sell drugs are more likely to be involved in delinquency.[15] Of the 2.4 million juvenile arrests in 2000, 78.4 percent (1.9 million) involved youth under the influence of alcohol or drugs while committing their crime.[16] Drug use was implicated in 69 percent of violent offenses, 72 percent of property offenses, and 81 percent of assaults, vandalisms, and disorderly conducts.[17] Reymundo committed violence while heavily under the influence of alcohol and other drugs. Of that 1.9 million who were under the influence of drugs at the time of arrest, only 68,600 juveniles received substance abuse treatment; yet, we know that without treatment, individuals are more likely to reoffend.

Peers

A consistent finding in delinquency research is that youthful offending most often occurs in a co-offending context, meaning youth are more likely to commit crimes with other youth. Who youth socialize with on a daily basis is very important. Those who hang out with delinquent friends are more likely to become delinquent themselves, even when all other factors, such as adult supervision and neighborhood crime rates, are taken into account.[18] The more time youth spend with delinquent peers, the more likely it is that they will commit delinquency. Delinquent peers are one of the best, if not *the* best, predictor for delinquency.[19] Of course, delinquent peers are not the only factor that can lead to delinquency, and some youth will commit delinquent acts on their own, without peers. As discussed in chapter 5, a combination of risk factors, like high family conflict and poor schooling experiences, also can be precursors to delinquency.[20]

From a life course perspective, peers and friendship networks are increasingly influential as youth enter adolescence, and gradually diminish in importance as youth enter their twenties. Most youth have friendship networks with both delinquent and nondelinquent friends, but it is friends' behavior that most influences the delinquent behavior of a youth.[21] One peer group structure that is particularly powerful in this regard is gangs. It is not surprising that gangs are one of the main avenues toward serious violent offending.

Gang membership increases involvement in crime and violent crime above and beyond association with delinquent peers.[22] The fact that gang members are more likely to be involved in crime, both violent and nonviolent, than other youth is important from a response perspective. Preventing gangs, gang joining, and gang violence is a critical task in reducing overall levels of violence in communities that have gangs.[23]

Gang members use violence to protect their turf and/or their economic enterprises, such as drug dealing. Despite this, the majority of gang activity does not involve violence. Most of the time gangs do very little beyond just hang out. The group context of gangs allows for learning of criminal behavior through deviant values and attitudes. Gangs do not specialize in a certain type of offending.

Instead, they, like most other youthful and adult offenders, engage in **cafeteria-style offending**, meaning they dabble in different types of crime.

UNDERSTANDING GANGS

What is a gang? One problem with trying to understand gangs is that not everyone has the same definition of a gang. The term *gang* is ambiguous, with no clear-cut distinctions. One definition that many agree to is as follows: "A self-formed group, united by mutual interests, that controls a particular territory, facility, or enterprise; uses symbols in communications; and is collectively involved in crime."[24] Would groups like football teams and fraternities fit into this definition? Alternatively, a critical-theory perspective on gangs would emphasize gang formation and crime as a result of resistance to social inequality.[25] In this sense, gangs have a positive function for those who have been otherwise marginalized. An additional issue is the different terms that are sometimes used as synonymous with gangs: cliques, posses, and crews (or crues). The question is, how are these groups different from gangs, if at all?

Gang researcher Buddy Howell proposes a definition that may be useful for those attempting to address gang problems in their communities. His definition consists of five components that can be further refined based on each community's local circumstances: a) A gang has five or more members; b) The members share an identity, such as a name and/or symbols; c) The members view themselves as a gang and are recognized by others as a gang; d) The group has some permanence and organization; and e) The group is engaged in criminal activity.[26] Ultimately, defining gang members is often based on self-reporting or external criteria, such as who individuals hang out with. Allowing individuals to self-report gang membership, however, has been found to be a reliable measure of true gang status.[27] Because there is likely to be continued disagreement about what defines a gang or gang member, best practice is to identify how "gangs" are defined for any given purpose.

The History of Gangs

Recent analysis of gang problems in the United States through police reporting shows that there are approximately 850,000 gang members nationwide, and 30,700 gangs.[28] Most of those gangs are in urban locations.

Gangs developed in the United States in the late 1800s during a time of rapid immigration into urban industrial areas.[29] The first gangs were of German and Irish descent, and later, Italian descent, who were discriminated against in finding jobs and housing. Their main activities were fighting and thievery. By the 1900s, however, the federal government had created new jobs and pockets of conventional employment for these people doing work that others did not want to do, including police officers, firefighters, and sanitation workers. Gang activity decreased as a result. The first academic study of street gangs occurred in the early 1900s.[30] During this time, new immigrants continued to populate gangs, and the marginalized population of gang membership shifted to newly arrived Eastern Europeans. Territory wars developed, and robbery was a common crime.

By the 1950s and 1960s, the majority of gang members were Latino and black, coinciding with the influx of blacks into northern cities from the South, and the

CAFETERIA-STYLE OFFENDING
Engaging in a variety of delinquent or criminal offenses.

immigration of Latinos into the United States. There was more national attention paid to the study of gangs, but discriminatory US policies, limiting who could live where, and lack of access to education and jobs for people of color, fueled gang formation and membership. Gangs of this era were more violent than before, and gangs became increasingly more violent between the 1980s and 2000, due in large part to access to guns. The number of gangs and gang members has also increased substantially since the late 1980s. Los Angeles, Chicago, and New York were dubbed "chronic gang cities" because of the consistent gang problems they experienced over decades. Gangs also began to emerge in smaller cities and suburban areas, and they proliferated in prisons. Consistent with previous eras, and like Reymundo, gang members today are typically from marginalized classes who lack access to opportunities for adequate housing, good education, and solid employment.

Gang Formation and Gang Joining

Several hypotheses exist as to why gangs form. Theories draw on those discussed in chapter 4, including social disorganization, general strain theory (GST), subcultural theory, and multiple marginality. From a social disorganization perspective, the lack of access to opportunities is a key reason for gang formation. Gangs develop in urban areas where social control is bereft and where there is little social or economic opportunity. Those who live in these under-resourced areas tend to be poor, and typically move out as soon as they are capable. GST proposes that we all want wealth, power, and prestige, but legitimate ways to achieve these are blocked for those living in the lower classes who do not have the same access to things like education and employment. Gangs are a way to obtain those desires through illegitimate means, while membership provides a coping mechanism for group members who have been marginalized by society.

Similar to GST, multiple marginality theory suggests that certain groups, particularly immigrants and people of color, are economically, socially, and culturally marginalized.[31] To deal with this, they form their own groups, or gangs, that have their own values and norms. In contrast to GST, they do not necessarily place equal value on the same things as the rest of society, and they value the street code as important. Another prominent theory of gang joining is through social learning. Older relatives or friends recruit youth into gangs, where they then learn gang behavior. Finally, another plausible theory of gang formation is social control: Youth who are not bonded to conventional institutions, such as family and school; who do not engage in prosocial activities; who do not have conventional belief systems, such as fighting is not acceptable; and youth who are not committed to a crime-free lifestyle, are likely to join gangs. Research finds some support for all of these theories.

Ultimately, as described in Reymundo's memoir, gangs provide a sense of belonging, respect, status, and power. All humans have these basic needs, which may be unfulfilled in the lives of youth who join gangs.[32] Key risk factors for gang joining vary depending on the age of the youth, but here is an example of a short list of factors that lead to gang joining in adolescence from an ecological context.[33]

Neighborhood problems (community domain), including crime, transience, and poverty are coupled in early childhood with a lack of parental attachment (family domain). The child engages in disruptive and aggressive behavior in the early school years (school domain), which leads to school sanctions and fewer opportunities to engage with prosocial peers in conventional activities. The youth then associates with deviant peers and engages in delinquent behavior in later childhood (peer domain). By the time the youth is in early adolescence (around twelve years old), these factors, combined with increasing school failure and lack of parental monitoring, lead to further delinquency and gang membership. Importantly, it is not the presence of any one of these risk factors, but the number of risk factors accumulated from across the different domains, that make the difference. Youth who have multiple risk factors from multiple ecological domains are more likely to become gang members than those who do not, although the exact forces which propel or buffer youth from gang membership are still unknown.[34]

Profile of Gangs and Members

Gangs are typically located in under-resourced urban cores where youth of color are more likely to take part as members. Latinos, followed by blacks, whites, and Asians are likely to be gang members. That said, only 14 to 30 percent of youthful community members ever become gang members, and their average tenure in gangs is less than two years.[35] Here, too, we see the importance of resiliency and the need to uncover the protective factors that buffer against gang joining.

Gangs tend to be organized around geographic locations, often forming single-ethnicity gangs, although most gangs do not exclude youth of other ethnicities. In this sense, "place" (where the youth is from), is more important than "race" (race or ethnicity of youth). The average age of gang members is about seventeen and half years old, and approximately 25 percent of gang members are females. Gang members typically, but not always, have higher needs, such as mental health problems, substance abuse issues, and academic concerns than other non-gang-involved youth, underscoring the importance of addressing the general well-being of these youth.[36]

Although the traditional view of gangs, and the one that is described in this chapter's case study, is that gangs are ethnically homogeneous and have an established territory, this is starting to change. Modern gangs are increasingly becoming ethnically diverse, and they may not have a specific territory. Gangs may not always have consistent symbols or colors, and they may quickly form alliances (or animosities) with other gangs. Gang members also may switch affiliations or be affiliated with more than one gang. This modern gang constitution is termed a **hybrid gang**. This new type of gang affiliation makes trying to prevent the formation of gangs and intervening in gang rivalries all the more difficult.

Gang Structure

Popular opinion may have us believe that most gangs are well organized. This is far from the truth. Most gangs are considered **emergent gangs**, or informal groups recognized by the community as a gang and developing organization and leadership.[37] Emergent gangs have engaged in criminal activity that is not chronic or severe. **Crystallized gangs**, in contrast, are those that have more organizational sophistication, membership, codes, and criminal involvement than emergent gangs, but are, for the most part, localized. **Formalized gangs** are more organized and are located throughout country, such as the Latin Kings,

HYBRID GANG
A gang that may span ethnic and geographic boundaries with no gang loyalty.

EMERGENT GANGS
Most common gang structure, with informal leadership and organization.

CRYSTALLIZED GANGS
Local gangs with more structure, organization, and involvement in criminal activity than emergent gangs.

FORMALIZED GANGS
Highly structured national and sometimes transnational gang organizations that function as criminal enterprises.

the Bloods, and the Crips. Reymundo joined a crystallized gang when he first moved to Chicago, and eventually folded into the formalized Latin King gang.

While some may believe that youth join gangs as a result of intimidation or coercion, this recruitment strategy is uncommon, usually employed only to beef up membership quickly to protect against rival gangs. Some youth also may ask to join a gang, believing that it is their "duty" to join because of their neighborhood or relative ties to the gang. Some youth may become a gang member without any formal process, just through hanging out with the gang. This was the case with Reymundo's first gang.

Youth commonly join or leave without any ceremony. There indeed is sometimes a "blood in, blood out" ritual, but this does not typically involve death to a gang member who leaves. Gang initiating and exiting strategies also may be a "jumping in/out," where a member, or potential member, has to endure a three-minute beating, like Reymundo. Some youth are "born into" a gang by virtue of their parents being gang members, while others must commit a crime to be part of a gang. Rarely, and only for female members, is there a "sex in," where female members must have sex with other gang members. Gang members typically age out of the gang by early adulthood, opting for a more conventional and less dangerous lifestyle. Sometimes gang members leave because of relocation or other life events. Obtaining a legitimate, quality job and becoming a parent are some of those reasons, as is experiencing extreme violence while in a gang that makes them reconsider their life choices.

Females and Gangs

Females tend to join gangs and leave gangs earlier than males. They may join earlier to remove themselves from domestic violence situations or child-care responsibilities at home. They may leave earlier due to earlier psychological maturation, pregnancy, or childbirth. Typically, females are not subjected to the same exit strategies as males, such as a "beating out." On the whole, female gang members do not commit acts that are as violent as those committed by their male counterparts. Though they are less delinquent than male gang members, they are more delinquent than non-gang male youth, and they are more delinquent when there are fewer female members in the gang.[38]

Females can be part of co-ed or mixed gangs, where both male and female members are part of the gang. This is the most common arrangement. Females also can act as auxiliary gang members to males in the gang. This means that they are more of a support system for the main male gang, but they are still actively involved in criminal activity. The Latin Queens, for example, may be considered an auxiliary gang to the Latin Kings. The least common type of female gang is independent gangs, which are exclusively female.

Females in co-ed gangs tend to form strong bonds with each other, in contrast to stereotypes of females being in competition with each other.[39] At the same time, females may be seen as less capable by male members, or viewed as sex objects rather than as true gang members. This may make females more vulnerable as victims by male members of their own gang and as retaliatory objects by members of rival gangs. There is a double standard for female gang members in many gangs, where violence is respectable within the gang, but if females commit too much violence, they are viewed negatively because this goes against the feminine ideal. Furthermore, although being sexed in may be their only route to membership, they are subsequently not respected by other gang members once they join.

Although females leave gangs earlier than males, they may have less ability to be conventionally successful later in life. Childbearing and child care may hasten their exit, but they may also hinder their ability to be productive and have a high quality of life. Child-care responsibilities are momentous, particularly for those without outside support systems. Female former gang members with children have a difficult time completing their education and finding and keeping quality employment without a caring, reliable adult to help with child care. Physical and mental health needs of females are less likely to be met than those of males, further impacting their chances of leading successful lives.[40]

Although gang membership is fleeting for both males and females—most are members for less than two years—the effects of gang membership are long-lasting, and may even extend to the offspring of gang members. Short-term effects of gang membership include limiting connections to prosocial people and prosocial activities that could otherwise provide positive influences and opportunities to these youth.[41] The increase in deviant and criminal involvement has previously been discussed, but victimization also increases with gang membership, contrary to the idea that gang members will be more protected. The long-term effects of gang membership are many, including low educational attainment; early and out-of-wedlock childbearing; financial strain; and adult mental and physical health issues, such as depression and obesity.[42] Recent research also has examined what happens to children of former gang members. Results show that these children are at higher risk for poor parenting and child maltreatment.[43] Addressing gangs has far-reaching consequences for ensuring the well-being of all children.

PROMISING INNOVATIONS ADDRESSING GANGS AND SVC OFFENDERS

Gang Responses

There is no foolproof method for either stopping the proliferation of gangs or for preventing youth from joining gangs, although there are a variety of responses.[44] Responses to serious, violent, and chronic (SVC) offenders overlap a great deal with gangs. Gang responses are discussed first, followed by SVC responses. Gang reduction measures range from primarily social service prevention efforts to all-out law enforcement suppression techniques. While some responses are specific to gangs or those most at risk for joining gangs, other responses cast a wider net to SVC youth who may not be gang members, but may be at risk for or involved in serious delinquency.

Streetworkers, or street outreach workers, are individuals, often former gang members themselves, who attempt to intervene in the lives of those entrenched in gangs and those who may not be gang members yet, but associate with them. Streetworkers often meet gang members in the "streets" or at their local hangouts to talk about alternatives to the gang lifestyle, and to provide opportunities to members to get out of "the life." Some of these opportunities include job training, alternative high school education programming, and counseling. Streetworkers can act as mentors to those who are ready to move on to more-conventional lifestyles. Because streetworkers have similar backgrounds and often were former gang members themselves, they have an easier time connecting with these youth.

STREETWORKERS
Community workers who engage gang members to help them find a way out of the gang lifestyle and who mediate gang disputes.

They also serve as "successful" role models for gang-involved youth in terms of showing them that it's possible to navigate life outside of the gang. Sadly, however, most streetworkers can barely eke out a living, and sometimes they themselves are not completely free from criminality.[45]

One particular program that has shown success in getting gang members off the street is Homeboy Industries, based in one of the most gang-entrenched areas of Los Angeles.[46] Homeboy Industries provides a gamut of services to gang members and former gang members, including counseling, employment, education, and tattoo removal. Founder Father Greg Boyle is fond of saying "Nothing stops a bullet like a job." A link to their website with more information and videos can be found at the end of this chapter.

Several school-based gang prevention programs are worthy of note. The Montreal Preventive Treatment Program has shown gang reduction effects with boys identified in kindergarten who received school instruction and counseling over the course of several years. These boys were less likely to join gangs and to be violent as teenagers and adults than similarly aggressive boys who did not participate in the program.[47]

Another school-based gang reduction program, the Gang Resistance Education and Training (G.R.E.A.T.)-revised program, is discussed further in chapter 7. G.R.E.A.T. integrates law enforcement officers into high-risk schools to provide instruction on the negative effects of gang membership; techniques to resist gangs; and role-playing scenarios that youth in neighborhoods with gangs are likely to encounter. Initial G.R.E.A.T. program evaluations did not show promising results, so the program was revised. This revised program has shown to result in a reduction in gang joining in the United States and in Central America.[48]

The **Comprehensive Gang Model** (CGM) is an approach to coordinate gang reduction efforts across diverse agencies such as social services, clergy, law enforcement, and the community. The CGM is an ambitious effort to focus a response to gangs that brings together entities that have a vested interest in reducing gangs, gang membership, and gang violence. Evaluations of the CGM show that it has achieved a measure of success in some locations, but has been unsuccessful in others.[49] Continued rigorous evaluations are needed to better understand whether or not this is an effective gang reduction approach.

Overall, comprehensive responses to gangs and SVCs are thought of as critical. This means that policy and programs must address those at risk for violence and gang membership; those who have engaged in some violence; and those "6 percenters" who make up a large share of crime in a given area. Responses of police and prosecution ideally are coupled with rehabilitative and counseling opportunities to support former gang members' transition toward becoming productive members of society. As noted, because of the high needs of many of these youth, law enforcement responses alone are not the total answer.

SVC Responses

Since the 1990s the US federal government has provided resources to understand and implement policies directed at those youth who may become serious, violent, and chronic juvenile offenders through dual foci: preventing delinquency, and graduated sanctions.[50] The prevention of delinquency has a community emphasis, involving community organizations and targeting factors known to cause delinquency, while building up youths' strengths in an age-appropriate

COMPREHENSIVE GANG MODEL (CGM)
A multi-stakeholder approach to addressing gangs utilizing coordinated strategies.

context. We will go into more detail about delinquency prevention strategies and programming in chapter 11. **Graduated sanctions** focuses on youth in the juvenile justice system. Under this strategy, there is an increased severity and intensity of consequences as youth commit more crimes. This means lighter sentences for first-time offenders, which may include diversion from the formal justice system altogether, to increasingly severe penalties, up to incarceration. Graduated sanctions will be discussed in more detail in chapter 9.

Several comprehensive community programs funded by the US federal government have been developed to address violent and serious crime with these dual foci. The majority of offenders who are committing theses offenses may have reached the age of adult criminal liability, but there are still some juveniles, and the prevention and early intervention portions of these programs most often are geared toward youth who have not yet reached the criminal majority age. Two such programs, Pulling Levers and Project Safe Neighborhoods, are discussed here in some detail to give you a sense of what types of initiatives have been used to reduce SVC offending, including gang offending.

The **Pulling Levers** strategy is a deterrence-based approach toward reducing serious crime and violence that provides options for identified SVC offenders. Often labeled "high-impact players," these offenders are put "on notice" by police that their behaviors are being closely watched. At the same time, they are given positive options to help them lead productive lives. Similar to those offered by streetworkers to gang members, options for high-impact players, of which hard-core gang members are a part, include GED classes, counseling, and job training. Providing prosocial options to these high-impact players is considered a "carrot" to get them to behave, while the consequences for continuing criminal activity is considered a "stick."

This strategy was first tried in Boston in the 1990s under the name of the Boston Gun Project, or, as it was more commonly known, Boston Ceasefire. It has also been dubbed "The Boston Miracle," although project leaders assert it was not a miracle, but a lot of hard work.[51] The Boston Police Department, the US Attorney's Office, social service providers, a coalition of clergy (known as the Ten Point Coalition), and researchers collaborated to reduce the rising violent crime rate in the city. Using data to help define the situation, researchers found that guns were a major source of the problem. Further, they discovered that it was a small group of highly SVC individuals, mostly gang members, who were committing most of the serious crimes.

Offender notification meetings with gangs, hosted by the alliance of agencies and community leaders, were held throughout the crime trouble spots in the city. Here, gangs were put on notice that they were being carefully watched by law enforcement, and anyone who committed a violent act would be prosecuted to the fullest extent of the law; in other words, every possible "lever" would be "pulled." The audience was also introduced to representatives from social services and clergy who could help them make positive changes. Over the next five years, violent crime, particularly homicides, dropped significantly; and although crime rates were dropping around the country, none dropped more substantially than those in Boston. Rigorous studies showed that this drop was due to the Pulling Levers strategy rather than other factors.[52] The Pulling Levers strategy is now being used throughout the United States and abroad.[53]

Project Safe Neighborhoods (PSN) developed in part out of the research from the Boston Gun Project. Started in 2001, the main objective of PSN is to

GRADUATED SANCTIONS
Increased system of penalties for continued delinquent or criminal behavior.

PULLING LEVERS
Approach that provides both severe penalties and prosocial opportunities to offenders.

PROJECT SAFE NEIGHBORHOODS (PSN)
A comprehensive community-based approach that prosecutes gun offenders while providing prevention programming for youth in the neighborhoods most exposed to gun crime.

target gun crime in order to reduce violent crime and gang crime. This is done through a coordinated, comprehensive, community-based approach that seeks to prosecute gun offenders to the fullest extent of the law, while providing prevention programming for youth in the neighborhoods that are most exposed to gun crime. A media campaign sends the message that gun crimes will not be tolerated and will be prosecuted federally, which typically involves more possible prison time than do state laws. Like the Pulling Levers strategy, those who do not comply with the law are prosecuted and held up as an example for others who continue to use guns. Evaluative results show that PSN is effective in reducing violent crime.[54]

Federally sponsored initiatives designed to reduce violent crime and gangs, as well as to prevent youth from taking part in these activities, will continue, but more attention to what is known to work effectively is important. We know that a small number of SVC young people commit the majority of these crimes, and that identifying these individuals is important; however, it's equally important to prosecute those who commit violent acts in order to provide real opportunities for those who wish to leave, or can be convinced of leaving the violence and gang life behind.

The contemporary juvenile justice system, covering police, courts, and corrections, will be discussed more fully in Part III, while prevention and intervention options will be the subject of chapter 11.

KEY TERMS

cafeteria-style offending Engaging in a variety of delinquent or criminal offenses.

Comprehensive Gang Model (CGM) A multistakeholder approach to addressing gangs utilizing coordinated strategies.

crystallized gangs Local gangs with more structure, organization, and involvement in criminal activity than emergent gangs.

emergent gangs Most common gang structure, with informal leadership and organization.

formalized gangs Highly structured national and sometimes transnational gang organizations that function as criminal enterprises.

graduated sanctions Increased system of penalties for continued delinquent or criminal behavior.

hybrid gang A gang that may span ethnic and geographic boundaries with no gang loyalty.

Project Safe Neighborhoods (PSN) A comprehensive community-based approach that prosecutes gun offenders while providing prevention programming for youth in the neighborhoods most exposed to gun crime.

Pulling Levers Approach that provides both severe penalties and prosocial opportunities to offenders.

serious, violent, chronic (SVC) offenders Term used to describe the small portion of youth who repetitively engage in crime, and serious and violent crime in particular.

streetworkers Community workers who engage gang members to help them find a way out of the gang lifestyle and who mediate gang disputes.

REVIEW AND STUDY QUESTIONS

1. What is meant by the term serious, violent, and chronic offender? Why is it important in the field of crime and justice?

2. Discuss the relationships between drugs, guns, peers, and delinquency. How does this vary by ethnicity? Why does the American Medical Association consider gun violence to be a public health crisis?

3. What are the defining characteristics of a "gang"?

4. Compare and contrast emergent, crystallized, and formal gang structures.

5. Why do gangs develop? Under what historical conditions did they develop? What are the characteristics of the communities within which gangs form?

6. Why do youth join gangs? Why do they leave? What do you believe prevents individuals from joining gangs?

7. Describe female participation in gangs. What kinds of roles do females play within the gang? How is female participation different from male participation?

8. Why is it important to prevent gangs and gang involvement?

9. Describe the role of the streetworker in the prevention of gang involvement and the reduction of gang violence.

10. Describe the Pulling Levers and Safe Neighborhood strategies. Explain how these comprehensive programs work to reduce serious and violent offending in urban communities.

CHECK IT OUT

Watch

Homeboy Industries:

www.homeboyindustries.org/

Trends in youth drug and alcohol use:

https://youtu.be/kZVaoRbr7vU

Why youth join gangs:

www.nationalgangcenter.gov/Content/HTML/Why-Youth-Join-Gangs/

Recommended Movies

Gangs of New York (2002)

Hoop Dreams (1994)

Peace Process (2006)

NOTES

1 Howell, J. C., Lipsey, M. W., and Wilson, J. J. (2014). *A Handbook for Evidence-Based Juvenile Justice Systems*. Lanham, MD: Lexington.

2 Office of Juvenile Justice and Delinquency Prevention. (2003). *Juveniles in Court*. Retrieved from www.ncjrs.gov/html/ojjdp/195420/page16.html.

3 Cook, P. J., and Goss, K. A. (2014). *The Gun Debate*. New York: Oxford.

4 Centers for Disease Control and Prevention. (2014). *Nonfatal Injury 2001–2013*. Injury Prevention and Control: Data and Statistics (WISQARS). Retrieved from www.cdc.gov/injury/wisqars/nonfatal.html; Federal Bureau of Investigations. Retrieved from https://ucr.fbi.gov/crime-in-the-u.s/2014/crime-in-the-u.s.-2014/tables/expanded-homicide-data/expanded_homicide_data_table_8_murder_victims_by_weapon_2010-2014.xls.

5 Cook and Goss, *The Gun Debate*.

6 Ridgeway, G., Braga A. A., Tita, G., and Pierce, G. L. (2011). Intervening in Gun Markets: An Experiment to Assess the Impact of Targeted Gun-Law Messaging. *Journal of Experimental Criminology, 7*, 103–9; Watchtel, J. (1999). Sources of Crime Guns in Los Angeles, California. *Policing: An International Journal of Police Strategies & Management, 21*, 220–39.

7 Ibid.

8 David-Ferdon, C., Dahlberg, L. L., and Kegler, S. R. (2013). Homicide Rates among Persons Aged 10–24 Years: United States, 1981–2010. *Morbidity and Mortality Weekly Report, 62*, 545–48. Retrieved from www.cdc.gov/mmwr/preview/mmwrhtml/mm6227a1.htm?s_cid=mm6227a1_w.

9 American Medical Association. Retrieved from www.ama-assn.org/ama-calls-gun-violence-%E2%80%9C-public-health-crisis%E2%80%9D.

10 Author's analysis of data from the Centers for Disease Control. Retrieved from www.cdc.gov/nchs/data/hus/2015/029.pdf.

11 National Institute of Drug Abuse. *High School and Youth Trends*. Retrieved from www.drugabuse.gov/publications/drugfacts/high-school-youth-trends.

12 Substance Abuse and Mental Health Services Administration. (2011). *Results from the 2010 National Survey on Drug Use and Health: Summary of National Findings*. NSDUH Series H-41, HHS Publication No. (SMA) 11-4658.

13 Neff, J. L., and Waite, D. E. (2007). Male versus Female Substance Abuse Patterns among Incarcerated Juvenile Offenders: Comparing Strain and Social Learning Variables. *Justice Quarterly, 24*, 106–32.

14 Crowe, A. J. (1998). *Drug Identification and Testing Summary*. Washington, DC: Office of Juvenile Justice and Delinquency Prevention; King, K. M., Meehan, B. T., Trim, R. S., and Chassin, L. (2006). Substance Use and Academic Outcomes: Synthesizing Findings and Future Directions. *Addiction, 101*, 1688–89; Tapert, S. F., Aarons, G. A., Sedlar, G. R., and Brown, S. A. (2001). Adolescent Substance Use and Sexual Risk-Taking Behavior. *Journal of Adolescent Health, 28*, 181–89.

15 Altschuler, D. M., and Brounstein, P. J. (1991). Patterns of Drug Use, Drug Trafficking, and Other Delinquency among Inner-City Adolescent Males in Washington, DC. *Criminology, 29*, 589–622.

[16] The National Center on Addiction and Substance Abuse. (2004). *Criminal Neglect: Substance Abuse, Juvenile Justice, Children Left Behind.* New York: Columbia University.

[17] Mulvey, E. P., Schubert, C. A., and Chassin, L. (2010). *Substance Abuse and Delinquent Behavior among Serious Adolescent Offenders.* Juvenile Justice Bulletin. NCJ 232790. Retrieved from www.ncjrs.gov/pdffiles1/ojjdp/232790.pdf.

[18] Watts, S. J., and McNulty, T. L. (2015). Delinquent Peers and Offending: Integrating Social Learning and Biosocial Theory. *Youth Violence and Juvenile Justice, 13,* 190–206.

[19] Gifford-Smith, M., Dodge, K. A., Dishion, T. J., and McCord, J. (2005). Peer Influence in Children and Adolescents: Crossing the Bridge from Developmental to Intervention Science. *Journal of Abnormal Child Psychology, 33,* 255–65.

[20] Spohn, R. E., and Kurtz, D. L. (2011). Family Structure as a Social Context for Family Conflict: Unjust Strain and Serious Delinquency. *Criminal Justice Review, 36,* 332–56.

[21] Haynie, D. L., and Kreager, D. (2013). Peer Networks and Crime. In F. T. Cullen and P. Wilcox (eds.). *The Oxford Handbook of Criminological Theory,* 257–73. New York: Oxford.

[22] Krohn, M. D., and Thornberry, T. (2008). Longitudinal Perspectives on Adolescent Street Gangs. In A. Liberman (ed.)., *The Long View of Crime: A Synthesis of Longitudinal Research,* 138–60. New York: Springer.

[23] Gebo, E., Foley, E., and Ross, L. (2014). Preventing Gang Violence. In P. J. Donnelly and C. L. Ward (eds.)., *Oxford Textbook of Violence Prevention: Epidemiology, Evidence, and Policy,* 213–17. London, UK: Oxford.

[24] Curry, G. D., Decker, S. H., and Pyrooz, D. C. (2013). *Confronting Gangs: Crime and Community* (3rd ed.). New York: Oxford.

[25] Durán, R. J. (2013). *Gang Life in Two Cities: An Insider's Journey.* New York: Columbia University Press.

[26] Howell, J. C. (2012). *Gangs in America's Communities.* Thousand Oaks, CA: Sage.

[27] Matsuda, K. M., Esbensen, F., and Carson, D. (2012). Putting the "Gang" in "Eurogang": Characteristics of Delinquent Youth Groups by Different Definitional Approaches. In F. Esbensen and C. Maxson (eds.)., *Youth Gangs in International Perspective: Results from the Eurogang Program of Research,* 17–33. New York: Springer.

[28] Egley, A., Howell, J. C., and Harris, M. (2014). *National Gang Center: Highlights of the 2012 National Youth Gang Survey.* Washington, DC: Office of Juvenile Justice and Delinquency Prevention.

[29] Howell, J. C. (2015). *The History of Street Gangs in the United States.* Lanham, MD: Lexington.

[30] Thrasher, E. (1927). *The Gang: A Study of 1,313 Gangs in Chicago.* Chicago: University of Chicago Press.

[31] Vigil, J. D. (2002). *A Rainbow of Gangs: Street Cultures in the Mega-City.* Austin: University of Texas Press.

[32] Maslow, A. H. (1968). *Toward a Psychology of Being.* New York: D. Van Nostrand Company.

[33] Howell, J. C., and Egley, A. Jr. (2005). Moving Risk Factors into Developmental Theories of Gang Membership. *Youth Violence and Juvenile Justice, 3,* 334–54.

[34] Decker, S. H., Melde, C., and Pyrooz, D. C. (2013). What Do We Know about Gangs and Gang Members and Where Do We Go from Here? *Justice Quarterly, 30,* 369–402.

[35] Thornberry, T. P., Krohn, M. D., Lizotte, A. J., Smith, C. A., and Tobin, K. (2003). *Gangs and Delinquency in Developmental Perspective.* New York: Cambridge.

[36] Gebo, E., and Sullivan. C. J. (2014). A Statewide Comparison of Gang and Non-Gang Youth in Schools. *Youth Violence & Juvenile Justice, 12,* 191–208.

[37] Maxson, C. L., and Klein M. W. (2006). *Street Gangs: Patterns and Policies.* New York: Oxford.

[38] Miller, J. (2001). *One of the Guys: Girls, Gangs and Gender.* New York: Oxford.

[39] Ibid.

[40] Odgers, C. L., Moffitt, T. E., Broadbent, J. M. . . . , and Caspi, A. (2008). Female and Male Antisocial Trajectories: From Childhood Origins to Adult Outcomes. *Development and Psychopathology, 20,* 673–716.

[41] Thornberry et al., *Gangs and Delinquency in Developmental Perspective.*

[42] Gilman, A. B., Hill, K. G., and Hawkins, J. D. (2014). Long-Term Consequences of Adolescent Gang Membership for Adult Functioning. *American Journal of Public Health, 105,* 938–45; Pyrooz, D. C. (2014). From Colors and Guns to Caps and Gowns? The Effects of Gang Membership on Educational Attainment. *Journal of Research in Crime and Delinquency, 51,* 56–87.

[43] Augustyn, M. B., Thornberry, T. P., and Krohn, M. V. (2014). Gang Membership and Pathways to Maladaptive Parenting. *Journal of Research on Adolescence, 24,* 252–67.

[44] Wong, J., Gravel, J., Bouchard, M., Morselli, C., and Descormiers, K. (2012). *Effectiveness of Street Gang Control Strategies: A Systematic Review and Meta-Analysis of Evaluation Studies.* Ottawa, Canada: Public Safety Canada.

[45] Varano, S., and Wolff, R. (2012). Street Outreach as an Intervention Modality for At-Risk and Gang-Involved Youth. In E. Gebo and B. Bond (eds.), *Looking Beyond Suppression: Community Strategies to Reduce Gang Violence,* 83–104. Lanham, MD: Lexington.

[46] Retrieved from www.homeboyindustries.org/why-we-do-it/.

[47] Tremblay, R. E., Masse, L., Pagani, L., and Vitaro, F. (1996). From Childhood Physical Aggression to Adolescent Maladjustment: The Montreal Prevention

Experiment. In R. D. Peters and R. J. McMahon (eds.), *Preventing Childhood Disorders, Substance Abuse, and Delinquency*, 268–98. Thousand Oaks, CA: Sage.

[48] Esbensen, F., Peterson, D., Taylor, T. J., and Osgood, D. W. (2012). Results from a Multi-Site Evaluation of the G.R.E.A.T. Program. *Justice Quarterly, 29,* 125–51.

[49] Gebo, E., Bond, B. J., and Campos, K. S. (2015). The Office of Juvenile Justice and Delinquency Prevention Comprehensive Gang Strategy: The Comprehensive Gang Model. In S. H. Decker and D. C. Pyrooz (eds.), *The Handbook of Gangs*, 392–405. New York: Wiley.

[50] Howell, J. C. (2003). Diffusing Research into Practice Using the Comprehensive Strategy for Serious, Violent, and Chronic Juvenile Offenders. *Youth Violence and Juvenile Justice, 1,* 219–45.

[51] Kennedy, D. (2011). *Don't Shoot.* New York: Bloomsbury.

[52] Braga, A. A., Kennedy, D. M., Waring, E. J., and Piehl, A. M. (2001). Problem-Oriented Policing, Deterrence, and Youth Violence: An Evaluation of Boston's Operation Ceasefire. *Journal of Research in Crime and Delinquency, 38,* 195–225.

[53] Braga, A., and Weisburd, D. (2012). The Effects of "Pulling Levers" Focused Deterrence Strategies on Crime. *Campbell Systematic Reviews, 6,* 1–90.

[54] McGarrell, E. F., Hipple, N. K., Corsaro, N., Bynum, T. S., Perez, H., Zimmerman, C. A., and Garmo, M. (2009). *Project Safe Neighborhoods: A National Program to Reduce Gun Crime: Final Project Report.* East Lansing: Michigan State University, School of Criminal Justice.

CHAPTER — 7

Youth, Schools, and Problem Behaviors

LEARNING OBJECTIVES

By the end of the chapter, you should be able to do the following:

- Identify the factors that promote positive school climate.
- Discuss solutions to bullying behavior.
- Discuss the effects of bullying on victims, bystanders, and bullies.
- Define zero-tolerance policies.
- Identify the effects of zero-tolerance policies on schools and students.
- Explain the school-to-prison pipeline.
- Articulate the challenges of school resource officers.
- Know basic trends in school violence.
- Understand the history of exclusion and intersectionality in public schools.
- Connect school climate with positive youth development.

Case Study 7: Understanding the Horror at Columbine High School

April 20, 1999, was an ordinary Tuesday. Eric Harris and Dylan Klebold carefully positioned a duffel bag containing two twenty-pound explosives attached to timing devices inside the door of the school cafeteria. The boys, seniors at Columbine High School, headed to an outside parking lot. Their plan was to trap fleeing students in a hailstorm of bullets as they tried to escape the inferno in the cafeteria.

At 11:14 a.m., a diversionary bomb in a nearby field exploded. Harris and Klebold, armed and ready, waited for the next set of explosions to drive the students into the sights of their 9mm semiautomatic weapons. But the devices failed to detonate. Instead, Harris and Klebold cloaked themselves in long coats packed with weapons, explosives, and ammunition and headed toward the cafeteria. The first students they encountered were eating lunch on the grass. Harris and Klebold opened fire, killing Rachel Scott and seriously injuring Richard Castaldo. The rampage had begun. Over the next forty-seven minutes Eric Harris and Dylan Klebold would shoot thirty-nine people, mostly students, including themselves.

The Devastation

The murderous path of the two boys began outside the school. Hearing the shots fired at the students, school resource officer Neil Gardner arrived on the scene and fired back at the two boys, driving them inside the building. After leaving the cafeteria they roamed the hallways, throwing fire bombs and pipe bombs. In the hall, they encountered Dave Sanders, the girls' basketball coach, who was racing through the hallways, urging students to run. They shot Sanders, inflicting a wound from which he would slowly bleed to death over the next three hours.

It was in the library, where fifty-two students and four adults had taken refuge, that Harris and Klebold spent the longest amount of time, hunting students crouched beneath desks and behind bookcases, taunting and teasing them before shooting them. It took the boys seven and half minutes to shoot twenty-two students, killing ten and wounding twelve.

Leaving the library, Klebold and Harris returned to the cafeteria to check on the defective explosives they had left there. They can be seen on videotape looking through a window at the nearly one thousand law enforcement and medical emergency personnel amassed outside the building. Returning to the hallway, they continued to shoot aimlessly as they made their way back to the library. During their absence, the police had managed to evacuate the living and wounded from the library, except for two students who lay unconscious among the dead.

It was here in the library, minutes after shooting at the police through the windows, that Harris and Klebold turned their weapons on themselves—Harris, to his mouth, and Klebold, to his temple. At 12:08 p.m., the pair committed the final element of their plan: double suicide. Fifteen people—fourteen students, including the shooters, and one adult—were dead. Another twenty-three were wounded by gunshots, including three who remain paralyzed below the waist today.

The Police and Emergency Response

Teacher Patti Nielson, who sought refuge in the library after being hit by flying glass in the hallway, was the first to call 911. As she hid, she yelled to the many students in the library to get under their desks. She dropped the phone as the two boys entered the library, and the dispatcher could hear the shots as Klebold and Harris teased and then killed students hiding beneath their desks.

Within minutes of the first reports of gunshots, six officers from the Jefferson County Sheriff's Department were on the scene. Three of them sighted at least one of the boys and exchanged gunfire outside the school or through a window. Four Denver police officers, one from the Gang Unit and three from the SWAT team, also arrived within minutes. They too exchanged gunfire with the boys. None of the law enforcement officers from Jefferson County or Denver City Police entered the building in pursuit of the two boys.

By 12:00 p.m., more SWAT teams were stationed outside the school, and ambulances were starting to take the wounded to local hospitals. Shortly after noon, the first SWAT teams entered, methodically clearing the building of students and faculty who were barricaded in classrooms and closets. Thirty bombs exploded at Columbine that day. Most were planted around the school, and others were hidden in their cars and in the parking lot. With pipe bombs exploding, sprinklers and fire alarms ringing, the scene was chaotic.

Although Dave Sanders had managed to crawl to a classroom, where he lay bleeding, the SWAT teams moved slowly, and they didn't reach Sanders until it was too late. At 3:30 p.m., the teams finally reached the library where they found the bodies of the two perpetrators. There was only one other surviving injured victim.

As SWAT teams outside found the explosives in the parking lot and on the roof, a bomb inside Klebold's car detonated when an officer tried to defuse it; fortunately, no one was hurt. The next day a bomb squad searched the entire school complex thoroughly before declaring it safe. By late afternoon of the following day, authorities had removed all of the fifteen bodies inside the school, including the two shooters.

Could This Have Been Prevented?

Simply put, Harris and Klebold were not the kids one would expect to turn violent. Harris and Klebold hailed from affluent two-parent families, and both did well in school. According to most adults, they were bright, articulate, and well-mannered. They enjoyed what many described as normal upbringings. Both had friends at school and were involved in school activities. Harris had played soccer until the year before, and Klebold was in the drama club. Klebold visited the University of Arizona with his parents earlier that year, where he had been accepted for the following year. The weekend before the slaughter, Klebold took a date to the prom. Harris joined afterward, celebrating with the students they were meticulously planning to murder in three days' time.

And plan they did. Klebold and Harris had plotted and prepared this attack for well over a year, carefully rehearsing each and every move. The boys did not "snap" or act impulsively; they had worked on their preparations under the noses of their parents and adults in school. They manufactured explosives in the garage; held target practice in the basement; and carefully documented their plans on paper, in videotapes, and on a website.

Even more detailed are five homemade videos created in the basement of Klebold's home discovered by police investigators immediately after the attack. These "basement tapes" contain footage of their growing gun arsenal, of the boys doing target practice, and the methods they used to deceive their parents about their plans. They loved to watch violent movies and speculated for the camera about which famous film director would bid for the rights to make a movie about them. Everything they did was done for a twisted fantasy: They would be known as the worst of the worst, and the tapes were intended to provide as much gruesome detail as possible.

On several of the videotapes Harris complained that because he had to move so many times with his military family, he was always the skinny white kid "at the bottom of the ladder." Klebold also complained about his popular athletic older brother and his friends, who constantly "ripped" on him and treated him like the runt of the litter. On the tape, they explained that all this abuse led to a pent-up rage that would find its outlet in a mass killing. Klebold looked into the camera and said, "I am going to kill you all. You've been giving us shit for years." In the library, the boys can be heard on the 911 tape calling for all the "jocks in white hats" to get up. During the rampage, they deliberately shot several well-known athletes in the school.

The tapes are full of complaints of their victimization at the hands of others who did not treat them with respect. They stated that this massacre was going to earn them "the respect they deserve." They spewed invective against blacks, women, Christians, and Jews, as well as jocks and popular types in Denver. They took pains to exonerate the people who helped them acquire the guns, explaining that those individuals knew nothing of their plans and were not to blame. One final video made only a half-hour before the attack documents them saying good-bye and apologizing to friends and family.

What Were the Warning Signs?

In the case of Columbine, there were many signs of trouble. One of their parents even walked in on them as they took turns trying on a black trench coat with a rifle hidden beneath it. Another time Harris's mother saw the butt of a rifle sticking out from a gym bag but she assumed it was a BB gun. There were allegations that Harris's father had once discovered a pipe bomb in his son's possession. And the boys described in their journals how the plan was nearly foiled days before the attack when Harris's father picked up a phone call alerting them that their order for ammunition clips was ready. Harris's father ended the call, assuming it was a mistake.

There were signs at school as well. In English class, Harris had written a violent essay. The teacher was so upset by the essay that she insisted on meeting with Harris's parents and a school counselor about the matter. The pair used Columbine High School video equipment for some of their tapes, displaying their arsenal and detailing their plans. Later students reported having seen these tapes while in the video lab at the school, yet no one told an adult what they had seen.

Harris and Klebold also had had prior involvement with local law enforcement. One year before the shootings, they were caught stealing tools from a parked electrical van. They pled guilty to the theft and completed a juvenile diversion program that required them to attend a class on anger management and participate in counseling. As part of their sentences, they paid fines, did community service, and wrote letters full of heartfelt remorse. Because of their excellent behavior in the diversion program, they were released early; charges were dropped; and their juvenile records wiped clean.

The school was never informed of the boys' criminal involvement with the police. Similarly, the police were not notified when the school apprehended the two boys hacking into the school computer. The school suspended them but did not inform the police about it.

Probably the most damning evidence known prior to the massacre was the suspicious incident reported by the parents of Brooks Brown, a former friend of Harris's. One year earlier, around the same time as the theft of equipment from the van, a student at Columbine discovered that Eric Harris was posting death threats against Brown on his website. It was actually Klebold who alerted Brown that he was identified as someone Harris wanted to kill. The site, first created in 1996, focused originally on tips for playing a popular online game, Doom. But increasingly it included expressions of hate and violence. By 1998, it was a vicious website with detailed descriptions of how to build and use explosives, explicit threats to kill,

and ranting and raving against all the rich people of Denver, "with their high and mighty snobby thinking."

Brown's worried parents notified the Jefferson County Sheriff's Office, and investigator Michael Guerra examined the website, which also contained violent threats toward other students and teachers at Columbine High School. Guerra monitored the site and noted that Harris was clearly admitting to possession of illegal explosives, and had created a hit list of individuals he planned to target. Guerra drafted an affidavit for a search warrant of the Harris home.

Deputy Mark Miller came out to the Browns' house to interview them about their allegations. Miller knew Harris and Klebold because he had been one of the arresting officers in the van break-in case. At the time, the boys were under the supervision of the juvenile authorities for that crime, but no one in the sheriff's office had informed them of these additional allegations against the boys. This was partly because the Browns did not want Harris to know that their son had reported the threats, fearing that it would incite him to even worse violence. And even though Brown's mother had been friendly with Klebold's mother for years, she failed to contact her to tell her what they knew about their son's involvement with Eric Harris.

The Browns did give the deputy the names and addresses of both families and followed up in the next couple of weeks to see if anything had been done. But the sheriff's office could no longer locate the web pages, and because the Browns wished to remain anonymous, the sheriff's office determined there was insufficient evidence to move forward with a search warrant. A suspicious incident report was filed and nothing else happened.

Distracted by what they saw as more serious matters, the sheriff's department let the allegation fall through the cracks. The sheriff's office did forward the report to the school's designated police officer. Neil Gardner now states that he observed the boys at school and felt there was nothing suspicious in their conduct. He failed to report any of this information to anyone else in the school. On the morning of the rampage, Brown was in the parking lot before it all began when Harris told him that he had better leave before he got hurt. Without saying anything to anyone, Brown took his advice and went home.

Who Is to Blame?

With both Klebold and Harris dead, the question of responsibility was divided among their parents; the failure of the school and sheriff's department to prevent the violence; and the legal context that made it possible for the boys to get their hands on such an array of weaponry.

The only individuals charged with crimes associated with Columbine were the two adults who helped them acquire guns. They were both convicted of providing a handgun to a minor and illegal possession of a firearm. One was sentenced to six years and the other to four and a half years. Perhaps more difficult than the prison terms was the requirement that both men listen to grief-stricken parents reading their victim impact statements in the only criminal court proceeding related to the case. While the boys had attempted to absolve the people who helped them acquire weapons, the parents of the slain children made it clear that they held these two individuals responsible for what the two boys did with those guns.

Parents also filed civil lawsuits against the parents of Harris and Klebold. In their anger and grief, many parents believed that Harris and Klebold's parents should be held responsible for failing to adequately supervise their children. Almost two years after the tragedy, a group of families agreed to a settlement paid out by the parents of Harris and Klebold.

For many of the victims, one goal of the lawsuit was to get more information about the two boys. They wanted to know what the boys' parents knew so they could better understand why and how this happened. Like many victims, they experienced a desire to have these questions answered, especially by those who were closest to the two boys. Yet, this need was never fully met. While the parents settled the lawsuit, as a whole, they refused to meet with victims or make any public disclosures, although they did send letters of apology to the victims in the immediate aftermath. Years later, Dylan Klebold's mother, Sue Klebold, did meet with some of the victims' families, and wrote a memoir about her feelings of guilt and her efforts to reach out to them.

In addition to the lawsuit against the parents, twenty families have filed notices of "intent to sue" local government agencies, including the Jefferson County Sheriff's Department and the school district. The school district could be subject to claims that it was negligent in failing to keep the school safe and to respond to warnings about Eric Harris. The sheriff's office may be subject to claims that they were negligent in not investigating or responding to complaints they had received about Harris's activities. Among

the families filing notices were the parents of Dylan Klebold. The Klebolds claim that the sheriff's office may have been negligent by failing to inform them of a 1998 complaint filed with the office that Harris had threatened to kill another student; and that the office had knowledge of a website maintained by Harris that contained menacing statements and references to mass murder, and in which he reportedly posted diagrams for building bombs. Had they known of this potential danger, the Klebolds say they could have taken steps to prevent it by restricting their son's contact with Harris.

Some parents focused on the issue of gun availability, feeling strongly that blame was equally shared among the gun manufacturers and sellers, and that the lack of gun laws contributed to the tragedy. Tom Mauser, who lost his son Daniel, made it his mission to change the nation's gun laws, under which weapons are easily accessible to teenagers. He was inspired by the success of a similar mission in the wake of a tragic shooting in Scotland, where families of victims joined together and successfully lobbied for a ban on handguns throughout the entire United Kingdom.

At first, this campaign was successful. In the wake of Columbine, voters in Colorado passed an initiative to require criminal background checks for those buying guns from private dealers, and state lawmakers introduced legislation that would raise the legal age to own a handgun from eighteen to twenty-one. Yet, with significant resistance from the National Rifle Association, few of these initiatives passed. Efforts to require background checks at gun shows, to require safe storage of guns in the home, and to increase the age of gun ownership all failed.

On a national level, attempts to enact stricter gun control measures in response to the tragedy also were unsuccessful. Since the Columbine High School shooting, not a single major gun control law has been passed by Congress. In fact, restrictions on certain weapons have actually been relaxed. In 2003, Congress passed a measure to prevent local enforcement agencies from consulting police in other states regarding firearms traces. In 2004 under the Clinton administration, the assault weapons ban expired. And in 2005, Congress passed legislation that prevented shooting victims or their families from instituting wrongful death lawsuits against gun manufacturers. In the words of one of the advocates, "It is as if Columbine never happened."

THINKING CRITICALLY ABOUT THIS CASE

1. What do you believe were the factors that contributed to this rampage? Do you believe any of these factors were preventable? Explain.

2. Do you believe that widespread tolerance for bullying in our nation's schools is a significant factor contributing to the problem of school rampages? Why, or why not?

3. Do you believe that reform of our nation's gun laws would reduce the incidence of future school rampages? Why, or why not?

4. Reflect back on your own high school experience. Did you feel physically safe in your school? Why, or why not? Did you feel psychologically safe? Why, or why not? What changes, if any, do you think would have made your own school environment a safer educational experience for students?

5. Do you support the presence of police officers in schools? Do you believe the presence of armed police officers in schools would prevent shootings such as Columbine? Why, or why not?

REFERENCES

This case is based on the following sources:

Adams, L., and Russakoff, D. "Dissecting Columbine's Cult of the Athlete; In Search for Answers, Community Examines One Source of Killers' Rage," *Washington Post*, June 12, 1999.

Brooke, J. "Teacher of Colorado Gunmen Alerted Parents," *New York Times*, May 11, 1999.

———. "Terror in Littleton: The Overview," *New York Times*, May 4, 1999.

———. "Diary of High School Gunman Reveals Plan to Kill Hundreds," *New York Times*, April 27, 1999.

Butterfield, F. "Students, Mindful of Columbine, Break Silence to Report Threats," *New York Times*, February 10, 2001.

Egan, T. "Terror in Littleton: The Police Response," *USA TODAY*, April 28, 1999.

Erickson, Hon. W. "The Report of Governor Bill Owen's Columbine Review Commission." Colorado: May 2001.

Garbarino, J. "Some Kids Are Orchids," *Time*, March 19, 2001.

Gibbs, N., and Roche, T. "The Columbine Tapes," *Time*, March 19, 2001.

Goldstein, A., Sanchez, R., and Fletcher, M. A. "In Choosing Victims, Gunmen Showed Their Prejudice," *Washington Post*, April 23, 1999.

Goldstein, A. "Victims: Never Again," *Time*, March 19, 2001.

Janofsky, M. "The Columbine Killers' Tapes of Rage," *New York Times*, December 14, 1999.

Kenworthy, T. "Columbine Gun Seller Gets 6-Year Term; In Videotape, 2 Shooters Thanked Friend But Said He Didn't Know of Their Plan," *Washington Post*, November 13, 1999.

Newman, K. S. *Rampage: The Social Roots of School Shootings*. New York: Basic Books, 2004.

Ochberg, F. M. "Bound by a Trauma Called Columbine," *Washington Post*, November 19, 2000.

O'Driscoll, P. "Duo Left Long Trail of Clues Leading Up to Massacre," *USA TODAY*, April 23, 1999.

O'Driscoll, P., and Tom Kenworthy, T. "A Year Later, School Massacre Still Haunts," *USA TODAY*, April 20, 2000.

Richardson, V. "Columbine Report Puts Blame on Sheriff; Says His Office Could Have Averted Killings," *Washington Times*, May 18, 2001.

———. "Columbine Killer's Activities Investigated Year Before Attack," *Washington Times*, April 16, 2001.

Thompson, C. W., and Suro, R. "Columbine Officer Received Warning of Gunman's Death Threats," *Washington Post*, May 1, 1999.

US Secret Service and US Department of Education. *The Final Report and Findings of the Safe School Initiative*. Washington, DC: 2002.

Von Drehle, D. "To Killers, Model School Was Cruel," *Washington Post*, April 25, 1999.

INTRODUCTION

GROWING UP, AMERICAN CHILDREN SPEND MORE waking hours in school than anywhere else. As noted in chapter 2, schools are a primary socializing agent in modern society. Next to parents and family, school-teachers and peer groups are profoundly influential in shaping the values, attitudes, and behaviors of youth. This is especially true as children enter adolescence, seeking to develop competency, independence, and an identity separate from home and parents. As we see in the tragic actions of Klebold and Harris, youth experience school as a highly positive or negative place, depending on the quality of their relationships with teachers and peers.

Learning at school extends far beyond the content of reading, writing, and arithmetic. Harry Gracey notes that even kindergarten should be seen as a kind of "boot camp," socializing young children and teaching them how to behave in the school environment.[1] For some children, this adaptation to school is highly successful: School is a place where they flourish in their relationships with peers and adults. For other children, the school environment is challenging and hostile. Positive school attachment is a powerful force in a young person's life, setting the stage for a successful transition to secondary education, a career, and adult roles. For other children, however, the experiences of academic failure and behavioral difficulty with adults and peers at school leads to a detachment from the school environment. School failure and detachment is a key factor associated with increased involvement in delinquent behaviors and involvement with the juvenile justice system.

This chapter takes a close look at the relationship between delinquency and schooling. Schools represent an opportunity to achieve one's potential and overcome the limitations of one's birth. We can see the importance of quality education in the life trajectory of Geoffrey Canada in Case Study 4, and in the next chapter's case study on the life of Victor Rios. Success at school helped both of these men transcend early disadvantages in their lives. But their stories are the exception rather than the rule. Schools more often reinforce the advantages of those who are privileged and compound the disadvantages associated with poverty and discrimination. Although the hope is that schools will provide opportunities to achieve for all children, the reality is that schools too often label, isolate, and reject the children most in need of additional support from adults.

In the twenty-first century, equal access to quality education regardless of location, income, race, gender, ethnicity, or sexual orientation remains part of the struggle to create equity within American society. Today, an education is even more important than it was fifty or one hundred years ago, yet many barriers to equal access to quality education persist. Schools, however, remain one of the most positive developmental institutions open to all youth. When school is a positive experience, it can literally change lives. We close this chapter by examining promising school-based programs of prevention and intervention.

EDUCATION AND INEQUALITY

Public education is the cornerstone of the American goal of providing equal opportunity for all citizens regardless of social background. The colonies of seventeenth-century Puritan society were the first to offer free schooling for all children. These early schools were rooted in Protestant religious doctrine and were created to instill proper values and skills in the next generation. Even in its infancy, however, there were different tracks for children depending upon their place in society. Thomas Jefferson believed that there were only a few bright children among the lower classes, and that education was a way of "raking a few geniuses from the rubbish."[2] Until the nineteenth century, only those wealthy enough could continue beyond the primary years of schooling. Girls were thought to only need education through the third grade to prepare them for marriage and motherhood. While Jefferson thought democracy required everyone to have a basic education in reading and writing, "everyone" did not include slaves or girls, both of whom were not eligible to participate in the political process.

In 1830, Horace Mann, a statesman from Massachusetts, was the first to advocate for publicly funded education for all, both rich and poor. Public education laws passed in many states, but with Protestant religious teaching as a central tenet of schools. Many immigrants at that time, particularly Irish Catholic, refused public school education and demanded their own schools be paid for with tax dollars. The compromise was the legal requirement that all specific religious teachings be removed from the public education curriculum.

Throughout early American history, African Americans were denied access to education. During slavery, whites feared that literacy among slaves would lead to discontent and rebellion. The education of slaves was therefore prohibited by law and punishable as a criminal offense. After the Civil War, Southern states responded to the end of slavery with the imposition of segregated public school systems, arguing that segregated schools were "separate but equal." Catherine Beecher, the sister of Harriet Beecher Stowe, the abolitionist who wrote *Uncle Tom's Cabin*, was also an advocate for education of women. She believed that all women should have access to education, and that they were the natural schoolteachers for young children.[3] For most of the nineteenth century, girls received single-gender education, but only if their parents approved and could afford it.

The Progressive Movement in the early 1900s provided the ultimate push to make public education open to all, and compulsory throughout the United States. Just as the juvenile court was created both to care for youth and to control immigrant children, the drive for universal public education was partly to ensure that the right "American" values were instilled in masses of immigrant youth. Public school laws were also a way to eliminate public funding for private and parochial, particularly Catholic, schools that had sprung up around the country. By the mid-twentieth century, all states required girls and boys to attend public school, at least through the eighth grade.

In the South segregated schools remained the norm until 1954, when the landmark Supreme Court case of *Brown v. Board of Education of Topeka* struck down the notion that segregated black and white schools could be separate but equal. The Court unanimously found that even if black and white schools provided equal education (which they did not), segregation itself was harmful to black students and unconstitutional under the Fourteenth Amendment. In the middle of the twentieth century, the Supreme Court required the racial integration of all publicly funded schools from elementary to high school to college, and all across the South angry whites protested the arrival of black students in previously all-white schools. In the North, de facto racial segregation was tied to residential segregation of blacks and whites. Efforts in the 1970s to integrate schools through forced busing also fueled racial tensions and conflict among whites and blacks within many Northern urban communities.

Today, public education from kindergarten through high school is a universal public program that most US citizens believe is essential. Each state has their own compulsory education law, which starts at age six and typically ends at age seventeen, though there are some exceptions. For example, Amish children are only required to attend some form of schooling through the eighth grade. Title IX of the Education Amendments Act in 1972 requires all students, including girls and youth of color, be granted equal access to education at the primary, secondary, and collegiate levels.[4] Yet, school segregation based on racially segregated residential neighborhood patterns remains a significant challenge to the American dream of equal education for all. Many inner-city school systems are more racially segregated today than they were in the 1950s when the Supreme Court ruled against legal segregation in *Brown v. Board of Education.*[5]

Although the United States was at the forefront of creating a universal education system, internationally, it is increasingly falling behind academically.[6] Certain schools are left even further behind. These schools are located in the poorer communities, often urban, and predominantly serving youth of color. Because local property taxes almost fully fund public schools, in poor communities with fewer tax dollars, schools lack substantial resources to provide equal opportunities.

Inequality and Academic Achievement

In the twenty-first century, educational attainment through college is increasingly necessary to achieve the "American Dream" of a stable job and family life. Data consistently show that college graduates earn far more than those with a high school diploma. The latest figures show that even after calculating the cost of college, those with bachelor's degrees earn over their lifetime in excess of $800,000 more than high school graduates.[7] Table 7.1 shows the education attainment level of persons in the United States ages twenty-five and older. These data are illustrative of a few things. First, whites generally have slightly higher high school achievement levels, but when we examine college achievement, we see that Asians are more likely to obtain degrees. Native Americans, while included in the Asian category by the federal government, have completion rates on par with Hispanics, who are the lowest-achieving category. Overall, black and Hispanic females fare better than their male ethnic counterparts in achieving higher-education diplomas.

Clearly, race, ethnicity, class, and gender are all related to who is likely to succeed in school and who is likely to drop out. Table 7.1 shows that Hispanics are most likely to drop out.[8] When children arrive in kindergarten, those from poor backgrounds are already behind their more-advantaged peers in knowledge, language acquisition, and social skills.[9] Children from disadvantaged backgrounds also have higher rates of special education and grade repetition. Chronic absences due to family dysfunction, residential instability, or homelessness also interfere with learning and increase the likelihood that a child will drop out of school.

For some youth, school conflicts with responsibilities at home. Youth may leave school to help support their families, especially if they are from single-parent, mother-headed households. Astonishingly, 51 percent of entering

TABLE 7.1	Educational Achievement by Ethnicity and Gender			
	High School Diploma		**Bachelor's Degree**	
	Male	**Female**	**Male**	**Female**
White	92.7%	93.2%	36.0%	34.4%
Black	84.9%	86.6%	20.2%	23.4%
Hispanic	64.6%	67.9%	13.9%	16.2%
Asian / Pacific Islander*	91.7%	88.9%	56.9%	51.3%

*Includes Native Americans, who have the lowest completion rates in the category, with rates on par with Hispanics.

high school freshmen in 2009 also held down full-time jobs while they were attending school.[10] Balancing full-time school with full-time work is a feat for any individual, especially for still-maturing youth. These students may get fewer hours of needed rest, and both school performance and their overall health and well-being are negatively affected.

Parents, who themselves have not achieved at least a high school diploma, typically are not as likely to encourage their children to finish school as parents with high school diplomas. For those families whose primary language is not English, school may be a particularly inhospitable place where youth feel destined for failure; thus, they may leave school early to find social support elsewhere, particularly on the street.[11] Schools, too, can be a culprit in dropout decisions, from harsh disciplinary rules that "push out" students to curriculum and school policies that alienate students from diverse backgrounds. Unfortunately, as we have seen from the beginning of the chapter, the history of American education is one of exclusion and isolation.

Youth who drop out of school are consistently shown to have poorer life outcomes in terms of physical and mental health and in terms of earning potential. Dropouts are more likely to access social services and earn less, affecting those far from their immediate families and neighborhoods. Further, black male high school dropouts are more likely to be sentenced to incarceration when all other factors are equal, showing the importance of education for justice system avoidance.[12]

DELINQUENCY AND SCHOOL FAILURE

There is a strong correlation, or relationship, between school failure and delinquency. Children who are chronic underachievers in school are among the most likely to become delinquent.[13] There are three possible relationships between doing poorly in school and engaging in delinquent behavior. First, it is possible that youth who do poorly in school become angry and frustrated at school failure and react by engaging in delinquent activities. This is a direct relationship in which academic failure leads to delinquency. This may be especially true for those with learning disabilities. Approximately 13 percent of public school students in primary or secondary education have learning disabilities, while that figure rises to 45 to 60 percent among youth held in the juvenile justice system.[14]

Alternatively, the relationship may be causal, but indirect, where youth who struggle academically are likely to be grouped with other struggling youth. Because they are together in alternative classrooms, these youth are likely to bond and engage in delinquency. Students who academically struggle also may be more likely to be suspended, leading to more unsupervised free time with other youth and young adults who may be involved in delinquent behavior.[15]

A final possibility is that students who struggle with academics may have negative relationships with teachers, which in turn leads them to reject school in favor of hanging out with delinquent peers. In all of these examples, the relationship is causal, but indirect: School failure increases the conditions—such as hanging out with peers away from supervising adults—that lead to delinquent behavior.

The relationship between school failure and delinquency also could be spurious, meaning that both variables are related to another variable that is causing the change.[16] The same factors that cause school failure, such as family dysfunction, neighborhood violence, poverty, or poor nutrition, also influence delinquent behavior. A large body of research finds support for all of these possible relationships, with no clear answers. Regardless of the causal pattern, however, the link between school failure and delinquency is well established.

School and Crime

The events at Columbine and other highly publicized school shootings raise a serious question: How safe are our schools? The National Center for Education Statistics reveals that in the 2013–2014 school year, there were twenty-six homicides and twenty suicides among both students and staff that took place on school grounds.[17] This may sound dramatic, but amounts to less than 2 percent of all youth homicides. This figure has remained constant over time, despite the increase in media coverage associated with Columbine and other school shootings.[18]

Another way to measure school crime is through the National Crime Victimization Survey, School Crime Supplement. Data show that while lethal violence is rare in school, there are a substantial number of other crimes reported at school by youth ages twelve to eighteen. Of those crimes, theft is the most common. In 2015, 33 students out of every 1,000 reported victimization at school, compared with 22 out of 1,000 who reported out-of-school victimizations. On average, about 3 percent of all students report being victimized at school during the last six months. Serious victimizations, such as aggravated assaults and larceny, are slightly more likely to happen outside of school. Figure 7.1 shows the rate of victimization at school and away from school for every 1,000 students from 1995 to 2013.[19]

In general, the number of students engaging in physical fighting has dropped from the early 1990s to 2013; approximately 8 percent of students in 2013 reported

FIGURE 7.1

Student Nonfatal Victimization Rate, Ages 12 to 18

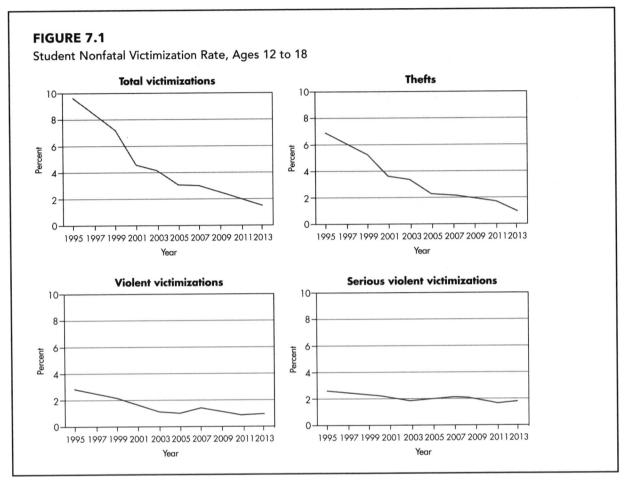

being in a physical fight in the last year, with more ninth graders reporting fights than those in upper grades.[20] Asian students report the least amount of fighting, followed by white students. As you might expect, males are more likely to engage in physical fights than females; 30 percent of males report being in a fight during the last year, compared with 19 percent of females.

Another question about school crime is how safe students feel while at school. Fear of school crime and violence can affect students' mental health as well as their ability to learn. Data show that 3 percent of students fear being victimized at school and 3 percent fear being victimized outside of school.[21] School is a space of safety for most students, but for a small percentage, school is seen as a place of danger. One of the key responses to the Columbine tragedy was a massive influx of security measures, such as metal detectors, security guards, police officers, and cameras. Between the 1996–1997 and 2007–2008 school years, the number of public high schools with full-time law enforcement and security guards tripled. Ironically, research shows that the presence of these security measures increases fear among students, rather than making them feel safer.[22]

Approximately 5 percent of students carry weapons on school grounds, and that has decreased since the early 2000s. The majority of students who carry weapons report doing so for safety reasons.[23] It is difficult to reconcile how to keep schools safe without raising more fear among students, and without students feeling as though they need to carry weapons for safety. Students who report gang presence in their schools are also more likely to feel fearful while at school.

Gangs, Weapons, and Drugs

Twelve percent of students report gang presence in their schools, and approximately 5 to 7 percent of high school students are gang members.[24] Schools are often recruiting grounds for gangs, and this is particularly true of some gangs, such as 18th Street.[25] Gang conflicts can also spill over from the community into the schools. Gang members are more likely to have behavioral problems in school; more likely to carry weapons; and more likely to use or sell drugs in schools.[26] Some gang members may engage in delinquent activity, however, not on behalf of their gangs, but for personal reasons. Thus, it is important for schools to focus on the behaviors and the needs of students who may be gang members, rather than on the fact that they are members of a gang.[27] At the same time, the presence of gangs is highly correlated with more security measures, higher levels of school crime, and increased safety fears among students.

School rampage shootings have led to heated debates about gun control. Both Colorado and Connecticut attempted to pass gun control legislation after such tragedies. The Colorado legislation was not successful, while legislation in Connecticut after the Sandy Hook massacre in Newtown passed with some modifications. The National Rifle Association (NRA) and its affiliates have spent large sums of money to ensure that access to guns is not restricted, and limit funding of research that addresses the effects of guns in society.[28] The effects of the lobbying arm of the NRA are one large reason why such measures have not passed.

As we see in the Columbine case, guns are relatively easy to obtain for those who are intent on doing so, even those who are underage, such as Harris and Klebold. This leads some to argue that gun legislation that restricts access is likely to have little impact on school or youth violence.[29] At the same time, smart technology—in the form of fingerprint identification that ensures guns can only be fired by legal owners—might prove to be more effective if the gun industry and the public are willing to adopt it. Such technological advances may hold promise in reducing violence by guns, but we also must examine the demand for guns themselves, and address the reasons why youth feel compelled to use them.

UNDERSTANDING SCHOOL RAMPAGES

Although the massacre at Columbine was of unprecedented scale and horror, it was not the first of its kind to hit the nation's schools. The US Secret Service's National Threat Assessment Center identified thirty-seven targeted-violence school shootings that occurred in the United States between 1974 and 2000.[30] Their report on school safety defines "targeted violence" as instances where the attacker was either a student or former student who deliberately chose the school as the site for the attack. The "target" of attack is often the social order among the students at the school, or the authority structure at the school itself.

Sociologist Katherine Newman calls a mass school shooting a "rampage," and argues that it is fundamentally different from the school violence that comes from a gang shooting, drug deal, or personal argument.[31] In the latter cases, the fact that the violence happens on school grounds is incidental. Rampage killings are different. In this kind of violence, the target is the school community itself. The killing takes place on a school-related public stage before an audience; there are generally multiple victims—some of whom are random, while others are chosen for their symbolic value as representative of some hated clique or group; and the perpetrators themselves are students or former students.

Who is the real target in school shootings like this? Similar to the Secret Service report, Newman finds that it is the entire school community, specifically, the hated social order which relegates some individuals to the top of the ladder and others to the bottom. Upper-middle-class Columbine High School is a far cry from the typical inner-city school associated with violence. But rampages are unlikely in inner-city schools. They occur almost exclusively in suburban and rural schools.

Rampages follow a relatively distinctive pattern, and Columbine was no exception. According to the Secret Service report, there is little to distinguish those who are planning these kinds of rampages from other teens at the school.[32] Youth who commit most other types of violence fit a predictable profile. They are youth with a history of neglect, broken families, abandonment, and victimization at the hands of adults. They have behavioral issues in school and tend to get in trouble with the law early and often. Rampage shooters, however, are almost always, at least on the surface, indistinguishable from other kids. Klebold and Harris appeared to be "normal" kids.

According to the Secret Service, however, rampages are never sudden or spontaneous events. Shooters have generally planned the crime in advance. They have talked about it; written about it; and often revealed pieces of the plans to other students. Most rampage perpetrators are generally obsessed with violence and weapons, and have access to those weapons. This obsession shows up in their writings in school, homemade videos, their choice of movies and books, as well as in conversations with friends.

Klebold and Harris were both obsessed with violence. For about a year before the actual attack, both boys kept journals in which they detailed their progress in creating explosives. They were inspired by the Oklahoma City bombing, in which 168 people died and hundreds were injured, and they hoped to achieve a level of destruction that would rival that massive explosion. Their journals revealed plans for escaping to Mexico by hijacking an aircraft, and even an idea about crashing the plane into buildings in New York City.

A key characteristic of school rampages, according to the Secret Service, is that many school shooters feel bullied or persecuted by other students and are often struggling to cope with a recent emotional loss, personal failure, or sense of social rejection. Psychologist James Garbarino believes that school shooters engage in a desperate bid to end their psychological pain through violence.[33] Despite outward appearances, did Harris and Klebold secretly hate the social order of their school community? Did they feel excluded or rejected by the student body? Harris and Klebold left abundant evidence that this was exactly how they felt. The videotapes reveal intense resentment at a litany of perceived rejections, insults, exclusions, and harassments by those at the top of the Columbine High pecking order. Like most school shooters, they felt bullied, persecuted, and oppressed, especially by wealthy student "jocks" who they believed were glorified and favored in the school environment as well as in the wider community.

Almost all of the perpetrators of rampage violence are male.[34] The desire to prove one's "masculinity," which may be called into question by poor athletic ability or lack of success with girls, is a common factor in the background of many of the youth who embark on these murderous rampages. The school is a stage where they enact the role of the masculine avenger, sending a message to all those who mistakenly thought they were "wimps" or "weak." That image is ubiquitous in the popular media, and is enacted over and over again in films like *Natural Born Killers*, which Klebold and Harris watched obsessively.

The use of guns is a central prop in that script, and easy access to guns is what makes it all possible. Most school shooters acquired their guns either from their own home or the home of a relative. Klebold and Harris acquired their guns from friends and other acquaintances old enough to purchase them legally. A fellow employee where Harris worked, Phillip Duran, along with his friend, Michael Manes, helped purchase the semiautomatic assault weapons for Harris and Klebold. A third acquaintance, Robyn Anderson, bought three guns at a local gun show.

Why did no one notice what Harris and Klebold were doing? In most school rampages, there are many warning signs, disturbing events, and troubling behavior that, in retrospect, foreshadow the horrific outburst. Yet these "leakages" typically are overlooked, ignored, or dismissed as insignificant, partly because no one person is in a position to see all the warning signs before it is too late. The Secret Service report recommends that schools and police, especially school resource officers, learn to share information. They acknowledge the importance of protecting student privacy, but in too many of the school rampage shootings, there are bits and pieces of information which, when put together, give a clear picture of a troubled adolescent. While it might be easy to shrug off one incident or unsettling interaction, the overall pattern would signal the need for intervention.

The Secret Service report also warns that profiling is not likely to be an effective approach because there is no typical "profile" of a potential school shooter. Instead of trying to identify a "type" of student who might commit violence, schools need to focus on troublesome behaviors. Again, the key is to share information across different entities, including the school, the family, and law enforcement. But the most important source of information sharing that needs to take place is between adolescents and adults. In almost all of the school rampages, there were students who knew about the violent threats, death lists, weapons, experiments with explosives, disturbing behavior, and secret plans. Often the students are unsure if a person is just showing off or joking, or if they really intend to take action. In fact, the prevalence of violent talk among adolescents makes it hard to distinguish between those who are just talking from those who might mean what they say.

Yet, in the aftermath of many of these shootings, there are many students who may have had strong feelings that something was unusually wrong. These students fail to notify adults before it is too late because of the student ethos to refrain from snitching on one another. Addressing this "code of silence" among adolescents is identified as one area where prevention efforts might genuinely help to keep schools safe from these kinds of attacks.[35] The challenge, according to the Secret Service, is to build a bond of trust between adults and young people in the schools. Adolescents need to know that they can turn to adults with their suspicions and that they will be treated with confidentiality and respect.

One component of building a culture of respect is getting serious about addressing bullying. An attitude on the part of adults that this kind of behavior is "normal" and "inevitable" fuels the misperception that bullying is acceptable.

School shooters often come to the conclusion that they have no escape other than through violence.

BULLYING

Bullying became part of the American lexicon in the 1990s as a result of its perceived connection to school rampages like Columbine. **Bullying** is abuse that is physical, verbal, and/or emotional that is repeated and causes someone physical or psychological discomfort.[36] The goal of bullying is to exert control over someone who is perceived to be weaker. The classic case of bullying is one in which a student hits or pushes a weaker student with the intent to cause bodily harm. Verbal abuse includes taunting, name-calling, or making fun of another; while emotional abuse can consist of actions such as purposeful exclusion from activities and isolation. These types of bullying behaviors often occur together. Bullying can have negative effects not only on those being bullied, but also on those doing the bullying, and bystanders, as well.

The problems of bullying and a culture of intolerance for diversity in schools are widely associated with school rampages. There were reports that Klebold and Harris had been subjected to a humiliating incident in which they were covered in ketchup and called "faggots" in the cafeteria by popular jocks while adults watched without intervening. There are others who dispute that this happened, and point out that these two boys were more often the ones doing the bullying.

About 22 percent of students reported being bullied at school in 2013.[37] This includes name-calling, starting rumors, purposeful exclusion, as well as threats of physical harm. Whites were most likely to report being bullied (25 percent), and Asians were the least likely to report being bullied (12 percent). Girls were slightly more likely to report bullying than boys. Bullying is most likely to occur during the middle school years and declines progressively during the high school years. Further, approximately 8 percent of all **hate crimes** happened at school in 2015.[38] More students of color reported being victims of hate-related words than did white students.

The effects of bullying and hate speech can include anxiety, fear, stress, psychological and/or physical pain, as well as poor school performance and decreased connection to school.[39] Youth who are bullies often engage in other high-risk behaviors, including using drugs and alcohol and early sexual activity; and they are likely to have juvenile and criminal justice system involvement.[40] Youth who witness bullying also are not immune. **Bystanders** to bullying are more likely to miss school and to have mental health problems than those who have not witnessed it.[41] Bullying can ultimately lead to death, as in the case of Columbine. Bullying can also result in suicide by the victim, as in the case of Phoebe Prince from South Hadley, Massachusetts, in 2012, who took her own life after she was bullied both in person and online by at least nine schoolmates.

There is growing concern over cyberbullying, which happens through electronic media. **Cyberbullying** includes the posting of derogatory remarks and pictures, or hurtful texts, instant, or e-mail messages. Victims often experience shame as a result of the bullying.[42] Unless parents or guardians are privy to their child's electronic communication, such bullying can go unnoticed. The proliferation of social media, its penetration into daily life, and the relative anonymity

BULLYING
Abuse that is physical, verbal, and/or emotional that is repeated and causes someone physical or psychological discomfort.

HATE CRIME
A crime motivated by prejudice that involves violence.

BYSTANDERS
Those present at an event who do not take part in it.

CYBERBULLYING
Electronic media posting of derogatory remarks and pictures, or hurtful texts, instant, or e-mail messages.

of the medium has increased the power of this kind of bullying behavior. Cyber-bullying is often reported in school crime statistics because it generally starts at school.[43] During the latest year for which there are public statistics, 9 percent of students reported being cyberbullied at some point during the school year. White students were more likely to report being cyberbullied than other students; and females were slightly more likely to report being cyberbullied than males. Males who reported bullying once, however, were more likely to report repeated bullying incidents.

As we have so often heard before, few students report the victimization. Less than half of students notified an adult that bullying was taking place. Females were more likely than males to do so, but most students—60 percent of them—did not tell adults. This raises questions about why students do not report harmful behavior to adults. If life had been different at Columbine High School for Harris and Klebold, or if either of the boys had connected with a positive adult, could the events of that terrible day been avoided? If other students had felt comfortable confiding in adults, could it have been possible to prevent the boys from executing their terrible plans?

Most states have enacted legislation that requires schools to take overt steps to prevent bullying and to respond to it when it does occur. Positive school climates, in which the atmosphere is warm and welcoming, parent-teacher conferences, and restorative circles may be part of an effective solution to bullying problems.[44] Promising school-based strategies to prevent bullying and to address problem behaviors are discussed at the end of the chapter.

SCHOOL CLIMATE

Schools are often a cornerstone of communities, a place for gathering and networking, and building bridges between individuals and institutions. One way to buffer against the deeply embedded problem of school exclusion is for schools to create a welcoming climate for all. Schools as social institutions have effects on the behavior of individuals who are connected to them. Seemingly mundane factors, such as the structure, organization, and climate of a school, can have powerful human effects that translate into action and inaction. We expect schools to prepare youth intellectually and socially while keeping them safe physically and psychologically while in the school's care. How can we ensure that schools meet the challenges of providing quality education and building a culture of care for our students in the modern age?

The National School Climate Center refers to **school climate** as the quality and character of school life based on perceptions of students, school personnel, and parents. School climate goes beyond learning and teaching to address interpersonal relationships, school norms, and school goals.[45] School climate is about the safety and relational aspects of the institution between and among individuals and the school's policies. School climate has a powerful effect on learning and on school delinquency.

A positive school climate goes hand in hand with positive youth development, and it includes the following: a) norms, values, and expectations that support people feeling socially, emotionally, and physically safe; b) engaged and respectful people; c) collaboration among students, families, and educators to develop, live, and contribute to a shared school vision; and d) modeling and nurturing

SCHOOL CLIMATE
The quality and character of school life based on perceptions of students, school personnel, and parents.

educators' attitudes that emphasize the benefits and satisfaction gained from learning.[46] In this way, each person contributes to the operations of the school and the care of the physical environment.

Schools reflect the community, in part, but they also can create an environment that is somewhat insulated from what happens in the community. As in the case of Canada (Case Study 4), the latter can be extremely important for youth who are exposed to chronic violence in their homes and neighborhoods. Yet, school rampage violence, such as Columbine, as well as interpersonal violence, such as verbal abuse between two students, is affected by the school climate. So the solution also lies within the school itself.

The purpose of schools has always been to educate students. As we saw from the history of schools, however, the latent function early on was to promote a particular Anglo-centered value system. Today, those "other" functions of developing students to be socially responsible and caring adults have become even more salient and important. Some may argue that it is unreasonable to place these burdens on schools, but most point out that schools have always been a place where societal values are transmitted and reinforced.[47]

A positive school climate has been linked to increases in student well-being, better interpersonal relationships, and more motivation to learn.[48] Less harassment and an increased perception of safety also is related to positive school climate. The importance of school climate factors varies by ethnicity. Latinos put more emphasis on teachers' fairness and the moral code of the school, while blacks rate student-teacher relationships more strongly than others.[49] The take-home message from this body of work is that schools must pay attention to the atmosphere of their institutions, and while the perceptions of factors related to school climate differ, schools should incorporate policies and ways of teaching and interacting that are both responsive to different cultures and consistent with a positive youth development approach for all students.

Social and Emotional Development and Schools

Positive school experiences buffer against delinquency and drug use and increase the likelihood of quality employment. These effects are particularly strong for girls.[50] Conversely, we have learned that school failure and lack of **school connectedness** are risk factors for delinquency and gang membership. Importantly, how teachers interact with students and their expectations for success for students can affect student school performance and feelings about school. Those students who are learning-disabled and who are perceived as problematic, often children of color from the lower class, are not encouraged to succeed and are placed in tracked, lower-achieving classrooms, further isolating and alienating them from mainstream society.[51] As discussed, this may lead to delinquency through classroom placement with deviant youth, negative labeling, and poor treatment.

School curriculum must be relevant to all students for critical social and emotional development to take place.[52] It was not long ago that school textbooks contained nothing about the persecution of Native Americans in the conquest of the United States, or Japanese internment camps during World War II; nor did most textbooks honestly cover issues of racial discrimination or the contribution of people of color to our nation's intellectual, artistic, and political achievements. Many students forced to read material about the proverbial blond-haired and

SCHOOL CONNECTEDNESS
Belief by students that adults at school care about students' learning and well-being.

blue-eyed "Dick and Jane," who portrayed a story so starkly different from their own reality, could not relate well enough to the characters to absorb and apply what they had learned. True **cultural competence** teaching and learning in schools can only be accomplished through exposure. Incorporation of cultural heritages and diversity are increasingly part of school curriculum, though the extent to which that is covered certainly varies across schools. Embracing cultural differences is key to creating a welcoming, positive school climate for all students in which social and emotional learning can take place.

DISCIPLINE AND THE SCHOOL-TO-PRISON PIPELINE

The violence at Columbine High School, along with other highly publicized school shootings, contributed to an increase in rigid disciplinary policies at schools across the nation, known as **zero-tolerance policies**. The idea of zero tolerance originated in the 1980s when the US military declared that there would be swift and harsh penalties for use of any illegal drugs in any amount by US military personnel. The purpose of this policy was to replace the attitude of tolerance toward recreational marijuana use with a blanket prohibition on illegal substances. This philosophy was first applied to schools with the passage of the federal Gun-Free Schools Act in 1994, which required all states to pass laws requiring school districts to automatically expel any student, for at least one year, who brings a weapon to school.

After Columbine, many school districts adopted zero-tolerance approaches, not just for weapons or drugs, but in response to all disciplinary infractions, including minor ones, such as disrespect, truancy, or disruption of school assemblies.[53] By the 1996–1997 school year, 79 percent of US schools had adopted zero-tolerance policies for all forms of violence, including schoolyard fights, pushing and shoving in the hallways, and cafeteria food fights. These policies went far beyond the original federal mandates. Nationally, the number of secondary school students suspended or expelled over the course of a school year increased roughly 40 percent, from one in thirteen in 1972–1973, to one in nine in 2009–2010.[54] Today, almost 32 percent of males in high school report having been suspended or expelled compared to approximately 16 percent of females.[55] Disability intersects with school discipline. Students with learning disabilities are twice as likely to receive out-of-school suspensions than students without disabilities.[56]

Major studies comparing schools with zero-tolerance policies and schools with more-flexible policies have found no credible evidence that zero tolerance either increases school safety or reduces misbehavior among students.[57] The research, however, has shown a substantial negative impact of zero-tolerance policies on certain segments of the school population—namely, youth of color. The term **school-to-prison pipeline** refers to the dynamic in which youth, especially youth of color, are literally pushed out of school through excessive and repeated suspensions and pushed into the adult prison system, starting with juvenile justice system involvement. The first step in the pipeline is being disciplined through multiple suspensions that disrupt learning, reduce school attachment, and increase hostility with adults at school.[58]

Research shows that zero-tolerance policies target children of color. Black youth receive 48 percent of out-of-school suspensions.[59] Teachers in

CULTURAL COMPETENCE
Incorporating cultural heritage and diversity within the curriculum and school environment to create welcoming school communities for students of all backgrounds.

ZERO-TOLERANCE POLICIES
Strict enforcement of severe consequences, such as suspension and expulsion, for prohibited behavior regardless of circumstances.

SCHOOL-TO-PRISON PIPELINE
Concept wherein youth are pushed out of school and into the justice system through harsh school policies.

under-resourced urban schools are more likely to respond to misbehavior with a punitive response compared to teachers in more affluent, suburban schools.[60] Overall, about 5 percent of white students are suspended compared to 16 percent of black students.[61] Nationally, nearly one-third (31 percent) of black youth in middle school were suspended at least once during the 2009–2010 school year.[62]

It is not difficult to understand the connection between multiple suspensions and more juvenile justice system involvement. Time away from the classroom undermines learning, and the more a student falls behind, the less likely he is to cooperate in the classroom. This sets off a vicious cycle that contributes to academic failure and dropping out of school. Research shows that a single suspension in the ninth grade doubles the likelihood a student will eventually drop out of school.[63] Those students who receive out-of-school suspensions are often those least likely to have an adult at home to supervise them. As discussed, when left on their own without adult supervision during the day, youth bond with other excluded youth, which can increase their involvement in delinquent behaviors. Youth who are alienated from adults both in school and at home are much more susceptible to joining gangs and engaging in drugs, theft, and other kinds of crime.[64]

Police in Schools

Many critics argue that security measures, including zero-tolerance policies, have led to the criminalization of the school environment, increasing the number of youth entering the juvenile justice system through school referrals. Contributing to this trend has been the growing presence of police officers assigned to schools. Upwards of 90 percent of schools have either police or security officers on school premises.[65] Police officers stationed at schools are typically known as **school resource officers** (SROs), though some locations may use other terms, such as school liaison officers. The main task of SROs is to ensure the safety of the school, but they are also sometimes charged with developing positive relationships with students. SROs may teach classes such as D.A.R.E. or G.R.E.A.T. to students, though outside police officers may come in to conduct those classes. (D.A.R.E. and G.R.E.A.T. programs are discussed in chapter 8.) Depending on the agreement between police departments and school departments, the exact duties of SROs may vary; some SROs may respond immediately to any student conflict, while others may wait until the school administration calls upon them to do so.

Schools in which administrators maintain control over when incidents are referred to the police are much more likely to resolve the incident at school, without juvenile justice system involvement.[66] When SROs are given the authority to respond to youthful misconduct, however, youth are more likely to be arrested and sent to juvenile court. SROs often respond with arrests, even for minor transgressions such as pushing in the hallways or disturbing a classroom by swearing.[67] The result is that many youth whose actions would have otherwise been dealt with at the school by teachers and principals are now caught up in the juvenile justice system for minor offenses. As we will see in chapter 9, there are serious negative consequences for youth when they are referred to juvenile court.

As SROs increasingly become part of the school landscape, it is clear that those who build positive relationships with students and staff are the most effective at

SCHOOL RESOURCE OFFICERS (SROS)
Police officers who are assigned to work in schools.

their jobs.[68] Not all police, however, are trained in such a non-authoritative role. Typical police training does not include information about adolescent development, peer dynamics, or mental health issues. In the case of Harris and Klebold, we are left to wonder about the relationship of the SRO with students in that school. SRO Neil Gardner was notified by the sheriff's department about the violent website Harris had created. Yet he only observed the two boys and did not speak with them or attempt to build a relationship. Nor did he reach out to the student who told his parents about the boys' plans. Would the outcome have been different for the families of Columbine High School if their SRO had chosen to have conversations with these boys?

SCHOOL-BASED PROGRAMS FOR POSITIVE CHANGE

Several school-based behavioral interventions and dropout prevention programs have been developed to counteract the negative outcomes discussed in this chapter. Some of these programs address the social and emotional needs of youth believed to be part of the root causes of behavioral problems in schools. Other school programs attempt to address the overall school climate and offer alternatives to the use of exclusionary forms of discipline.

The international Olweus Bullying Prevention Program is among the most successful school-based interventions in increasing positive school climate and reducing bullying and antisocial behaviors among students.[69] In this program, elementary and middle school students are exposed to messages in school and in the community that encourage positive peer relationships and connections to adults. Students talk about bullying in a supervised environment with their peers. Individual attention is provided to students who have been bullied, as well as to those who did the bullying.

Positive Action is another school-based program that has been shown to increase positive behaviors, improve social and emotional learning, and promote a positive school climate.[70] The program is administered in classrooms to children ages five to fourteen, teaching them to understand their anger cues and utilizing anger management techniques. Students also practice how to positively interact with others. Positive Action has been shown to work across ethnic lines, though it may be slightly more effective in reducing violence and sexual activity for boys than for girls.[71]

Another major school-based program implemented in an attempt to reduce the overuse of suspensions and expulsions is restorative practices. Restorative justice was covered in chapter 3, and restorative practices are an outgrowth of that. Restorative practices are methods to address behaviors and process feelings. **Restorative circles** within the classroom, among students, staff, and parents, help to establish positive norms and develop a sense of belonging and connection among the students. By building a strong community, these practices develop an attachment to the school that increases academic achievement and positive social behavior among students.[72]

When a disciplinary response is needed, restorative conferences, along with peer mediation and other forms of conflict resolution, bring the wrongdoer and the victim face-to-face to discuss the incident in order to resolve it through constructive actions designed to repair the relationship. With traditional suspensions, students return to school without having resolved the issues that led

RESTORATIVE CIRCLES
A restorative practice to establish positive norms and develop a sense of belonging and connection, resolve conflict, and provide alternatives to exclusionary discipline.

to the suspension. If there was a fight between students, the hostility is still there when the students come back; if there was a disruption in the classroom, angry feelings between the teacher and the student often persist long after the student has returned to the classroom. These hurt and angry feelings undermine learning and positive attachment to school. A restorative conference restores the relationship so that strong bonds to the school community are preserved or re-created.

Based on these principles, the state of Minnesota implemented legislation and guidelines about how to produce positive outcomes and develop healthy youth in the school setting.[73] Adopting schoolwide behavior systems where there are genuine and consistent conversations among students, parents, and staff; creating behavioral expectations that are fair and equitable; and reaching beyond the school walls to connect with students and their families in the community are key ways to encourage healthy youth development. The overall goal is to create inclusive schools where students, staff, and visitors feel welcome and are an integral part of the process.

Schools are an important focus in any book devoted to understanding youth, crime, and justice, and an impactful touchstone in the lives of young people. When we think about prevention and intervention to help young people, schools play a critical role. Policies such as zero tolerance have undermined the mission of positive youth development by creating tense atmospheres that criminalize normal adolescent behavior. It is clear from tragedies like Columbine that positive connections between students and staff are a key element to realizing the mission of schools as educational and socializing institutions.

KEY TERMS

bullying Abuse that is physical, verbal, and/or emotional that is repeated and causes someone physical or psychological discomfort.

bystanders Those present at an event who do not take part in it.

cultural competence Incorporating cultural heritage and diversity within the curriculum and school environment to create welcoming school communities for students of all backgrounds.

cyberbullying Electronic media posting of derogatory remarks and pictures, or hurtful texts, instant, or e-mail messages.

hate crime A crime motivated by prejudice that involves violence.

restorative circles A restorative practice to establish positive norms and develop a sense of belonging and connection, resolve conflict, and provide alternatives to exclusionary discipline.

school climate The quality and character of school life based on perceptions of students, school personnel, and parents.

school connectedness Belief by students that adults at school care about students' learning and well-being.

school-to-prison pipeline Concept wherein youth are pushed out of school and into the justice system through harsh school policies.

school resource officers (SROs) Police officers who are assigned to work in schools.

zero-tolerance policies Strict enforcement of severe consequences, such as suspension and expulsion, for prohibited behavior regardless of circumstances.

REVIEW AND STUDY QUESTIONS

1. Access to public education is one of the key means for creating an equal society. Using the lens of intersectionality, discuss the differential access to education by race, class, ethnicity, and gender in American history.

2. Explain the impact of race, ethnicity, class, and gender on who is likely to succeed in school and who is likely to drop out.

3. Describe the three possible relationships between poor school performance and engaging in delinquent behavior.

4. Are students safe from crime at school? Explain your answer.

5. What are the sociological origins of school rampages? What do you think are the best strategies to prevent school rampages?

6. Define the concept of bullying. How extensive is bullying, and what are the most effective forms of prevention and intervention?

7. What is school climate, and why is it important for positive youth development? How are school climate and student connectedness important for the prevention of bullying and delinquency?

8. How do schools play an important role in delinquency prevention and positive youth development? Describe restorative justice programs within the school environment.

9. What are zero-tolerance policies, and what has been the impact of these policies? Using the lens of intersectionality, discuss which students have been the primary target of these policies.

10. What is the role of school resource officers in public education? What has been the impact of increasing police presence within the school community?

CHECK IT OUT

Watch

Bowling for Columbine (2002)

School: The Story of American Public Education (2001)

Waiting for Superman (2010)

Read

Case: *Brown v. Board of Education of Topeka* (1954)

NOTES

[1] Gracey, H. L. (2004). Learning the Student Role: Kindergarten as Academic Boot Camp. In J. H. Ballantine and J. Z. Spade (eds.), *Schools and Society: A Sociological Approach to Education* (2nd ed.), 144–48. Belmont, CA: Wadsworth.

[2] Mondale, S. (ed.). (2001). *School: The Story of American Public Education*. Boston, MA: Beacon Press.

[3] White, B. (2003). *The Beecher Sisters*. London: Yale University Press.

[4] US Department of Justice. (2012). *Equal Access to Education: Forty Years of Title IX*. Washington, DC: Author.

[5] Madigan, J. C. (2009). The Education of Girls and Women in the United States: A Historical Perspective. *Advances in Gender and Education, 1,* 11–13.

[6] Index of Cognitive Skills and Educational Attainment. Available at http://thelearningcurve.pearson.com/index/index-ranking.

[7] Barrow, L., and Rouse C. E. (2005). Does College Still Pay? *The Economist's Voice, 2,* 1–8.

[8] Ibid.

[9] Rumberger, R. W. (2011). *Dropping Out: Why Students Drop Out of High School and What Can Be Done about It*. Cambridge, MA: Harvard University Press.

[10] Dalton, B., Ingels, S. J., Fritch, L., and Christopher, E. M. (2015). *High School Longitudinal Study of 2009 (HSLS:09) 2013 Update and High School Transcript Study: A First Look at Fall 2009 Ninth-Graders in 2013*. Available at http://nces.ed.gov/pubs2015/2015037.pdf.

[11] Conchas, G. Q., and Vigil, J. D. (2010). Multiple Marginality and Urban Education: Community and School Socialization among Low-Income Mexican-Descent Youth. *Journal of Education for Students Placed at Risk, 15,* 51–65.

[12] Ibid.

[13] Hoffman, J. P., Erickson, L. D., and Spence, K. R. (2013). Modeling the Association Between Academic Achievement and Delinquency: An Application of Interactional Theory. *Criminology, 51,* 629–60.

[14] US Department of Education, National Center for Education Statistics. (2015). *Digest of Education Statistics, 2013* (NCES 2015-011), chapter 2; National Institute of Child Health and Human Development. Cognition, Brain Function, and Learning in Incarceration Youth Workshop July 2010. Available at www.nichd.nih.gov/about/meetings/2010/pages/72310.aspx.

[15] Achilles, G. M., McLaughlin, M. J., and Croninger, R. (2007). Sociocultural Correlates of Disciplinary Exclusion among Students with Emotional, Behavioral, and Learning Disabilities in the SEELS National Dataset. *Journal of Emotional and Behavioral Disorders, 15,* 33–45.

[16] Simons, R. L., Whitbeck, W. B., Conger, R. D., and Conger, K. J. (1991). Parenting Factors, Social Skills, and Value Commitments as Precursors to School Failure, Involvement with Deviant Peers, and Delinquent Behavior. *Journal of Youth and Adolescence 20,* 645–64.

[17] *Digest of Educational Statistics.* Available at https://nces.ed.gov/programs/digest/d16/tables/dt16_228.10.asp?current=yes.

[18] Killingbeck, D. (2001). The Role of Television News in the Construction of School Violence as a "Moral Panic." *Journal of Criminal Justice and Popular Culture, 8,* 186–202.

[19] Rober, S., Kemp, J, Rathbun, A., and Morgan, R. (2014). Indicators of School Crime and Safety: 2013. Available at https://nces.ed.gov/pubsearch/pubsinfo.asp?pubid=2014042.

[20] Ibid.

[21] Ibid.

[22] Bachman, R., Randolph, A., and Brown, B. L. (2010). Predicting Perceptions of Fear at School and Going to and From School for African American and White Students: The Effects of School Security Measures. *Youth & Society, 43,* 705–26.

[23] Rober et al., Indicators of School Crime and Safety: 2013.

[24] Gebo, E., and Sullivan, C. J. (2014). A Statewide Comparison of Gang and Non-Gang Youth in Schools. *Youth Violence & Juvenile Justice, 12,* 191–208.

[25] Howell, J. C. (2012). *Gangs in America's Communities.* Thousand Oaks, CA: Sage.

[26] Naber, P. A., May, D. C., Decker, S. H., Minor, K. I., and Wells, J. B. (2006). Are There Gangs in Schools? It Depends on Whom You Ask. *Journal of School Violence 5,* 53–72.

[27] Gebo and Sullivan, A Statewide Comparison of Gang and Non-Gang Youth in Schools, 191–208.

[28] See www.jhsph.edu/research/centers-and-institutes/johns-hopkins-center-for-gun-policy-and-research/.

[29] Walker, S. (2015). *Sense and Nonsense about Crime, Drugs, and Communities* (8th ed.). Stamford, CT: Cengage.

[30] US Secret Service. (2001). *The Final Report and Findings of the Safe School Initiative: Implications for the Prevention of School Attacks in the United States.* Washington, DC: Author.

[31] Newman, K. S. (2005). *Rampage: The Social Roots of School Shootings.* New York: Basic Books.

[32] US Secret Service, *The Final Report and Findings of the Safe School Initiative.*

[33] Garbarino, J. (2015). *Listening to Killers: Lessons Learned from My Twenty Years as a Psychological Expert Witness in Murder Cases.* Oakland: University of California Press.

[34] US Secret Service, *The Final Report and Findings of the Safe School Initiative.*

[35] Ibid.

[36] American Psychological Association. (2004). *American Psychological Association Resolution on Bullying among Children and Youth.* Available at www.apa.org/about/policy/bullying.pdf.

[37] US Department of Education. *Trends in Bullying.* Available at https://nces.ed.gov/pubs2016/2016004.pdf.

[38] FBI Hate Crime Statistics. Available at https://ucr.fbi.gov/hate-crime/2015/tables-and-data-declarations/10tabledatadecpdf.

[39] Wolke, D., and Layere, S. T. (2015). Long-Term Effects of Bullying. *Archives of Disease in Childhood, 100,* 879–85.

[40] Swearer, S., and Hymel, S. (2015). Understanding the Psychology of Bullying. *American Psychologist, 70,* 344–53.

[41] Olweus, D. (2001). Peer Harassment: A Critical Analysis and Some Important Issues. In J. Juvonen and S. Graham (eds.)., *Peer Harassment in School,* 3–20. New York: Guilford.

[42] Hoff, D. L., and Mitchell, S. N. (2009). Cyberbullying: Causes, Effects, and Remedies. *Journal of Educational Administration, 47,* 652–65.

[43] Ibid.

[44] Ayers, S., Wagaman, M. M., Geiger, J., Bermudez-Parsai, M., and Hedberg, E. E. (2012). Examining School-Based Bullying Interventions Using Multilevel Discrete Time Hazard Modeling. *Prevention Science, 13,* 539–50.

[45] See www.schoolclimate.org/climate/.

[46] Wilson, D. (2004). The Interface of School Climate and School Connectedness and Relationships with Aggression and Victimization. *Journal of School Health, 74,* 293–99.

[47] Omar, L. (1999). Schools as Agents of Cultural Transmission and Social Control. *Revue Sciences Humaines, 12,* 41–51.

[48] Thapa, A., Cohen, J., Guffey, S., and Higgins-D'Alessandro, A. (2013). A Review of School Climate Research. *Review of Educational Research, 83,* 357–85.

[49] Ibid.

[50] Zhan, M.A., Agnew, R., Fishbein, D., Miller, S., Winn, D., Dakoff, G., et al. (2010). *Causes and Correlates of Girls' Delinquency.* Girls Study Group: Understanding and Responding to Girls' Delinquency. Washington, DC: Office of Juvenile Justice and Delinquency Prevention.

[51] See, for example, Yogan, L. J. (2000). School Tracking and Student Violence. *Annals of the American Academy of Political and Social Science, 567,* 108–22.

[52] Gay, G. (2010). *Culturally Responsive Teaching* (2nd ed.). New York: Columbia University, Teachers College Press.

[53] Smith, M. L. (2015). A Generation at Risk: The Ties between Zero-Tolerance Policies and the School-to-Prison Pipeline. *McNair Scholars Research Journal, 8,* 125–41.

[54] Children's Defense Fund. (1975). *School Suspensions: Are They Helping Children?* Washington, DC: Washington Research Project; Losen, D. J., and Martinez, T. A. (2013). *Out of School & Off Track: The Overuse of Suspensions in American Middle and High Schools.* Los Angeles, CA: The Civil Rights Project, Center for Civil Rights Remedies.

[55] Losen, D. J., and Gillespie, J. (2012). *Opportunities Suspended: The Disparate Impact of Disciplinary Exclusion from School.* Available at http://civilrightsproject.ucla.edu/resources/projects/center-for-civil-rights-remedies/school-to-prison-folder/federal-reports/upcoming-ccrr-research.

[56] Ibid.

[57] Skiba, R. J. (2000). *Zero Tolerance, Zero Evidence: An Analysis of School Disciplinary Practice.* Bloomington, IN: Indiana Education Policy Center.

[58] Skiba, R. (2014). The Failure of Zero Tolerance. *Reclaiming Children and Youth, 22,* 27–33.

[59] Kang-Brown, J., Trone, J., Fratello, J., and Daftary-Kapur, T. (2013). *A Generation Later: What We've Learned about Zero Tolerance in Schools.* New York: Vera Institute of Justice.

[60] Payne, A. A., and Welch, K. (2010). Modeling the Effects of Racial Threat on Punitive and Restorative School Discipline Practices. *Criminology, 48,* 1019–62.

[61] US Department of Education. (2014). *Rethinking School Discipline*: Remarks of US Secretary of Education Arne Duncan at the Release of the Joint DOJ-ED School Discipline Guidance Package. Available at www.ed.gov/new/speeches/rethining-school-discipline.

[62] Kang-Brown et al., *A Generation Later: What We've Learned about Zero Tolerance in Schools.*

[63] Center for Civil and Human Rights. (2012). *Sent Home and Put Off-Track: The Antecedents, Disproportionalities,* *and Consequences of Being Suspended in the Ninth Grade.* Atlanta, GA: Author.

[64] Maddox, S. J., and Prinz, R. J. (2003). School Bonding in Children and Adolescents: Conceptualization, Assessment, and Associated Variables. *Clinical Child and Family Psychology Review, 6,* 31–49.

[65] Gray, L., Lewis, L., and Ralph, J. (2015). *Public School Safety and Discipline: 2013–2014.* Washington, DC: Department of Education.

[66] Brown, B. (2006). Understanding and Assessing School Police Officers: A Conceptual and Methodological Comment. *Journal of Criminal Justice, 34,* 591–604.

[67] Ibid.

[68] Finn, P., and McDevitt, J. (2005). *National Assessment of School Resource Officer Programs: Final Project Report.* Washington, DC: National Institute of Justice.

[69] Olweus, D., Limber, S., and Mihalic, S. F. (1999). *Bullying Prevention Program: Blueprints for Violence Prevention, Book Nine.* Blueprints for Violence Prevention Series. Boulder, CO: University of Colorado, Institute of Behavioral Science.

[70] Review from Blueprints for Healthy Youth Development. Available at www.blueprintsprograms.com/factsheet/positive-action.

[71] Flay, B. R., and Allred, C. G. (2003). Long-Term Effects of the Positive Action Program. *American Journal of Health Behavior, 27,* S1, 6–21.

[72] Fronius, T., Persson, H., Guckenburg, S., Hurley, N., and Petrosino, A. (2015). *Restorative Justice in U.S. Schools: A Research Review.* San Francisco, CA: Wested.

[73] Minneapolis Public Schools. (nd). *Positive School Climate Toolkit.* Available at http://sss.mpls.k12.mn.us/positive_school_climate_tool_kit.

THE CONTEMPORARY JUVENILE JUSTICE SYSTEM

I

PART

II

PART

III

PART

Youth and Police

LEARNING OBJECTIVES

By the end of the chapter, you should be able to do the following:

- Discuss the various roles of police officers.
- Explain procedural justice and its importance to the justice process.
- Identify the main factors in police discretion.
- Identify important civil rights for youth.
- Understand the juvenile justice system case flow.
- Describe the key policing practices of stop, question, and frisk; crackdowns; hot spots; and zero tolerance, and their influences on police–youth relations.
- Discuss the dynamics of police–youth interaction by ethnicity and gender.

Case Study 8: Victor Rios—Changing What Police See

Victor Rios never expected to be standing on a stage at the Los Angeles Convention Center nervously facing an audience of five thousand educators and parents. Growing up, he never expected anyone would listen to what he had to say, much less read books he had written. Like so many poor young men of color, Rios expected he would be locked up or dead long before he reached his twenties. As the speech ended, the room exploded with a standing ovation. Rios thought of his two close friends whose lives turned out pretty much as everyone had expected: Rambo was doing life in a six-by-eight-foot cell at San Quentin State Prison, and Smiley was buried in an eight-by-three-foot box six feet underground.

Against the odds Victor Rios made it out of poverty and into a prominent position as an award-winning sociologist whose life's work is dedicated to telling the struggles of young boys of color growing up poor and facing constant harassment and oppression by the very institutions that should be there to support and protect them—schools and police. With one or two all-important exceptions, Rios felt he had been treated like a criminal long before he had done anything to violate the law. This hostility and humiliation, day in and day out, takes its toll. Rios knows well the hurt and anger it invokes in the hearts of young boys. He knows too the urgent need to uphold a sense of dignity and respect regardless of the risks and costs.

At one point Rios decided he wanted to change his life. And when he was ready, there was someone who made good on her promise to support and help him. Now Rios wants that to be possible for others. As a sociologist employed by a major university in California, Rios is in a position to ask: What if police stopped treating poor kids as criminals just because they are poor and black or brown? What if instead of punishing kids, police were there to help? And, if police change how they see kids on the street, would this change how kids see themselves?

Rejected

Victor's childhood was harsh. His mother was only thirteen the first time she was kidnapped, raped, and forced into marriage with an older man in Mexico. Her cousin rescued her from this violent man by beating and killing him. Soon after, Raquel became pregnant with Victor's older brother, JT. She later became pregnant with Victor. Raquel tried to end the pregnancy. In jail for injuring a woman in a bar fight, Victor's mother lugged heavy jugs of water for hours, trying to induce a miscarriage of the unwanted baby. The jail authorities intervened against her will. Rios was born to a mother who had done all she could to end his life.

Growing up, Victor's mother told him many times how hard she tried to get rid of him. As a vulnerable child, Victor remembers hiding in lonely spots, concealing his tears in a stairwell or behind a building, feeling unwanted and unloved. As an adult, Rios has more compassion and understanding for his marginalized mother. A single mother with a four-year-old and a newborn, she had no one to comfort and care for her. She did what she needed to do to survive.

The demands on her strength were unimaginable. As a baby, Rios contracted stomach parasites from unsanitary milk which left him writhing in pain, requiring several hospitalizations by the time he was a toddler. Sleeping on the dirt floors in the crowded shantytowns of Mexico City, there was little Raquel could do to keep her son from getting sick again and again.

Crossing the Border

It was Raquel who dreamed of something better and decided to risk everything to make the journey north to America, the land of opportunity. It was Raquel who slowly saved her pesos to go to the border town of Tijuana and buy passage for herself and her two young sons, now seven and three. Begging on the streets, reaching her hand out to strangers, she gathered her coins until she had enough to pay for a bus ride across the border, only to be turned back by the US authorities because she did not have papers.

Crossing the border at age three was the earliest memory Rios had of an encounter with a US law enforcement officer. Saddled with the two young boys, Raquel was quickly apprehended by the authorities the first time she tried to enter the country. Rios remembers the cruel lie the officer told him and his brother. Held together in a prison-like van in the desert, the officer laughed at their wailing faces as he told them their mother was going to jail for life and that they would never see her again.

Not to be defeated, back in Tijuana, Raquel starting saving again, this time for money to pay a coyote—a person who will smuggle human beings across the border for a fee. Raquel did not give up. This time she separated herself from her two young sons to improve their chances of making it across. Victor and JT were taken by a strange man across the desert and then locked in an apartment, where they waited ten days with little adult supervision or food for their mother to come, not knowing if she made it, was jailed, or was sent back to Mexico.

Victor later learned that the coyote had lost his mother's address. Meanwhile, Raquel searched frantically in the strange new city of Los Angeles to find her sons. Raquel could have simply abandoned her children in her quest for a better life, or she could have left them behind in Mexico City or Tijuana, but she did not. Raquel may never have shown her children much love or affection, but she never left them behind. Despite her talk about getting rid of him, all her life she did her best to feed and shelter Victor and JT. And that, Rios came to understand, was a kind of love.

Parasites, Rats, and Cockroaches

Rios still remembers the stabbing pain in his stomach from the parasites he contracted as a baby in Mexico, but some of his worst childhood memories were of rats as large as cats and cockroaches infesting his food and swarming his bed in the promised land of America. With only a third-grade education and no English, Raquel got a job cleaning tables and sweeping floors in a restaurant for $2 an hour, while Victor and his brother sat alone all day in the apartment.

Soon relatives from Mexico joined them: cousins, uncles, and aunts who crowded together in the decrepit apartments in Oakland, California, where the rats continued to plague them, especially the children. Victor remembers one night when a particularly vicious rat attacked his baby cousin, asleep in his crib, chewing on the infant's cheeks, lips, and gums before an adult woke to drive it away. It took doctors three months of intensive hospital care to rebuild his face.

Growing Up in the Land of Opportunity

Eventually Rios's mother enrolled him and his brother in school. More than anything else, she thought school was her sons' one chance to escape the trap of poverty. To Rios, though, school was not a place where he felt he belonged, or could succeed. Rios suffered endless taunting from the other kids when they found out he had no father: "Bastard" was his nickname. No amount of fighting in the schoolyard would make it go away. Rios learned that he was "stupid" from the teachers. In the third grade, Rios was sent to the principal because he couldn't read the word written on the blackboard. No one asked Rios why he couldn't read the word; the teacher assumed he was being defiant and ordered him out of the room. No one took the time to find out that Rios badly needed glasses and actually could not see the word on the blackboard. Having never had his eyes checked, Rios had no idea what the problem was, and his mother was too overwhelmed with putting food on the table to take him for an eye exam. It was not until the tenth grade that Rios got the glasses he needed to see properly.

At age thirteen, Rios came to his own conclusions about the value of school for his survival. He dropped out to take a job mowing lawns for $2 an hour. For three months Rios didn't show up to school. The school tried to call his house, but the phone had been disconnected for nonpayment of bills; the school sent letters, but Rios intercepted them before his mother could see them. Rios knew his mother wanted him to go to school, but he thought it would be better if he could earn money to help his family get out of poverty. He pushed those lawn mowers in the blazing heat in hopes that he would one day get his family away from the rats.

When a neighbor told his mother that Victor had left school, Raquel wasted no time in bringing out the man's belt she had purchased just for this purpose. As she beat Rios on his soft flesh, she screamed at him that all her hard work was so that he could be in

America, get an education, and do a different kind of work—where he used his brains, not his body. She had fought so hard to be here for just one reason: so her children could have a better life. School was the only way that would happen.

The Lure of the Gang

Rios got the message from his mother loud and clear, but at that age, he was tuning in to different and much louder messages in his world. On the surface, he listened to his mother and returned to school, but his real attention was on the older boys in the neighborhood: the so-called "shot callers," older gang members in their late teens who seemed to have it all—money, girls, cars, respect, and power.

The reality of gangs had been made clear to Rios earlier, when he was eleven. A stranger had held a gun to his head, demanding that he reveal which gang he was loyal to. He received warnings from his mother to just stay away. She couldn't understand that for young males, being part of a gang was often perceived as a necessity, not a choice. At the same time, the police treated everyone in the neighborhood as if they were gang members, calling them names, stopping and frisking for no reason. Not long after that, Rios was beaten up by a group of boys when he couldn't answer this same question. Tired of being afraid, of being treated like he was in a gang by police, and seeing no alternative, Rios wanted "in."

As an adult, Rios still remembers the feeling he had when he downed a forty-ounce bottle of malt liquor after being "jumped in" by the gang. Bruised and battered, it was the best feeling he had ever had up until that point. For the first time in his life, Victor felt "important." The lure of that good feeling was even greater than the fear of being physically hurt. His first test came one day later, when Victor "proved" himself by picking up a gun, stealing a car, and heading to enemy territory to settle a score. Victor missed his shot to avoid killing anyone, but no one knew that; his street reputation was off to a good start, and police began to take more notice of him.

One year later, with many car thefts, brawls, and break-ins under his belt, Rios was riding high. Police rarely came into the neighborhood to address the violence, only to harass the young boys who lived there, including Rios. One afternoon, walking in the park, Rios picked a fight with a rival gang on their own turf. Winning easily, Rios felt a surge of pride and power.

His homies congratulated him on a job well done as he was walking away. It should have ended there, but Rios realized his hat was missing and went back to retrieve it. His buddy Rambo came with him, and when he saw someone wearing the hat, Rambo demanded it back. A punch was thrown. In response, Rambo pulled a knife that he sank deep in the throat of the boy wearing the hat. Two lives ended that day: One boy was dead from his wounds, and the other, Rambo, was consigned to spend the rest of his life inside prison. This was the beginning of a wake-up call for Rios about the waste and tragedy of it all.

Dealing with Police: A Game of Cat and Mouse

One day Rios was arrested for driving a stolen car. The police dragged him from the car, kicked him in the stomach and head, and yelled, "You want to be a fucking criminal, then we will treat you like one." By this time, Rios was used to being stopped, searched, frisked, shoved, cursed, kicked, and accused of being a gang member. This happened regularly. It was made clear to Victor that in the eyes of the police, even as a young boy, he was already a criminal not worthy of protection.

In the interrogation room, an officer told Rios that the judge would go easier on him if he wrote a letter of apology to the owner of the car. Naively Rios did what he was told, writing and signing his own legal confession. The officer also used a ruse to trick Rios into revealing his gang affiliation, nickname, and tattoos: all information that went into the gang database and branded Victor as a gangbanger in the eyes of the system. During this time, Victor did several stints in juvenile hall, each time learning how to be a better criminal and gangster from his fellow inmates. Doing time in juvie boosted his reputation on the street and elevated his status in the gang.

What was happening to Victor was happening to other boys in the neighborhood. Smiley, his other best friend, seemed to be a magnet for aggressive police attention. Life for Smiley was worse than for Victor. He had a drug-addicted mother who beat him regularly and often kicked him out onto the street, yet Smiley went through life with a huge smile on his face. This disturbed his teachers, who interpreted his smile as an act of defiance and personal insult. To the police, his baggy pants and crazy grin signaled he was no good, and he too was harassed countless times for being a gang member before he officially joined at age fourteen.

One day Rios, Smiley, and a few other boys were flirting with a group of girls on the stoop in the neighborhood of a rival gang. Soon, they were surrounded by a group of eight, and a fight began. When the gunshots started, Rios fled, ducking between two cars for protection. When Rios emerged, he discovered Smiley facedown, struck by a single bullet to his head. Still alive, Rios threw his friend in a car and sped to the emergency room. He knew from experience that no ambulance would come to this neighborhood to treat the victim until after police had cleared the crime scene. The only chance to save Smiley's life was to drive him.

Smiley died a few hours after being brought to the hospital. Grief-stricken, Rios turned to the policeman in the ER and asked if they were going to catch the shooter. The officer shrugged his shoulders and said, "What for? We want you to kill each other off." The officer then warned Rios that he had better leave before he was arrested on an accessory-to-murder charge. Rios returned to his neighborhood to find his homeboys already preparing to retaliate, the words "We want you to kill each other off" still ringing in his head.

This was it for Rios. While the others went to seek revenge, Rios went home, knowing it was time to make a change. Thinking of Smiley, who had wanted to be liked by everyone, Rios knew the best way to honor his slain friend was to get himself out of this vicious cycle.

It Only Takes One

There was one person Rios felt he could turn to—a teacher who was always glad to see him, who always asked how he was, and who had told him she would be there if he ever wanted to talk. After Smiley's death, Rios went to see her, not really knowing why, or what to say. Her immediate concern and interest in Victor hit a nerve. Of all the adults he came into contact with—the police officers who stopped him and harassed him every day; the teachers who looked right through him as they droned on with lessons; the judges, probation officers, and juvenile detention staff who processed him through the system—none ever seemed to "see" him, none ever asked how he was feeling, or seemed to even care enough to listen to what he had to say, except for Ms. Russ.

In his darkest hour, Rios turned to her and told her all of it: the pain of losing his friend; the fear of being on the street; the intense anger at police and the courts; the daily humiliations of being searched, jabbed, harassed, taunted, and dismissed as nothing better than a criminal destined for jail or the grave. In the middle of a hallway full of kids, Rios sobbed, letting Ms. Russ hold him while she told him, right then and there, that if he was ready to work, she was ready to support him, advocate for him, and not give up on him.

Ms. Russ proved good to her word in the weeks, months, and years to come. Victor had years of education to catch up on. It was Victor who had to do the work, but it was Ms. Russ who gave him what he had believed the gang could provide: a sense of being important and valued, and someone he could count on and trust. It was Ms. Russ who showed him that, unlike his experiences with police, some people with authority could be trusted and kind. Above all, Ms. Russ offered Rios a choice: If he wanted a different future and was willing to work for it, she was going to help him get there.

A New Vision for Police?

Years later Rios returned to the streets of his childhood and adolescence, publishing a powerful book about the feelings and experiences of the young boys of color growing up in the same impoverished world. Over and over, he heard familiar stories about police taunting boys, mocking them, labeling them as gang members, beating them up, and setting them up for arrests and charges.

Even with his status as a university professor, Rios found he was still vulnerable to bad treatment from police. More than once Rios tried to convince youth that they could stand up for their civil rights by reporting abuse when it occurred. But when Rios tried to report an officer who slammed him against the door of a cruiser and ripped the interior of his car apart, the officer's superiors shrugged it off as a baseless accusation. Victor realized that even as a professional and privileged adult, he too was powerless.

It did not need to be that way. Rios recalled one encounter when a police officer had shown him kindness and consideration that he never forgot. It happened when he was just beginning to turn his life around. Visiting with his friends at a local high school, a fight broke out, with Rios in the middle of it. The officer on the scene recognized Rios and knew he was on probation; an arrest would send him back to juvie. But the officer chose not to arrest him. Rios told him he was trying to turn his life around and the officer cut him a break. Just this time, the officer warned; next time he'd go away for good. There was no next time for Rios, and to this day, Rios remains deeply grateful for the chance that officer gave him to make a better future for himself.

Today, Rios runs his own mentoring program for gang members and those "at promise." He believes we need to shift our language from "at-risk" youth to "at-promise" youth, to show that adults believe in and support young people. How young people are treated by adults matters, especially those adults in key institutions such as police departments and schools, as well as family members. He states that he is living proof that through adult belief and support, youth can change their lives for the better.

THINKING CRITICALLY ABOUT THIS CASE

1. Compare Rios's experience with police officers to your own. How are they different? How are they similar?

2. Do you think the officer who let Rios go home instead of arresting him for fighting did the right thing? Why, or why not? Do you believe police should use their discretion to allow youth a second chance? Why, or why not?

3. Do you think Rios would have received the same treatment if he were white or if he lived in an upper-class neighborhood? Explain.

4. How did the youth in this case study exacerbate tensions between police and residents? What do you think youth can do to improve interactions with the police? What do you think police can do?

5. Do you agree with Rios's assessment that youth were hyper-criminalized by social institutions like police and schools? Explain your answer.

REFERENCES

This case is based on the following sources:

Fritz, M., and Brown, A. (2012). *One Man's Journey from Gang Member to Academia*. PBS Newshour. Available at www.pbs.org/newshour/updates/american-graduate-jan -june12-victor_rios/.

Monaghan, P. A. Sociologist Returns to the Mean Streets of His Youth. *Chronicle of Higher Education*, July 17, 2011.

Rios, V. M. (2012). *Punished: Policing the Lives of Black and Latino Youth*. New York: New York University Press.

———. (2011). *Street Life: Poverty, Gangs, and a PhD*. California: Five Rivers Press.

———. TED Talk. Available at http://tedxtalks.ted.com/ video/TEDxUCSB-Victor-Rios-From-At-Ri.

INTRODUCTION

Growing up, Rios experienced harsh treatment by police, but he also attributes his success to the compassion shown by one officer that prevented him from getting arrested while on probation. This one decision allowed Rios to continue to turn away from the street life and focus on getting an education. According to the law, the police officer could have arrested a young man already on probation engaged in a fight. Rios was no angel: By this point in his life, he had committed a fair amount of crime. Yet the officer used his discretion to let him go with a warning. This choice made all the difference; instead of treating Rios as a delinquent, the officer showed faith in Rios's effort to change his life.

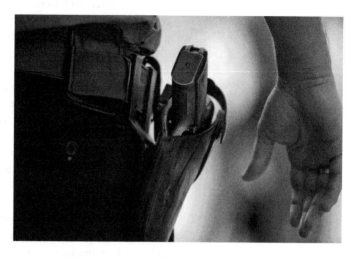

This chapter looks at the role of police in the juvenile justice process. In a very real sense, police are the gatekeepers of the entire juvenile justice process. If the police officer had made the decision to arrest Rios, most likely Rios would have gone back to juvenile hall. This, in turn, would have increased the odds that he would not have graduated from high school, and would not have gone on to college, or graduate school to earn a PhD; nor would he have been able to one day stand on a stage, addressing an audience. In hindsight, we can see that the police officer made a critically important decision: He used his discretion to divert Rios because he believed Rios was making a genuine effort to change. This act of leniency was the exception rather than the rule. Rios's experience was that police in his community generally treated all youth, regardless of whether or not they had done anything illegal, as if they were already serious criminals.

We will examine the formal and informal role police play in the regulation of the behavior of youth in this chapter. We also will look at how police historically have interacted with youth, as well as how that varies by intersectional concerns, including race, ethnicity, gender, and geography. We will look at the strategies that police use to intervene in crime and delinquency. A key consideration in this chapter is the dynamic interaction between youth and law enforcement, and how that plays a role in youth involvement in the juvenile justice system.

HISTORY OF POLICING YOUTH IN AMERICA

Before the rise of the juvenile court, there was no legal age distinction in the criminal justice system, so police often treated youth the same as adults. Youth were detained alongside adults in cells that held all types of offenders, from drunks to petty thieves, to murderers. As society began to recognize children and youth as distinct from adults, however, police were expected to view children as vulnerable and in need of guidance. This gave rise to separate units in police departments to address juveniles.

The first juvenile units in police departments, often called juvenile bureaus, appeared in the early years of the twentieth century.[1] The first female police officers were designated police "social workers," whose sole job was to handle juvenile cases. In the early days of the juvenile court, before the development of probation systems, police also were assigned to act as police probation officers. The main role of police probation officers was to decide if a youth should be referred to the juvenile court or if the case should be subject to informal adjustment.

Informal adjustment simply meant that the youth was not processed further into the juvenile system, but was handled by the police. The officer might have simply warned the youth to stay out of trouble, as Rios was; or the youth might have been held at the station for a while and then released; or the child might have been escorted home to parents. It might also mean the police issued **rough justice** in the form of a physical beating, to teach the youth a lesson. Between 1918 and 1930, in Cook County (Chicago), police probation officers referred only 11 percent of all cases to the juvenile court, choosing to informally adjust 89 percent on their own.[2]

Historically, police disproportionately referred immigrant youth to the juvenile court for formal processing. This is consistent with the focus of the child-saving movement that removed many immigrant children from what were perceived as inadequate homes. Between 1918 and 1926, 82 percent of cases referred to the Chicago Juvenile Court were for immigrant youth.[3] As states began to pass compulsory education laws beginning in the late nineteenth century, police were authorized to arrest any child who skipped school; was out in public during school hours; or who disobeyed teachers at school. For immigrant families, police as well as social workers were authority figures that threatened to take children away from families. Historians note that families often warned children, "The cops are gonna take you!" if they misbehaved.[4] As you read through this chapter, think about how these traditional policing practices have or have not changed today.

JUVENILE JUSTICE SYSTEM CASE FLOW

To understand where police fit into the juvenile system it is important to review the overall processing of cases through the system. Historically, police acted as gatekeepers to the juvenile court, relying on wide discretion to decide whether to arrest a youth, informally adjust, or refer to the juvenile court. Police continue to act in the role of gatekeeper to the juvenile justice system today. Figure 8.1 outlines the flow of a case in the juvenile justice system.[5] States vary slightly in how they formally process juveniles, but the key decision points in each state are the same.

The first stage in the process is **arrest** and booking. Police often have a lot of discretion at this stage, and we will discuss that more fully later in the chapter. If the case against the youth is serious enough, or if the youth is considered a flight risk, youth can be held in **detention** awaiting further case processing. Detention can be a youth facility or a jail cell where youth await release to a parent or guardian, or await further court processing. The 2002 reauthorized Juvenile Justice and Delinquency Prevention Act requires that youth be placed in a cell that is "sight and sound"–separated from adult detainees.[6] The Act further requires that youth be held for no more than four hours in jail cells in facilities that are not specifically designed for youthful offenders.

The remaining stages of the juvenile justice system relate to court involvement and are discussed in more detail in chapters 9 and 10, but are outlined here. *Arraignment* is the stage where a youth answers to the petition—similar to a

INFORMAL ADJUSTMENT
Discretionary decision by police to not refer youth to further juvenile justice processing.

ROUGH JUSTICE
Unfair treatment of a suspect by police to teach a "lesson."

ARREST
Taking someone into custody by legal authority.

DETENTION
Keeping someone temporarily in official custody.

FIGURE 8.1

Justice System Case Flow

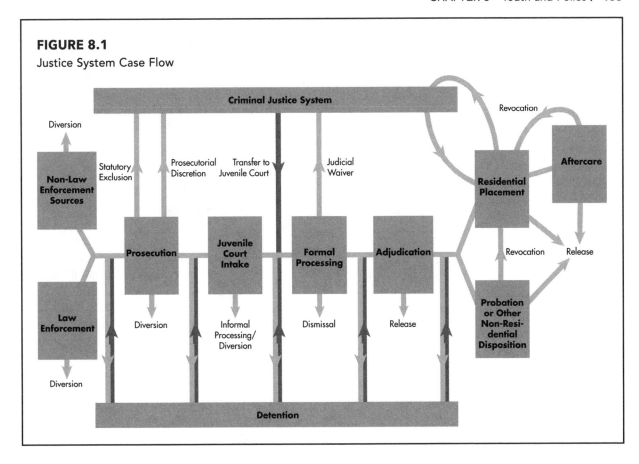

charge in adult court terms—in court in front of a judge. Youth can plead "true" (guilty) or "not true" (not guilty). Most cases are heard before the juvenile court, though if the offense is serious enough, youth can be tried as adults in all states. (Recall that chapter 1 has a table identifying the ages at which youth can be tried as an adult in each state.)

Adjudication is the trial stage. The petition can be found true or not true. If a petition is found true, the youth is considered adjudicated delinquent, and a probation officer completes an investigational report in order to make sentencing recommendations to the judge. If the petition is found not true, the youth is free to leave. The *disposition*, or sentencing stage, occurs at another hearing time separate from adjudication. Most youth receive probation, though disposition can include residential placement, an out-of-home placement, in a facility geared toward needs of youth, or the state's training school, a youth prison. Some states have aftercare, or parole, once youth return from residential treatment or training schools, in order to help reintegrate them within their families and communities. With the overall juvenile justice system processing in mind, we turn back to our examination of police.

POLICE ROLE IN JUVENILE JUSTICE

Three core functions of modern policing are order maintenance, which means keeping peace on the streets; crime-fighting, which covers responding to and investigating crime; and a social service function, which is helping those in need.[7] Police investigate crimes, collect evidence, present evidence, and testify in court. Officers also respond to complaints, patrol streets, and break up fights. They disperse groups of rowdy individuals and generally help to keep peace and order in the community. Finally, police are expected to help citizens who need assistance. This may mean removing a child in cases of maltreatment, or taking runaway or homeless youth into custody so that other agencies, such as child welfare services, can care for the child.

Increasingly, an added police function is to work collaboratively with the community to prevent crime.[8] This has become particularly important in preventing youth violence. Police work alongside other community agencies, local and state government entities, and community groups and leaders to problem-solve youth violence issues and better coordinate their work with the end goal of reducing violence. Indeed, juvenile arrests have gone down since their peak in the late 1980s and early 1990s. Some of this is due to the decriminalization of drug offenses, as well as the general downward shift in offending, but it may also be due to these youth-violence-reduction community collaboratives.

In 2013, the latest information available, police referred over 867,000 cases to juvenile court.[9] Of all police juvenile cases, 68 percent went to juvenile court, 22 percent were handled informally, 7 percent were referred to criminal court, and 3 percent were sent to child welfare agencies or another entity. Disproportionate minority contact (DMC) is a reality. Blacks are more likely to be funneled into the system than other ethnicities. Youth of color are 1.6 times more likely than whites to be arrested.[10] Comparing blacks to whites exclusively shows that black youth are more than twice as likely to be arrested. Minority youth are also more likely to be placed in detention; more likely to be processed through juvenile court; and more likely to be sent to a juvenile detention facility or prison than white youth. Cumulatively, the impact of these decision points creates the DMC pattern that results in an overrepresentation of minority youth in the juvenile as well as the adult criminal justice system. Rios's perception of being overpoliced and hassled is the same perception shared by most other black and brown youth. Arrest statistics demonstrate this harsh reality.

Juvenile Officers, Units, and Specialized Training

Today, working with youth is the job of all police officers, but some departments, especially larger ones, have specialized juvenile units to address all juvenile issues and supervise informal diversion agreements. In other departments, designated officers are assigned to handle juvenile cases. Additionally, other officers may have specialized duties, such as a school liaison officer, where they are the main contact between school officials and the police department. In some jurisdictions officers are designated school resource officers (SROs), whose main function is to remain on school grounds each day to provide safety, investigate crime, and to build positive relationships with students. Police officers also lead educational and skill-building programs, such as Drug Awareness Resistance Education (D.A.R.E.) and Gang Resistance Education and Training (G.R.E.A.T.) programs.

In some departments, officers who have an interest in working with youth are recruited to serve in these positions. In other departments, juvenile officers may be appointed. As a result, there may not be motivation on the part of the officer to learn how best to work with young people and to mentor youth. A juvenile officer position may be seen as just "doing time" until the officer can move into a more-desirable post.[11] This attitude can have an impact on how officers treat youth, and ultimately, how youth view police. The widely publicized incidents of police brutality, particularly in communities of color, have brought the importance of police professionalism and training to the forefront.

State law enforcement training centers spend little to no time training officers in how to deal with youth or juvenile cases, even though a significant portion of a patrol officer's time will be spent on such issues.[12] In response, the federal government, in collaboration with the International Association of Chiefs of Police, now offer juvenile training to help improve those relationships and to teach juvenile rights to police officers. Some information about youth does flow through training given to specialized units, such as gang units, gun units, and narcotics units. That content, however, often only addresses specific subtopics of gangs, guns, or narcotics, rather than how youth should be treated.

There are negative stereotypes on both sides of the police–youth relationship that interfere with effective interactions among them.[13] There has been a growing recognition that police training on adolescent development is critical to dealing effectively with youth. Key areas of training include understanding adolescent developmental stages, cultural and gender differences, disproportionate minority contact, effective strategies for interacting with youth, and perception of youth as assets rather than threats.[14] Training ensures that police understand juvenile competencies, particularly during questioning, and may influence the degree to which police are seen by youth across the color and socioeconomic spectrums as legitimate and trustworthy.[15]

POLICE DISCRETION

One of the hallmarks of policing is latitude in discretion, or judgment. Police are expected to use their discretion to decide on the best course of action in each situation. Discretionary responses for police–youth encounters range from ignoring incidents completely, to issuing formal arrests, to the use of lethal force. At the most basic level of intervention, officers may choose to process an incident informally, such as what happened with Rios when he was trying to make good. Officers are not required to file any paperwork for this street-level adjustment. It is not possible to know precisely how many youth–police encounters end with street-level adjustments because there are no official records in these instances.

Alternatively, officers may choose to bring youth to the police station for a **stationhouse adjustment**, where youth are reprimanded, information is taken, and youths' parents/guardians are called to the station to pick up their children. Stationhouse adjustments are still considered informal because youth are diverted away from the formal juvenile justice system. Such encounters generate little to no official paperwork for the officer.

It is also possible for the police to decide to combine formal and informal processing: Youth may be arrested and then diverted to a program not run through the court. These diversion programs may require community service, attendance at prosocial activities, and classes on various topics, including anger management and substance abuse. Upon program completion, charges against the youth are dropped. If a youth fails to complete the program, a court petition is filed. Informal handling can also mean that youth go to juvenile court,

STATIONHOUSE ADJUSTMENT
Discretionary decision by police to detain a youth at the police station and call a parent or guardian without further juvenile processing.

but the case is continued without a finding by a judge for a period of months. Upon good behavior during those months, the case is then dismissed from the system.

Beyond the delinquent act itself, several other factors play a role in police discretion. The ability of families to meet with police, provide supervision to their children, and enroll their children in needed mental health or substance abuse treatment programs are often important in the decision-making process. Police—and judges—are more likely to informally process youth whose parents have the employment flexibility to go to the police station immediately upon request and who have the financial means to seek treatment outside the juvenile justice system. This reality has led to what some have called the **two-track system**, where youth with the financial means (often white) are released, while poor youth (often black or brown) are funneled into the juvenile justice system and given a "delinquent" label in order to be supervised and to receive needed mental health services or substance abuse treatment.[16]

Dynamics of Police Discretion

Rios believes that police in his community adopt a stereotypical attitude toward black and brown youth that leads them to treat youth as criminals, regardless of the actual behavior of the youth. This means that youth who are struggling with the burdens of poverty, family dysfunction, and community violence are also treated to a daily dose of suspicion and hostility by those officially charged with the responsibility to "protect and serve." By the time these youth reach adolescence, this treatment triggers a defiant response that further escalates police suspicion and hostility.

Research confirms that nonlegal factors, such as **demeanor**, influence who is arrested. Six main influences on police discretion are broken down into legal factors, environmental factors, victim–offender relationship, department culture, suspect demeanor, and suspect characteristics. And, when it comes to juveniles, parents' cooperation, their ability to supervise their children, and their financial means to obtain treatment for their children, lead to the two-track system. The lack of oversight of officers on the street means that there is the potential for abuse of police powers, particularly with youth who may not understand their rights. The story of Victor Rios shows that on more than one occasion, police verbally, emotionally, and physically abused him.

Legal factors that influence police discretion are the seriousness of the crime and the suspect's prior juvenile/criminal history. Most people would agree that legal factors should be the most important—and, some believe, the only legitimate—factors to be considered in the decision to arrest. We know that the more serious the crime, the less discretion is used.[17] Police tend to use the most discretion in how they handle less-serious offenses. Given that most juvenile delinquency is minor, this means that police use a lot of discretion in handling juvenile offenses. There is enormous variation in how cases of underage drinking, marijuana use, running away, simple assault, vandalism, truancy, disturbing the peace, and so on, are handled by police.

A key environmental factor in police discretion is the availability of arrest alternatives in the community. While diversion is a popular alternative, its legality has been questioned. Youth are not formally charged, and they may feel

TWO-TRACK SYSTEM
Differential treatment by class wherein those with financial means avoid the system, while those without do not.

DEMEANOR
Attitude, manner, and body language of youth during interaction with police which influences police discretionary decision-making.

coerced to "voluntarily" enter into a program, believing that other avenues, such as court proceedings, may be far worse.[18] Another environmental factor influencing arrest is prevailing community values. What is acceptable in one community, such as possession of a small amount of marijuana, may not be acceptable in another. Getting caught in one neighborhood may lead to a simple warning, while getting caught in another may lead to an arrest.

Victim–offender relationships also make a difference in an officer's decision to arrest. If the victim and offender know each other, and the offense is not a serious felony, the officer is more likely to handle the situation informally.[19] This can be good in some situations, where offenses are relatively inconsequential, as in a minor fight between two youth. Processing through the juvenile justice system would not only result in the delinquent label, but would also be a strain on limited system resources. This is not, however, the case for all situations. Physical violence among family members is often handled informally. Yet if this occurred between strangers, it would be seen as deserving of arrest.[20] Lack of arrest when there is violence within the family often places youth more at risk for future violence, and it may send a message that violence within the family is acceptable.

The culture of police departments, particularly with regard to youthful crime, also plays a role in who gets arrested.[21] If the department, or individual officers, believes that juveniles are a threat to public safety, then police question, stop, and frisk youth more often. This is considered *overpolicing*. At the same time, the police may not readily respond to youth calls for service for a myriad of reasons, one of which may be officer safety. This is considered *underpolicing*. The case study at the beginning of this chapter describes the **overpolicing–underpolicing paradox** experienced by Rios and his peers. In urban minority neighborhoods, youth often face the worst of both worlds when it comes to law enforcement. On the one hand, they are constantly under suspicion and subjected to daily frisking, searches, and other aggressive forms of police surveillance.[22] On the other hand, police fail to offer them protection, either for fear of their own safety, or because they do not see youth as genuine "victims," assuming they are participants in the criminal incident.

Of all nonlegal factors, a suspect's demeanor has the strongest effect on police discretion, more so than suspect characteristics like ethnicity, gender, and class.[23] The demeanor of youth, or outward behavior, is influenced by a host of factors; one of the most salient is their opinion of police officers. Youth generally do not have opinions of police that are as positive as those held by adults. This is especially true in poor, nonwhite communities.[24] Given the overpolicing–underpolicing paradox, it is not surprising that research finds black and brown youth do not hold favorable opinions of police.

Youth who are respectful and deferential to police officers are less likely to be arrested than those who are not, as Rios points out from his experience in growing up on the streets of Oakland. Youth who are perceived to have a poor attitude toward officers, and those who resist arrest, are more likely to be arrested. This is the vicious cycle observed by Rios: Hostile treatment by the police engenders defiant attitudes by the youth, which in turn triggers more aggressive behaviors from the police. As youth garner more charges on their record, legal factors alone—a prior history of arrest, and contact with the police—means they will continue to be arrested even for minor offenses.

OVERPOLICING-UNDERPOLICING PARADOX
Policing practices that are heavy-handed for minor transgressions (overpolicing) and lack of prompt response to resident calls for service (underpolicing).

GENDER AND POLICE TREATMENT

Several decades ago, research consistently found that girls were less likely to be arrested for offenses than boys. This may have been due to what is termed the **chivalry hypothesis**, wherein girls were viewed by police as needing protection from the system, resulting in a greater likelihood that they would be released to parents/guardians. Boys who committed "typical" delinquent crimes were more likely to have a police record than girls who committed "typical" delinquent crimes, because of differential treatment by law enforcement.[25] As we have discussed in chapter 5, this view has begun to change.

Today, girls are more likely than boys to be arrested for prostitution, and almost as likely to be arrested for some status offenses, particularly running away from home and truancy. Girls account for almost 50 percent of status offenses, compared to only about 25 percent of delinquency cases, though arrests for delinquency have gone up for girls.[26] The existence of a double standard based on gender results in differential patterns of police arrest: For more-serious crimes, girls are treated as less-serious offenders, but when it comes to behavior that is seen to place them at risk, particularly sexual involvement, girls are more likely to be arrested and detained by the system.[27]

Girls are more likely to get into physical altercations with family members, especially mothers or mothers' boyfriends, than boys. Girls are more likely to be arrested in these situations than adults. Police may make this decision for a variety of reasons: There may be other children in the home that need to be cared for by the adult; the arresting officer may believe the adult's version of the story over the girl's; or the officer may take the girl into custody to protect her from an abusive parent. A paternalistic attitude by police means girls are removed from the family far more quickly than boys, generally "for their own good."[28]

POLICING PRACTICES

The methods police use to do their job and interact with the community has been the subject of much scrutiny over the last few years. Story upon story has been brought to light of police killing young black and brown men who were unarmed; and the federal government has declared that some police departments, such as Ferguson, Missouri, and Chicago, Illinois, routinely violated the civil rights of individuals from communities of color.[29] This has further damaged police–community relations. What guides police in their work and how they think about individuals and communities? The most prominent practice has been the espousal of community policing.

Community Policing

The concept of **community policing** developed during the 1980s. It is a vision of police in which it is the responsibility of the officer to partner with the community in order to prevent crime and to address community concerns.[30] This philosophy recognizes that police need to work with schools, social services, youth agencies, and public health organizations in order to address the root causes of crime. Increasingly, officers are charged with crime prevention aimed particularly at forms of delinquency, including reducing youth violence, substance

CHIVALRY HYPOTHESIS
Belief that girls are in need of protection influencing the way agents of the justice system handle girls' cases.

COMMUNITY POLICING
Police partner with the community to reduce crime and problems within the community.

abuse, truancy, and sex trafficking. More a philosophy than a practice, community policing encompasses a variety of programs and strategies with varying levels of effectiveness. A review of existing research shows that community-oriented policing strategies do not necessarily prevent crime, but they do have positive effects on resident satisfaction with police and perceptions of police legitimacy.[31] Positive relationships between community and police are desperately needed in many poor, urban communities.

D.A.R.E., or Drug Abuse Resistance Education, is one example of a community policing program. D.A.R.E. aims to reduce the use of drugs, tobacco, and alcohol by youth through structured educational classes in school taught by police officers trained in providing the curriculum. The program is administered primarily in middle school where students engage in role plays, practicing saying "no" to peer pressure. Evaluation results show that the initial version of the D.A.R.E. program was ineffective in reducing students' substance use.[32] D.A.R.E. was subsequently revised as the Keepin' it REAL program, based on those research recommendations. Preliminary evaluation results show that it is effective in reducing substance use by young people.[33] Although Keepin' it REAL has been shown to be much more effective than D.A.R.E., the D.A.R.E. program continues to be popular among police and in communities throughout the United States.

The G.R.E.A.T. program is similar to D.A.R.E. in that it is taught by police officers in middle schools in communities at the highest risk for gangs. Structured curriculum teaches youth to resist peer pressure and build life skills. Initial evaluations of G.R.E.A.T. showed few positive gang resistance effects, so, like the D.A.R.E. program, it was revised. The revised G.R.E.A.T. program has shown positive effects with regard to increasing negative perceptions of gangs among youth and increasing students' capacity to resist peer pressure.[34] The roles of police officers in drug abuse prevention programs and G.R.E.A.T. are commensurate with their role as a crime prevention partner.

Other examples of community-oriented policing strategies that connect with youth include youth–police academies and police athletic leagues. These programs provide hands-on skills and recreational opportunities for youth with the goals of building relationships between youth and police and keeping youth out of trouble by providing healthy alternatives to delinquency. Another youth-focused community policing strategy is ride-alongs between police and probation officers. Together, these authorities visit local youth hangouts and homes of youth on probation to ensure that youth are adhering to their conditions. Ultimately, a key idea of community policing is that police will partner with other agencies and with the community to share information on prevention and intervention strategies, as well as information about particular incidents, in order to work collaboratively toward solutions.

Procedural Justice, Zero Tolerance, and Hot Spots

One concern about the aggressive policing described by Victor Rios is that these practices may reduce the perceived legitimacy of law enforcement by community members, especially youth. As we discussed already, youth view police more negatively than adults, and this is particularly true among youth of color.[35] We know that the more people perceive the authority as legitimate, the more they are willing to comply with the law.[36] It is therefore in the best interests of everyone,

PROCEDURAL JUSTICE
The perception of fairness and respect in the process, not the outcome, of a situation.

RECIDIVATE
To reoffend.

CONCENTRATED DISADVANTAGE
Areas that have a combination of heterogeneous population, high population mobility, and high poverty.

INSTITUTIONALIZED RACISM
Organizational practices and policies that systematically discriminate against certain races.

CRACKDOWNS
Sudden increases in police presence and sanctions for specific offenses or in specific areas.

HOT-SPOT POLICING
Assignment of police resources to areas where crime is concentrated.

ZERO-TOLERANCE POLICING
Policing strategy that involves a crackdown on all offenses, including public order disturbances, in an effort to show that even petty crime will not be tolerated.

BROKEN WINDOWS THEORY
Proposition that reducing all forms of disorder in a neighborhood, including fixing broken windows and removing abandoned cars, will reduce crime.

police and community members, to treat each other with respect. This is part of a **procedural justice** perspective.

Procedural justice is a growing area of research and application in the field of crime and justice. It is about human interaction, emphasizing the process, not the outcome. Individuals may still be arrested and detained, but if they believe that they have been treated fairly, they are *less likely* to reoffend, or **recidivate**, and they are more likely to believe that the agents of the government (police) are legitimate.[37] Procedural justice has broad implications for how and why youth, and people overall, comply with authority figures. When police are seen to violate the law in their own conduct toward youth and others in the community, the legitimacy of the law itself is called into question. If youth believe the system is fair, they are more likely to cooperate with it, even if they are being prosecuted; if they believe the system operates unfairly, they are less likely to comply.

Youth, particularly youth of color, are vulnerable to perceived unfair treatment by law enforcement.[38] Policing practices result in certain high-crime locations and individuals being subject to more police scrutiny and surveillance. Neighborhoods with high rates of poverty and unemployment, and high levels of population mobility, are described by the term **concentrated disadvantage**. People of color tend to reside in these areas. Crime is more pronounced in areas of concentrated disadvantage. While targeted policing practices may be a response to crime, police use of discretionary powers in these locations is controversial. Some citizens, particularly young community members, perceive constant police surveillance as a form of **institutionalized racism**, in which police dole out negative treatment consistently to groups of people based on their race.

Policing practices in high-crime areas include crackdowns, hot spots, and zero tolerance. **Crackdowns** can take many forms, from intense police presence in a certain area to intensive search and arrest for a specific type of crime, such as gun possession or drug dealing. Sweeps may take place where police systematically target neighborhoods in search of illegal firearms or drugs. Those in possession are prosecuted to the fullest extent of the law. **Hot-spot policing** involves utilizing crime data to reveal where crime is concentrated, the types of crime committed, and the hours crime occurs. Police efforts are then deployed based on those data to combat the highest-crime areas during peak criminal activity. Focused policing using data to identify hot-spot areas and crimes has been shown to be effective, at least in the short term, in reducing crime rates—if implemented correctly.[39] Importantly, however, as noted above, procedural justice is key to long-term effectiveness.

Zero-tolerance policing is meant to crack down on *all* offenses, including public order disturbances, such as panhandling, in an effort to show that crime, even petty crime, will not be tolerated. These policies originated from the **broken windows theory**, in which reducing all forms of disorder in a neighborhood—quite literally including fixing broken windows and removing abandoned cars—will reduce crime.[40] Zero-tolerance policies were behind the New York City crime reduction efforts in the 2000s, led by then police commissioner William Bratton. Crime rates did decrease in the city, with some attributing the drop to zero-tolerance policies, and others disputing that claim.[41]

The social cost of such policing practices, however, may be antithetical to procedural justice. Perceived police harassment by community members—again, especially by male youth of color—fuels negative police perceptions and interactions. Research consistently shows that people of color are more likely to experience negative police interactions, and their demeanor is influenced by prior experiences.[42] Youth may be more likely to "cop an attitude," and police may perceive that as resisting arrest. Perceptions influence actions on both sides.

POLICE AND CIVIL RIGHTS

What rights do juveniles have in the midst of authorities? Juveniles are generally afforded the same due process rights as adults. The Fourth Amendment to the US Constitution protects all individuals from unnecessary search and seizure by legal authorities. Police must obtain a **search warrant** from a court in order to search the individual, or the individual's property. Search warrants are only issued upon **probable cause**, which means more than suspicion, but less than beyond a reasonable doubt. A police officer must submit an affidavit to court stating the grounds for a search warrant request. This affidavit must specify the place to be searched and the property to be seized.

Several exceptions exist to the search warrant law. Warrantless searches are allowed a) when there is a search incident to arrest; b) during Terry stops; and c) upon consent of the individual. The first two exceptions deserve further elaboration. A **search incident to arrest** is a search made soon after a valid lawful arrest. The purpose of the search is to protect an officer from danger and to secure evidence. During these searches, the officer is looking for evidence, a means of escape, weapons, or **contraband**. The suspect can be searched, as well as the area under the suspect's immediate control, which is generally thought to be within arm's length of the suspect, such as the cab of a truck.

A **Terry stop**, otherwise known as stop, question, and frisk, allows police officers to question individuals, including juveniles, without probable cause, only **reasonable suspicion**, to investigate potentially criminal situations. Police can frisk the outer clothing and body of a person to uncover weapons or evidence of criminal activity, such as contraband, and to question the person. The landmark case that first allowed police officers this search was *Terry v. Ohio*. In this case, a police officer saw an individual go by a storefront several times. The officer's suspicions were aroused that the individual was casing the store in order to commit robbery. The officer stopped and frisked the suspect and found a gun. The Supreme Court ruled that such a search was necessary for the officer's safety, not just government interest in investigating crime. The Court found it reasonable for officers to take measures to neutralize the threat of physical harm.

Terry stops have been the subject of much debate, as they are perceived as a pretense to harass individuals, particularly those that fall into traditional stereotypes of typical "criminals"—nonwhites and youth. Nonwhites and youth indeed are subjected to more Terry stops, and that has negatively impacted their view of police and legitimacy.[43] Rios is a living example of that. While courts generally have upheld the stop-and-frisk doctrine on the grounds of crime prevention and officer safety, that is changing. A New York City judge ruled that the police department's "stop, question, and frisk" policy, under which more young, nonwhite youth of color were stopped, violated a person's Fourth Amendment rights, and while the city appealed, the new New York City mayor decided to abandon the tactic.[44] As we move further into the twenty-first century, police–citizen encounters may be altered based on case law and general public climate about police interactions.

SEARCH WARRANT
Search order issued by the court allowing police to search particular areas for specific property and to bring that property to court.

PROBABLE CAUSE
More likely than not that a law has been violated.

SEARCH INCIDENT TO ARREST
Physical examination of a suspect and the area under a suspect's control upon an arrest.

CONTRABAND
Any item that is illegal to be possessed or sold.

TERRY STOP
A brief detention of a person by police on reasonable suspicion of involvement in criminal activity allowing for stop, frisk, and questioning.

REASONABLE SUSPICION
Specific facts/ circumstances that allow police to stop and frisk that do not rise to the level of probable cause.

Custodial Interrogations and Miranda Rights

Youth suspects have the Fifth Amendment right to remain silent when detained. The Supreme Court case discussed in chapter 3, *In re Gault*, extended the Miranda warning to juveniles, affording them the right to know that they can remain silent and to have an attorney present. This means that once an arrest is made, police are required to read **Miranda rights** to youth and ensure that they understand those rights before officers commence questioning. A youth can waive his/her right to an attorney if the totality of circumstances suggests that he understands the rights and is doing so intelligibly and competently.[45]

What is the capacity of youth to understand their right to an attorney and to grasp the implications of talking to police? Recall the case of Cristian Fernandez at the start of chapter 3. Although the officer had Cristian read the rights aloud and then sign the document stating he was willing to waive his right to an attorney, the courts ruled that a twelve-year-old could not have genuinely understood the implications of putting his signature on that piece of paper. It is clear that Cristian was being obedient to the authority of the adult police officer, just as he would a teacher or a parent.

Thomas Grisso and Elizabeth Scott have conducted extensive research on youths' capacity to understand Miranda and to testify in court, linking their research to adolescent brain development.[46] Youth under fourteen years old are significantly different than adults in their capacity to understand. They found that youth up until the age of eighteen are still more likely to waive counsel due to their desire to comply with authority figures, rather than any genuine understanding of their legal rights. These realities may be changing police interrogation tactics, as more police departments are declining to question youth until legal counsel or parents are present.[47]

CHANGING ROLE OF POLICE?

The Black Lives Matter protest movement was instigated when George Zimmerman, a white man acting as a volunteer member of a neighborhood watch program, shot and killed Trayvon Martin, an unarmed black teen walking home from the neighborhood candy store. The protest movement has continued to call attention to fatal shootings of unarmed black and brown individuals, beginning with the police shooting of teenager Michael Brown in Ferguson, Missouri. The failure to hold law enforcement accountable to the rule of law, and the disrespect shown to Brown and his family when law enforcement left his body on the street for hours, cements the widespread perception that the justice system lacks procedural justice for people of color. This movement, along with the growing field of procedural justice, is likely to shape policing practices of the future.

Victor Rios believes that it is both necessary and possible to change the attitude and behavior of the police from a mind-set centered on suspicion and control to one focused on encouragement and support. This in turn would help to improve community perception of police. He believes that police should partner with schools, probation, and other agencies to provide a comprehensive system of positive support for poor youth desperately in need of constructive adult supervision and guidance. Critics of community policing argue that current partnerships only increase the all-encompassing system of harassment of

MIRANDA RIGHTS
Legal safeguards of the right to remain silent and the right to an attorney that must be provided by police to a suspect before questioning.

minority youth because they are based in a control mind-set, generating negative dynamics that lead to juvenile justice involvement.[48] If, however, adults shift from an attitude of control to one of support, these same agencies could provide vital adult mentors that encourage positive youth development.

Youth–police dialogues and similar programs are attempting to change the police–youth dynamic from negative to positive. As noted, there is mistrust on both sides of the relationship. Teen Empowerment, a youth development agency with locations in Massachusetts and Rochester, New York, conducted a survey in Rochester of over three hundred youth on problems in the community, and found that issues with police were among the youths' top concerns.[49] Over 70 percent reported being stopped and questioned by the police without reason, and over half felt that police treated youth unfairly. Using these results, the agency organized conferences; youth–police reconciliation dialogues; a police–youth unity day; and other activities aimed at increasing understanding on both sides. Evaluations showed that both police and youth felt that they had gained better awareness of the perspective of the others, but both also realized it would require significantly more work to change behaviors.

For many, these dialogues are a positive step toward the ultimate goal that Rios envisions. The problem of secondary deviance—in which youth are propelled toward an entrenched delinquent identity because of negative interactions with law enforcement and perceptions of police illegitimacy—makes it crucial to continue efforts to alter negative police–youth interactions. Because that one officer was willing to see Rios as more than just a gangbanger, Rios was able to achieve far beyond the expectations for youth from his neighborhood. Rios argues that all poor youth should be given the same opportunities and support, and a different vision of policing must be embraced by both police and communities for that to happen.

KEY TERMS

arrest Taking someone into custody by legal authority.

broken windows theory Proposition that reducing all forms of disorder in a neighborhood, including fixing broken windows and removing abandoned cars, will reduce crime.

chivalry hypothesis Belief that girls are in need of protection influencing the way agents of the justice system handle girls' cases.

community policing Police partner with the community to reduce crime and problems within the community.

concentrated disadvantage Areas that have a combination of heterogeneous population, high population mobility, and high poverty.

contraband Any item that is illegal to be possessed or sold.

crackdowns Sudden increases in police presence and sanctions for specific offenses or in specific areas.

demeanor Attitude, manner, and body language of youth during interaction with police which influences police discretionary decision-making.

detention Keeping someone temporarily in official custody.

hot-spot policing Assignment of police resources to areas where crime is concentrated.

informal adjustment Discretionary decision by police to not refer youth to further juvenile justice processing.

institutionalized racism Organizational practices and policies that systematically discriminate against certain races.

Miranda rights Legal safeguards of the right to remain silent and the right to an attorney that must be provided by police to a suspect before questioning.

overpolicing–underpolicing paradox Policing practices that are heavy-handed for minor transgressions (overpolicing) and lack of prompt response to resident calls for service (underpolicing).

probable cause More likely than not that a law has been violated.

procedural justice The perception of fairness and respect in the process, not the outcome, of a situation.

reasonable suspicion Specific facts/circumstances that allow police to stop and frisk that do not rise to the level of probable cause.

recidivate To reoffend.

rough justice Unfair treatment of a suspect by police to teach a "lesson."

search incident to arrest Physical examination of a suspect and the area under a suspect's control upon an arrest.

search warrant Search order issued by the court allowing police to search particular areas for specific property and to bring that property to court.

stationhouse adjustment Discretionary decision by police to detain a youth at the police station and call a parent or guardian without further juvenile processing.

Terry stop A brief detention of a person by police on reasonable suspicion of involvement in criminal activity allowing for stop, frisk, and questioning.

two-track system Differential treatment by class wherein those with financial means avoid the system, while those without do not.

zero-tolerance policing Policing strategy that involves a crackdown on all offenses, including public order disturbances, in an effort to show that even petty crime will not be tolerated.

REVIEW AND STUDY QUESTIONS

1. Describe the roles that police play in communities.
2. How much discretion, if any, should police have in cases involving youth? Why?
3. How would you feel if officers in your local police department were mandated to receive training in procedural justice techniques?
4. How are boys and girls treated differently by police? How has this changed over time?

5. How are black and brown youth treated differently by police? Has this changed over time? Explain.
6. What is community policing?
7. Define crackdowns, hot spots, and zero-tolerance policing. What are the challenges with these policies?
8. How can communities best balance the possible public safety benefits of stop and frisk with procedural justice concerns around experiences of youth, particularly black and brown youth?
9. Should parents or legal guardians be required to be present when their children are given the Miranda warning? Justify your response.

CHECK IT OUT

Listen

"New Yorkers Weigh Safety and Harassment in 'Stop and Frisk' Police Policy":

www.pbs.org/newshour/bb/nation-july-dec13-stopfrisk_08-13/

Watch

Color of Justice, Connecticut Office of Policy and Management:

www.ct.gov/opm/cwp/view.asp?a=2974&q=383632

Victor M. Rios TED Talk:

www.ted.com/talks/victor_rios_help_for_kids_the_education_system_ignores

Cases Cited

Terry v. Ohio 392 US Supreme Court 1 (1968)

NOTES

[1] Walker, S. (1979). *A Critical History of Police Reform.* Lexington, MA: DC Heath.

[2] Wolcott, D. B. (2001). "The Cop Will Get You": The Police and Discretionary Juvenile Justice, 1890–1940. *Journal of Social History, 35,* 349–71.

[3] Ibid.

[4] Ibid.

[5] Retrieved from www.ojjdp.gov/ojstatbb/structure_process/case.html 2/25/14.

[6] Act available at www.ojjdp.gov/about/jjdpa2002titlev.pdf.

[7] Wilson, J. Q. (1968). *Varieties of Police Behavior: The Management of Law and Order in Eight Communities.* Cambridge, MA: Harvard University Press.

[8] Plant, J. B., and Scott, M. S. (2009). *Effective Policing and Crime Prevention.* Washington, DC: DOJ, COPS. Available at www.popcenter.org/library/reading/pdfs/mayorsguide.pdf.

[9] Hockenberry, S., and Puzzanchera, C. (2015). *Juvenile Court Statistics 2013.* Available at www.ojjdp.gov/ojstatbb/njcda/pdf/jcs2013.pdf.

[10] Puzzanchera, C., and Hockenberry, S. *National Disproportionate Minority Contact Databook.* Developed by the National Center for Juvenile Justice for the Office of Juvenile Justice and Delinquency Prevention. Available at www.ojjdp.gov/ojstatbb/dmcdb/.

[11] Hurst, Y. G., and Frank, J. (2000). How Kids View Cops: The Nature of Juvenile Attitudes Toward the Police. *Journal of Criminal Justice, 28,* 189–202.

[12] Strategies for Youth: Connecting Cops and Kids. (2013). *If Not Now, When? A Survey of Juvenile Justice Training in America's Police Academies.* Cambridge, MA: Author.

[13] Piquero, A. (2008). Disproportionate Minority Contact. *The Future of Children, 18,* 57–79.

[14] Strategies for Youth. Available at http://strategiesforyouth.org; Forman, J., Jr. (2004). Community Policing and Youth as Assets. *Journal of Criminal Law and Criminology, 95,* 1–48.

[15] Malloy, L. C., Shulman, E. P., and Cauffman, E. (2014). Interrogations, Confessions, and Guilty Pleas among Serious Adolescent Offenders. *Law and Human Behavior, 38,* 181–93; Shusta, R. M., Levine, D. R., Wong, H. Z., Olson, A. T., and Harris, P. R. (2015). *Multicultural Law Enforcement: Strategies for Peacekeeping in a Diverse Society* (6th ed.). Upper Saddle River, NJ: Prentice Hall.

[16] Chensey-Lind, M., and Pasko, L. (2013). *Female Offenders: Girls, Women, & Crime.* Thousand Oaks, CA: Sage.

[17] Goldstein, J. (1960). Police Discretion Not to Invoke the Criminal Process: Low-Visibility Decisions in the Administration of Justice. *The Yale Law Journal, 69,* 543–94.

[18] Flynn, W. J., and McDonough, B. (2004). Police Work with Juveniles: Discretion, Model Programs, and School Police Resource Officers. In A. R. Roberts (ed.), *Juvenile Justice Sourcebook: Past, Present, and Future,* 199–215. New York: Oxford.

[19] Ibid.

[20] Gebo, E. (2007). A Family Affair: The Juvenile Court and Family Violence Cases. *Journal of Family Violence, 22,* 501–9.

[21] Chappell, A. T., MacDonald, J. M, and Manz, P. W. (2006). The Organizational Determinants of Police Arrest Decisions. *Crime & Delinquency, 52,* 287–306.

[22] Hipp, J. R. (2007). Income Inequality, Race, and Place: Does the Distribution of Race and Class within Neighborhoods Affect Crime Rates? *Criminology 45,* 665–97.

[23] Engel, R. S., Sobol, J. J., and Worden, R.E. (2000). Further Exploration of the Demeanor Hypothesis: The Interaction Effects of Suspects' Characteristics and Demeanor on Police Behavior. *Justice Quarterly, 17,* 235–58; Allen, T. T. (2005). Taking a Juvenile into Custody: Situational Factors that Affect Police Officers' Decisions. *Journal of Sociology & Social Welfare, 32,* 121–29.

[24] Bruson, R. K., and Weitzer, R. (2009). Police Relations with Black and White Youths in Different Urban Neighborhoods. *Urban Affairs Review, 44,* 858–85.

[25] Morash, M. (2006). *Understanding Gender, Crime, and Justice.* Thousand Oaks, CA: Sage.

[26] Puzzanchera, C., Adams, B., and Hockenberry, S. (2012). *Juvenile Court Statistics 2009.* Pittsburgh, PA: National Center for Juvenile Justice.

[27] MacDonald, J. M., and Chesney-Lind, M. (2001). Gender Bias and Juvenile Justice Revisited: A Multi-Year Analysis. *Crime & Delinquency, 47,* 173–95.

[28] Cauffman, E. (2008). Understanding the Female Offender. *Future of Children, 18,* 119–42.

[29] Gilbert, K., and Ray, R. (2016). Why Police Kill Black Males with Impunity: Applying Public Health Critical Race Praxis (PHCRP) to Address Determinants of Policing Behaviors and Justifiable Homicides in the USA. *Journal of Urban Health, 93,* Supplement 1, 122–40.

[30] See US Department of Justice Community-Oriented Policing Services Office. Available at https://cops.usdoj.gov/html/dispatch/january_2008/nugget.html.

[31] Gill, C., Weisburd, D., Telep, C. W., Vitter, Z., and Bennett, T. (2014). Community-Oriented Policing to Reduce Crime, Disorder, and Fear and Increase Satisfaction and Legitimacy among Citizens: A Systematic Review. *Journal of Experimental Criminology, 10,* 399–428.

[32] Berman, G., and Fox, A. (2009). *Lessons from the Battle over D.A.R.E.: The Complicated Relationship between Research and Practice.* New York: Center for Court Innovation; Rosenbaum, D. P. (2007). Just Say "No" to D.A.R.E. *Criminology & Public Policy, 6,* 815–24.

[33] Hecht, M. L., Marsiglia, F. F., Elek, E., Wagstaff, D. A., Dustman, P., and Miller-Day, M. (2003). Culturally Grounded Substance Use Prevention: An Evaluation of the Keepin' It REAL. Curriculum. *Prevention Science, 4,* 233–48.

[34] Esbensen, F., Peterson, D., Taylor, T. J., Freng, A., Osgood, D. W., Carson, D. C., and Matsuda, K. N. (2011). Evaluation and Evolution of the Gang Resistance Education and Training (G.R.E.A.T.) Program. *Journal of School Violence, 10,* 53–70.

[35] Taylor, T. J., Turner, K., Esbensen, F., and Winfree, L. (2001). Coppin' an Attitude: Attitudinal Differences among Juveniles toward Police. *Journal of Criminal Justice, 29*, 295–305.

[36] Tyler, T. R., and Huo, Y. J. (2002). *Trust in the Law: Encouraging Public Cooperation with the Police and Courts.* New York: Russell-Sage.

[37] Sunshine, J., and Tyler, T. R. (2003). The Role of Procedural Justice and Legitimacy in Shaping Public Support for Policing. *Law & Society Review, 37*, 513–48.

[38] Lurigio, A. J., Greenleaf, R. J., and Flexon, J. L. (2009). The Effects of Race on Relationships with the Police: A Survey of African American and Latino Youths in Chicago. *Western Criminology Review, 10*, 29–41.

[39] Braga, A., Papachristos, A., and Hureau, D. (2014). The Effects of Hot Spots Policing on Crime: An Updated Systematic Review and Meta-Analysis. *Justice Quarterly, 31*, 633–63.

[40] Wilson, J. Q., and Kelling, G. L. (1982). Broken Windows. *The Atlantic.* Available at www.theatlantic.com/doc/print/198203/broken-windows.

[41] Harcourt, B. E., and Ludwig, J. (2006). Broken Windows: New Evidence from New York City and a Five-City Social Experiment. *University of Chicago Law Review, 73*, 271–320.

[42] Ibid.

[43] Gellman, A., Fagan, J., and Kiss, A. (2005). *An Analysis of the NYPD's Stop-And-Frisk Policy in the Context of Claims of Racial Bias.* Available at www.stat.columbia.edu/~gelman/research/unpublished/frisk7.pdf; Fratello, J., Rengifo, A. F., and Trone, J. (2013). *Coming of Age with Stop and Frisk: Experiences, Self-Perceptions, and Public Safety Implications.* New York: Vera Institute of Justice.

[44] See www.pbs.org/newshour/bb/nation-july-dec13-stopfrisk_08-13/.

[45] *State v. Sugg* 456 S.E.2D 469 (W.VA. 1995).

[46] Scott, E., and Grisso, T. (2005). Developmental Incompetence, Due Process, and Juvenile Justice Policy. *North Carolina Law Review, 83*, 101–47.

[47] Feld, B. C. (2006). Police Interrogation of Juveniles: An Empirical Study of Policy and Practice. *The Journal of Criminal Law & Criminology, 97*, 219–316.

[48] Xu, L., Fiedler, M. L., and Flaming, K. H. (2005). Discovering the Impact of Community Police: The Broken Windows Thesis, Collective Efficacy, and Citizens' Judgment. *Journal of Research in Crime and Delinquency, 42*, 147–86.

[49] Dougherty, J., Flemming, P., and Klofas, J. (2014). *Teen Empowerment's Youth Police Dialogues Evaluation: Final Report to the Fetzer Institute.* Rochester, NY: Rochester Institute of Technology, Center for Public Safety Initiatives.

Youth and the Courts

LEARNING OBJECTIVES

By the end of the chapter, you should be able to do the following:

- Identify competing explanations for the origins of the juvenile court.
- Describe the juvenile court process.
- Describe the roles of the main actors in the juvenile court process.
- Identify the key functions of the juvenile court.
- Know the procedural safeguards provided to juveniles.
- Discuss the mechanisms by which juveniles can be tried as adults.
- Discuss the nuances of intersectionality in juvenile court processing.
- Identify the effect of adolescent development research on juvenile court practices and laws.

Case Study 9: Judging Our Youth

Hillary's mom set off the investigation. Hillary Transue had just turned fifteen when she stood before Judge Mark Ciavarella, trembling and confused. Less than one minute after she heard him say "Adjudicated delinquent," officers had her handcuffed, shackled, and whisked away. Hillary's mother, Laurene, stood helpless as court personnel told her to go home, explaining that her daughter was now a legal ward of the Commonwealth of Pennsylvania. She was handed a business card with a probation officer's name and number scrawled on the back. She was told to call and he would explain.

Hysterical, Laurene stood sobbing on the sidewalk. How could this be happening? How could they take her daughter away? She began what was a series of relentless phone calls: to the local public defenders' office; to county officials; the governor's office; the ACLU; university professors; and finally, to a law center in Philadelphia dedicated to protecting the legal rights of children. The law center agreed to take the case.

This began the uncovering of one of the worst judicial scandals in the state's history. By the end, two senior judges would be serving long sentences in federal prison; the owners and managers of two private juvenile detention facilities would be convicted; and the state Supreme Court would overturn the delinquency convictions of over 2,400 juveniles. It began with Hillary's story and the revelation that Hillary had stood before the judge without her constitutional right to an attorney.

No-Nonsense

Known as "Mr. Zero Tolerance," Judge Mark Ciavarella had a tough reputation and was proud of it. Schools across the county invited him to speak at assemblies. On the podium facing hundreds of schoolchildren, he preached: "Whatever sins you have committed, you can't go back and undo it." The judge issued this warning: "If you want to experience prison, I'll be glad to put you there."

Ciavarella's platform running for a ten-year term as a judge in the mid-1990s was as a tough-on-crime advocate who would not hesitate to prosecute juveniles as adults. His campaign ads were full of threatening images of teens committing serious crime. He was elected in 2002. Four years later, he was elected by his peers to be the presiding judge of the juvenile court in Luzerne County, Pennsylvania. By the time Judge Ciavarella heard Hillary's case, he had become somewhat of a celebrity in the county.

A local boy made good, Ciavarella was a pillar of the community. School superintendents, mayors, and other officials clamored for him to speak at local events. He loved the spotlight and spoke with great animation as he paced back and forth onstage. His rulings and folksy comments were covered in the press, espousing the importance of accountability, obedience to the law, and the obligation of parents to be strict disciplinarians. He made constant reference to his own parenting, to the way his parents raised him, and the choices he had made in his own life.

School officials especially embraced Ciavarella's judicial philosophy as part of the larger zero-tolerance school discipline policy. Ciavarella partnered with the county commissioners to create school programs designed to use the "fear factor" to prevent kids from wrongdoing. The program began with a visit to the county courthouse to hear a lecture by Ciavarella and continued with a tour through an adult prison, where the children were taunted by inmates, ordered to stop smiling, and to pull up their baggy pants. Kids who smirked or rolled their eyes were pulled out of line and made to stand facing a wall.

Ciavarella often repeated his favorite warning: "If you do something in school and I see you in my courtroom, I will send you away. This is your one warning." One strike was all you got in Ciavarella's courtroom. When kids appeared in court, he would remind them: "Do you remember what I told you? I warned you. Well, now you have to live with the consequences." Judge Ciavarella made good on his promise every time.

The Problem Is Bad Parents

Judge Ciavarella lectured parents as much as he did their children, accusing them of being too lenient and neglecting to discipline or hold children accountable. He often threatened the parents with charges, and had on occasion jailed a parent for failure to pay the court-related fines incurred by the child. To Ciavarella, the parents were as much to blame as the youth. The pleas from anxious parents to allow them to take their children home fell on deaf ears. He chastised them for being "overprotective" and indulgent. He saw his role as a stern judge necessary because parents were failing to do their job.

In defense of his philosophy, Ciavarella often shared a story from his own upbringing. He grew up in a rough neighborhood. His father worked in a brewery, his mother, as a telephone operator. When he was a teenager, he and some friends had a few beers and attempted to go joyriding in a neighbor's car. The police caught them trying to break into the car. The detective drove him home. While his mother wept, lamenting that her son was a criminal, his father hit him so hard that he was knocked out cold. To Ciavarella this was the epitome of "tough love." Ciavarella claimed that he didn't need intervention by the juvenile justice system because his father had already "taken care of it." In his courtroom, Ciavarella said it was his job to deliver the judicial equivalent of the knockout blow.

The Doctrine of *Parens Patriae* and Due Process

In the original design of the juvenile court, the judge held absolute power to decide the fate of a child before the court. Because this power was intended to be benevolent and exercised "in the best interests of the child," there was no need for defense counsel; no need to prove guilt; hear witnesses; use rules of evidence; or invoke the protections of due process. According to the doctrine of *parens patriae*, the judge literally could take over for the parents if the judge determined the parents were doing an inadequate job. With the assistance of reports written by social workers and probation officers, the judge would examine the details of the child's life and make that judgment.

Even in the nineteenth century there were many who questioned the basic fairness of the juvenile court. Judges were given enormous legal power to deprive children of their liberties and parents of their parental rights without due process of law. Many worried that children would be vulnerable to a possible abuse of power on the part of the system that might not always be acting in their best interests, or with compassion or fairness.

Locking kids up without due process seemed to subject children to what Supreme Court justice Abe Fortas said was "the worst of both worlds." Children were being deprived of their liberty in juvenile facilities that were often no different from adult prisons without the protections of fundamental fairness given to adults. The question was: Are children "people" who are entitled to the same constitutional rights as adults?

By 1967, in the famous *In re Gault* case, the US Supreme Court emphatically decided the answer was yes. In Gault, the court said children, like adults, were entitled to a host of due process protections. Foremost among these was the right to legal counsel. Yet four decades later, children came before Ciavarella's court without benefit of legal counsel. How could this happen?

Facing Ciavarella

Hillary quickly admitted what she had done when the police called. At fourteen, she and her friends thought it would be funny to create a fake Myspace page about her assistant principal. The content was pretty mild: A drawing captured the assistant principal's red hair and typical green pants suit, and the fake text read, "I spend most of my days reading silly teen magazines and daydreaming about Johnny Depp in nothing but his tidy whities—ooh la la!" It was a parody posted months ago, and she had forgotten all about it.

The police officer made the incident sound far more serious. He told her mother that he was coming to arrest Hillary. Alarmed, Laurene said, "Wait a minute. You are not going to arrest my daughter until I get a lawyer!" The officer then warned her not to get lawyers involved or he would charge Hillary with the federal crime of Internet stalking. If she cooperated, he told her mother that the charge would be reduced to a misdemeanor. He reassured Laurene that since Hillary had no record of system involvement, she would be put on probation. Laurene agreed to cooperate.

Months later Hillary and Laurene appeared in court as instructed without having consulted an attorney. The pair entered the waiting room where they were directed to a table along with other children and their parents. The clerk asked Hillary if she had an attorney with her. She said, "No," and was handed an entirely blank form. Both mother and daughter were told to sign the document, which they did, as they saw others doing the same. Laurene thought she was signing up for a public defender. Then they waited. When Hillary's name was called, they assumed they were going to meet the public defender. Instead, they were brought directly to the courtroom to face Judge Ciavarella.

The first thing Ciavarella said to Hillary was, "What makes you think you can do this kind of crap?" Then he asked her if she had attended the assembly at her school. She said she had, but could not recall what he'd said. Ciavarella was annoyed. "It's going to come back to you, because I didn't go to that school just to blow smoke. I'm a man of my word. You're gone." With that, he adjudicated her a delinquent and sentenced her to three months in detention, saying, "Send her up and let her think about what she has done!" Hillary was cuffed, shackled, and gone; in ninety seconds it was all over.

When Laurene finally called the Juvenile Justice Law Center in Philadelphia, attorneys Marsha Levick and Bob Schwartz already had suspicions about what was going on in Luzerne County. This was not the first call they had received about Judge Ciavarella.

The Same Story Over and Over

Charlie Balasavage was fourteen when the police came to his front door. Charlie had been riding his moped, a birthday present from his parents, in his neighborhood. Charlie thought the police were there because he wasn't wearing a helmet. Instead they told him that the scooter was stolen property. He called his parents, who rushed home to explain that they had purchased the scooter from a family member and had no receipt. The police arrested all three.

At the station, police explained that if Charlie agreed to the charge of receiving stolen property, the police would drop the charges against his parents. Charlie had never been in trouble with the law or at school. Awkward and chubby, he preferred to stay close to home; a speech impediment made him a target for teasing by other kids, and Charlie's mother often let him stay home from school. Police reassured his parents that punishment for Charlie would be mild: probation at most. In court, the family went through the same process that Hillary's mother described. They were directed to a table and handed a blank form and told to sign. With no explanation, both parents and child signed. They too thought they were signing up for a public defender.

Judge Ciavarella took one look at Charlie's record of school absences and said, "Clearly you have behavioral problems." He never asked Charlie how he had come to possess the moped, nor did he ask his parents where they had purchased it. These facts were irrelevant in his determination that Charlie was a delinquent youth.

"[It appears to me] that [these] parents have lost control of a child, and it's up to me to get this child back under control."

When Charlie's mother tried to object, Judge Ciavarella accused her of being "overprotective." He sentenced Charlie to three months in Camp Adams, a boot camp for seriously delinquent boys. Like Hillary, Charlie was cuffed, shackled, and taken away—as were thousands of other youth who went through Judge Ciavarella's courtroom without a lawyer.

The Worst of Both Worlds

Children from Ciavarella's courtroom were sent to detention facilities that housed youth from across the state. Most youth were sent there for far more serious offenses. Like so many other juvenile detention facilities, these places resembled prisons more than caring, home-like environments. For most of the children, the hardest part was the separation from their families. Hillary's mother explained that in the first week of Hillary's detention she was allowed a single one-minute phone call; in the second week, it was a five-minute phone call; and in the third week, it was raised to eight minutes. Visits, like many other "perks," were privileges that had to be earned. It took Charlie several weeks to earn the privilege of having a pillow at boot camp.

The psychological consequences of court processing for children can be grave. Amanda, another "delinquent" from Ciavarella's courtroom, described being shackled. Officers told her to get down on her knees so they could put chains on her ankles; then they cuffed her hands behind her back; and finally, they put a belt around her waist with a kind of leash so they could pull her along. Amanda said of lockup, "I was scared every day." Almost immediately she fell apart psychologically. In desperation, she wrote Ciavarella a letter begging to go home to her parents, promising that she had learned her lesson, offering to do any kind of punishment as long as she was allowed to go home. She never received a reply and sank into a severe depression.

Hillary was one of the lucky ones: Because of the investigation, she served only three weeks of the original ninety-day sentence. Countless others were not so fortunate. For many, the sentence stretched from months to years as the system continued to detain them inside punitive facilities that provided no education, little treatment, and exposed them to significant trauma. The damage was extensive: the loss of innocence, childhood, mental health, education, and, in some instances, their lives.

Once In, Hard to Get Out

A detention sentence was usually just the beginning. Policies and procedures in the juvenile justice system make it difficult to get out of the system. If youth violate rules in a detention facility or conditions of probation, they can be brought back before the judge. Given Ciavarella's judicial philosophy, youth in his courtroom found themselves ordered back to juvenile facilities again and again. For Amanda, the endless rounds of placements lasted for five years and eleven months. Amanda left with a diagnosis of PTS and the need to be on medication.

Charlie remained under the supervision of the juvenile court for four years and ten months. Again without a lawyer, Charlie naively admitted to the judge that he had tried marijuana for the first time in boot camp. Ciavarella sentenced him to three more months at a treatment facility for drug abuse. The longer Charlie was away from school, the more difficult it was for him to succeed at school when he was sent back home. Each time Charlie was released, a probation violation for truancy brought him back before Judge Ciavarella, who sentenced him to yet another juvenile facility. Between the ages of fourteen and eighteen, Charlie celebrated every single birthday behind bars.

It is not hard to violate conditions of probation that typically include attending school and obeying school rules; obeying curfew and other parental rules; and abstaining from alcohol and drugs. As part of the zero-tolerance policies created by Ciavarella and school officials, probation officers were placed directly in the schools. Instead of being sent to the principal, kids like Amanda and Charlie were sent directly to their probation officers. Violation of conditions of probation is a delinquent offense. Judge Ciavarella returned kids like Amanda and Charlie back to detention every time.

Irreparable Damage

For all youth, being locked up is traumatic, but for some kids, the consequences are lethal. By his senior year Ed Kenzakoski was a star wrestler in line for a full athletic scholarship to college. At age seventeen, however, Ed's parents were worried about the choices he was making. In the summer between his junior and senior years, they thought he was partying too much, and they didn't want him to ruin his chances at a scholarship.

Ed's father and several of his high school buddies who were now police officers hatched a plan to "teach Ed a lesson" that would "scare" him into more-responsible behavior. They conspired to plant a marijuana pipe inside his vehicle and then arrest him and charge him with possession of drug paraphernalia. They expected the court to issue a warning or stint on probation that would serve as a wake-up call to stay on the straight and narrow.

But with Judge Ciavarella on the bench, the plan backfired badly. Like everyone else, Ed was adjudicated, shackled, and taken away within minutes. The look on his face when they led him away remains seared forever in his mother's memory. With that went Ed's hopes for a scholarship. He missed his senior year's wrestling season; the scouts stopped calling; his chances were over. Ed never returned to school or wrestling again.

Ed came out of the facility a changed person, his mother said. "He went in there a free-spirited seventeen-year-old kid, and came out a hardened man." He refused to talk about what happened while he was there; all his mother knew was that he was angry and bitter. Shortly after being released, he got into a fight. The incident went to adult court and was dismissed. But Ed was still on juvenile probation with Judge Ciavarella. Rather than risk being sent back, Ed ran away to Florida.

Ed returned home after a month. He got a job in construction and seemed to be getting his life back together. Two whole years went by. But there was still an outstanding warrant from Judge Ciavarella. When Ed got into a minor car accident, he was forced to appear before the judge, who sent him back to juvenile detention for another three months. This time when he was released, he was "a ball of fury." He got into another fight, and this time he was sentenced in adult court to two years in state prison for aggravated assault. Five months after his release from prison, Ed killed himself with a single bullet to his heart.

All for Profit?

During his time on the bench, Ciavarella sentenced 6,500 kids. Over half of these children (54 percent) appeared before him without the benefit of a lawyer. In the spring of 2008, the Juvenile Justice Law Center filed a petition with the state Supreme Court asking for reversals of all convictions and to expunge the records for these youth on the grounds that they had all been denied right to counsel.

Around this time, the Law Center received a call from the FBI asking for information about Ciavarella's courtroom. Independently, the justice department had been investigating suspicious flows of money in the county juvenile justice system. The costs associated with incarcerating juveniles are high; the average is about $88,000 each year. Unlike other jurisdictions where the dollars spent on detention fluctuated from year to year, Luzerne County figures were steady from year to year. This was suspicious.

The FBI investigation found that Chief Judge Conahan and his good friend Ciavarella had lobbied hard to build two new privately run, for-profit facilities. The builders and owners of those facilities were business associates of Conahan. Conahan signed an agreement guaranteeing that the county would send juveniles to the facilities. Conahan also cut off funds to the county facility, leading to its closing. The FBI investigation discovered that both judges had received financial payments as part of the deal—a total of $2.6 million—concealed in a series of hidden bank accounts.

When the facts of this corruption were reported in the media, a firestorm broke out as parent after parent came forward to talk about what had happened to their children. A reporter for the local paper said, "We ran the story and our phones rang off the hook. Everyone told the exact same story." People of the county came to the devastating conclusion that all this time Judge Ciavarella had been sentencing children to detention in exchange for cash payments. The media dubbed it "Kids for Cash." Initially Ciavarella and Judge Conahan pled guilty to tax evasion and fraud in exchange for eighty-seven months in prison, but a federal judge refused to accept the plea deal. Ciavarella insisted he was innocent and went to trial.

The Documentary: Kids for Cash

It was the trial of the century in Luzerne County. In the end, Ciavarella was convicted of only four counts against him, but the federal judge sentenced him to twenty-eight years in prison. This was a huge victory for so many who wanted the judge to be held accountable for what he had done.

Yet many wonder: Did Ciavarella really commit kids to detention just to make money? The investigative reporter who followed the case from the start points out that Ciavarella was jailing kids long before he received any money. What about the schools, probation officers, police, and prosecutors who all went along with the zero-tolerance system he had orchestrated in the county? Why did everyone else go along with this scheme?

When Robert Mays, an accomplished filmmaker, read about the case in 2009 just after the two judges had entered guilty pleas, he decided to tell the story from both points of view: the families who were the "victims," and the judges who by now were widely seen as the "villains." Remarkably both judges agreed to be extensively interviewed for the film. While the events unfolded in the dramatic trial, they too told their story. What emerges is a tale of greed and corruption, but also a story about the enormous power of the juvenile court and its potential to harm the very children they are supposed to protect.

THINKING CRITICALLY ABOUT THIS CASE

1. Why do you think that schools, police, and probation went along with Judge Ciavarella's practices?

2. Would access to legal counsel have changed the outcome for these youth? Explain.

3. Should judges be allowed broad discretionary powers in the juvenile court? Why, or why not?

4. Do you think the justice system's handling of the corrupt court officials was appropriate? Explain.

5. Thinking about the concept of procedural justice, what, if anything, can be done to improve the perceptions of the juvenile justice system held by these youth and families? Should the state provide any monetary compensation or other forms of restitution?

6. Some countries have a court system in which three judges hear the case at one time in order to protect against judicial bias. Do you think this would help in the United States?

REFERENCES

This case is based on the following sources:

Associated Press. (2/11/2009). Pennsylvania. Judges Accused of Jailing Kids for Cash. Available at www.nbcnews.com/id29142654/ns/us_news-crime_and_courts/t/pa-judges-accused-jailing-kids-cash/#.VzOXaPkrK70.

Juvenile Law Center. Luzerne County Kids-for-Cash Scandal. Available at http://jlc.org/luzerne-county-kings-cash-scandal.

National Public Radio. "Kids for Cash" Captures a Juvenile Justice Scandal from Two Sides. All Things Considered. Available at www.npr.org/2014/03/08/28786626/kids-for-cash-captures-a-juvenile-justice-scandal-from-two-sides.

INTRODUCTION

THE KIDS FOR CASH SCANDAL ILLUSTRATES the broad reach of the juvenile justice system as well as the limits on the juvenile court in the modern era. This chapter highlights the role of the juvenile court in the larger juvenile justice system. The Latin term *parens patriae* describes the purpose of the court: to act as a "super" parent and make decisions in the best interests of the child. Judge Ciavarella relied on this doctrine to remove children from parents he believed were not acting as strict disciplinarians. However, the Supreme Court ruled in 1967 that children do possess constitutional rights and cannot be deprived of their liberty without the protections of due process.

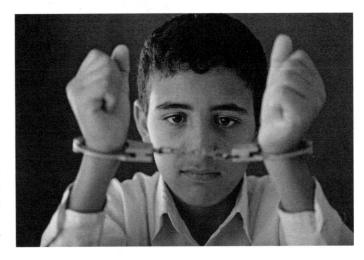

Over two thousand delinquency convictions were overturned because Ciavarella illegally denied youth due process of law in his courtroom.

JUVENILE COURT EVOLUTION

The first juvenile court was started in Cook County (Chicago), Illinois, in 1899. The court was an outgrowth of the Progressive Era child-saving movement discussed in chapter 3. It was rooted in a rehabilitative philosophy, as opposed to the adult system, which is focused on punishment.[1] The idea that the whole child should be taken into account was paramount in juvenile court. This meant that legal factors, such as the offense and prior offense history, would be secondary to the needs of the child. This also meant that court decisions were not always reflective of delinquency histories, as evidenced by the youth who went through Ciavarella's courtroom. Dispositions could be disproportionate to offense because the "whole child" was taken into account. Juvenile judges had ultimate discretion in their dealings with youth as long as they thought they were acting in the "best interests of the child."

Until 1967, lawyers were not a part of the juvenile court process, and formal rules of evidence—such as guilty beyond a reasonable doubt—did not apply. The belief was that adherence to formal court rules might interfere with rehabilitating young persons. Lawyers were thought to make the process adversarial rather than rehabilitative. Court hearings were confidential in order to insulate children from outside labels. **Dispositions**, or sentences, were indeterminate, meaning that it was up to the system to decide when a child was rehabilitated.

Some believe that the *parens patriae* philosophy legitimized the poor treatment of immigrants and those in the lower class; that discretion invited discrimination; and that confidentiality could cover up abuses and limit public sympathy for youth.[2] As discussed in Part I, most of the youth processed in juvenile court in the early years were poor and of immigrant descent. They were sent to institutions for minor infractions under the guise of being in their best interests. The public generally paid little attention to what was happening.

DISPOSITION
Juvenile court sentence.

The juvenile court has not been immune to societal changes, explored in chapter 3. The court has evolved from the idea of a benevolent parent, to a pattern of treating behavioral problems through medical methods, to granting civil rights to youth involved in court proceedings, to diverting minor delinquency acts from the court system entirely, to taking a "get tough" stance on youthful offenders. Each of these eras had important implications for how youth were treated.

Today the juvenile court sees more cases than ever before, even though juvenile crime, especially violent crime, has decreased significantly since its early-1990s peak. Delinquency cases in juvenile court rose almost 300 percent between 1960 and 2009.[3] The main reason for this increase is that youth are more likely to be formally sanctioned for more minor offenses today than in the past. School problems and family problems are more likely to be on the juvenile court docket today, and girls are more likely to be involved in the juvenile justice system than they were twenty years ago.[4] Alternatives to juvenile court and different types of courts have been created to help ensure that youth are not receiving the "worst of both worlds." Those initiatives are discussed at the end of this chapter.

JUVENILE COURT STAGES

Youth in Judge Ciavarella's court were often denied counsel and sent away, and, as we see from Hillary's case, denied the proper court process of arraignment, adjudication, and disposition (see figure 9.1). Typically, there is a funnel process that removes some cases from juvenile court through an **intake screening**. In this stage, an intake officer, typically a court or probation officer, reviews a case to determine which steps, if any, should be taken by the juvenile court. Options include dismissal, further formal court processing, or informal diversion. Diversion at the court stage is similar to that at the police stage. The case can be placed on file without a finding for a period of time, or an informal agreement can be made to attend a diversion program. If the youth behaves and/or completes the diversion program successfully, the charges are dropped.

Some youth may be detained at a juvenile facility prior to the next court hearing. Youth who are considered a risk to the community, or a "flight" risk—meaning, they might leave the area before the next court hearing—can be held in detention. Increasingly, jurisdictions are using a risk assessment tool to help an intake officer determine whether or not the youth is a high-enough risk to be placed there. A detention hearing, also called an initial hearing, must be held to assess the continued secured confinement of the youth prior to arraignment. Youth have a constitutional guarantee of a lawyer for a detention hearing. Clearly, Ciavarella's courtroom did not always honor that.

Bail is afforded to juveniles in some states, but there is no federal legal right to bail in juvenile court.[5] Bail is the release of an accused youth from juvenile court custody in exchange for money, or other assurance, that the youth will appear for subsequent court hearings. Bail is forfeited should the youth fail to appear in court. In most cases, the burden of obtaining bail assurance would fall to parents/guardians, given that most youth have yet to acquire substantive resources to provide bail for their future court appearance.

In an **arraignment**, a youth must respond to the delinquency petition(s) before the court. Ideally, youth have received adequate attorney representation

INTAKE SCREENING
Review of juvenile case to determine next steps in court process.

BAIL
The release of accused juvenile prior to the next court date in exchange for money, or other assurance, of court appearance.

ARRAIGNMENT
Court stage where the youth must respond to a delinquency petition.

at this stage and clearly understand the charges and implications of either admitting "true" (guilt) or pleading "not true." Youth move on to the disposition phase of the court system if they plead true. If they plead not true, youth go to an adjudicatory hearing. Far too many youth, as

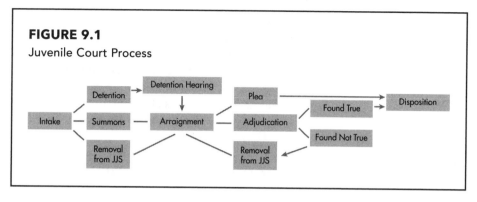

FIGURE 9.1
Juvenile Court Process

we have seen from this chapter's case study, as well as the stories of Cristian Fernandez and Victor Rios, do not understand the legal implications of their actions.

Juveniles can agree to a **plea bargain** in which the prosecutor, with the judge's consent, offers a lesser sentence to the youth in exchange for a true plea. There are no figures available for the percentage of youth who plea bargain in juvenile court. The benefits to plea-bargaining are that the youth ostensibly receives a lighter disposition and the court removes a case from the docket. Yet, there is a question of whether youths, even with adequate legal counsel, fully understand the implications of the agreement, and whether or not they feel compelled to go along with the authorities in agreeing to a plea.[6]

The adjudicatory hearing is the trial stage of the juvenile court process. During this phase, the facts of the case are presented and the prosecution and defense can call witnesses to the stand and enter evidence to be reviewed. The judge hears the evidence against the youthful defendant. Most states do not allow a jury trial for juvenile cases. Just as with adults, the state's representative, a prosecutor or district attorney, must prove that the youth in question committed the delinquent act beyond a reasonable doubt.

A petition that is found not true means that the youth is free to leave with no other court involvement. A petition that is found true means that the youth is **adjudicated delinquent**. The judge sets a date for a disposition hearing, known in the adult system as a sentencing hearing. The judge also may order a **predisposition investigation (PDI)** report, also known as a social background investigation, to be completed by a probation officer. This report documents the youth's current and prior offenses, his/her educational, social/medical, and family history, and makes dispositional recommendations to the court.

The dispositional phase of the juvenile court is akin to the sentencing stage in adult court. The judge decides what will happen to the youth. Most youth receive probation at disposition.[7] Approximately 24 percent of youth receive the disposition of a correctional institution or residential home.[8] Increasingly, judges are using structured decision-making tools for disposition. Like detention risk-assessment instruments, these are scoring instruments that utilize information about the youth, such as offense history and substance abuse, to determine appropriate placement. Disposition also can involve adult court supervision in juvenile cases where a serious offense has been committed or youth are regarded as serious and violent offenders. This is called **blended sentencing**, where supervision begins in the juvenile justice system and is extended into the adult criminal system once the youth ages out of the juvenile system.

PLEA BARGAIN
An agreement offered by the prosecutor to the defendant that allows the youth to plead "true" to lesser offenses in exchange for a lighter penalty.

ADJUDICATED DELINQUENT
Label for youth on a petition that has been found true.

PREDISPOSITION INVESTIGATION (PDI)
Report detailing a youth's social history by a probation officer that makes sentencing recommendations to the judge.

BLENDED SENTENCING
Juvenile and adult court jurisdiction over a case at disposition.

Most of the youth in Ciavarella's court had multiple **revocation hearings**. When a youth has not obeyed court orders, a judge may "revoke" the previous court orders and impose new ones. As we have seen, this may include out-of-home placements. Finally, a **review hearing**, or post-disposition review, is held to discuss the status of a juvenile case. Some of these hearings are routine to ensure that the youth is attending to court orders, while for others, the purpose is to change the disposition, or to close the case entirely.

KEY COURT PERSONNEL

Judge, prosecutor, defense attorney, and probation officer are the four central personnel in the juvenile court. Other parties to juvenile delinquency and status offense cases may include police officers, school staff, social workers, and child advocates. As we saw in Luzerne County, the judge is the most powerful figure in juvenile court. It is the judge who decides how the court will proceed; what will be allowed into evidence; whether or not the state proved its case; and dispositional sanctions. Some juvenile court judges are part-time employees. While juvenile court judges are the cornerstone, like police, they do not necessarily receive training in juvenile justice issues or adolescent development. An appointment in juvenile court is not always welcomed by judges, and some states rotate judges through the juvenile court.[9]

Referees are used in some locations in lieu of judges in order to relieve the caseload pressures of the juvenile court. Referees are individuals appointed by the court to hold hearings and make recommendations to the judge on juvenile justice matters. They must learn the laws in their states, but do not always have to be attorneys. Referees have broad powers to make procedural decisions and rule on substantive issues, although ultimately the juvenile court judge has power over them. These decision-making methods have broad implications for how youth will be treated.

The **prosecutor**, often a district attorney, is usually a practicing lawyer who represents the interests of the state that has filed a petition against a youth. The prosecutor must prove beyond a reasonable doubt that the youth has committed the act(s) outlined in the filed petition. In smaller jurisdictions that lack the resources to have a prosecutor's office, a police officer who has some legal training represents the state's interest. These officers must follow the law and fulfill the same obligations as prosecutors.

The defense attorney in juvenile court is often a **public defender** who is hired by the state to represent youth who are **indigent**, or cannot afford a lawyer. Some states require that practicing lawyers must "pay their dues" by rotating in to juvenile court to represent youth for a period of time or for a certain number of cases. In other states, new lawyers gain skills through the public defender's office before moving on to private practice. These practices have resulted in questioning whether youth have adequate legal representation. The American Bar Association (ABA) formed the National Juvenile Defender Center after an ABA national study found that juvenile court attorney representation was woefully inadequate.[10] Results showed that most law schools provided no juvenile training; that there were limited resources to conduct investigations by defense attorneys; and that youth were denied access to representation at crucial stages of the juvenile justice process, including detention hearings.[11]

REVOCATION HEARING
A court hearing occurring when court orders have not been obeyed.

REVIEW HEARING
Post-disposition review of a case.

REFEREES
Individuals appointed by the court to hold hearings and make recommendations to the judge on juvenile justice matters.

PROSECUTOR
State's attorney; often a district attorney.

PUBLIC DEFENDER
Attorney provided to the defendant free of charge.

INDIGENT PERSON
Person deemed poor and eligible for a court-appointed attorney.

The **probation officer** plays a prominent role in juvenile court by providing the judge with a PDI prior to the dispositional hearing that investigates the history of the youth and provides recommendations to the judge about sentencing. Most of the time, judges go along with these recommendations.[12] Probation officers not only supervise youth who are released into the community to ensure that they are complying with court orders, but they also appear in court whenever there is a review hearing, and may request a revocation hearing if youth are not following court orders. Probation officers are often referred to as the "eyes and the ears" of the court in the community.

Court actors—judges, prosecutors, defense attorneys, and probation officers—often work together in what is called a **courtroom workgroup**. They effectively manage high caseloads and provide a sense of stability for themselves in a job that does not have prescribed routines by giving similar "going rates" for certain types of offenses.[13] This may help to explain why there was no immediate public outcry about Judge Ciavarella's sentencing practices from the start. The existence of a courtroom workgroup calls into question the juvenile court goals of providing individualized justice that is in the best interests of the child.

A parent/guardian is required to attend hearings in most, but not all, states. Parents have an obligation to assist the child in meeting their court orders. Just as Ciavarella did countless times, judges may give instructions or lectures to parents about the gravity of the situation and the needs of the child. Parents can be held liable for the actions of their children in all fifty states under parent responsibility laws. Examples of when parent responsibility laws have been invoked include cases where youth have accessed household firearms, and cases of drinking by minors at the parents' home without their knowledge.

COURT PRACTICES AND EFFECTIVENESS

States generally adhere to the guidelines set forth in the Uniform Juvenile Court Act (1968) in crafting their own juvenile court statutes, purpose, scope, and procedures.[14] This document, produced by the National Conference of Commissioners on Uniform State Laws, identifies the offenses to be included in juvenile court and sets the age of court jurisdiction as under eighteen, although states can, and do, vary from that.

In general, juvenile records are kept confidential from the public as part of a rehabilitative orientation. Confidentiality does not typically apply when youth are tried as adults. States have imposed mandatory time limits for the processing of juvenile cases, typically one month, in order to ensure that the needs of the youth are addressed as quickly as possible in keeping with the original purposes of the court. The reality, however, is that delays and requests for extensions are a frequent occurrence in the juvenile court system.

The primary goal of the juvenile justice system is rehabilitation. This involves addressing the needs of the youth so s/he does not recidivate. While the public generally supports treatment for youthful offenders, particularly for those who have committed nonviolent offenses, the uptick in juvenile crime in the late 1980s and early 1990s, coupled with the increasingly conservative political climate, caused many states to transform their juvenile justice statutes to include a second purpose: punishment. In practice, juvenile court sentencing also often includes restitution and restoration geared toward ensuring that the delinquent repairs the harm that was done by his/her acts.

PROBATION OFFICER
Person who investigates, reports on, and supervises youth while under court control.

COURTROOM WORKGROUP
Court actors who work together to develop a routine to manage their caseloads.

Restitution refers to the youthful offender "giving back" to the community and/or the victim. Restitution can include monetary remuneration for material damage caused by the youth—for example, paying for a smashed car window—and/or it can include community service, such as working at soup kitchens or in parks, to repay debt through labor. Restitution can lead to greater victim satisfaction with the process.[15] Restorative justice also is increasingly being used in the juvenile justice system, where the focus is to "restore" the offender, victim, and community to their previous states. Restorative justice as a correctional practice is discussed more fully in the next chapter.

Intersectionality and Effectiveness

Of cases referred to juvenile court in 2013, 45 percent were dismissed or not adjudicated delinquent.[16] Cases may be dropped by a prosecutor or judge for a variety of reasons, including lack of evidence, due process problems, and informal diversion agreements. Cases that went to trial and were not adjudicated delinquent could be because of a lack of evidence, or because of a diversion agreement. That said, youth of color are disproportionately represented at all stages of the juvenile justice system, and the disparity increases throughout the juvenile justice process. What this means is that more white youth are funneled out of the system at earlier stages of the juvenile justice process, while black and brown youth are more likely to remain in the system and end up institutionalized.[17]

"Race matters" in the juvenile justice system.[18] Overt discrimination does not usually play a role, but **extralegal factors** are significant, leading to a two-track system. For example, parents who can afford private treatment and are able to work only one job, or flexible hours, to provide more supervision for their children are likely to have their children diverted away from the juvenile system.[19] Youth whose parents cannot afford private treatment or who have jobs that prevent them from providing supervision, or are incarcerated, are much more likely to be funneled into the system. These youth are also more likely to come from neighborhoods with high crime rates and are more likely to be youth of color.[20]

Addressing these disparities is a federal mandate, which means that the federal government is requiring that states correct the disparity or they will not receive money from the federal government. States have responded by creating community-based alternatives, increasing cultural awareness of court staff, and reducing barriers to family involvement, such as providing child care and holding court hearings around parents' work schedules.[21] The juvenile court process can have a profound effect on youth and their families. We saw this in the case study, and research that finds that youth who are processed through the court and given out-of-home placements, such as Hillary, Charlie, Amanda, and Ed, are more likely to become adult offenders than those who are given alternatives to court.[22]

SIGNIFICANT JUVENILE JUSTICE CASES

Many procedural safeguards for juveniles were enacted during the juvenile rights era when Chief Justice Earl Warren was at the helm of the Supreme Court in the 1960s and early 1970s. The most significant case was *In Re Gault* (1967), mentioned in chapter 3, providing juveniles with a number of due process rights,

RESTITUTION
Refers to the offender "giving back" to the community and/or the victim.

EXTRALEGAL FACTORS
Factors other than present offense and offense history that play a role in decision-making.

including the right to counsel. This case, along with several others, began the juvenile court shift in delinquency proceedings from informality and guilty by preponderance of evidence to more formality and proof beyond a reasonable doubt.

The facts of the case were that fifteen-year-old Gault, who was on probation, made a prank call with his friend to a neighbor. The police arrested him and took him to a detention facility. Gault's parents were not home, but were notified of the detention when they returned to their house. At his trial, Gault was denied many due process rights afforded to adults, including access to the charges against him; a formal court transcript; ability to confront witnesses; and attorney representation. Gault was found true and committed to a training school for the remainder of his minority, which meant until he turned twenty-one—six years later. Had Gault been an adult, his maximum punishment for this crime would have been either a $50 fine, or no more than two months in jail. The appeal went to the Supreme Court.

The Supreme Court ruled that juveniles have the right to due process, through the Fourteenth Amendment. As a result of *Gault*, juveniles were afforded key rights: a) adequate notice of hearing/charges; b) right to counsel when the penalty could be institutionalization; c) right to confront/cross-examine witnesses; d) right against self-incrimination; e) Miranda application; f) right to appeal; and g) court-recorded hearings (transcripts). The Supreme Court felt that they did not interfere with the benevolence of the juvenile court by providing such safeguards only in cases where confinement was a possibility. Critics of the juvenile court, however, believe that granting these safeguards legitimized the punitive practices of the court that disproportionately affected black and brown youth. They charged that the juvenile court was now a scaled-down criminal court that did not offer the full array of adult procedural safeguards.[23]

Several other cases decided during the juvenile rights era shaped the juvenile court of today. *Kent v. United States* (1966) mandated that youth could not be waived to adult court without a hearing to determine whether or not that was appropriate. *In re Winship* (1970) afforded the standard of proof to be "beyond a reasonable doubt" in delinquency cases of possible confinement. The case of *Breed v. Jones* (1975) ensured that **double jeopardy** did not apply to juveniles, meaning that, like adults, juveniles cannot be tried twice for the same crime. Finally, in the case of *McKeiver v. PA* (1971), the Supreme Court held that juveniles did *not* have the right to a jury trial. This decision was meant to distinguish the benevolent nature of the juvenile court from the adversarial nature of the adult court.

Today, youth in juvenile court do not have access to four main constitutional rights that are afforded to adults: a) the right to trial by jury; b) the right to bail; c) the right to a grand jury indictment; and d) the right to a public trial. A few states do offer some of these rights, but they are not required by the Constitution to do so. The lack of the full array of constitutional rights, along with the recognition that the juvenile court can still act capriciously and instill punishment, has led some to question whether the juvenile court should be reformed or abolished. Those issues will be taken up later in the chapter.

The Supreme Court recently made several landmark decisions relative to the disposition of juveniles. The result of *Roper v. Simmons* (2005) was to make it unconstitutional to put to death youth under the age of eighteen. Citing recent neuroscience research on the developing brain, the majority opinion concluded

DOUBLE JEOPARDY
Being tried twice for the same crime.

that youth under eighteen were not fully capable of understanding their actions or the consequences of them, and thus, they should not be subjected to the death penalty. Executing juveniles would violate the Eighth Amendment's ban against cruel and unusual punishment. More recently, the Supreme Court ruled in *Graham v. Florida* (2010) and *Miller v. Alabama* (2012) that sentencing juveniles to life without parole, both for non-murder and murderer offenses, also violates the cruel and unusual punishment clause of the Eighth Amendment. Collectively, these recent cases show a shift in the Supreme Court view of youth informed by current neuroscience.

From Juvenile to Adult Court

Although the Supreme Court has recently recognized youths' lack of maturity, there are several legal mechanisms that continue to process youth as adults for their crimes. Most states reacted to the uptick in juvenile crime in the 1980s and 1990s by reducing the age limit for criminal responsibility from eighteen years old to sixteen or seventeen years old. This meant that youth who met the age criteria would be tried in adult court for all offenses. Yet at the same time, youth of this age were not emancipated, which meant that youth still had to obey parental rules and were not considered adults in other aspects of their lives. They could not drop out of school without parental consent, obtain full-time employment, or vote.

Some perceived that lowering the age of criminal liability devalued youth, giving them more behavioral "responsibility" only when it was convenient for adults to do so.[24] Recently, some states have increased the criminal age limit to eighteen years old (see figure 9.2). This shift has been spurred on by a variety of factors, including neuroscience research, as well as recent federal legislation that requires that states housing youth under age eighteen who have been convicted in adult court be held separate from the general population of offenders ages eighteen and older.[25]

Transfers to adult court are the most widely known mechanisms to process juveniles as adult offenders, yet less than 1 percent of cases are typically transferred.[26] Transfer mechanisms came to the forefront in *Kent v. United States*, where the Supreme Court ruled that a waiver hearing must take place to determine the appropriateness of a transfer to adult court. This traditional form of transfer is called a **judicial waiver**. The prosecutor typically has a preponderance-of-evidence burden of proof to show that a youth should be tried in adult court. The judge must decide on the basis of vague criteria what is in the best interests of the child and the public.

Some states have imposed a **reverse waiver**. Under this waiver, if certain criteria are met (i.e., the charge is capital murder), the case is automatically sent to adult court unless the prosecutor asks for a hearing to move the case to juvenile court. A **prosecutorial waiver**, also called a direct file, leaves the decision of whether to try the case in juvenile or adult court up to the prosecutor. Under this waiver, the decision of where the case should be heard is taken out of the judge's hands and given to the prosecutor. Finally, there is **statutory exclusion**, also called legislative exclusion, in which certain offenses and/or the age of the offender automatically excludes the case from juvenile court and makes it mandatory that the case be heard in adult court.

Race, ethnicity, and social class can indirectly affect transfer decisions, through extralegal factors such as family situation and community environment.[27]

JUDICIAL WAIVER
Judge has discretion to transfer a juvenile case to adult court.

REVERSE WAIVER
Mechanism to move a juvenile case from adult court to juvenile court.

PROSECUTORIAL WAIVER
Prosecutor has discretion to transfer a juvenile case to adult court; also known as direct file.

STATUTORY EXCLUSION
State law exempting certain crime(s) and/or juvenile(s) from juvenile court; also known as legislative exclusion.

For example, a discretionary juvenile transfer to adult court by a judge or prose-cutor may be influenced by lack of family supervision, which may be a function of growing up in a single-parent household with other siblings and a parent who must work two jobs to make ends meet. Black youth are more likely to be in these living arrangements, and therefore more likely to be affected by such decisions.[28]

Research on adult court transfers shows negative outcomes. There also does not appear to be convincing evidence that sentencing juveniles as adults acts as a general deterrent for other youth.[29] Most importantly, among youth with similar offense histories, those tried in adult court are more likely to reoffend than those tried in juvenile court.[30] Why does adult court increase recidivism? It may be that adult conviction carries a stigma and a criminal record that is public. Youth convicted in adult court may then be more likely to commit crimes because they have internalized a criminal label, as labeling theory would suggest. Criminal records also make finding employment and stable housing more difficult.[31] Youth convicted in criminal court do not have access to the same programs as juvenile offenders that may increase their competencies in a positive youth development approach.[32]

FIGURE 9.2

Age of Criminal Responsibility[33]

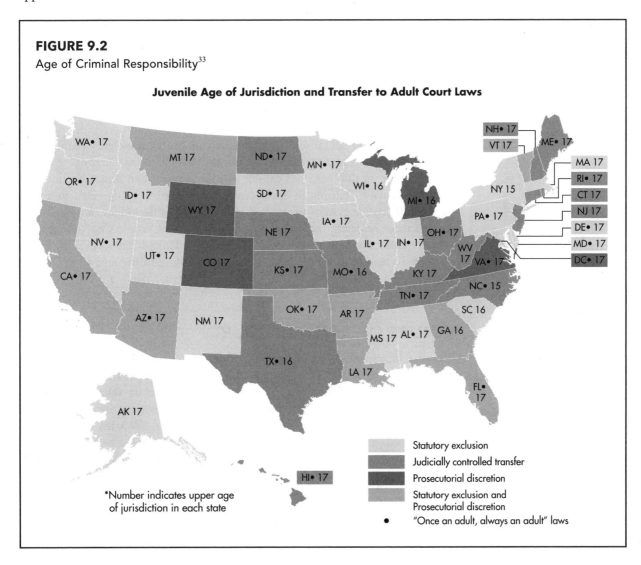

Juvenile Age of Jurisdiction and Transfer to Adult Court Laws

For all of these reasons, adult court transfers are not helpful for juveniles. Some states also have a **Once an Adult, Always an Adult statute**. These laws stipulate that once a youth has been transferred to adult court for a crime, any subsequent cases will also be heard in adult court, regardless of the age of the youth. These policies further amplify racial disparities found at earlier stages of the juvenile justice system.

Developmental Competency

Developmental immaturity characterizes the teen years, and nothing but time can increase maturity. Age itself is a crude indicator of development. Current research shows that almost all youth under the age of fifteen, as well as many sixteen- and seventeen-year-olds, do not have the **developmental competence** to stand trial in adult court.[34] Scientists identify four domains critical to assessing development: neurological, intellectual, emotional, and psychosocial.[35] *Neurological development* is heightened in the mid-teenage years, and slows through late adolescence. In relation to delinquent activities, this means that youth cannot fully think through consequences of their actions. *Intellectual development* affects a person's capacity to think in hypotheticals. This makes it hard for youth to understand that others may have different opinions. *Emotional development* refers to impulse control. Youth lack some capacity to delay gratification. *Psychosocial development* addresses the perception of risk, the influence of others, and future orientation. This means that youth may believe that their actions are not risky; they may be easily influenced by their peers; and they may be unable to think about what the consequences could mean for their futures.

Neuroscientists call for reforming the juvenile court competency requirement by giving consequences that are attuned to the developmental stage of the youth, and by ensuring that penalties cannot be more severe than those administered by adult court.[36] Training in adolescent development is being given to a host of juvenile justice system personnel, including juvenile judges. As a result of neuroscience research, the Association of Juvenile and Family Court Judges, the largest member organization of such judges in the United States, is calling for an increase in standards for all court personnel training in the area of adolescent development and culpability.[37]

FUTURE OF JUVENILE COURT

How can kids in juvenile court thrive? What can prevent a Kids for Cash scandal from happening again? The reality is that the juvenile court has been criticized both for being too soft on crime and for not holding to the rehabilitative ideal. It has been a conduit for discriminating against the poor, youth of color, and girls; and it has been condemned for not offering the full array of procedural safeguards to juveniles that are offered to adults.[38] There have been various proposals, sometimes opposing, to rectify the problems faced by the juvenile court.

Youth Specialty Courts

Specialty courts, also called **problem-solving courts**, have been touted as a way to improve the juvenile justice system.[39] Several types of specialty courts exist

ONCE AN ADULT, ALWAYS AN ADULT STATUTE
Law stipulating that once a youth has been processed in adult court, all subsequent court cases will be processed in adult court.

DEVELOPMENTAL COMPETENCE
Ability to navigate social, emotional, cognitive, and behavioral tasks at different developmental stages of maturity.

PROBLEM-SOLVING COURTS
Courts that focus solely on a specific problem; also known as specialty courts.

that hear juvenile court cases. They include youth court, family court, and drug court. The emphasis of these courts is on creativity, and ensuring that personnel who work in these courts actually want to work with youth. Court personnel are trained in youth development and issues specific to the court, such as the pharmacology of drugs. The approach of these courts is that the process fits the problem, so family courts address family issues and drug courts specialize in drug issues. These courts also partner with other agencies and schools to coordinate cases. Youth who go through these courts are monitored more closely by judges, and these courts make decisions based on ongoing data assessment of youth program involvement.

Teen or **youth courts** are an alternative to juvenile court wherein youth volunteers are trained in legal procedure. Supervised by adults, they take on the roles of judge, prosecutor, defense attorney, and jury to adjudicate their peers who have committed misdemeanor offenses. Jury members are comprised in part of youth who have gone through the youth court process. Youth courts operate in schools and communities. A code of ethics is at the forefront of such programs, emphasizing confidentiality, and the community of youth engaged in the process must be supportive of the offender rather than shaming in order for youth courts to work.[40] Some evaluations of youth courts show lower subsequent juvenile justice system involvement among those who have successfully completed the program.[41] Other research, however, has pointed to increased recidivism among teen court graduates.[42] Differences in outcomes may be the result of how the program was implemented and the training of volunteers.[43]

In most family courts, one judge hears all cases related to family matters. This one-family, one-judge model translates into the judge knowing more about the family and ostensibly making better decisions based on that knowledge. Family court cases include delinquency, child maltreatment, divorce, and probate. Evaluation outcomes of family courts are scarce. One study of delinquency cases heard in family court found that while family court judges took more time with cases and learned more about the youths and their families than juvenile court judges, in the end, there was no difference in dispositional outcomes given.[44] Alternatively, another study found that clients and community members perceived that procedural justice was more likely to take place in family and other specialty courts than in traditional courts, which may lead to lower recidivism rates.[45]

Juvenile drug courts attempt to redress substance abuse problems through in-depth knowledge of addiction. Traditional juvenile courts have been criticized for not paying attention to addiction issues, and it has been postulated that part of the reason for youths' failure to remain delinquency-free is due to substance abuse problems.[46] Juvenile drug courts take into account the cycle of dependency. Evaluations of juvenile drug courts do not generally show positive outcomes. One recent multisite evaluation found that drug court youth recidivated more than youth in a comparison site, and questioned whether drug courts should be used with juvenile offenders, given that drug courts require more investment on the part of the youth and there are more opportunities to "fail."[47]

Juvenile Court Revision or Abolishment?

The American Bar Association (ABA), the national association of lawyers, advocates for the continuation of the juvenile court, with revisions. The ABA

YOUTH COURTS
Alternative to juvenile court, where trained youth volunteers hear their peers' cases as judges, attorneys, and jury members; also called teen courts.

JUVENILE DRUG COURTS
Problem-solving courts to redress substance abuse problems through in-depth knowledge of addiction.

believes youth entering juvenile court should have all the due process rights of adults.[48] The ABA also believes that the juvenile court should provide graduated sanctions, or increasing penalties, for continued delinquent behavior; and they advocate for status offenses being removed from juvenile court jurisdiction. Alternatively, legal scholar Barry Feld believes the juvenile court cannot continue with its current practices, as the original purpose of the juvenile court has been lost through legal reforms. He believes that providing social welfare is a societal function, not a judicial one, and providing community protection will always undermine social welfare concerns in any juvenile court.[49]

Arguments to abolish the juvenile court go further, stating that judges' discretion is subjective, rather than based on objective science; and that a closed juvenile court invites abuses of discretion. These critics argue for a criminal court designed to hear both juvenile and adult cases, in which judges could give a "youth discount" at sentencing, so that youth would not receive penalties as severe as those received by adults.[50] Advocates of this approach state that youth would then receive the full procedural safeguards granted to adults, and sentencing disparities for youth tried in adult versus juvenile court would be eliminated.[51] Supporters of abolishing the juvenile court further argue that a single court would save money by eliminating the juvenile court and its related personnel and resources.

Status Offense Removal

Recall that status offenses are offenses that if committed by an adult would not be considered a crime, such as truancy, running away, and incorrigibility. Status offenses have been removed from juvenile court jurisdiction in some states, while others are considering doing so. The strongest argument for removing status offenses from juvenile court jurisdiction is that such acts typically need assistance from social service agencies, not juvenile court involvement, which may "criminalize" behavior and widen the reach of the court.[52] Status offenses involve behavior that in some cases may be within the normal range of adolescent *Sturm und Drang*, or turmoil, that accompanies growing up in America. Juvenile court may not adequately address the underlying family problems, and the process of juvenile court itself may be detrimental to youth. Those who argue for keeping status offenses in juvenile court point to research that shows that status offenses are likely to occur prior to delinquent activity for both boys and girls; thus, effective early intervention with status offending could prevent future delinquent acts.[53] As juvenile courts continue to evolve, the question of court jurisdiction over status offenses is likely to do so as well.

Regardless of the shape or existence of juvenile court in the future, it is likely to have more scientifically derived instruments to assist court personnel in making appropriate decisions for youth. These structured decision-making tools help to assess the risk youth pose as well as the needs of youth through a matrix that is rooted in scientific knowledge about youth and offending. Assets are not yet built into many of these structured decision-making tools. Ensuring that such tools are equitable across gender, ethnic, racial, and geographic populations, however, is a current task of research.

How the juvenile court may be transformed in the coming years is the subject of much debate. What is clear, however, is that the pivotal role played by the court in the juvenile justice process cannot be underestimated. Consequences of court involvement are severe, as we saw in the case study example. Juvenile court judges wield the power to adjudicate youth, to release youth to the community, or confine them to institutions. All of these decisions have implications for a young person's future.

The next two chapters will examine those dispositional options in more depth.

KEY TERMS

adjudicated delinquent Label for youth on a petition that has been found true.

arraignment Court stage where the youth must respond to a delinquency petition.

bail The release of accused juvenile prior to the next court date in exchange for money, or other assurance, of court appearance.

blended sentencing Juvenile and adult court jurisdiction over a case at disposition.

courtroom workgroup Court actors who work together to develop a routine to manage their caseloads.

developmental competence Ability to navigate social, emotional, cognitive, and behavioral tasks at different developmental stages of maturity.

disposition Juvenile court sentence.

double jeopardy Being tried twice for the same crime.

extralegal factors Factors other than present offense and offense history that play a role in decision-making.

indigent person Person deemed poor and eligible for a court-appointed attorney.

intake screening Review of juvenile case to determine next steps in court process.

judicial waiver Judge has discretion to transfer a juvenile case to adult court.

juvenile drug courts Problem-solving courts to redress substance abuse problems through in-depth knowledge of addiction.

Once an Adult, Always an Adult statute Law stipulating that once a youth has been processed in adult court, all subsequent court cases will be processed in adult court.

plea bargain An agreement offered by the prosecutor to the defendant that allows the youth to plead "true" to lesser offenses in exchange for a lighter penalty.

predisposition investigation (PDI) Report detailing a youth's social history by a probation officer that makes sentencing recommendations to the judge.

probation officer Person who investigates, reports on, and supervises youth while under court control.

problem-solving courts Courts that focus solely on a specific problem; also known as specialty courts.

prosecutor State's attorney; often a district attorney.

prosecutorial waiver Prosecutor has discretion to transfer a juvenile case to adult court; also known as direct file.

public defender Attorney provided to the defendant free of charge.

referees Individuals appointed by the court to hold hearings and make recommendations to the judge on juvenile justice matters.

restitution Refers to the offender "giving back" to the community and/or the victim.

reverse waiver Mechanism to move a juvenile case from adult court to juvenile court.

revocation hearing A court hearing occurring when court orders have not been obeyed.

review hearing Post-disposition review of a case.

statutory exclusion State law exempting certain crime(s) and/or juvenile(s) from juvenile court; also known as legislative exclusion.

youth courts Alternative to juvenile court, where trained youth volunteers hear their peers' cases as judges, attorneys, and jury members; also called teen courts.

REVIEW AND STUDY QUESTIONS

1. What are the competing explanations for the creation of juvenile court?

2. What are typical extralegal factors that influence the dispositions handed out by the juvenile court? Explain how these factors contribute to a two-track system and to the problem of DMC in the juvenile justice system.

3. Using the concept of developmental competency, take a stand on whether or not adolescents should be tried in adult court.

4. At what age should youth be held criminally responsible? Support your argument.

5. What are the arguments for and against juvenile court revision and abolishment?

6. Describe what happened in the *In re Gault* case. What specific legal changes resulted from this Supreme Court decision?

7. Identify the due process rights afforded to juveniles. How do the constitutional rights of juveniles differ from the constitutional rights of adults? Do you believe this is fair? Why, or why not?

8. What is a revocation hearing? How did the revocation hearing process contribute to the lengthy sentences served by youth profiled in this chapter's case study?

9. What is the courtroom workgroup? How might that explain what happened in Judge Ciavarella's courtroom?

10. How do specialty courts operate differently from juvenile court? Which of these innovative courts would you support? Provide evidence for your answer.

CHECK IT OUT

Watch

Reclaiming Futures: Helping Kids Caught in the Cycle of Drugs, Alcohol, and Crime:

www.youtube.com/watch?v=Oq1nRHHkun8#t=289

Film: *Kids for Cash*:

kidsforcashthemovie.com

Listen

www.oyez.org/cases/1960-1969/1965/1965_104

Cases

Breed v. Jones 421 U.S. 519 (1975)

Graham v. Florida 560 U.S. 48 (2010)

In Re Gault 387 U.S. 1 (1967)

In Re Winship 397 U.S. 358 (1970)

Kent v. United States 383 U.S. 541 (1966)

McKeiver v. PA 403 U.S. 528 (1971)

Miller v. Alabama 567 U.S. 460 (2012)

Roper v. Simmons 543 U.S. 551 (2005)

NOTES

[1] Fox, S. J. (1996). The Early History of the Juvenile Court. *The Future of Children, 6*, 29–39.

[2] Platt, A. M. (2009). *Child Savers: The Invention of Delinquency* (40th anniversary edition). New Brunswick, NJ: Rutgers University Press.

[3] Puzzanchera, C., Adams, B., and Hockenberry, S. (2012). *Juvenile Court Statistics 2009*. Pittsburgh, PA: National Center for Juvenile Justice.

[4] Aull, E. H. (2012). Zero-Tolerance, Frivolous Juvenile Court Referrals, and the School-to-Prison Pipeline: Using Arbitration as a Screening-Out Mechanism to Help Plug the Pipeline. *Ohio State Journal on Dispute Resolution, 27*, 179–206; Ukert, B., Sagatun-Edwards, I., Crowe, A., . . . Kameda, D. (2006). *Juvenile Domestic and Family Violence: The Effects of Court-Based Intervention Programs on Recidivism—Final Report*. Washington, DC: Department of Justice; Zahn, M. A., Brumbaugh, S., Steffensmeier, D., . . . Kruttschnitt, C. (2008). *Violence by Teenage Girls: Trends and Context*. Washington, DC: Office of Juvenile Justice and Delinquency Prevention, Girls Study Group.

[5] Dominguez, D. (2007). Community Lawyering in the Juvenile Cellblock: Creative Uses of Legal Problem Solving to Reconcile Competing Narratives on Prosecutorial Abuse, Juvenile Criminality, and Public Safety. *Journal of Dispute Resolution, 2*, 387–416.

[6] Scott, E. S., and Steinberg, L. (2009). *Rethinking Juvenile Justice*. Cambridge, MA: Harvard University Press.

[7] Furdella, J., and Puzzanchera, C. (2015). *Juvenile Cases in Court, 2013*. Washington, DC: Office of Juvenile Justice and Delinquency Prevention.

[8] Ibid.

[9] Ibid.

[10] Puritz, P., Burrell, S., Schwartz, R., Soler, M., and Warboys, L. (2002). *A Call for Justice: An Assessment*

of Access to Counsel and Quality of Representation in Delinquency Proceedings. Washington, DC: American Bar Association, Juvenile Law Center, and Youth Law Center.

[11] Ibid.

[12] Freiburger, T. L., and Hilinski, C. M. (2011). Probation Officers' Recommendations and Final Sentencing Outcomes. *Journal of Criminology and Justice, 34,* 45–61.

[13] Gebo, E., Stracuzzi, N. F., and Hurst, V. (2006). Juvenile Justice Reform and the Courtroom Workgroup: Issues of Perception and Workload. *Journal of Criminal Justice, 34,* 425–33.

[14] National Council of Juvenile and Family Court Judges. (2005). *Juvenile Delinquency Guidelines: Improving Court Practice in Juvenile Delinquency Cases.* Reno, NV: Author.

[15] Latimer, J., Dowden, C., and Muise, D. (2005). The Effectiveness of Restorative Justice Practices: A Meta-Analysis. *The Prison Journal, 85,* 127–44; Lipsey, M. W. (2009). The Primary Factors That Characterize Effective Interventions with Juvenile Offenders: A Meta-Analytic Overview. *Victims and Offenders, 4,* 124–47.

[16] Furdella and Puzzanchera, *Juvenile Cases in Court, 2013.*

[17] Chapin Hall Center for Children. (2008). *Understanding Racial and Ethnic Disparity in Child Welfare and Juvenile Justice.* Chicago, IL: University of Chicago, Chapin Hall Center for Children; Rodriguez, N. (2010). The Cumulative Effect of Race and Ethnicity in Juvenile Court Outcomes and Why Preadjudication Detention Matters. *Journal of Research in Crime & Delinquency, 47,* 391–413.

[18] Engen, R., Steen, S., and Bridges, G. (2002). Racial Disparities in the Punishment of Youth: A Theoretical and Empirical Assessment of the Literature. *Social Problems, 49,* 194–220.

[19] Fader, J. J., Kurlychek, M. C., and Morgan, K. A. (2014). The Color of Juvenile Justice: Racial Disparities in Dispositional Decisions. *Social Science Research, 44,* 126–40.

[20] Rodriguez, N., Smith, H., and Zatz, M. S. (2009). "Youth Is Enmeshed in a Highly Dysfunctional Family System": Exploring the Relationship among Dysfunctional Families, Parental Incarceration, and Juvenile Court Decision Making. *Criminology, 47,* 177–208.

[21] Cabaniss, E. R., Frabutt, J. M., Kendrick, M. H., and Arbuckle, M. B. (2007). Reducing Disproportionate Minority Contact in the Juvenile Justice System: Promising Practices. *Aggression and Violent Behavior, 12,* 393–401.

[22] Gatti, U., Tremblay, R. E., and Vitaro, F. (2009). Iatrogenic Effect of Juvenile Justice. *The Journal of Child Psychology and Psychiatry, 50,* 991–98.

[23] Feld, B. C. (1997). Abolish the Juvenile Court: Youthfulness, Criminal Responsibility, and Sentencing Policy. *Journal of Criminal Law and Criminology, 88,* 68–88.

[24] Munn, N. (2012). Reconciling the Criminal and Participatory Responsibilities of Youth. *Social Theory & Practice, 38,* 139–59.

[25] Justice Policy Institute. (2009). *The Costs of Confinement: Why Good Juvenile Justice Policies Make Good Fiscal Sense.* Washington, DC: Author.

[26] Knoll, C., and Sickmund, M. (2012). *Delinquency Cases in Juvenile Court 2009.* Juvenile Offenders and Victims National Report Series Fact Sheet. Washington, DC: Office of Juvenile Justice and Delinquency Prevention.

[27] Burgess-Proctor, A., Holtrop, K., and Villarruel, F. A. (nd). *Youth Transferred to Adult Court: Racial Disparities.* Policy Brief. Washington, DC: Campaign for Youth Justice.

[28] Family Structure and Children's Living Arrangements. (2012). Available at www.childstats.gov/americaschildren/famsoc1.asp.

[29] Burgess-Proctor et al., *Youth Transferred to Adult Court: Racial Disparities.*

[30] Redding, R. E. (2010). *Juvenile Transfer Laws: An Effective Deterrent to Delinquency?* Juvenile Justice Bulletin. Washington, DC: Office of Juvenile Justice and Delinquency Prevention.

[31] Burgess-Proctor et al., *Youth Transferred to Adult Court: Racial Disparities.*

[32] Butts, J. A., Bazemore, G., and Meroe, A. S. (2010). *Positive Youth Justice: Framing Justice Interventions Using the Concepts of Positive Youth Development.* Washington, DC: Coalition for Juvenile Justice.

[33] Teigen, A. (2014). *Juvenile Age of Jurisdiction and Transfer to Adult Court Laws.* Available at www.ncsl.org/research/civil-and-criminal-justice/juvenile-age-of-jurisdiction-and-transfer-to-adult-court-laws.aspx.

[34] Grisso, T., Steinberg, L., Woolard, J., . . . Schwartz, R. (2003). Juveniles' and Adults' Competence as Trial Defendants. *Law and Human Behavior, 27,* 333–63.

[35] Ibid.

[36] Scott, E. S., and Steinberg, L. (2009). *Rethinking Juvenile Justice.* Cambridge, MA: Harvard University Press.

[37] National Council of Juvenile and Family Court Judges. (2005). *Juvenile Delinquency Guidelines: Improving Court Practice in Juvenile Delinquency Cases.* Reno, NV: Author.

[38] Feld, B. C. (1999). *Bad Kids: Race and the Transformation of the Juvenile Court.* New York: Oxford University Press.

[39] Gebo, E. (2005). Do Family Courts Administer Individualized Justice in Delinquency Cases? *Criminal Justice Policy Review, 16,* 190–210.

[40] Godwin, T. M. (2000). *National Youth Court Guidelines.* Lexington, KY: American Probation and Parole Association.

[41] Butts, J. A., Buck, J., and Coggeshall, M. B. (2002). *The Impact of Teen Court on Young Offenders.* Washington, DC: Urban Institute.

[42] Stickle, W. P., Connell, N. M., Wilson, D., and Gottfredson, D. (2008). An Experimental Evaluation of Teen Courts. *Journal of Experimental Criminology, 14,* 137–63.

[43] Ibid.

[44] Ibid.

[45] Lee, C. G., Cheesman, F., Rottman, D., . . . Curtis, R. (2013). *A Community Court Grows in Brooklyn: A Comprehensive Evaluation of the Red Hook Community Justice Center.* Williamsburg, VA: National Center for State Courts.

[46] Latessa, E. J., Sullivan, C., Blair, L., Sullivan, C. J., and Smith, P. (2013). *Final Report Outcome and Process Evaluation of Juvenile Drug Courts.* Washington, DC: US Department of Justice.

[47] Ibid.

[48] Puritz et al., *A Call for Justice: An Assessment of Access to Counsel and Quality of Representation in Delinquency Proceedings.*

[49] Ibid.

[50] Zimring, F. (1998). *American Youth Violence.* New York: Oxford.

[51] Redding, *Juvenile Transfer Laws: An Effective Deterrent to Delinquency?*

[52] Chubink, C., and Kendal, J. (2007). Rethinking Juvenile Status Offense Laws: Considerations for Congressional Review of the Juvenile Justice and Delinquency Prevention Act. *Family Court Review, 45,* 384–98.

[53] Gorman-Smith, D., and Loeber, R. (2005). Are Developmental Pathways in Disruptive Behaviors the Same for Girls and Boys? *Journal of Child and Family Studies, 14,* 15–27.

CHAPTER 10

Youth and Corrections

LEARNING OBJECTIVES

By the end of the chapter, you should be able to do the following:

- Articulate a continuum of graduated sanctions for youth offenders.
- Compare and contrast various correctional options.
- Describe the risk principle and its importance.
- Describe how disproportionate minority contact (DMC) is being addressed.
- Discuss the ways in which restorative justice can be used in conjunction with, or as an alternative to, the traditional juvenile justice process.
- Be familiar with key issues in residential placements, including mental health, victimization, education, and privatization.

Case Study 10: From Punishment to Rehabilitation

The name of the facility was like a cruel joke. Located fifteen miles north of Washington, DC, the Oak Hill Center—along with its annex facility, called the Children's Center—was the place the court sent youth for over thirty years to reform them. The name "Oak Hill" evoked an image of a serene, tree-filled campus, and the "Children's Center" implied a facility with a loving staff dedicated to the nurturing care of needy children.

The reality could not have been more different. When Vince Schiraldi, former youth services commissioner, first visited, his comment was, "I wouldn't kennel my dog at Oak Hill Center."

Not Fit for a Dog

Built in 1967, the Oak Hill facility consisted of eleven one-story buildings surrounded by twelve-foot-high razor-wire fencing. One building on the outskirts, just inside the fencing, Unit 6, housed girls; the rest were reserved for boys aged fifteen to nineteen years old.

Inside the brick buildings were cold tile floors, harsh fluorescent lighting, and metal beds, sinks, and toilets, all bolted to the floor. Most of the windows were so damaged they could not be opened, and the glass, long since broken, had been replaced by thick Plexiglas so yellowed it was impossible to see outside. Without fans or air-conditioning, the indoor temperature in summer rose above 100 degrees. And then there were the vermin—snakes, mosquitoes, rats, and roaches—that infested the facility from beds to bathrooms. Boys stuffed T-shirts down the toilets to keep pests from climbing out. The smell of urine permeated the place.

The conditions were filthy, chaotic, and violent. Periodic investigations revealed that staff routinely used fists as well as bricks, knives, and chairs to physically restrain and punish youth. Spending twenty-two hours locked in a cell as punishment for some infraction was not unusual, and lockdowns for the entire facility were a frequent occurrence. As one youth put it, "Kids peed and crapped on the floor if they did not have a toilet in their room and couldn't get out."

The institutional routine consisted of a set of rules and scheduled activities entirely controlled by staff. Youth wore shirts color-coded by the seriousness of their offense: green for violent; purple for "at risk"; gray for those due to be released in thirty days. Youth walked in straight lines with arms folded behind their backs, each hand grasping the opposite wrist. Three times a day, during the change in shift, all activities ceased so officers could take an official count. Staff controlled all activities: when to shower, access to privileges and to basic necessities, including food and hygiene products, such as tampons. Drug use was widespread, aided and abetted by corruption among the staff.

Many at Oak Hill were repeat offenders. In their world, being sent to "reform school"—Oak Hill—was a rite of passage on the streets of Washington, DC. Mixed in among them were first-time offenders, truants, and runaways. There was no separation between those awaiting trial and those who had been convicted, a violation of federal law. Without alternative group homes and community-based placements, Oak Hill was the all-purpose placement for all DC youth in need of supervision.

One of the biggest problems for the facility was the high number of escapes. In one year alone, between January 1988 and January 1989, more than 300 youth escaped—128 from the facility itself, while 191 failed to return after weekend visits with their families. Other times youth disappeared during trips to the hospital or by cutting a hole in the wire fence surrounding the facility. Staff sometimes took bribes to help youth escape. During one dramatic escape widely reported in the press, a young man holding a gun walked into a crowded pediatric waiting room and freed two youth from the facility who were waiting for medical treatment. He himself had escaped by bribing two staff members to take him to the hospital where he could more easily slip away.

Suing to Make a Change

In 1985, a group of lawyers sued the District of Columbia, alleging that the Oak Hill facility and Department of Youth Services were violating the constitutional rights of youth. The Eighth Amendment prohibits cruel and unusual forms of punishment, and conditions at Oak Hill were far below the worst conditions, even for adult offenders. The case was known as *Jerry M. v. District of Columbia*.

It only took a visit or two to the facility to prove the truth of the allegations: The judge ruled that conditions at Oak Hill were in violation of the Eighth Amendment. In 1986, a court consent decree mandated that DC make sweeping reforms across its juvenile justice system adhering to three key principles: First, youth should be held in the least-restrictive environments possible; second, youth should always be placed in a community-based facility rather than secure confinement where possible; and third, all youth placed in secure confinement awaiting trial should be there for as short a time as possible. These principles complied with the Juvenile Justice and Delinquency Prevention Act.

The court went on to issue highly detailed goals and timelines for the reformation of Oak Hill itself. The consent decree detailed the staff-youth ratio and the level of required staff training. Each youth was mandated to receive individualized treatment, education plans, and aftercare plans. The decree set qualification standards for mental health and social workers in the facility, and specified the amounts of daily exercise and recreation youth must have. The decree went on to limit the length of time in isolation for discipline and limit the use of physical restraint, such as leg irons and handcuffs.

The facility was required to have on-site medical care and institute educational programming that met the same standards as the DC public schools. Finally, the court order also focused on the physical condition of Oak Hill, demanding adherence to set standards for food, housekeeping, laundry, waste disposal, vermin control, plumbing, temperature controls, fire safety, and the size of each room. The court appointed a legal monitor to ensure that the department made the necessary changes according to the timetable and to report back to the court on the progress made.

Eighteen Years of Resistance

Every year the court monitor issued one or two reports on the progress the DC juvenile system was making toward instituting these mandatory reforms. Year after year these reports cataloged a dismal failure to implement these reforms. In 2004, in the fifty-second and final report, the monitor made a depressing assessment: "Unfortunately, much of the halting, stutter-step movement toward compliance seen for much of the past eighteen years [has] continued." Little had changed: The court monitor recommended the court close down the whole agency and place it in receivership to be taken over by an authority from outside the jurisdiction in order to provide for the constitutional rights of youth.

A Genuine New Beginning

In 2003, a new DC mayor was sworn in, coinciding with the emergence of a new movement in juvenile justice among the public and policymakers. Informed by the research on trauma and adolescent brain development, this movement balked at the "get tough" idea that punitive approaches for youth were effective and ethical. The mayor appointed a blue-ribbon commission that called for sweeping reforms. The mayor also brought in Vince Schiraldi, who had reformed the juvenile justice system in Missouri, transforming it from a prison-like nightmare to a national model in small-scale therapeutic and community-based treatment for youth. As head of the newly renamed Department for Youth Rehabilitation Services, Schiraldi vowed to finally implement all the changes that the court had ordered eighteen years earlier. The first item on his agenda was to reform Oak Hill.

From Correctional Officer to Youth Development Specialist

For eighteen years, despite the legal mandate from the court, Oak Hill had resisted change. Many of the staff at all levels undermined the court order in every way possible, ignoring all the new rules. They continued to use isolation, violence, and physical restraints. They continued to bring in drugs and alcohol, profiting from the trade and using them to reward favored youth. Whenever pressure mounted for change, staff simply allowed youth to escape, ensuring that media coverage of a dangerous criminal loose in the community would distract policymakers from the reform agenda. Staff-aided escapes were a powerful form of staff sabotage. A staffer from Oak Hill told a reporter, "Many of the old staff are angry . . . and there is a feeling that they may be letting the kids go and looking the other way in an attempt to make the place look like it's falling apart."

Vince Schiraldi knew what he was up against because he had done this before. In 2007, Schiraldi told city officials that his top management problems were keeping staff from beating up kids and figuring out how to cut down on the sex-for-overtime trade between managers and line staff. He knew that in a very real sense, reforming a juvenile correctional facility is a battle for control between the new and the old.

Schiraldi also knew that the most critical challenge for implementing reform was changing the mind-set of the staff. He wanted the corrections officers to see themselves as "youth development specialists" whose job it was to help children turn their lives around. He wanted staff to see youth not as criminals or inmates, but as young people whose life experiences had led them to act a certain way. He wanted staff to see the youth as young people full of potential and promise.

Schiraldi introduced the requirement that each staff member needed to earn at least sixty hours toward their bachelor's degree, ideally in youth development or human services. He instituted training and professional development for staff, so they would have the skills necessary to work with troubled youth. According to Schiraldi, "In the past, a kid who'd spat in a guard's face would have been locked up for twenty-four, maybe even seventy-two hours. Today, if an employee gets spat on, he's encouraged to wash his face off, recover his calm, and then lead the youths in a session on respect and dignity."

This transition was not easy. The biggest obstacle was overcoming the resistance on the part of the staff who didn't want to see their responsibilities change; they had been hired as prison guards, and that's the job they wanted to do. Many of them also believed that punishment, or the threat of it, was necessary to get youth to conform. They did not embrace the new philosophy and sought to get Schiraldi fired. In the end, about sixty staff left the institution or took early retirement, while the rest, along with newly hired staff, embraced the new paradigm of a modern era in juvenile corrections.

The Shuttering of Oak Hill and the Start of New Beginnings

The new generation of policymakers no longer wanted to reform Oak Hill. Instead, they wanted to replace it with an entirely new facility that would look, feel, and run on the principles of positive youth development. The timetable was set for 2009. Many were skeptical; that seemed unrealistic. After all, nothing much had changed for nearly twenty years, despite all the timetables, mandates, consent decrees, and reports. But things were different. In just four years, the District had found the funds to build a top-of-the-line facility called New Beginnings Youth Development Center, and right on schedule. In 2009, the doors of Oak Hill were closed forever.

Today, DC is held up as a model for other juvenile systems across the country: If juvenile justice reform can happen in the District of Columbia, it can happen anywhere. The $46 million, sixty-bed facility includes a library and lunchroom, and buildings that let in plenty of natural sunlight through the multitude of windows. New Beginnings has on-site medical, mental health, and substance abuse care, as well as vocational training. It has a Maya Angelou Academy to educate youth by focusing on a rigorous, culturally relevant curriculum, helping to create meaningful relationships between students and teachers. Some youth development specialists were at one point in their lives themselves incarcerated at Oak Hill. Today they are professionals helping others to turn their lives around.

All staff members at the facility are trained in the "DC model," an evidence-based behavioral modification program modeled after one in Missouri which holds youth accountable for their actions in a humane way. The model emphasizes a positive youth development approach in which youth are seen as future productive citizens, and utilizes cognitive behavioral therapy to help youth change their thinking and responses to life events.

A core element of the new facility is family engagement and reentry planning. There are weekly calls by staff to family members to discuss youths' progress. There also is a free shuttle service on weekends from downtown DC to help make it possible for family members to visit their children while they are incarcerated. New Beginnings has tried to better connect the pieces of the puzzle for youth, so that when they do return to society, they are better equipped to navigate their lives successfully, with the support of caring adults and a network of compassionate institutions. One community worker says, "What is important is where they want to go, not where they've been."

So far, the shift seems to be working. There are fewer youth going back to the facility, and there are community-based alternatives to placement, such as afterschool and evening reporting centers that supervise youth, help them stay on track in school, and provide support and mentoring. This approach has been so successful that DC won the prestigious Harvard Award for Innovation in American Government. Says Schiraldi, "What we had before was a training school for them to become adult inmates. We want them to aspire to college, to be in a place that looks like you care about them."

That said, Vince Schiraldi still argues for the abolition of all reform schools, replacing them with more-humanistic systems of care that follow a positive youth development model and seek to rehabilitate youth within their own families and in their own communities.

THINKING CRITICALLY ABOUT THIS CASE

1. What do you think caused staff to act the way they did at Oak Hill? What does this say about the influence of organizations on individual behavior, and vice versa?

2. What is the difference between the job of the correctional officer and the job of the youth development specialist? Which job appeals to you? Why?

3. Why do you think it took years for court-ordered changes to occur? Do you believe that the race and class background of the youth played a role in the length of time that it took to implement reform?

4. What kinds of supports should be available in the community for youth who return from lockup? Describe the ideal structure of support.

5. Do you agree with Schiraldi that reform schools should be abolished? Provide a rationale for your answer.

REFERENCES

This case is based on the following sources:

Anderson, J. "Officer Beaten in an Escape Attempt at New Beginnings," *Washington Times*, April 18, 2011.

Blog Talk Radio. (9/22/2011). Available at www.blogtalkradio.com/jjmatters/2011/09/22/discussion-with-formerly-incarcerated-youth-michael-kemp.

Forman, J., Jr., and Weingarten, R. H. "New Hope at Oak Hill," *Washington Post*, December 24, 2007.

Kemp, M. "A Double Life Is Nothing but Trouble," *Washington Post*, March 6, 2012.

Labbé, T. "Behind Oak Hill's Fences, Violence and Uncertainty," *Washington Post*, August 2, 2004.

Okonkwo, R. D., and de Kervor, D. N. (2012). There are Two Sides to Every Story: Collaboration between Advocates and Defenders in Achieving Systemic Juvenile Justice Reform. *University of Pennsylvania Journal of Law and Social Change*, 15, 435–54.

Pierre, R. E. "Oak Hill Center Emptied and Its Baggage Left Behind," *Washington Post*, May 29, 2009.

Taskier, A. (12/19/2013). DC Youth Face Solitary Confinement in DC Jails and Federal Prisons. Solitary Watch. Available at http://solitarywatch.com/2013/12/19/dcs-youth-face-solitary-confinement-district-jails-federal-prisons/.

INTRODUCTION

O AK HILL IS A REMINDER TO US THAT intervention can be harmful, and that it is the responsibility of the juvenile justice system to care for children in ways that will lead to healthy youth development. Long gone are the days when experts thought that *any* type of intervention with youth who had committed delinquent acts would be for the better. Today we know that incarceration can disrupt the developmental process for youth and increase the likelihood of negative outcomes such as recidivism, dropping out of school, mental health problems, and suicide. The idea that juvenile justice intervention could "do no harm" is a relic of the Progressive Era. Although there were dissenting voices, their concerns were not heeded until the 1970s, when research clearly showed that juvenile justice intervention could be harmful if not provided properly and to the right youth.[1]

This chapter will examine those correctional interventions from community-based options, like probation, to secure confinement, like Oak Hill. We see a noticeable shift from a punitive, crime-control paradigm at Oak Hill to a community / restorative justice, positive youth development paradigm. The facility went from a retributive system of total control to a focus on healthy youth development that incorporated different systems, including parents and community members, in the process of rehabilitating the youth.

Probation is the most common form of community corrections. More-severe penalties are often called *intermediate sanctions*. These intermediate sanctions also are used as a means to transition youth from institutionalization in residential settings to the community. This is called **reentry** into society. Residential intermediate sanctions are covered in the last half of the chapter.

INTERVENING WITH YOUTH

We know that most youth who are arrested will not be rearrested regardless of whether or not there is a correctional intervention.[2] Why is this? The primary reason is that much delinquency is part of normal adolescent behavior: Most youth age out of crime with the onset of employment, higher education, and/ or marriage. As we saw in the case of Oak Hill, correctional intervention can do more harm than good, underscoring the need to "get it right" when the juvenile justice system does intervene. Complicating this problem is the fact that research has found that there is some juvenile justice system **net-widening**. This means that more youth, often those involved in very petty delinquency activities, are brought into the system when it is of no benefit—and, in fact, could actually be harmful—to them.[3]

Who is likely to benefit from juvenile justice system intervention? This is a difficult question to answer without taking a broader look at what we offer as a society to youth who are at risk or who have engaged in delinquent acts. In recent years, we have gotten better at understanding what makes a delinquency intervention program successful. First, matching the youthful offender with the right correctional program is critical. Second, programs that build on the youth's strengths, especially through a positive youth development approach, must be available. Finally, interventions must holistically address the ecological spheres of the youth's everyday life, including individual, relational, school, and community domains.[4]

REENTRY
An offender's return to society after being institutionalized.

NET-WIDENING
Increasing the number of persons involved in the justice process.

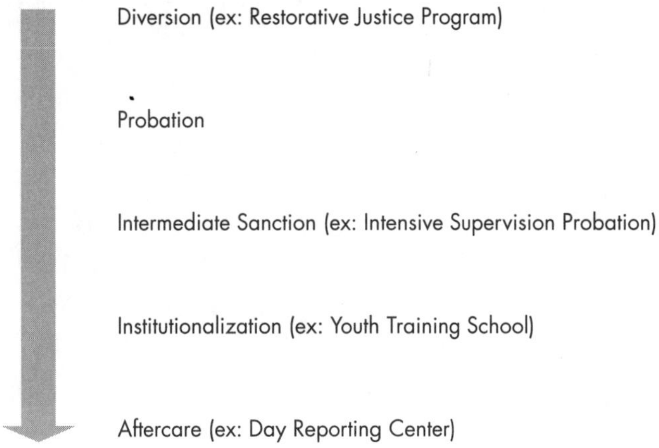

Here is an example to help translate that research: A youth who has committed a nonserious act should not be placed in an intervention program with chronic, serious juvenile offenders. Ideally he would be provided with a program that allows him to build upon his strengths, as no "one size fits all" approach is effective. The reality is, however, that because so many youthful offenders are processed through an under-resourced system, individualized interventions are not the norm. States and correctional entities have practical difficulties in following such research guidelines.

For the most part, youth are treated differently than adults in correctional systems. From a treatment perspective, research shows that youth are more malleable to behavioral interventions than adults.[5] This finding, coupled with the norm of **desistance** from delinquent and criminal behavior, is a major reason why studies show that interventions with youth are more successful than interventions with adults.[6] **Graduated sanctions** are often employed at sentencing, where penalties increase in severity and intensity as youth continue to offend. Formal surveillance and control also increase with sanctions. A typical continuum of graduated sanctions would be diversion, probation, intensive probation, community confinement, and finally, training (reform) school, or youth prison, as seen in figure 10.1. Each of these sanction types are discussed in this chapter.

FIGURE 10.1

Continuum of Juvenile Justice Corrections

Diversion (ex: Restorative Justice Program)

Probation

Intermediate Sanction (ex: Intensive Supervision Probation)

Institutionalization (ex: Youth Training School)

Aftercare (ex: Day Reporting Center)

DIVERSION

Diversion has been discussed in the last two chapters as an alternative to official system involvement, although the reality is that youth have had some system contact prior to being offered a diversion program. Diversion can take place at the police stage of the justice process, at the intake stage, at the arraignment stage, or even at the adjudication stage. Regardless of when it is offered, diversion is a community-based correctional sanction meant to avoid a delinquency label and, secondarily, to reduce the number of cases in the system. Examples include teen court and restorative justice programs. Most states have provided general statutory guidelines that define diversion eligibility, processes, procedures, and legal protections.

The success of diversion programs varies widely. Studies that were conducted prior to the mid-1980s generally show that diversion widened the net of the juvenile justice system, bringing more youth into contact with the system. Some evaluations show positive effects on recidivism, and other evaluations show negative effects.[7] More-recent diversion program evaluations, however, have shown that when a structured decision-making tool identifies the right youth for diversion, and these youth are given quality programming, juvenile diversion

DESISTANCE
Stopping delinquent/ criminal activity.

GRADUATED SANCTIONS
Increased system of penalties for continued delinquent or criminal behavior.

is more successful at reducing recidivism than doing nothing.[8]

Community / Restorative Justice

Restorative justice, discussed in chapters 3 and 7, can be used in a diversion process or as part of an adjudication process through which youth help to "restore" the victim and the community. In this process victims and community members have a voice in the process to let the youthful offender know what can make them whole again. Youth are able to learn empathy by listening to the impact of their behavior on others, and they are able to develop key competencies by taking responsibility and engaging in constructive repair of the harm.

Restorative processes can take many forms. It can be a victim-offender mediation wherein the victim talks with the offender about the offense and its repercussions. The offender also has a chance to speak on his own behalf. A mutually agreeable solution to move forward is then agreed upon, and a neutral party ensures follow-through. If the youth does not follow through, then s/he goes to or returns to court and may receive a more-stringent graduated sanction. Restorative justice also can be a family group conference or restorative circle where family, friends, and neighbors all participate in the process.

Evaluations of restorative justice programs show positive outcomes, in terms of reduced recidivism, completion of court/program requirements, and greater satisfaction with the process felt by both the victim and the offender.[9] It is likely that community / restorative justice as a paradigm for the direction of the juvenile justice system will continue, given the flexibility of the approach, the inclusion of victim and community stakeholders, and the evidence of positive results.

Economic Sanctions

Economic sanctions are court-ordered penalties that have economic costs associated with them. They include restitution, fines, and fees. They can be used to supplement diversion and probation requirements, and they can be used as intermediate sanctions. Restitution can involve victims working to repay their debt, but a large majority of the time, restitution is monetary, wherein offenders monetarily pay their victims back for offenses committed. For example, a youth may have to pay a victim's car insurance deductible for vandalizing his car. Most youth do not pay their restitution debts in full, and restitution alone is unlikely to prevent recidivism, but restitution is one mechanism to help repair harm and promote accountability that has wide public support.[10]

In contrast, **fines** are monetary sums paid to the court, and usually given out in misdemeanor and lesser offenses. Fines are problematic in juvenile justice because youth often do not have their own sources of income from which to pay fines. To hold youth accountable for their actions, fines must be doable

FINES
Court-imposed monetary sanction on the offender.

for the youth; but, to prevent delinquent activity, it is commonly believed that something further must be done. **Fees**, on the other hand, involve "paying" for services, such as the court's time, or probation supervision.

PROBATION

Probation, the most common community sanction, is community supervision of adjudicated youth who are under the court's control. Probation started in Boston, Massachusetts, in 1847 when a shoemaker, John Augustus, stood up in court and told the judge that he would bail out youth accused of crimes and oversee them in the community. He returned to court on occasion to report on these youth who were required to be in school or to be employed. Augustus selected youth to be released to him on the basis of his own inklings about their ability to "make good," and based on their age, criminal history, and general disposition. This innovation was then termed *probation*. Probation officers were not paid for their work until 1878. Soon after the turn of the twentieth century, probation officers became a fixture in courts around the country and created their own professional organization. Estimates today show that approximately 54 percent of adjudicated juveniles are on probation.[11]

As we learned in the last chapter, probation officers can be involved at the intake process to determine whether or not youth should be detained.

Probation Functions

The two primary functions of probation officers after the intake phase are investigation and supervision. *Investigation* includes examining a youth's relevant history as it pertains to writing the predisposition investigation report for the court. Probation officers will interview family members, examine school records, talk with employers, obtain relevant physical and mental health histories, and interview victims as part of this function. Probation officers also will investigate any new offenses that the probationer is alleged to have committed while on probation. The bulk of the new offense investigation is done by police officers, but probation officers can provide evidence or statements made by the probationer to aid the investigation. In some states, probation officers have the legal power to arrest probationers for their actions.

Under the *supervision* function, probation officers monitor youth to ensure the safety of both the youth and the community. Probation officers also see to it that the youth's rehabilitative needs are being met. **Case management** refers to the combination of these two elements, supervision and support. Good case-management approaches address both. The strengths, risks, and needs of the youth are assessed, and probation officer contact and supervision is based on that assessment. Probation officers also connect youth with services to address areas of need, which may include educational placement and tutoring, counseling, substance abuse treatment, and employment training. State statutes may emphasize supervision or case management. A clear manifestation of the social control (supervision) function of the job is that some state statutes authorize juvenile probation officers to carry handguns. Critics claim that offender management and supervision are the main focus of modern-day probation instead of rehabilitation.[12]

FEES
Court-imposed payment for criminal justice–related services.

CASE MANAGEMENT
Planning, supervising, and supporting clients to meet individual and community safety needs.

Probation officers themselves may have role conflict as a result of their supervision and support roles. On the one hand, they act as police officers in a surveillance capacity, investigating possible wrongdoing by youth, and ensuring that they meet court orders. On the other hand, they attempt to help youth by connecting with them and linking them to services they need, such as mental health counseling. The dual social control and service function may lead some probation officers to emphasize one function over another. Because of their dual role, probationers may not fully trust their probation officers (POs), knowing that they can bring them back to court on a probation violation charge. Indeed, this may have been true in the case study of Victor Rios from chapter 8.

A recent probation advancement has been the use of structured decision-making tools to assist probation officers in making supervision and support decisions. Similar to how these tools help in judicial decision-making, structured decision-making instruments for correctional staff identify the level of supervision a youth needs, whether that is low, medium, or high. They also identify areas in which the youth needs rehabilitative support, and they provide feedback on the degree to which youth are responding to treatment. Some of the guesswork from Augustus's time is removed from the job. These tools have not yet become commonplace in probation offices across the nation, even though studies show that when probation officers rely on their own "expert" judgment, it is not as accurate and reliable as these tools.[13]

The **Youth Level of Service / Case Management Inventory (YLS/CMI)** is one of the better-known structured decision-making tools that assesses risk and identifies needs and responsiveness to treatment. The YLS/CMI has been shown to work across diverse ethnic populations and with both males and females.[14] The YLS/CMI assesses eight risks and need factors: prior and current offenses and dispositions; education and employment; family circumstances and parenting; peer relations; substance abuse; personality and behavior; attitudes and orientation; and leisure and recreation.

In states that have **aftercare**, known as *parole* in the adult system, a juvenile parole officer may be assigned to a youth. The role of the parole officer is the same as a probation officer: supervision and support. Typically, however, the supervision role is emphasized more, as these youth are returning from institutionalization. Sometimes states authorize juvenile probation officers to serve in both roles. They are often called juvenile probation / parole officers.

Probation Rules

Youth on probation/parole must abide by the **conditions of probation**. Conditions are statutory, meaning they are written in law and apply to all probationers. Additional conditions are discretionary, where judges tailor additional conditions to individual youth circumstances. Typical statutory conditions of probation are often attending school/work; refraining from substance use; abstaining from weapon carrying; and refraining from committing new crimes. While discretionary conditions differ, there are standard requirements that they must meet. They must: a) relate to crime and to offender's rehabilitation; b) be doable; and c) be safe for society.

YOUTH LEVEL OF SERVICE / CASE MANAGEMENT INVENTORY (YLS/CMI)
A structured decision-making tool that assesses risk, and identifies needs and responsiveness to treatment.

AFTERCARE
Community correctional intervention after incarceration; also called juvenile parole.

CONDITIONS OF PROBATION
Stipulations of behavior placed on probationers by the court.

An example of discretionary stipulations are for a youth to stay away from those with whom he has committed delinquent acts (his coconspirators), and to stay away from certain places known to attract delinquent and criminal activity, such as a particular city park or an arcade. Community service, and economic sanctions, also are popular discretionary conditions of probation, where youth work in the community as a way to pay back the community (restitute) for the damage they have done and the resources (police and courts) that have been used to address their delinquency. Community service work varies, but can include cleaning up parks and cemeteries, and working in soup kitchens.

Those who do not follow the conditions of probation can be brought back to court where probation can be "revoked," and where they may incur further penalties, including being institutionalized. Probation officers file a violation of probation with the court to request a court hearing. Violations of probation can be for a new delinquent offense or a technical violation. A **delinquent offense** is a new offense. A **technical violation** is a violation of the conditions of probation, such as staying out after a curfew or failing a drug test. Most probation violations are for new offenses, though technical violations constitute approximately one-third of all violations.[15] Probation revocation hearings usually have a lower burden of proof (preponderance of evidence), and hearsay is admissible.

Probation today is evolving from a nine-to-five, primarily office job, to one that meets youth in communities and schools, and one that tracks the outcomes of its work.[16] Good probation practices recommend that probation officers engage with key people and institutions in the lives of their probationers and in the wider community. Like community policing, community members can assist the probation process by providing opportunities to youth and helping them to become productive members of society. Good probation work also addresses community and victim concerns in a more holistic manner, evaluating the harm done by the actions of youth on probation and the needed restoration to those parties.[17]

Probation and Intersectionality

As discussed, youth of color are disproportionately represented at all stages of the justice system, and this includes probation.[18] All other things being equal, when they have committed similar offenses, white youth are more likely to receive probation, and black and brown youth, both males and females, are more likely to receive institutional placement.[19] Youth of color also may be treated differently while on probation. One study found that black youth were four times more likely than white youth to be noted as "noncompliant" with probation conditions, all other things being equal.[20] This means that these youth can be further processed into the deep end of the system through a probation violation.

A probation violation can lead to detention or residential placement, as we saw with youth in Judge Ciavarella's court. Many times, a probation violation results in a detention, and youth who are detained proceed deeper into the juvenile justice system, which further places youth of color at risk for their deemed failures while on probation.[21] This is called **cumulative disadvantage**: Indirect factors, such as race, ethnicity, and class, are compounded throughout the juvenile justice process, so that youth of color increasingly become disproportionately involved in the system at each stage. Cumulative disadvantage is one reason

DELINQUENT OFFENSE
An act committed by a juvenile that is considered a crime.

TECHNICAL VIOLATION
Noncriminal offense for which probation can be revoked.

CUMULATIVE DISADVANTAGE
Indirect factors of race, ethnicity, and class are compounded throughout the juvenile justice process, resulting in more-disproportionate involvement in the system at each stage.

many advocate for using structured decision-making tools in detention and probation as a way to reduce racial disparities.[22]

Overall, studies of racial and ethnic effects show that race effects are strongest at the earliest stages of the juvenile justice process.[23] The strongest race effect is seen between the early processing of black and white youth. Less research has been conducted on correctional treatment differences by gender. As we saw in the last chapter, girls may be treated more leniently or more harshly than boys, depending on the type of offense. We know even less about how multiple intersections, such as being a brown female, affect correctional treatment. There is a call to examine these issues more carefully using theoretical approaches that guide research.[24]

INTERMEDIATE SANCTIONS

Intermediate sanctions are penalties that are more severe than probation, but less severe than institutional placement. Originally developed in the adult system because of prison overcrowding, intermediate sanctions quickly caught on in the juvenile justice system. They are popular for a number of reasons. First, they reduce correctional costs. It is much less costly to keep a youth offender in the community than to incarcerate. Second, because surveillance is increased under intermediate sanctions, it appeases those who take a "tough on crime" approach. Third, punishments and interventions can be individually tailored to youth risks and needs in line with research on effective rehabilitation. Finally, intermediate sanctions can be used as a reintegration and aftercare mechanism to help youth transition from institutionalization to the community, which sits well with those who want more emphasis on community corrections.

That said, there are several problems with intermediate sanctions as a community sanctioning mechanism. As we saw with diversion, there is concern over net-widening. Some youth who would otherwise be placed on probation, and who may be more appropriate for probation, are given an intermediate sanction because that option is available. Youth who commit technical violations may be placed in more-restrictive environments, such as institutional placements, as a way to be "taught a lesson," rather than because their actions are deserving of that consequence. There also is a real concern of bias in who is given what correctional sanction.[25]

Intensive interventions, such as those that are provided by intermediate sanctions, should only be used with those who are at high risk of reoffending and who have high needs. Providing intensive services to low-risk individuals can actually *increase* their chances of reoffending.[26] In other words, interventions can do more harm than good if the risk principle is not adhered to. The **risk principle** is the likelihood of an individual reoffending, which is captured through structured decision-making tools. This means that the system itself can be the cause of more offending, so justice system professionals must pay careful attention to which youth are given which sanctions. Several types of intermediate sanctions are described: 1) intensive supervision probation, also called intensive supervision program; 2) day reporting centers; and 3) house arrest and electronic monitoring. Each of these is nonresidential. Youth continue to live at home, but they have additional requirements that they must meet beyond traditional probation.

INTERMEDIATE SANCTIONS
Penalties between probation and incarceration.

RISK PRINCIPLE
Risk of recidivism taken into account in determining appropriate level of supervision and programming.

Intensive supervision probation (ISP) differs from probation not in content, but in more-frequent contact as a means to provide for community safety. Youth under ISP have multiple weekly contacts with their probation officers, stringent conditions of probation, random drug tests, and, typically, community service. ISP is often conducted in teams, where some probation officers have the primary responsibility of supervision and others have the primary responsibility of case management. Two main problems arise with ISP. First, intensive scrutiny leads to more violations of probation for minor infractions that may be overlooked in regular probation, such as being late for curfew. Also, intensity alone is insufficient to make a behavior change; it must be combined with effective treatment.[27] When more-serious, violent, or chronic juvenile offenders are given ISP along with attention to their needs, ISP can be more successful in reducing recidivism than traditional probation, though the opposite can result from not paying attention to the risk principle and the needs of the youth.[28]

Day reporting centers (DRC) were first created in Great Britain and imported into the United States through Massachusetts in the 1990s. DRCs are facilities where youth on probation, or aftercare, report daily for structured activities. These centers can be used in conjunction with ISP and as a transition from institutionalization back to the community, or reentry.[29] DRCs must be carefully structured so that the youthful offenders reporting to the center do not learn negative behaviors from their peers at the center. Youth at high risk for reoffending are more easily influenced by peer behavior than are those at low risk of reoffending.[30] The few evaluations of DRCs that exist are of adult-only programs, which show cost-effectiveness, but not always lower recidivism among DRC participants.[31] The use of DRCs for youth may be growing, but like other correctional sanctions, it is important to uncover under what circumstances and for which individuals DRCs may be effective.[32]

Finally, house arrest and electronic monitoring are intermediate sanctions used to ensure that youthful offenders are where they are supposed to be. They are often used with probation. **House arrest** means that youth are court-ordered not to leave their houses with minor exceptions, such as to attend school. **Electronic monitoring** refers to technological advances that allow the movements of the youthful offender to be tracked by computer. Offenders wear watches or ankle bracelets to track their whereabouts. If the electronic monitoring device is tampered with, an alarm is set off to notify probation of the tampering. If probationers are not where they are supposed to be, the probation office and/or law enforcement is notified. The sole function of house arrest and electronic monitoring is surveillance, but again, it is often used in combination with treatment modalities discussed previously, such as ISP and DRCs.

RESIDENTIAL CORRECTIONS

Out-of-home placements are considered more-serious juvenile justice options. They include detention, boot and wilderness camps, treatment facilities, and training/reform schools. As discussed, federal and state law mandates that youth offenders be placed in the least-restrictive alternative as possible. Again, this doctrine developed from the notion that removing youth from their home environments could be detrimental to their development. This means that youth who are placed in facilities should be placed in staff-secure environments prior

INTENSIVE SUPERVISION PROBATION (ISP)
Probation with a high degree of surveillance.

DAY REPORTING CENTER (DRC)
Facility that houses daily supervision and programming for offenders, but does not include overnight accommodations.

HOUSE ARREST
Court mandate to remain in house with few exceptions.

ELECTRONIC MONITORING
Technological device connected to offender that records offender's location at various times throughout the day and night.

to locked facilities. Staff-secure, or nonsecure, facilities are staff-supervised and unlocked. They include wilderness camps and ranches, residential treatment facilities, group homes, foster care, and shelter care facilities. Secure facilities, such as detention centers and **training schools**, are locked at all times.

There has been a downward trend in the number of youth in secure placement, particularly among white youth. Secure placement populations dropped 50 percent nationally between 1997 and 2013, the latest statistics available.[33] Yet, youth of color make up 68 percent of youth in placement, which underscores the need to address juvenile justice policies and practices that lead to cumulative disadvantage.[34] The overall drop in confinement is due to legislation that prohibits certain low-level offenders from being placed in secure facilities; the increase in the use of intermediate sanctions; and reductions in the length of stay in residential facilities.[35]

A 2013 census of juveniles in residential placements showed that there were 54,148 youth residing in such facilities.[36] Males made up 86 percent of those placements, and were more likely to be placed in these facilities for person offenses, such as murder, robbery, and drug offenses. Females were more likely to be placed out-of-home for status offenses and assaults.[37] These statistics underscore the points made in earlier chapters that females can be treated more severely by the juvenile justice system for more-minor offenses. Females' placement in these facilities for minor offenses calls into question the least-restrictive alternative doctrine as it relates to gender.

This same census showed that black and brown youth were placed in residential facilities at rates far higher than those for white youth. Black youth are fifteen times more likely to be confined to secure placement than white youth.[38] Looking at commitments to secure facilities, table 10.1 shows that for every 100,000 white juveniles in the population, 69 of them were committed in 2013 on the date the census was taken. Compare this with 294 committed black juveniles out of every 100,000 black youth, and 254 Native American youth committed for every 100,000 Native Americans. The federal government has recognized ethnic disparities, and reducing DMC is identified as a top priority. Proposed solutions are discussed later in this chapter.

TABLE 10.1	Committed Juveniles in 2013[39]
Race/Ethnicity	**Rate per 100,000**
White	69
Black	294
Hispanic	111
Native American	254
Asian	18

TRAINING SCHOOL
Incarceration for sentenced youth; also called reform school.

Staff-Secure Placements

Youth who have been taken away from their guardians because of maltreatment constitute the majority of youth in staff-secure placements, though minor delinquents and status offenders also may be placed here. **Shelter care** is typically a short-term facility for youth who are awaiting further court action, while **group homes** are meant to provide a home-like atmosphere for youth involved with the court system. Group homes have "house parents," who supervise and care for the youth. **Halfway houses** are similar to their adult counterparts, where youth transitioning from training schools are sent to live for a short amount of time, usually three to four months, while they adjust to life in a community setting before returning home. Youth live in congregate with other youth in these placements.

Foster care represents a family setting that, like shelter homes and group homes, is typically used for victims of abuse and neglect, though it may include delinquent youth. Foster care differs in that typically there is only one youth per foster family. Unfortunately, victimization issues are not necessarily addressed in such placements, especially for girls, which may lead to delinquency. Recall that there are also dual-system youth, involved in child protection and delinquency, and those who are maltreated are at a higher risk of later involvement in the juvenile justice system.[40]

These realities led to the development of multidimensional treatment foster care (MTFC), a system of care that trains and closely supervises foster families while also providing foster youth with intensive services in school and in the home. MTFC has been shown to significantly reduce problem behaviors and juvenile justice system involvement for *all* youth who may be appropriate for secure placement, regardless of gender and ethnicity. It is a considered a "model" program.

Beyond MTFC, very little research has been conducted on other types of nonsecure residential placements, such as halfway houses, for juvenile offenders. There is wide variability in how these facilities operate, as well as how staff members are trained. Some of these facilities are more appropriate for youth with certain characteristics, whether those characteristics are ascribed (born) statuses, such as sex or ethnicity, or whether those characteristics are achieved statuses, such as a chronic, low-level offending or substance abusing. Further, it is unknown whether such placements facilitate or deter future delinquent activity.

Wilderness Camps and Ranches

Ranches and wilderness camps for youth offenders are meant to remove youth from their environments and place them in unfamiliar settings that will strengthen their competencies, increase their self-esteem, build positive interpersonal skills, and reduce delinquency. While varied in length, these programs generally are between six and ten weeks long. A national survey of such programs found that the most common types of activities at these camps were academic education, backpacking, and canoeing.[41] An example of a wilderness program is a youth-offender variation of Outward Bound, in which youth must work together to figure out solutions to problems without the help of teachers. The self-discovery experience is then discussed with program staff so youth can generalize it to their daily lives.

SHELTER CARE
Staff-secure, short-term community facility housing youth awaiting court or placement.

GROUP HOME
Congregate living out-of-home placement supervised by a house parent.

HALFWAY HOUSE
Temporary community placement for youth transitioning from training school to home.

FOSTER CARE
Out-of-home placement for youth in a family setting.

A research synthesis of wilderness programs found that they can reduce anti-social behavior and recidivism among white male youth offenders, particularly if programs have an intense physical component, such as a remote backcountry camping trip, and a therapeutic component that provides cognitive-behavior treatment to participants and their families.[42] We do not know if these programs have positive effects for youth of color and girls. Those areas require further examination.

Juvenile Boot Camps

Juvenile **boot camps**, also known as shock intervention or shock incarceration, evolved from boot camps in the adult criminal justice system and proliferated during the 1990s, the "get tough" era of juvenile justice. There are fewer boot camps today than there were during that time, but they remain an important dispositional option in some locations. Boot camps are an intermediate sanction aimed at youth who may have failed probation but are not serious enough to warrant training schools. Boot camps typically last between 90 and 180 days.[43] Two main goals of boot camps are to reduce recidivism and to reduce institutional correctional populations through highly structured schedules, obedience to authority, and rigorous physical training.[44] The core assumption of boot camps is that strict adherence to rules and a highly structured schedule will lead to improvement in youths' behaviors and reduce offending. Present-day juvenile boot camps also include an education component, a counseling/treatment component, and an aftercare component, though there is wide variation in the emphasis of these other components across camps.

Some boot camps are privately run, contracting with the state to provide juvenile justice services. These agencies also may provide separate camps as an option for parents outside of the juvenile justice system who are frustrated with their disobedient teens. Boot camps are a cost savings to the juvenile justice system as an alternative to incarceration.[45] Yet, they have been criticized as net-widening when youth are sent to camp as a first alternative, and for the fact that participants who are dismissed from the program for noncompliance may be subsequently placed in secure facilities. Although camps are meant to promote respect for humans, some believe that they demean individuals and are at odds with the rehabilitative goal of the juvenile justice system.[46]

Little research has been devoted to the types of youth who may succeed in a boot camp setting, yet boot camps have received a fair share of negative press due to maltreatment incidents that have occurred.[47] One of the most highly publicized was the death of Martin Lee Anderson, who was sentenced to a Florida boot camp as a result of stealing his grandmother's car while on probation.[48] On the first day of camp, he collapsed during a running session. Guards beat him when he did not get up. In an attempt to revive him, they placed ammonia under his nose. Anderson died thirty minutes later. The result of the first autopsy was that he died from sickle cell trait complications. A second autopsy, ordered in the ensuing criminal investigation into the guards' behavior, cited cause of death as suffocation from the ammonia. A jury acquitted the guards and a nurse of his death, but the public charged that the verdict was racially motivated: Anderson was black and the jury was all white. Florida boot camps were closed down as a result of the controversy, and replaced with a less-militaristic, nonphysical intervention alternative in a legislative bill named after Anderson.

BOOT CAMP
Short-term correctional placement in military-like setting typically with education and treatment components; also called shock intervention / shock incarceration.

Are boot camps effective? First, boot camps must treat all individuals as human beings. A recent review of boot camp studies found that youth who attended boot camps with a strong treatment component, and where they were treated as human beings, had lower recidivism and better academic and employment outcomes than similarly situated youth who did not attend boot camp.[49] Overall, it appears that boot camps can help reduce participant chances of reoffending and help improve their academic and employment records only if strong emphasis is placed on treatment over military-style disciplinary tactics, although understanding boot camp effects for females and nonwhites needs more examination.

Residential Treatment Facilities

Residential treatment centers are often used in conjunction with probation. There are a variety of treatment centers to address youths' needs, including substance abuse, emotional and behavioral difficulties, sex offending, and pregnancy. Treatment facilities are often the last stop before training schools on a graduated sanction continuum. Treatment facilities can sometimes house a diagnostic center that may, on a short-term basis, house youth who need to be evaluated for substance abuse or behavioral health functioning. Private agencies often contract with state governments to provide residential services.

Evaluations of residential treatment facilities show that they can be effective if they include several critical components: They must serve higher-risk youth based on the risk principle; and they must address cognitive behavioral changes, as well as what is called dynamic risk factors, or factors that can change, such as social support, motivation to change, and living situations. Further, programs must be implemented properly (called program integrity); monitored for effectiveness; and employ qualified, trained staff for success.[50] Unfortunately, these things are difficult to implement simultaneously, and the reality is that staff typically receive low pay and little training, and turnover is high.[51] As we have seen with other types of correctional sanctions, what works with regard to differences in ethnicity, class, and gender is in need of further research.

Secure Placements

Detention, as discussed in previous chapters, is a pre-adjudicatory locked facility intended to house youth who are at risk of committing further crime or absconding before their next court hearing. Forty states also use detention as a consequence for violations of probation or as a dispositional option at sentencing.[52] The practice of using detention as a post-adjudicatory punishment goes against best practices and contributes to overcrowding. Intermediate sanction options, from house arrest to day reporting centers, have been suggested as ways to eliminate this problem.[53] A detention risk-assessment instrument (RAI) is a structured decision-making tool that helps intake officers and judges determine whether or not the youth should be placed in secure detention.

Decreasing the use of detention is important for several reasons. First, research shows that detention itself has an effect on out-of-home placement, even when all other things, such as severity of offense and prior history, are equal.[54] This means that although youth may have approximately the same offenses and backgrounds, detained youth are likely to have more-severe dispositions than those who were not detained. Further, deep-end juvenile justice interventions, such as

DETENTION
Keeping someone temporarily in official custody.

detention, can increase the risk of further justice system involvement into adult-hood.[55] Detained youth receive official labeling and may subsequently be treated as a "criminal"; they can develop deviant social networks with peers housed in detention; and detention can result in negative mental health impacts.[56]

Most youth stay in detention for about twenty-two days, though many states are trying to reduce that stay through ensuring that detention is not used as a "first resort" for probation violators, and by expediting how quickly juvenile cases move through the system.[57] The educational, social, and emotional disruption that occurs when youth are taken out of community settings can be reduced with shorter detention stays. This is particularly critical given research that shows juveniles in detention have more educational and mental health needs than the general population of youth.[58] Finally, there also is an economic incentive for shorter detention stays and lower detention populations: A 2009 report showed the average cost of youthful confinement in the United States is $240.99 per day.[59]

Training Schools / Reform Schools

Training schools are the juvenile equivalent of adult prison. They are also known as reform schools, industrial schools, and secure treatment facilities. Youth committed to training schools are typically placed in security levels commensurate with their public safety risk, similar to adult correctional facilities. Training schools developed out of the Houses of Refuge movement of the late 1800s, discussed in chapter 2, with the notion that these facilities were better for youth than prisons and jails, and that they would do more good than harm. Those assumptions came under attack in the 1970s during the noninterventionist era (see chapter 3).

Reports of widespread abuse in these institutions and high recidivism rates led many to question the utility of training schools. In the 1970s, Jerome Miller, the commissioner of youth services in Massachusetts, set out to change the "system." Miller made an unprecedented move to close all training schools in the state. He and a small cadre of supporters believed that youth offenders were better off in community care, and that the removal of training schools would not compromise public safety. The task was arduous and politically explosive, but he succeeded in closing all of the schools.

The results of the "Massachusetts Experiment," as some called it, showed lower recidivism rates as well as a cost savings.[60] Other states followed suit, but closing reform schools was by no means the norm across the United States. Rising youth crime in the 1980s led to the return of committed placements in Massachusetts and other locations, but with different names, such as secure residential treatment facilities. Correctional scholars note that youth correctional facilities are likely here to stay, but they are in need of a major overhaul involving changes in management practices and staffing; facility design and layout; and in the types and quality of youth programming.[61] Facilities such as New Beginnings have been at the forefront of that change.

Management must use what is known about effective organizations and what works for youth who are institutionalized. Creating a facility climate that is perceived as just and fair by youth and staff alike is critical.[62] There must be clear rules and consequences applied consistently, as well as a grievance process that can be accessed and understood by all. The original architecture of training schools after the Houses of Refuge movement was a cottage system where youth would reside in small houses on a campus with a bucolic atmosphere, going to a main building for education and programs. This structure evolved to a single building that housed dormitory living and all programming, including education and mental health services, under one roof. The changing conception of juvenile justice is reflected in these architectural arrangements—from home-like, to congregate—and, like the evolution in DC, returning to small groups with an emphasis on fulfilling individual needs.[63]

It is clear from decades of research that the more youth interact with deviant peers, the more likely they are to be delinquent.[64] It can be expected that unless interactions are highly structured and there is a high staff-to-youth ratio in these facilities, the negative effects of isolating deviant peers will surface.[65] Absent careful planning and implementation, interactions with deviant peers can reinforce negative values and antisocial behaviors, and reduce any positive intervention effects.[66] The creators of New Beginnings paid careful attention to these research findings in crafting their facility, and that is a key consideration in juvenile justice facility building and renovation today.

KEY ISSUES IN RESIDENTIAL PLACEMENT

Disproportionate Minority Confinement

As we discussed in chapter 1, the term disproportionate minority contact (DMC) is used to discuss the overrepresentation of youth of color in the juvenile justice system compared to their numbers in the population. Disproportionate minority *confinement*, especially in secured facilities, is a major problem, as we saw in table 10.1. The federal government has responded to this problem by stipulating that states must have plans in place to reduce DMC in order to receive federal funding. Almost all states have done so, although few have conducted formal evaluations to understand whether or not their DMC efforts are effective.[67]

Figure 10.2 illustrates the crucial stages and cyclical process of DMC reduction as laid out by the Office of Juvenile Justice and Delinquency Prevention (OJJDP).[68] States must identify the problem; assess the extent of the problem; implement interventions to reduce DMC; and finally, evaluate the effectiveness of interventions. If evaluations are positive, then the process must be monitored. This cyclical process is ongoing because, as we have seen in multiple case studies in this text, the juvenile justice system is dynamic—what may work at one time in

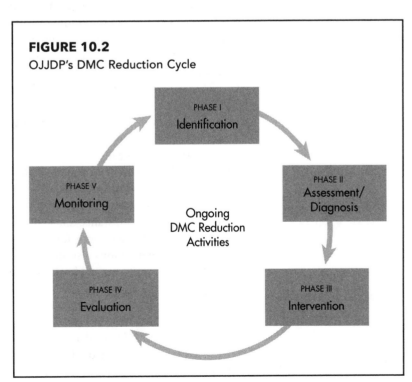

FIGURE 10.2
OJJDP's DMC Reduction Cycle

PHASE I
Identification

PHASE II
Assessment/
Diagnosis

PHASE III
Intervention

PHASE IV
Evaluation

PHASE V
Monitoring

Ongoing
DMC Reduction
Activities

one place, and for one set of youth, may not work in another setting and with other types of youth. Interventions developed to reduce DMC include utilizing risk-assessment instruments; ensuring that there are alternatives to secure placement, particularly for probation violators; and raising awareness of DMC among juvenile justice administrators and staff.

Mental Health

Awareness of mental health issues in the juvenile justice system has increased substantially in the last decade. Between 15 to 25 percent of youth in the general public have mental health disorders, compared to one-half to two-thirds of youth in the juvenile justice system, with those in secure facilities on the upper end of that estimate.[69] Importantly, most youth with mental health disorders are *not* juvenile justice–involved. There also is a call to ensure that normal adolescent developmental behaviors, as discussed in Part I of the book, are not funneling criminalized youth into the system.[70]

Youth with post-traumatic stress (PTS), irritable mood disorder, conduct disorder (CD), and attention deficit hyperactivity disorder (ADHD) are more likely to attract the attention of the juvenile justice system as a result of their outward aggressive and/or impulsive behaviors.[71] One study in Texas estimated that *approximately 98 percent* of youth entering state juvenile correctional facilities had a mental health disorder, which included substance abuse disorders.[72] This study also examined intersectionality issues and found that the prevalence of PTS was higher in females, while white males had the highest prevalence of ADHD. Hispanic males and females in the study were more likely to have substance abuse disorders. Mental health issues cut across gender and ethnicity.

There is a concerted effort to incorporate mental health services into the juvenile justice system through **trauma-informed care**, where treatment and rehabilitation address the trauma youth have experienced. Trauma can include child maltreatment, witnessing fights and shootings, and feelings of being in a constant state of alert. Youth in secure placements are more likely to have experienced trauma than are youth in the general public.[73]

To assist in rehabilitation, mental health professionals recommend that youth in placement undergo a mental health screening that includes assessments for substance abuse, suicide potential, anger, and impulse control.[74] Those youth who have chronic and serious mental health issues should be housed in special units that can clinically address needs, and exit screening should be given to these youth with follow-up plans. All youth who need mental health services should have access to them. Based on a federally sponsored census of youth in custody, approximately 70 percent of juvenile justice residential facilities evaluated all youth for substance abuse problems, while approximately 57 percent of facilities evaluated all youth for mental health needs. Not surprisingly, mental health recommendations also include keeping youth out of facilities where possible, as community mental health treatment is likely to be more effective.[75]

TRAUMA-INFORMED CARE
Addressing trauma within the context of treatment.

Victimization

A survey of youth in residential placement found that almost half (46 percent) reported being victimized while in residential facilities.[76] Most youth were victimized by other residents. The most common type of victimization was theft

(46 percent of youth experienced), and the least common was forced sexual activity (4 percent of youth experienced). Those with the highest rates of victimization were youth with physical or sexual abuse backgrounds; those with learning disabilities; and those living in units with the most serious offenders. This underscores the importance of low youth-to-staff ratios, and providing individualized services to youth based on needs, as pointed out in the case study at the beginning of this chapter.

Lesbian, gay, bisexual, transgendered, or queer (LGBTQ) youth are also vulnerable to victimization because they are perceived to be "different" from the general population. Prior to 2000, there was very little discussion of LGBTQ issues in the juvenile justice system, and there are no national estimates. One study found that between 4 and 10 percent of youth in the New York juvenile justice system are LGBTQ.[77] Updates to best-practices programming include staff training on LGBTQ issues, respect of confidentiality, providing support services, and residential housing selection that maximizes inclusiveness and reduces chances of victimization.[78]

Education

Education of youth in residential placements is mandatory, but not uniform across states. Various state agencies administer it, including juvenile justice in some states and the department of education in others, and the quality of education may vary substantially as a result.[79] We know that youth in juvenile justice facilities have poorer academic achievement relative to youth in traditional school settings, particularly for those with serious learning disabilities and emotional problems.[80] Currently, approximately 87 percent of juvenile justice residential facilities, housing 86 percent of youth offenders in the United States, screen all entering youth for educational needs and grade level.[81] A number of initiatives have sought to address educational problems in residential facilities. These initiatives range from private foundation support for educational alternatives to federal lawsuits and legislation, like that in DC, which attempt to reduce education problems for youth in residential facilities. The Maya Angelou public charter schools in Washington, DC, and at the New Beginnings facility are part of that private solution movement.

Educational research shows that teacher connectedness is linked to fewer school behavioral problems and better academic performance.[82] Positive connections between students and teachers are a cornerstone of the educational philosophy at the Maya Angelou schools. A lack of research exists on education in juvenile justice settings, but one study of a detention center found that youth offenders who perceived high levels of connectedness to their teachers were less likely to engage in high-risk sexual and substance abuse behaviors.[83] Education must be a priority of residential facilities in order to attract teachers who can engage and connect with students.

Aftercare and Community Involvement

The administration at New Beginnings acknowledges that effective juvenile justice systems do not only occur in locked facilities, but through services on the front and back end of any residential placement. While the Maya Angelou Academy in New Beginnings has small class sizes and committed teachers, all conducive to helping kids thrive, once back in the community's educational system, youth often stumble with poorly resourced schools, large class sizes, and a revolving door of teachers. Community services that provide further opportunities for youth to connect with positive adults; practice the positive skills they learned in the facility; and access therapeutic services need to be available not only for DC youth, but for all youth.

This chapter tells us that there is a graduated sanction continuum of corrections. Community corrections are preferable where possible over out-of-home placements, and those are likely to increase in the coming years, as they cost far less than placements in facilities. A study of an alternative to institutionalization for youth in Ohio found that the state saved between $11 and $45 per youth on alternatives to institutionalization, depending on youths' risk of reoffending levels and processing costs.[84] Lower costs may drive the utilization of community corrections, but there also is a call to the juvenile justice system to take on the challenge of successfully rehabilitating and reintegrating youth. Corrections scholars have pointed to three ways of doing so: a) reducing the number of offenders supervised by community corrections officers; b) ensuring that correctional agencies have the capabilities to implement evidence-based practices; and c) supporting the needs of offender populations, as well as the needs of the professionals who work in community corrections.[85] The content and quality of correctional interventions matter, and that is the subject of the last chapter.

KEY TERMS

boot camp Short-term correctional placement in military-like setting typically with education and treatment components; also called shock intervention / shock incarceration.

aftercare Community correctional intervention after incarceration; also called juvenile parole.

boot camp Short-term correctional placement in military-like setting typically with education and treatment components; also called shock intervention / shock incarceration.

case management Planning, supervising, and supporting clients to meet individual and community safety needs.

conditions of probation Stipulations of behavior placed on probationers by the court.

cumulative disadvantage Indirect factors of race, ethnicity, and class are compounded throughout the juvenile justice process, resulting in more-disproportionate involvement in the system at each stage.

day reporting center (DRC) Facility that houses daily supervision and programming for offenders, but does not include overnight accommodations.

delinquent offense An act committed by a juvenile that is considered a crime.

desistance Stopping delinquent/criminal activity.

detention Keeping someone temporarily in official custody.

electronic monitoring Technological device connected to offender that records offender's location at various times throughout the day and night.

fees Court-imposed payment for criminal justice–related services.

fines Court-imposed monetary sanction on the offender.

foster care Out-of-home placement for youth in a family setting.

graduated sanctions Increased system of penalties for continued delinquent or criminal behavior.

group home Congregate living out-of-home placement supervised by a house parent.

halfway house Temporary community placement for youth transitioning from training school to home.

house arrest Court mandate to remain in house with few exceptions.

intensive supervision probation (ISP) Probation with a high degree of surveillance.

intermediate sanctions Penalties between probation and incarceration.

net-widening Increasing the number of persons involved in the justice process.

reentry   An offender's return to society after being institutionalized.

risk principle   Risk of recidivism taken into account in determining appropriate level of supervision and programming.

shelter care   Staff-secure, short-term community facility housing youth awaiting court or placement.

technical violation   Noncriminal offense for which probation can be revoked.

training school   Incarceration for sentenced youth; also called reform school.

trauma-informed care   Addressing trauma within the context of treatment.

Youth Level of Service / Case Management Inventory (YLS/CMI)   A structured decision-making tool that assesses risk, and identifies needs and responsiveness to treatment.

REVIEW AND STUDY QUESTIONS

1. What is "net-widening"? What are the harms associated with this widespread practice within the juvenile justice system?

2. How would you respond to someone who said that locking up juveniles should be our response to juvenile crime? Use the risk principle in your answer.

3. Describe the role of the probation officer and the parole officer within the juvenile justice process. Identify the role conflicts within these occupations. What do you believe should be the primary function of these jobs? Explain.

4. What should happen to youth who continue to break their conditions of probation on technical violations, such as repeatedly missing curfew?

5. Should families be charged for the cost of processing and placing their children in the juvenile justice system? Explain. If they should be charged, what happens when they cannot pay the costs?

6. Should chronic, low-level offenders ever be placed in residential facilities? Why, or why not?

7. What are some of the reasons for DMC, and what are some of the solutions?

8. What reasons would you give to someone who asked why there has been a decrease in residential placement?

9. Why should training schools be a "last resort" correctional option? Identify key issues in residential placement and key considerations in the effective design of residential programs?

10. Why is community engagement and involvement important in the continuum of juvenile corrections?

CHECK IT OUT

Watch

Example of a juvenile boot camp demonstration for parents:

www.youtube.com/watch?v=oBu5Vzi_cWs

Transformation of juvenile justice system in DC:

https://youtu.be/YnhvuT5zzls

Listen

Cost of Juvenile Justice:

https://youthradio.org/player/?audio=7495

NOTES

[1] Lowenkamp, C. T., Latessa, E. J., and Holsinger, A. M. (2006). The Risk Principle in Action: What Have We Learned from 13,676 Offender and 97 Correctional Programs? *Crime & Delinquency, 52,* 77–93.

[2] Moffitt, T. (1993). Adolescence-Limited and Life-Course Persistent Antisocial Behavior: A Developmental Taxonomy. *Psychological Review, 100,* 674–701.

[3] Bohnstedt, M. (1978). Answers to Three Questions about Juvenile Diversion. *Journal of Research in Crime and Delinquency, 24,* 109–23.

[4] Bronfenbrenner, U. (1979). *The Ecology of Human Development: Experiments by Nature and Design.* Cambridge, MA: Harvard University Press.

[5] Scott, E., and Steinberg, L. (2008*). Rethinking Juvenile Justice.* Cambridge, MA: Harvard University Press.

[6] Loeber, R., and Farrington, D. P. (2000). Young Children Who Commit Crime: Epidemiology, Developmental Ori-

gins, Risk Factors, Early Intervention, and Policy Implications. *Development and Psychopathology, 12*, 737–62.

[7] Blomberg, T. G. (1983). Diversion's Disparate Results and Unresolved Questions: An Integrative Evaluation Perspective. *Journal of Research in Crime and Delinquency, 20*, 24–38.

[8] Kim, B., Merlo, A. V., and Benkos, P. J. (2013). Effective Correctional Intervention Programmes for Juveniles: A Review and Synthesis of Meta-Analytic Evidence. *International Journal of Police Science & Management, 15*, 169–89; Patrick, S., and Marsh, R. (2005). Juvenile Diversion: Results of a 3-Year Experimental Study. *Criminal Justice Policy Review, 16*, 59–73; Jones, P. R., and Wyant, B. R. (2007). Target Juvenile Needs to Reduce Delinquency. *Criminology & Public Policy, 6*, 763–71.

[9] Bazemore, G. and Elis, L. (2007). Evaluation of Restorative Justice. In G. Johnstone and D. Van Ness (eds.), *Handbook of Restorative Justice*, 397–425. London, UK: Willan.

[10] Haynes, S. H., Cares, A. C., and Ruback, R. B. (2014). Juvenile Economic Sanctions: An Analysis of Their Imposition, Payment, and Effect on Recidivism. *Criminology & Public Policy, 13*, 31–60.

[11] *Office of Juvenile Justice and Delinquency Prevention Statistical Briefing Book.* Retrieved from www.ojjdp.gov/ojstatbb/probation/qa07102.asp?qaDate=2013.

[12] Feeley, M. M., and Simon, J. (1992). The New Penology: Notes on the Emerging Strategy of Corrections and Its Implications. *Criminology, 30*, 449–74.

[13] Schwalbe, C. S., Fraser, M. W., Day, S. H., and Cooley, V. (2006). Classifying Juvenile Offenders According to Risk of Recidivism: Predictive Validity, Race/Ethnicity, and Gender. *Criminal Justice and Behavior, 33*, 305–24.

[14] Olver, M. E., Stockdale, K. C., and Wormith, J. S. (2009). Risk Assessment with Young Offenders: A Meta-Analysis of Three Assessment Measures. *Criminal Justice and Behavior, 36*, 329–53.

[15] Austin, J., Johnson, K. D., and Weitzer, R. (2005). *Alternatives to the Secure Detention and Confinement of Juvenile Offenders.* Washington, DC: Office of Juvenile Justice and Delinquency Prevention.

[16] Griffin, P., and Torbett, P. (eds.). (2002). *Desktop Guide to Good Juvenile Probation Practice.* Pittsburgh, PA: National Council on Juvenile Justice.

[17] Edwards, L. P. (1996). The Future of the Juvenile Court: Promising New Directions. *The Future of Children, 6*, 131–39.

[18] Bechtold, J., Cauffman, E., and Monahan, K. (2011). *Are Minority Youth Treated Differently in Juvenile Probation?* Knowledge Brief. Available at www.modelsforchange.net/publications/314.

[19] Rovner, J. (2016). *Racial Disparities in Juvenile Commitments and Arrests.* Washington, DC: The Sentencing Project. Retrieved from file:///C:/Users/egebo/Downloads/Racial-Disparities-in-Youth-Commitments-and-Arrests.pdf.

[20] Smith, H., Rodriguez, N., and Zatz, M. (2009). Race, Ethnicity, Class, and Noncompliance with Juvenile Court Supervision. *Annals of the American Academy of Political and Social Science, 623*, 108–20.

[21] Leiber, M. J., and Peck, J. H. (2013). Probation Violations and Juvenile Justice Decision Making: Implications for Blacks and Hispanics. *Youth Violence and Juvenile Justice, 11*, 60–78.

[22] Lieber, M. J., and Boggess, L. (2012). Race, Probation Violations, and Secure Detention Decision Making in Three Jurisdictions. *Youth Violence and Juvenile Justice, 10*, 333–53.

[23] Engen, R. L., Steen, S., and Bridges, G. S. (2002). Racial Disparities in the Punishment of Youth: A Theoretical and Empirical Assessment of the Literature. *Social Problems, 49*, 194–220.

[24] Veysey, B. M., and Hamilton, Z. (2007). Girls Will Be Girls. *Journal of Contemporary Criminal Justice, 23*, 341–62.

[25] Rovner, *Racial Disparities in Juvenile Commitments and Arrests.*

[26] Lowenkamp et al., The Risk Principle in Action: What Have We Learned from 13,676 Offenders and 97 Correctional Programs?, 77–93.

[27] Lipsey, M. W. (2009). The Primary Factors that Characterize Effective Interventions with Juvenile Offenders: A Meta-Analytic Overview. *Victims and Offenders, 4*, 124–47.

[28] Kim, B., Merlo, A. V., and Benkos, P. J. (2013). Effective Correctional Intervention Programmes for Juveniles: A Review and Synthesis of Meta-Analytic Evidence. *International Journal of Police Science & Management, 15*, 169–89; Lane, J., Turner, S., Fane, T., and Sehgal, A. (2007). The Effects of an Experimental Intensive Juvenile Probation Program on Self-Reported Delinquency and Drug Use. *Journal of Experimental Criminology, 3*, 201–19.

[29] Parent, D. G., and Corbett, R. P., Jr. (1996). Day Reporting Centers: An Evolving Intermediate Sanction. *Federal Probation, 60*, 51–54.

[30] Dishon, T. J., McCord, J., and Poulin, F. (1999). When Interventions Harm: Peer Groups and Problem Behavior. *American Psychologist, 54*, 755–64.

[31] Craddock, A. (2004). Estimating Criminal Justice System Costs and Cost-Savings Benefits of Day Reporting Centers. *Journal of Offender Rehabilitation, 39*, 69–98; Boyle, D. J., Ragusa-Salerno, L. M., Lanterman, J. L., and Marcus, A. F. (2013). An Evaluation of Day Report Centers for Parolees: Outcomes of a Randomized Trial. *Criminology & Public Policy, 12*, 119–43.

[32] Altschuler, D. M. (1998). Intermediate Sanctions and Community Treatment for Serious and Violent Juvenile

Offenders. In R. Loeber and D. P. Farrington (eds.), *Serious & Violent Juvenile Offenders: Risk Factors and Successful Interventions*, 367–85. Thousand Oaks, CA: Sage.

[33] Hockenberry, S. (2016). *Juveniles in Residential Placement, 2013*. Available at www.ojjdp.gov/pubs/249507.pdf.

[34] Ibid.

[35] Davis, A., Irvine, A., and Ziedenberg, J. (2014). *Stakeholders' View on the Movement to Reduce Youth Incarceration*. Oakland, CA: National Council on Crime & Delinquency.

[36] Hockenberry, *Juveniles in Residential Placement, 2013*.

[37] Sedlack, A. J., and Bruce, C. (2010). *Youth's Characteristics and Backgrounds: Findings from the Survey of Youth in Residential Placement*. Juvenile Justice Bulletin. Washington, DC: Office of Juvenile Justice and Delinquency Prevention.

[38] Rovner, *Racial Disparities in Juvenile Commitments and Arrests*.

[39] Hockenberry, *Juveniles in Residential Placement, 2013*.

[40] Widom, C. S. (1990). Child Abuse, Neglect, and Violent Criminal Behavior. *Criminology, 27*, 251–71.

[41] Fuentes, A. I., and Burns, R. (2002). Activities and Staffing in Therapeutic Wilderness Camps: A National Survey. *Journal of Offender Rehabilitation, 35*, 41–62.

[42] Wilson, S. J., and Lipsey, M. W. (2000). Wilderness Challenge Programs for Delinquent Youth: A Meta-Analysis of Outcome Evaluations. *Evaluation and Program Planning, 23*, 1–12.

[43] Wilson, D. B., MacKenzie, D. L., and Mitchell, F. N. (2008). *Effects of Correctional Boot Camps on Offending*. Campbell Collaboration Reviews. Available at www.campbellcollaboration.org/lib/project/1/.

[44] MacKenzie, D. L., and Parent, D. G. (2004). Boot Camp Prisons for Young Offenders. In D. L. MacKenzie and G. S. Armstrong (eds.), *Correctional Boot Camps: Military Basic Training or a Model for Corrections*, 16–25. Thousand Oaks, CA: Sage.

[45] Meade, B., and Steiner, B. (2010). The Total Effects of Boot Camps That House Juveniles: A Systematic Review of the Evidence. *Journal of Criminal Justice, 38*, 841–53.

[46] Cullen, F. T., Blevins, K. R., Trager, J. S., and Gendreau, P. (2005). The Rise and Fall of Boot Camps: A Case Study in Common-Sense Corrections. *Journal of Offender Rehabilitation, 40*, 53–70.

[47] But see Glover, Angela R. (2005). Native American Ethnicity and Childhood Maltreatment as Variables in Perceptions and Adjustments to Boot Camp vs. "Traditional" Correctional Settings. *Journal of Offender Rehabilitation, 40*, 177–98.

[48] Caputo, M., Fineout, G., and Miller, C. M. (November, 28, 2006). "Seven Guards, Nurse Charged in Boot Camp Death," *Miami Herald*.

[49] Wilson et al., *Effects of Correctional Boot Camps on Offending*.

[50] Lipsey, M. W. (1999). Can Intervention Rehabilitate Serious Delinquents? *The Annals of the Academy of American Political and Social Sciences, 564*, 142–66; Lowenkamp, C. T., Makarios, M. D., Latessa, E. J., Lemke, R., and Smith, P. (2010). Community Corrections Facilities for Juvenile Offenders in Ohio: An Examination of Treatment Integrity and Recidivism. *Criminal Justice and Behavior, 37*, 695–708.

[51] Mendell, R. A. (2011). *No Place for Kids: The Case for Reducing Juvenile Incarceration*. Baltimore, MD: The Annie E. Casey Foundation.

[52] National Center for Juvenile Justice. (2006). *State Juvenile Justice Profiles*. Pittsburgh, PA: Author.

[53] Steinhart, D. (2001). *Special Detention Cases: Strategies for Handling Difficult Populations*. Pathways to Juvenile Detention Reform #9. Baltimore, MD: Annie E. Casey Foundation.

[54] Jordan, K. L. (2012). Preventative Detention and Out-of-Home Placement: A Propensity Score Matching and Multilevel Modeling Approach. Available at www.journalofjuvjustice.org/JOJJ0201/article04.htm.

[55] Bernburg, J. G., Krohn, M. D., and Rivera, C. J. (2006). Official Labeling, Criminal Embeddedness, and Subsequent Delinquency: A Longitudinal Test of Labeling Theory. *Journal of Research in Crime and Delinquency, 43*, 67–88.

[56] Holman, B., and Zeidenberg, J. (nd). *The Effects of Detention*. Washington, DC: Justice Policy Center.

[57] Hockenberry, *Juveniles in Residential Placement, 2013*.

[58] Teplin, L. A., Abram, K., McClelland, G. M., Dulcan, M. K., and Mericle, A. A. (2002). Psychiatric Disorders in Youth in Juvenile Detention. *Archives of General Psychiatry, 59*, 1113–43.

[59] Justice Policy Institute. (2009). *The Costs of Confinement: Why Good Juvenile Justice Policies Make Good Fiscal Sense*. Washington, DC: Author.

[60] Miller, J. G. (1998). *Last One Over the Wall: The Massachusetts Experiment in Closing Reform Schools* (2nd ed.). Columbus, OH: Ohio State University Press.

[61] Bartollas, C., Miller, S. J., and Dinitz, S. (2007). Managerial Styles and Institutional Control. *Youth Violence and Juvenile Justice, 5*, 57–70.

[62] Sedlak, A., McPherson, K. S., and Basena, M. (2013). *Nature and Risk of Victimization: Findings from the Survey of Youth in Residential Placement*. Washington, DC: Office of Juvenile Justice and Delinquency Prevention.

[63] Bernard, T. J., and Kurlychek, M. C. (2010). *The Cycle of Juvenile Justice* (2nd ed.). New York: Oxford.

[64] See, for example: Akers, R. L. (2009). *Social Learning and Social Structure: A General Theory of Crime and Deviance*. New Brunswick, NJ: Transaction Publishers.

[65] Dodge, K. A., Dishion, T. J., and Lansford, J. E. (eds.). (2007). *Deviant Peer Influences in Programs for Youth: Problems and Solutions.* New York: Guilford.

[66] Ibid.

[67] Office of Juvenile Justice and Delinquency Prevention. (2012). *Disproportionate Minority Contact.* Washington, DC: Author.

[68] See Office of Juvenile Justice and Delinquency Prevention. (2009). *DMC Technical Assistance Manual* (4th ed.). Available at www.ojjdp.gov/compliance/dmc_ta_manual.pdf.

[69] Ibid.; Skowyra, K., and Cocozza, J. J. (2007). *Blueprint for Change: A Comprehensive Model for the Identification and Treatment of Youth with Mental Health Needs in Contact with the Juvenile Justice System.* Delmar, NY: The National Center for Mental Health and Juvenile Justice Policy Research Associates.

[70] Wasserman, G., McReynolds, L. S., Schwalbe, C. S., Keating, J. M., and Jones, S. A. (2010). Psychiatric Disorders, Comorbidity, and Suicidal Behavior in Juvenile Justice Youth. *Criminal Justice and Behavior, 37,* 1361–67.

[71] Grisso, T. (2008). Adolescent Offenders with Mental Disorders. *The Future of Children, 18,* 143–64.

[72] Harzke, A. J., Baillargeon, J., Baillargeon, G., . . . Parikh, R. (2012). Prevalence of Psychiatric Disorders in the Texas Juvenile Correctional System. *Journal of Correctional Health Care, 18,* 143–57.

[73] Ford, J. D., Chapman, J., Connor, D. F., and Cruise, K. R. (2012). Complex Trauma and Aggression in Secure Juvenile Justice Settings. *Criminal Justice and Behavior, 39,* 694–724.

[74] Underwood, L., Warren, K. M., Talbott, L., Jackson, L., and Dailey, F. L. L. (2014). Mental Health Treatment in Juvenile Justice Secure Care Facilities: Practice and Policy Recommendations, *Journal of Forensic Psychology Practice, 14,* 55–85.

[75] Harzke, et al., Prevalence of Psychiatric Disorders in the Texas Juvenile Correctional System, 143–57.

[76] Sedlak, et al., *Nature and Risk of Victimization: Findings from the Survey of Youth in Residential Placement.*

[77] Feinstein, R., Greenblatt, A., Hass, L., Kohn, S., and Rana, J. (2001). *Justice for All: A Report on Gay, Bisexual, and Transgendered Youth in the New York Juvenile Justice System.* New York: Urban Justice Center.

[78] Wilbur, S., Reyes, C., and Marksamer, J. (2006). The Model Standards Project: Creating Inclusive Systems for LGBT Youth in Out-of-Home Care. *Child Welfare, 85,* 133–49.

[79] Blomberg, T. G., Blomberg, J., Waldo, G. P., Pesta, G., and Bellows, J. (2006). Juvenile Justice Education, No Child Left Behind, and the National Collaboration Project. *Corrections Today, 68,* 143–46.

[80] Leone, P., and Weinberg, L. (2010). *Addressing the Unmet Educational Needs of Children and Youth in the Juvenile Justice and Child Welfare Systems.* Washington, DC: Georgetown University, Center for Juvenile Justice Reform.

[81] Hockenberry, S., Watcher, A., and Sladky, A. (2016). *Juvenile Residential Facility Census, 2013: Selected Findings.* Washington, DC: Office of Juvenile Justice and Delinquency Prevention.

[82] See, for example: Mrug, S., and Windle, M. (2009). Moderators of Negative Peer Influence on Early Adolescent Externalizing Behaviors: Individual Behavior, Parenting, and School Connectedness. *The Journal of Early Adolescence, 29,* 518–40.

[83] Voisin, D. R., Salazar, L. F., Crosby, R., . . . Staples-Horne, M. (2005). Teacher Connectedness and Health-Related Outcomes among Detained Adolescents. *Journal of Adolescent Health, 37,* 337.e18-337.e23.

[84] Lowenkamp, C., and Latessa, E. (2005). *Evaluation of Ohio's RECLAIM Funded Programs, Community Correctional Facilities, and DYS Facilities: Cost Benefit Analysis Supplemental Report.* Cincinnati, OH: University of Cincinnati.

[85] Lutze, F. E., Johnson, W. W., Clear, T. R., Latessa, E. J., and Slate, R. N. (2012). The Future of Community Corrections Is Now: Stop Dreaming and Take Action. *Journal of Contemporary Criminal Justice, 28,* 42–59.

Prevention, Intervention, and the Future of the Juvenile Justice System

LEARNING OBJECTIVES

By the end of the chapter, you should be able to do the following:

- Distinguish among primary, secondary, and tertiary prevention and intervention.
- Understand key components of what works.
- Compare and contrast evidence-based programming and best practices.
- Discuss problems with using solely evidence-based programs.
- Identify two evidence-based practices that prevent/intervene in delinquency.
- Identify a program that has been shown *not* to work through rigorous evaluation.
- Articulate the risk and protective factor model and positive youth development model for delinquency prevention and intervention.
- Articulate the values and beliefs of the community / restorative justice paradigm.

Case Study 11: A Matter of Degrees

On a February evening in 1996, Reginald (R.) Dwayne Betts and a friend, armed with a borrowed gun, went to the mall. They found a white man sleeping in his car and decided to carjack him. Dwayne pointed the gun at him through the window. He and his friend took the man's wallet and drove away with his car. The next day they tried to use the man's credit card at another mall to buy $300 worth of clothes from Macy's. The store clerk called Security. The boys ran, but the police apprehended them outside the mall. Dwayne would later say, "I did it for all kinds of reasons I can't clearly reason out. At that moment I wanted to do it, and I had no idea that it would define me for the rest of my life." It was the first time Dwayne had held a gun; the safety was still on.

When Dwayne found out he wouldn't be going home for Christmas, he cried. He didn't realize the enormity of his actions. He still grapples with what happened, especially because he now has two young children of

his own. He calls it a "bad decision." He felt he had no wherewithal or courage to turn away. He was Mirandized without a lawyer or parent present and confessed to police, believing that it was the right thing to do. His thought process was: He was wrong; he got caught; and he needed to make amends. He was not allowed a phone call. Only later, after talking with his lawyer, did he understand why people choose to remain silent. It was then he realized that he couldn't assume adults would make decisions that would be in his best interest.

Dwayne was sixteen at the time of the crime, but the Commonwealth of Virginia allowed juveniles who committed serious felonies to be sent to adult court if a juvenile court judge deemed they could be tried as adults. Because it was the 1990s, at the height of the "get tough" era and the "super-predator scare," no real conversation about whether or not it was appropriate to send Dwayne to adult court took place. The defense could have argued that Dwayne was a first-time offender: He had no juvenile court record, and he did well in school. Instead the prosecution's argument on the dangerousness of the crimes, and the fact that Dwayne had a gun, prevailed. Dwayne was certified as an adult and sent to adult court for processing.

Adolescent brain research tells us that it is very likely Dwayne was not thinking like an adult, and he very likely did not understand the consequences of his actions. He believed talking with the police was what he was supposed to do to help make amends. That thought process is consistent with research showing that juveniles do not fully understand their legal rights. Such research, however, was just emerging and largely unknown in juvenile justice circles when Dwayne Betts came before the court.

Dwayne's confession was entered into the record. He was found guilty of carjacking, attempted robbery, and using a firearm while committing a felony. He received a sentence of nine years in adult prison, although the judge could have sentenced him to life in prison. The sentencing judge remarked, "I'm under no illusions that sending you to prison will help you." These words are forever cemented in Dwayne's memory. Seemingly everyone understood that prisons weren't designed to help those housed within their walls.

In accordance with the federal Juvenile Justice and Delinquency Prevention Act, Dwayne was placed in an adult prison with other young offenders, sight and sound away from adult inmates while he was still a juvenile. He was transferred several times as a juvenile and placed in the adult population when he was eighteen years old. All told, Dwayne would be transferred to five prisons over the course of his sentence, in which he served eight and a half years out of the nine given. These prisons were not rehabilitative. In fact, one facility where he spent some of his sentence, Red Onion State Prison, was charged as abusive by Human Rights Watch for using gunshots to control inmates. There were a number of reports of rubber bullets from these guns landing in people's eyes, causing blindness.

Young, Smart, and in Trouble

Growing up, Dwayne, the son of a single mom, was restless. His mother, Gloria Hill, states that she often would get a phone call from teachers at school letting her know that her son was disruptive in class. He was on the honor roll without much effort, and he was part of the gifted and talented program. His disruptions stopped in the fourth grade when a teacher started giving him books to read whenever he became antsy. This kept him quiet. As he got older, however, his social life became increasingly more important. He started cutting school and using drugs. Like Geoffrey Canada, he saw that the street code of instilling fear through violence was powerful and status-generating. For his part, Dwayne never fully embraced the code; books became a crucial escape for him.

Dwayne was suspended several times in the eighth grade for being wise to his teachers. His mother later told the press that when she questioned him about his behavior, he said, "Malcolm X had to go to prison to become the man he was meant to be." Some of that street life began to take hold. One year later, Dwayne was cutting more classes and smoking pot, although he had never been in trouble with the police. Dwayne was considered a leader in school, and he was the treasurer of his junior class. He had good grades and college aspirations, but he didn't discuss them with his friends. He dreamed of playing point guard for the Georgia Tech basketball team and getting an engineering degree. Yet, he hung out with friends who barely went to school; stole things; used and sold drugs. His drift from conventional society went unnoticed. There were no clear signs. Said one high school teacher, "We really didn't know that side of him that was slipping away. He was too smart, too sharp, too articulate."

Because of Dwayne's poor attendance record and bad attitude, he was barred from competing on his high school's Academic Team. This, coupled with his favorite teacher's maternity leave, led him further away from school and further into drug use. The culminating event of this downward spiral was what got him prison time. In trying to make sense of his actions, and not excuse his behavior, Dwayne later said he saw carjacking as an opportunity for him, while conventional activities were just not available. The options he saw for himself and his friends were more often than not harmful and would land them in trouble with the juvenile justice system. Later on in life, he would create a program to help change both that perception and that reality for young boys of color.

Reflecting back, Dwayne witnessed the lack of support for kids in his community, and saw the dominoes set up against him. Dwayne's need, and later, his creation of positive programming, emphasizing mentorship, quality teachers, and quality content, is backed up by decades of research that show kids thrive when they are provided opportunities to build on their skills and have caring adults there to support them in that process. Creating and nurturing positive adult connections is a centerpiece of Dwayne's work today, and central to a positive youth development approach.

Life on the Inside

While in prison, Dwayne returned to books as an escape from the harsh realities of prison life, where degradation, isolation, violence, and beatings were commonplace at the hands of other inmates and guards. At one point, Dwayne was written up for talking back to a CO (correctional officer) and attempting to stop the CO from closing his cell. He spent three months in solitary confinement for that. There he began to write, later stating, "I wrote my way out of that world." He was in solitary several other times, for infractions which included "giving the finger" to someone. He wrote a memoir about prison life, *A Question of Freedom*, which won a 2010 NAACP Image Award.

Dwayne was concerned that being around so much violence would make him into a violent person. This was especially troubling after he became desensitized to the brutality that existed around him. He wondered if he could ever make it on the "outside," because the only way to survive in prison was to become hardened. Reflecting on his sentencing while sitting in prison, he wrote, "I can't understand why the state would send me to prison for nine years where I'd get no rehabilitation, no skill training, no education training, but enough violent images to last a generation." Books, writing, and several individuals helped him through.

Dwayne built positive connections with a few people while incarcerated who proved to be critical in his transformation. There was Ms. Elman, a jail GED teacher, who saw how smart Dwayne was and brought him books, which she allowed him to read in class in exchange for him writing a response paper to each of them. There was Pop Jenkins, who was from his father's generation, and from whom he could hear about the experiences of an older black man. These people and his family were the connections that Dwayne would need to survive in prison and to thrive once on the outside. In prison, he was called Shahid, meaning "the witness" in Arabic, because he wanted to "become someone else he wasn't," though he never fully identified with any religious or moral group while in prison. He came to believe that prison broke people, exposing them to more harm and trauma. Society would further discriminate against the formerly incarcerated on the outside because of their past.

Being smart in prison brought him some respect from other inmates, and it was there, in his early twenties, that he had his first serious conversation with Pop Jenkins. Older black males were not part of the community in which he was raised. His father, who didn't raise him, and for whom he was named, was a convicted felon. Dwayne said, "The men in my family had disappeared before I was old enough to know they were missing." Dwayne often cites research stating that one in nine African-American children has a parent in prison. He felt like he was another black male who had become part of that statistic. "Judges learned to read our complexions, crimes, and communities as reasons why we needed the bars of a jail."

Dwayne was motivated in prison. He taught himself Spanish and received his high school diploma. When his mom visited, he showed her the diploma through the Plexiglas. She cried, and they probably were both thinking about the milestones he was missing—getting his driver's license, the prom, high school graduation, first day of college.

The Mark of a Criminal Record

After returning from prison in 2005, Dwayne once again sought comfort in books, and met Yao Glover, co-owner of a local bookstore, who was so impressed with "the way he was dialoguing with literature" that he offered him an assistant manager position. Dwayne was amazed that Glover would entrust him with the store even though he knew of Betts's criminal history. Dwayne stated, "I got three felonies, and this guy is letting me make $3,000 deposits." Importantly, Betts came back to a stable home with his mother. With support from his family, he was able to work on his dreams of going to college and being a writer. He had those critical connections to positive adults to make positive change.

Once out, Dwayne sometimes felt as though his life was defined by his crime, as many people acted differently toward him once they knew. That became even more painful when he was denied a full scholarship to Howard University, a historically black college, even though he was president of the honor society at his community college and had a 3.85 GPA. As a result of the Howard experience, he felt compelled to discuss his criminal record at an internship interview with a prestigious magazine, *The Atlantic*. Despite his record, he got the position right alongside students from Yale, Columbia, and New York University. That internship and his academic accomplishments earned him a full tuition scholarship to the University of Maryland. During his college career, Dwayne spoke with groups of young people about how to prevent crime and implement positive policies for young people in communities where violence is an everyday occurrence. He received an English degree from the University of Maryland in 2009, becoming the first person in his family to receive a college degree. He gave the university's commencement address.

Moving Forward

While Dwayne has served his prison time, those memories still haunt him. He continues to dream about prison and forces himself to wake up. He knows that although he never had contact with police prior to his arrest, his friends had been harassed and beaten by them; he distrusted them. Like Victor Rios, who eventually went from the street to a professorship, Dwayne found other ways to direct his frustration and anger about the system into writing. And like Victor's friends, some of Dwayne's friends took out that frustration by committing crimes.

Betts is now an accomplished writer whose work appears in national publications. He was named by then president Barack Obama as a member of the

Coordinating Council on Juvenile Justice and Delinquency Prevention in 2012. He has won awards for his books, and he has committed himself to giving back to his community. He started a book club for middle school and high school boys through the local bookstore that helped him land on his feet. YoungMenRead is a place for male youth of color to hang out and talk. It is a place where it's cool to be smart. These youth read many black literature giants, such as James Baldwin and Nikki Grimes, filled with themes and characters they can identify with. Dwayne teaches poetry workshops for middle schoolers; he is a mentor and a role model. About his crime, he states, "I made one mistake. It was not the sum total of who I was." He regrets his actions, and says that he drifted because there were not enough supports for young men of color in his neighborhood, and no support at school to keep him on the right path. His work is about changing that.

His book, *Bastards of the Reagan Era*, is a comment on the war on drugs and the mass incarceration perpetuated in low-income communities of color where young boys grow up without father figures in fragmented neighborhoods. His poetry captures the poignant and very real problems of his community: a black youth shot by a white police officer who is never charged; the revolving door of prison; and no viable economic opportunities within these communities. These are things he has viscerally experienced.

Dwayne Betts graduated from Yale Law School in 2016. Reflecting on his life, Betts says, "Part of the problem is that society wants to forever judge you by the crime you committed, no matter what you do. There are roadblocks in your way even though you went to court and you've served your debt to society." He was rejected from jobs and from universities because of his criminal record. He tried to make the best of a terrible situation and converted that into a movement for positive change. At first, Dwayne wanted to be a public defender, but now he's working on post-conviction employment discrimination, especially for those with a criminal record who are fighting to work.

Today, Dwayne has reformulated his view of how system-involved individuals are perceived. He said that it is possible to "have a society that doesn't judge me for my past mistakes. That it is possible to create the notion that pre- and post-arrest, even pre- and post-incarceration, you're still a part of society." His work with those who are caught up in the system is living proof that conventional notions of how people should be classified need to be challenged. He intends to continue doing that in the next chapter of his life, so that he is looked upon as the rule rather than the exception to what is possible for those who have been system-involved.

THINKING CRITICALLY ABOUT THIS CASE

1. Knowing what you now know about Dwayne Betts and about adolescent brain development, do you think he should have been certified as an adult when tried for his crimes? Why, or why not?

2. Although Betts was a good student, he began to "drift" away from school during his high school years. What were the reasons for his gradual detachment from school? What interventions could have helped to keep Betts engaged in school instead of crime?

3. What message do you think this story sends to young men of color growing up in lower-middle-class and poor communities?

4. Betts states that the juvenile facility was much like the adult facility, with a lot of violence, few programs or activities, and a lot of doing nothing. How should correctional facilities for youth be different from correctional facilities for adults?

5. Do you think it would have been easier for Betts to flourish and be successful after serving his sentence if he had been left in the juvenile justice system? Explain.

REFERENCES

This case is based on the following sources:

Betts, D. (2010). *A Question of Freedom: A Memoir of Learning, Survival, and Coming of Age in Prison*. New York: Avery.

Chen, A. (9/9/2009). Ex-Con Tells Story of Prison Lessons and Second Chances. CNN. Available at www.cnn.com/2009/CRIME/09/09/prison.life.lesson.memoir/index.html.

Fresh Air. (12/8/15). Poet R. Dwayne Betts. National Public Radio. Available at http://freshairnpr.npr.libsynfusion.com/size/25/?search=dwayne+betts.

Parker, L. O. "From Inmate to Mentor, through Power of Books," *Washington Post*, October 2, 2006.

Vella, V. "From Jail to Yale: Ex-Offender Graduates with Law Degree 10 Years after Release," *Hartford Courant*, May 29, 2016.

INTRODUCTION

DWAYNE BETTS SEEMS TO BE THE EXCEPTION rather than the rule for success after incarceration. We must ask ourselves what could have been done to prevent him from getting into trouble in the first place? We discussed in chapter 1 the importance of asking the question: How well are *all* children in our society? When we think about the prevention of delinquency we must think holistically about how children and their families are treated in society. Are all children given equal opportunities and supports to make positive choices as they grow and mature? The positive youth development and community / restorative justice emerging paradigm discussed in chapter 3 is built upon the core assumption that healthy communities will pay large dividends in reducing delinquency and deviant behavior. In this final chapter, we examine delinquency prevention and intervention strategies developing within this paradigm.

Despite the common refrain of "Nothing works," the truth is, there *are* things that do work and do make a difference in the lives of youth. The evidence is clear. A key lesson from past decades of juvenile justice research is that not every intervention or prevention program is right for each and every youth. What worked for Dwayne is not necessarily the right intervention for another youth. Evidence-based practice and programming are critical elements in understanding what works, for whom, and when, and we need to know more about how intersectionality plays a role in that. We end the chapter with discussing what this means for the future of youth justice.

THREE LEVELS OF PREVENTION

We first must define what is meant by prevention. Prevention means to stop something, such as delinquency, from happening. From the perspective of ensuring that *all* of our children are well, crime prevention can be thought of in a public health framework, where at a base level, all society must be examined.

There are three different levels of prevention. **Primary prevention** is to stop something from happening with supports and opportunities available to all youth. This type of prevention may be out of the purview of the juvenile justice system, yet it is part of a broad youth justice platform. As we saw in chapters 1 and 2, making sure that there is adequate housing, employment with living wages, quality educational institutions with caring adults, access to quality health care, and laws that are equitable across diverse populations are critical requirements for society to thrive. Time and again, Betts reflected on these issues, both while he was incarcerated and upon release. These policies, programs, and laws provide the foundation which, in turn, helps families to provide positive supervision and support to their children.

Secondary prevention is more likely to fall under the juvenile justice umbrella. The goal is to stop something from happening for specific groups of youth typically identified as high-risk populations. The Gang Resistance Education and Training Program (G.R.E.A.T.), discussed in chapter 8, is an example of secondary prevention. This program is targeted at schools where there is a high risk of gang membership. In this program, students in certain grades within those schools are given lessons and practice skills to resist the attraction of gangs.

PRIMARY PREVENTION
Stop delinquency from occurring in the general population of youth.

SECONDARY PREVENTION
Stop delinquency from occurring among those at a heightened risk for delinquency.

Tertiary prevention is to stop something from happening in individuals who have already committed delinquent/criminal acts. Many of the correctional treatments discussed in chapter 10, such as probation and boot camps, are examples of tertiary prevention, but so too are counseling and job training for offenders. Oftentimes, the term **intervention** is used to discuss any type of treatment at the secondary or tertiary levels.

Primary prevention is part of a holistic view of promoting positive youth development and reducing delinquency, but it is often pushed aside to focus on those most at risk and those already delinquent. Prevention has financial, emotional, and social cost savings, but much of the justice research focuses on secondary and tertiary levels. At the primary level, there is less of a toll on victims, offenders, and others affected by negative actions and less concern for heightened safety measures.[1] These realties—coupled with findings that consistently show, both in the United States and internationally, that approximately 6 percent of offenders commit over half of all crimes—result in juvenile justice efforts being directed toward those at the highest risk of crime, although, as we have seen, it is often not just those youth who get caught up in the system.[2]

It is crucial that any type of intervention, at any of the three levels, be effective. The idea that providing services to youth can "do no harm" is inaccurate, as we have seen throughout this book. Some programs do more harm than good, and for some minor acts, it may be best for the juvenile justice system to do nothing at all. Furthermore, not all programs work for all youth, a point that has been underscored in the previous chapters. The familiar refrain of "Nothing works" also is inaccurate. We do know some things about what works with what youth. A broad discussion of primary prevention policies is beyond the scope of this book. We instead focus on the rich literature of "what works" in terms of delinquency prevention at the secondary and tertiary levels.

Before we move on to that discussion, we note the distinction between programs and policies. These terms are sometimes used interchangeably. For our purposes, **programs** are defined as set courses of action for individuals or groups of youth. **Policies** are defined as procedures that address how something should be done. Putting these two together in an example, a substance abuse program may involve a series of individual and group counseling sessions, as well as classes on pharmacology and skill building. One policy for the substance abuse program may be that after three "dirty" drug tests (meaning, where a youth tested positive for a substance), the youth has to leave the program. Another example is that the federal government may provide funding for programs that promote resiliency, or build upon the strengths of youth. Resiliency is the policy agenda, while actions taken to promote resiliency are the programs.

WHAT WORKS

We use the term *prevention* to indicate any intervention with youth to prevent or reduce delinquency. Delinquency prevention programming is examined first.

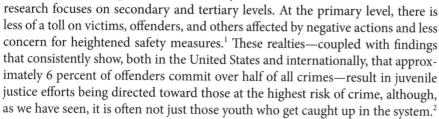

TERTIARY PREVENTION
Stop further recidivism after delinquency has occurred.

INTERVENTION
Stop any further delinquency after it has occurred.

PROGRAMS
Courses of action to address delinquency.

POLICIES
Management of actions/plan to address delinquency.

There are two key factors that must be taken into account in order for programs to be successful: a) program integrity; and b) matching. The first factor has to do with designing and implementing programs that will be effective, utilizing what is known about good programming. The second factor means taking into account the needs and risks of the youth. These factors help us to understand what works and what does not, for whom, and under what conditions.[3]

Program Integrity

Prevention programs must be of high quality in order for them to work.[4] There are two dimensions to quality programs: dosage and fidelity. **Dosage** means the intensity, frequency, and duration of programming matters. Programs must be delivered with enough intensity, or youth involvement, that youth can think and act upon the messages being delivered by the program. Programs must meet frequently enough that the youth perceives connection and continuity in the program content. Finally, programs must be of long-enough duration so that a change within the youth has a chance to occur. Duration is particularly important, because behavior change does not necessarily happen quickly, nor is it necessarily linear,[5] meaning that it may take several times for youth to try to stop doing something, such as using substances, before the youth stops permanently. Staff training, as we saw in chapter 10, is an important component of program integrity. Programs must have high-quality staff who have been well trained and who continue to keep pace with knowledge in the field.[6] It is often staff members who youth point to as helping them move on to leading productive lives.[7] From a positive youth development perspective, caring adults are critical to overall program integrity and positive change.

The **fidelity** dimension of program quality refers to the careful attention that must be paid to the implementation of a program, to ensure that it operates at the highest standards. Many programs, particularly those of the highest caliber, called evidence-based programs, have manuals that identify each step of program implementation, monitoring, and evaluation. Fidelity, in these cases, refers to following those instructions to ensure optimal operation. A major challenge of implementing evidence-based programs has been that the providers often want to add their own stamp to the program, thereby changing the way the program is delivered. The outcomes achieved may not be the same when changes are made.[8] Programs that meet evidence-based criteria are discussed in the next section.

Matching

Matching is the second prong of program integrity. Ensuring that the "right" youth is placed in the "right" program is critical to success. Not all youth are appropriate for all types of programs. In particular, placing youth at low risk of delinquency in intensive programs can lead to more recidivism.[9] One method of ensuring that youth are matched with the right programs is to use structured decision-making tools. Recall that these types of instruments can help intake officers make detention decisions and judges make sentencing decisions (see chapter 9). They also exist to help probation officers and program staff make treatment decisions (see chapter 10). Used at the intervention or correctional phase, these instruments not only assess the youth's risk of reoffending, but also their needs, and their success with intervention(s).

DOSAGE
The intensity, frequency and duration of an intervention.

FIDELITY
The degree to which a program is implemented according to protocol.

MATCHING
Ensuring the right youth is placed in the right program for the purposes of optimal delinquency prevention.

TABLE 11.1	What Works: Clearinghouses for Delinquency Prevention	
Name	**Description**	**Website**
Blueprints for Healthy Youth Development	Identifies evidence-based prevention and intervention programs that reduce antisocial behavior and promote healthy youth development	www.blueprintsprograms.com
Campbell Collaboration	Provides systematic reviews on the effects of interventions	www.campbellcollaboration.org
Coalition for Evidence-Based Policy	Nonprofit, nonpartisan organization that disseminates information on what works	www.coalition4evidence.org
Crime Solutions	Identifies programs and practices that work to reduce crime	www.crimesolutions.gov
Office of Juvenile Justice and Delinquency Prevention Model Programs Guide	Part of Crimesolutions.gov, but with more-specific youth programming information	www.ojjdp.gov/mgp

Continual assessment helps to ensure that interventions are meeting the needs of the youth (responsivity), and that the youth's progress can be tracked. Structured decision-making tools that are used for care and treatment decisions are often called **risk-need-responsivity instruments**. One of the most popular risk-assessment instruments is the Youth Level of Service / Case Management Inventory (YLS/CMI), discussed in chapter 10. This particular tool has been shown to be predictive of success across gender and ethnicity, thereby incorporating elements of intersectionality.

Programs that have been shown to prevent (secondary prevention) and reduce (tertiary prevention) delinquency through rigorous evaluation are called *evidence-based programs*. Evidence-based practices that are known to promote positive outcomes also are critical to what works. Table 11.1 lists websites that describe known evidence-based programs and practices. While not all of the programs identified through these websites address youths' needs comprehensively, many do take into account most ecological domains of youths' lives, while also holding youths accountable for their actions.

EVIDENCE-BASED PRACTICES

Employing evidence-based practices, or best practices, is something that is built into many evidence-based programs, and also may be a part of other programs that have not yet achieved an "evidence-based program" status. These practices include a broad array of procedures, from how best to operate an organization to how best to interact with offenders to ensure that goals are met. Best practices (BP), or evidence-informed practices, are terms that are more loosely applied

RISK-NEED-RESPONSIVITY INSTRUMENTS Structured decision-making tools that are used when making supervision and treatment decisions for offenders.

than the evidence-based program term. Best practices are supported by research evidence and grounded in theory, though they may not have gone through the rigorous scientific testing or achieved the consistent results that evidence-based practices have.

Throughout this book, many strategies that may be included under evidence-based practices and the broader BP umbrella have been discussed. Motivational interviewing, for example, is a BP used in counseling settings that helps clients to meet their goals through "client-centered" techniques, such as reflective listening, expressing empathy, and asking open-ended questions. Use of motivational interviewing can increase positive outcomes for clients, such as increased self-sufficiency and employment.[10]

Programs employing cognitive behavioral change practices rather than punishment alone are more effective in reducing recidivism, even among serious offenders.[11] **Cognitive behavioral training (CBT)** is a BP that has been shown to be successful in helping youth to reorient their thoughts about risks and rewards. CBT helps them to resist temptation through skill building and mental retraining as to how they weigh costs and benefits. CBT is especially effective with youthful offenders.[12] As we saw in the last chapter, CBT can be incorporated into community or residential settings. It is part of a therapeutic approach to youth development that includes coordinated services across the ecological domains of youths' lives.[13]

There are also BP at the organizational level that help to achieve positive outcomes for youthful offenders. At the organizational, or agency, level, techniques include the continual collection and analysis of quality data for program monitoring, ensuring that staff are held accountable, and employing leaders who have excellent managerial skills.[14] Organizational features are often overlooked in the juvenile justice field, where the focus tends to be on what can be done at the individual level with offenders. Organizational policies, staffing, and structure, however, matter in success.

One example of implementing evidence-based programs and practices (EBP) as part of an overall transformation of the juvenile justice system is Models for Change, which encourages organizations to use EBP as part of a juvenile justice system response to youthful offenders. Models for Change seeks to bring together government, public and private agencies, community members, and youth and their families to work together to implement research-based techniques "to make the juvenile justice system more fair, effective, rational, and developmentally appropriate."[15] Models for Change is funded by a private foundation, with efforts focused on system-wide change in four states (Pennsylvania, Illinois, Louisiana, and Washington), the results of which may influence the way other states run their juvenile justice systems in the future.

Another innovation in BP has been the development of **social impact bonds (SIBs)**, which seek to reduce the social and financial costs associated with social problems, such as delinquency, through a pay-for-success program. This means that the government reimburses social service providers for their programming *only when* better-than-average outcomes are achieved. Outcomes can refer to reduced recidivism, which lowers the cost to taxpayers, who are funding the programs. The up-front funding of a program is provided by private investors. These investors get repaid if the program is successful, and they receive a small dividend. If the program is unsuccessful, they could lose all the money they invested.

COGNITIVE BEHAVIORAL TRAINING (CBT)
A best practice technique that assists youth in understanding the connection between thinking and actions.

SOCIAL IMPACT BONDS (SIBs)
Contract between an agency and the government to pay for services only if the program is successful.

SIBs started in the United Kingdom, and have only recently been introduced in the United States. The very first SIB programs were started in New York City and Massachusetts. In New York City, the Adolescent Behavioral Learning Experience (ABLE) project for incarcerated youth aims to reduce the recidivism rate of youth between the ages of sixteen and eighteen who have been incarcerated at Rikers Island by more than 10 percent using evidence-based programming and practices. This 10 percent figure is based on findings that showed approximately 50 percent of this population of youth was reincarcerated within one year of release.[16] An 11 percent reduction in reincarceration would result in a cost savings to the city of approximately $1.7 million. SIBs are a very new addition to the field of justice; some believe that providing a monetary incentive may lead to unethical decisions or leave some of the most difficult youth without programming, so that success goals can be met. It is still too early to know whether SIBs do indeed deliver positive outcomes.

EVIDENCE-BASED PROGRAMS

There are few programs that meet the very highest standards of evidence for effectively preventing and/or reducing delinquency. The highest standards involve a **randomized control trial (RCT)** of the program, also called a true or classical experimental research design, in which participants are randomly (meaning, by chance) placed either in a control group, which does not receive the treatment, and an experimental group, which does receive the treatment. Randomization ensures that participants are equivalent across the two groups in terms of factors that may affect their performance. Participants are then examined before the program and afterward for changes in outcomes, such as behaviors and academic performance. Any differences can be attributed to the intervention, rather than some outside factor. RCTs are expensive and time-consuming, and sometimes unfeasible to conduct, so they are not used frequently in evaluation work. This is why some entities advocate drawing on knowledge from well-conducted research that may not have included an RCT.[17]

Replication is another requirement of determining an evidence-based program (EBP). A program may work in one area at one time, but in order to promote the program as effective, another experiment must be conducted in another location. Programs must be subjected to replication that also finds positive results in order for the program to be considered effective. Because of this gap, and the reality that some programs *not* evaluated may still be effective, researchers in the juvenile justice field have developed a tool to compare elements of intervention programs that might not meet the EBP standards, but may have key components that have been shown to reduce delinquency. This comparison tool, called the Standardized Program Evaluation Protocol (SPEP), can be used by states and programs alike to link research knowledge to practice.[18]

Blueprints for Healthy Youth Development has identified several model programs for delinquency prevention and intervention that had lasting positive effects over one year. Multidimensional treatment foster care (MTFC) has already been discussed in chapter 10. Other model programs include LifeSkills Training (LST), Functional Family Therapy (FFT), Multisystemic Therapy (MST), MST for Youth with Problem Sexual Behaviors (MST-PSB), and Positive Action.

> **RANDOMIZED CONTROL TRIAL (RCT)**
> Research design that randomly assigns participants to treatment and control groups; considered the "gold standard" to understand effects of programs; also called true or classical experiment.

LifeSkills Training (LST) is an evidence-based primary prevention program in middle / junior high schools aimed at providing students with social skills and social resistance skills addressing tobacco, alcohol, marijuana, and violence.[19] Youth who have gone through LST are less likely to abuse substances and use violence than their peers who did not go through the program. Full accounts, including costs and benefits, of these EBPs can be found on the Blueprints website (www.blueprintsprograms.com/).

At the family level, *Functional Family Therapy* (FFT) has been shown to be successful in reducing delinquency, violence, and substance abuse by focusing on family dynamics with the help of a supportive trained therapist. Families work on increasing support for each other and improving communication while recognizing and trying to stop dysfunctional behavioral patterns.

Alternatively, *Multisystemic Therapy* (MST) is an intervention program that addresses juvenile delinquency through therapists who work intensively not only with youth and their families, but with others, such as teachers, within the other socio-ecological domains in the youths' lives. The focus is on increasing youths' protective factors and reducing their risk factors. A cost-benefit analysis estimated that MST saves taxpayers and families $26,545 per youth in justice processing and treatment costs.

One final example from the school realm is *Positive Action*, which teaches positive behaviors through a school-based curriculum in grades K through eight.[20] This curriculum helps students to understand the links between thoughts, feelings, and actions. The program also has a school climate change initiative that addresses inclusiveness with regard to intersectionality and reintegration for students who have been punished.

COMPREHENSIVE COMMUNITY PROGRAMS

Apart from individual programs discussed previously, at the community level there is a focus on **comprehensive community initiatives** (CCIs) that address delinquency, as well as a myriad of other social problems, from multiple angles. The core belief is that social problems, such as delinquency, do not have a single cause of origin, so the solution must be multifaceted and involve the community itself, not just the juvenile justice components. Some examples of federally funded CCIs include Weed & Seed, which aims to reduce crime through improving a community's economic outlook; Project Safe Neighborhoods, which aims to reduce crime through targeting gun crimes, while also helping formerly incarcerated individuals reintegrate into the community; and the Comprehensive Gang Model, which aims to reduce gangs and gang crime while providing positive activities for those in high-crime neighborhoods. While these programs emphasize crime reduction, they do so in ways that coordinate policy and practices among public and private entities, emphasize community involvement, and promote a wide range of noncriminal benefits.

Increasingly, CCIs are being linked to public health approaches in which violence is seen as a preventable problem, through collaborative efforts engaging a cross section of the community.[21] The community must be mobilized for success and sustainability over the long run. The community is perceived as a copartner in crime prevention and control, which means that non-criminal justice entities are a critical part of the prevention puzzle. These include employment centers,

COMPREHENSIVE COMMUNITY INITIATIVES (CCIs)
Community-level initiatives that address large-scale social problems from multiple angles.

schools, housing departments, health-care institutions, and community leaders. Research has found that when community members and community organizations take an active role in the "health" of their youth, positive outcomes occur, including lower crime rates.[22] This is due, in part, to collective efficacy, or citizens' trust in each other and shared expectations of social control to address needs.

Coordinating such strategies in a cohesive way across organizations and entities with different missions and goals may be one of the biggest challenges faced by such collaborations.[23] Organizations must change the way they do business in order to effectively collaborate with each other. This means that they must share information with others, bring in the community as a partner, and agree to change some practices in order to effectively address youth violence. This may be particularly hard for schools and police departments who have traditionally not shared practices and procedures, even when void of personal information.

Evidence-based practices are only beginning to be utilized on the organizational front. CCIs do not necessarily employ evidence-based practices and programs for individuals and groups. While this is not yet common practice throughout the United States, the use of practices and programs informed by evidence is growing in application, but attention to intersectionality must be part of that approach. For example, the LifeSkills Training program has been shown to be effective with youth from different economic strata, gender orientations, and across racial and ethnic differences, yet we still do not know if Functional Family Therapy can work with serious and violent youth who are at the highest poverty levels.

Overall, comprehensive strategies have not been well researched. Studies point to multiple problems with implementing such complex, comprehensive strategies. On the face of it, such approaches seem logical. Youth delinquency and violence stem from a multitude of factors, so it is natural for solutions to be broadly based. Some programs, such as the Comprehensive Gang Model, have been rated as "promising" in their quest to reduce youth delinquency, but understanding how components best work together to implement these strategies is a key task of future CCI efforts.[24]

WHAT DOES NOT WORK

Attention also must be paid to what does not work. Many programs have received rigorous evaluations using RCTs in multiple locations, with the evidence clearly showing a failure to create positive outcomes. Several of these are highlighted here.

Scared Straight

The Scared Straight program is typically used as a secondary or tertiary prevention mechanism to reduce recidivism in young people who are considered the most at risk for delinquency, or who have already engaged in some sort of delinquent behavior. These youth are taken into a jail or prison where inmates try to "scare" them into being conventional—or going "straight"—by telling them their stories, including incarceration problems. Inmates use foul language and may yell at them at close range to get their messages across.

Scared Straight was first used at Rahway State Prison in New Jersey in the late 1970s. Although the program was later found to be ineffective, it proliferated in other places because of its tough-on-crime message. A more-recent systematic review of Scared Straight–type programs continues to show that they are more harmful to youth than doing nothing at all; these programs actually increase delinquency.[25] Unfortunately, while the evidence is clear that Scared Straight does not work, it continues to be implemented in locations around the country. This is likely due to the persistent belief on the part of policymakers and the public in its deterrent effects.[26]

Juvenile Justice System Processing

The lack of effectiveness of system processing for minor delinquents has been discussed in chapter 9, along with the disproportionate impact of justice processing on youth of color. A systematic review of literature has shown that juvenile justice processing is *criminogenic*—meaning, it increases delinquency as compared with doing nothing at all, or placing youth in diversion programs.[27] Further evidence points to the fact that transferring or waiving serious juveniles from juvenile court jurisdiction to adult court jurisdiction for processing is also ineffective, and may increase delinquency.[28] Dwayne Betts's story shows us that youth often do not understand what is happening, and that the effects of incarceration can reverberate for a lifetime. Despite the overwhelming evidence against system processing for minor transgressions and the processing of juveniles through adult court, these policies continue to be fueled by political will, and a perceived public demand for crime control and accountability, even as studies show that the public is generally sympathetic toward low-level offenders.[29]

Zero-Tolerance Policies

As discussed in chapter 7, schools that have implemented zero-tolerance policies as a way to increase school safety have not seen reductions in disciplinary problems, nor have students perceived their schools to be safer as a result of such measures. Furthermore, these policies disproportionately affect youth of color and those with disabilities; and they have been correlated with poorer academic outcomes.[30] The reverberation of zero-tolerance policies in schools has been felt in the juvenile justice system, and has led to the development of the concept of a "school-to-prison pipeline" to describe what happens to these youth. First, they get in trouble at school; then they are referred to juvenile court; and eventually, they end up in adult prison. This is directly related to the system processing findings: Youth who come into contact with the justice system are more likely to continue that contact, eventually leading to adult system contact and possibly prison time.[31]

There are other programs that have received both negative and positive findings from evaluations, such as juvenile curfews and neighborhood watch programs. Though the weight of the evidence shows they are ineffective, not enough rigorous evaluations have been completed to brand these programs as "ineffective." Recall from our discussion of the police in chapter 8 that the initial version of D.A.R.E. was shown to be ineffective, but a retooling of the program has led to better results. It remains to be seen, however, whether those positive findings will hold true over time.

An important point to keep in mind when we consider what works and what doesn't is that programs are revised over time, and circumstances and youth may change over time. A program that is not effective in one location at one time with certain individuals may be effective in other locations at another time. In addition, changing a variable, or a factor—such as the target population for the intervention—could drastically improve results. This is why continual program monitoring and assessment is needed.

THE FUTURE OF YOUTH AND JUVENILE JUSTICE

As we look to the future of youth justice broadly, and juvenile justice specifically, our knowledge of what works is likely to guide programs and policies directed at youth, and to play a more-prominent role in juvenile justice system revision. Yet, an overall framework or paradigm for the future is essential. Such a framework helps to organize the way we think about the topic; to classify new information; to examine various assumptions rooted in theoretical underpinnings; and to identify strengths and weaknesses of the approach. A paradigm encompasses research-based understandings, as well as core values and beliefs about youth development; the roles and responsibilities of families and communities; and the ethics of social justice.

Chapter 3 discusses the emerging positive youth development and community / restorative justice paradigm. This paradigm takes into account what works by emphasizing prevention and community responses to youthful misbehavior based on an ethic of care. This paradigm embraces the core value that all children deserve supportive adults, and that all children can thrive if given the opportunities and supports necessary for healthy development.

The positive youth development (PYD) framework emphasizes youth assets and human development throughout childhood and adolescence instead of focusing on crises and problem behaviors. This is considered a life course perspective of the issue. PYD emphasizes prevention: Youth supported early in their lives are less likely to develop problem behaviors. These problems include a broad spectrum of behaviors, not just a single focus on delinquency. The logic is that a healthy childhood will lead to a healthy and productive adult life.[32]

In this last section, we take a look at how the PYD framework can address delinquency prevention through examining the risk, protective, and promotive factors in the socio-ecological domains of a youth's life.

The community / restorative justice framework refocuses attention back on the development of a healthy community within which families are able to provide for the needs of their children. Restorative justice teaches accountability and individual responsibility. Youth develop empathy by becoming aware of the impact of their behavior on others, and they are taught how to repair the harm and restore relationships with people they have hurt. Learning how to admit and correct mistakes is a key part of learning to become a responsible adult. This framework also recognizes that the community is responsible for conditions in which children grow and develop. Stressed and broken families, inadequate schools, poor housing, lack of recreational and positive outlets—all of these elements need to be addressed in order to encourage positive youth development. Creating and maintaining these elements is a collective community responsibility. This framework acknowledges the need for collective accountability as well as individual accountability. Creating healthy communities and families for all of our children is the shared responsibility of everyone within society.

Risk and Protective Factors Revisited

A public health approach uses data on known risk and protective factors to help design intervention efforts. As we discussed in chapter 5, risk and protective factors are influences on youths' lives that help to propel them in different directions. Risk factors increase the chances of negative outcomes, while protective factors buffer against those outcomes. Much of the risk and protective factor research through the 1990s dealt almost exclusively with uncovering the risk factors, while ignoring factors that might insulate youth from negative behaviors. It is now generally understood that risk and protective factors are intertwined; both exert influence on youth; and both must be addressed in the multiple spheres of youths' lives.[33]

Risk and protective factors change throughout the life course. This means that some elements may not be an influential factor at one stage of the youth's life, or may increase in importance as the youth ages, and vice versa. School attachment and peer influence are two examples. These factors are of little importance at a very young age, but increase in importance as the youth ages. Table 11.2[34] displays a brief list of risk and protective factors in different ecological domains, followed by research on their influences.

Importantly, depending on the constellation of risk and protective factors in individual youth, the presence of protective factors and absence of risk factors may not *always* lead to positive results; this is because of unknown factors, or because of the interaction between the various factors mentioned. Further, risk factors may be influenced by promotive factors that interrupt the downward trajectory. In general, however, more protective factors and fewer risk factors lead to better outcomes. We need to know more about risk, protective, and promotive factors as they relate to intersectionality. Some factors may be more damaging, or more protective, to some populations—for example, girls—than they are for boys, and that also may vary by ethnicity.

Positive Youth Development and What Works

Research shows that capitalizing on existing strengths—protective factors—in the ecological spheres of youths' lives can have many positive effects, including reducing delinquency and increasing self-esteem.[35] This has been the thrust of positive youth development (PYD). Programming with a PYD focus has moved beyond the traditional approach to delinquency prevention—looking at deficits—to focusing on strengths as a way to increase competencies in youth themselves, and in their broader ecological spheres.[36] While PYD concepts continue to be refined, table 11.3[37] presents a short list of the most salient features of programs employing the PYD perspective.

The main purposes of a PYD approach are for youth to build better connections to their families and communities; to become self-confident and self-reliant; and to increase social, emotional, cognitive, behavioral, and moral competencies. As we move further into the twenty-first century, using PYD in- and outside of the juvenile justice system is likely to continue. Dwayne Betts's program,

TABLE 11.2	Sample of Risk and Protective Factors

Community Domain Risk Factors	
Community and Personal Transitions and Mobility	Neighborhoods with high rates of residential mobility are likely to have higher rates of juvenile crime, while children who experience frequent residential moves and stressful life transitions are likely to have higher risk for school failure, delinquency, and drug use.
Community Disorganization	Neighborhoods with high population density, lack of natural surveillance of public places, physical deterioration, and high rates of adult crime also have higher rates of juvenile crime.
Low Neighborhood Attachment	A low level of bonding to the neighborhood is related to higher levels of juvenile crime.
Perceived Availability of Drugs and Handguns	The availability of cigarettes, alcohol, marijuana, and other illegal drugs is related to the use of these substances by adolescents. The availability of handguns is related to a higher risk of crime and substance use by adolescents.

Community Domain Protective Factors	
Opportunities for Prosocial Involvement	When opportunities are available in a community for positive participation, children are less likely to engage in problem behaviors.
Rewards for Prosocial Involvement	Rewards for positive participation in activities help children bond to the community, thus lowering their risk for problem behaviors.

Family Domain Risk Factors	
Family Conflict	Children raised in families high in conflict, whether or not the child is directly involved in the conflict, appear at risk for delinquency.
Poor Family Management	Parents' use of inconsistent and/or unusually harsh or severe punishment with their children places them at higher risk for problem behaviors.

Family Domain Protective Factors	
Family Attachment	Young people who feel that they are a valued part of their family are less likely to engage in problem behaviors.
Rewards for Prosocial Involvement	When parents, siblings, and other family members praise, encourage, and attend to things done well by their child, children are less likely to engage in problem behaviors.

(continued)

TABLE 11.2 | *(Continued)*

School Domain Risk Factors	
Academic Failure	Beginning in the late elementary grades (grades 4–6), academic failure increases the risk of delinquency.
Low Commitment to School	Factors such as liking school, spending time on homework, and perceiving the coursework as relevant are negatively related to problem behaviors.
School Domain Protective Factors	
Opportunities for Prosocial Involvement	When young people are given more opportunities to participate meaningfully in important activities at school, they are less likely to engage in problem behaviors.
Rewards for Prosocial Involvement	When young people are recognized and rewarded for their contributions at school, they are less likely to be involved in problem behaviors.
Peer–Individual Risk Factors	
Early Initiation of Problem Behavior	The earlier the onset of problem behavior, the greater the likelihood of further problem behavior.
Friends' Use of Drugs	Young people who associate with peers who engage in alcohol or substance abuse are much more likely to engage in the same behavior.
Interaction with Antisocial Peers	Young people who associate with peers who engage in problem behaviors are at higher risk for engaging in antisocial behavior themselves.
Rewards for Antisocial Behavior	Young people who receive rewards for their antisocial behavior are at higher risk for engaging further in antisocial behavior.
Sensation Seeking	Young people who seek out opportunities for dangerous, risky behavior in general are at higher risk for participating in problem behaviors.
Gang Involvement	Youth who belong to gangs are more at risk for antisocial behavior.
Peer–Individual Protective Factors	
Religiosity	Young people who regularly attend religious services are less likely to engage in problem behaviors.
Social Skills	Young people who are socially competent and engage in positive interpersonal relations with their peers are less likely to use drugs and engage in other problem behaviors.

TABLE 11.3	PYD Program Characteristics

- Promote bonding.

- Foster resilience.

- Promote social, emotional, cognitive, behavioral, and moral competence.

- Foster self-determination.

- Foster spirituality.

- Foster self-efficacy.

- Foster clear and positive identity.

- Foster belief in the future.

- Provide recognition for positive behavior and opportunities for prosocial involvement.

- Foster prosocial norms (healthy standards for behavior).

YoungMenRead, is part of the PYD movement, promoting bonding through books, increasing positive identities and self-efficacy for young men of color.

CONCLUDING THOUGHTS

Throughout this chapter, we have discussed what we know (and do not know) about delinquency prevention and intervention. Recent developments in the criminology field have focused on ensuring that policy is better matched with theoretical links in order to better utilize knowledge, to understand what policies may be effective, and to provide more of an impact on what policies are adopted by government.[38]

But not all policies and programs that we know to work are adopted, and some policies and programs that we know do not work are in place throughout the United States. There are multiple reasons for the disconnection between what works and what is implemented. They include political reasons, such as a program being popular among politicians and/or a perceived popularity among the general public (i.e., Scared Straight); lack of knowledge of what is effective and ineffective for preventing and intervening in delinquency; and lack of funding to implement programs that work. Research might offer us useful guides for implementing programs, but there must also be the political will to implement these programs as a society. Political will is a matter of power, values, and choices. If we want a society in which all children are thriving, then we must commit to investing in the well-being of all communities.

As important as our extensive discussion of what works and what doesn't work is the fact that the knowledge of what may work for some youth in some locations is still unknown. We have only begun to gather evidence for what works across different segments and populations by applying the lens of intersectionality. We *do* know some things about what works, but our knowledge of the needs of girls, the needs of youth of color, and cultural competencies is in its infancy.

It is also important to recognize that using EBP to the exclusion of other knowledge can sometimes be dangerous. Some programs may be achieving positive results, but the number of youth going through the programs may be so small that no rigorous quantitative statistical analysis, as discussed with RCTs, would be able to ascertain whether or not it is effective. Further, not every agency that provides services has the resources to implement evidence-based programs and practices. This is particularly true for those agencies that are in the most underserved areas, serving some of the most vulnerable populations. Here we see intersectionality coming into play: Are we willing to invest the necessary resources to establish "what works" for all of our youth, living in all communities? Are we, as a society, able to hold our policymakers accountable for creating the conditions for positive youth development across every neighborhood, school, and household, especially those who are most marginalized and excluded?

It is clear that we must invest in our youth in general, not just selectively. Then we can affirmatively answer the question: "Yes, all of our children are well." In the language of public health, this means that there are universal programs for children and families that ensure healthy well-being through promoting individual strengths and addressing deficits in ways that are supportive, and where positive relationships are developed. This is the foundation of the positive youth development, community / restorative justice paradigm we have discussed throughout the book.

Since 1994, a cross section of US federal agencies has come together to provide a broad picture of the well-being of our nation's children. They have examined key areas of youths' lives, including family and social environment, economics, health, education, and safety. The 2015 report reveals that while there is always room for improvement, leaps have been made in providing health care to children, and in increasing rates of high school graduation.[39] Yet, the sheer number of youth who continue to flow through the juvenile justice system is troubling, as are their indicators of well-being, which are significantly below youth in the general population. This has been recognized by scholars and practitioners, and acknowledged by the federal government. We believe it is time to put what we know works, for whom and in what contexts, into practice, so that all children are indeed well.

KEY TERMS

cognitive behavioral training (CBT) A best practice technique that assists youth in understanding the connection between thinking and actions.

comprehensive community initiatives (CCIs) Community-level initiatives that address large-scale social problems from multiple angles.

dosage The intensity, frequency, and duration of an intervention.

fidelity The degree to which a program is implemented according to protocol.

intervention Stop any further delinquency after it has occurred.

matching Ensuring the right youth is placed in the right program for the purposes of optimal delinquency prevention.

policies Management of actions/plan to address delinquency.

primary prevention Stop delinquency from occurring in the general population of youth.

programs Courses of action to address delinquency.

randomized control trial (RCT) Research design that randomly assigns participants to treatment and control groups; considered the "gold standard" to understand effects of programs; also called true or classical experiment.

risk-need-responsivity instruments Structured decision-making tools that are used when making supervision and treatment decisions for offenders.

secondary prevention Stop delinquency from occurring among those at a heightened risk for delinquency.

social impact bonds (SIBs) Contract between an agency and the government to pay for services only if the program is successful.

tertiary prevention Stop further recidivism after delinquency has occurred.

REVIEW AND STUDY QUESTIONS

1. Explain the three levels of prevention in juvenile justice programming. Where do we currently invest most of our resources? Where do you believe we should focus our investment of resources? Why?

2. Design a prevention or intervention program in your city. Specify the following details for your program: Who is the target population, and why; what kinds of qualifications should staff hold, and why; what services will be provided, and why; and how will success be measured?

3. Explain the difference between a "program" and a "policy," and provide an illustration of each.

4. What are structured decision-making tools, and why are these tools an important component of evidence-based juvenile justice programming?

5. Explain the importance of the following elements of a program: dosage, fidelity, and matching.

6. How would you respond to someone who said nothing works to prevent delinquency? Use evidence in this chapter to discuss what we know about effective juvenile justice programming.

7. According to evidence-based research, which widely used programs do not work to reduce recidivism? Why are these programs unsuccessful in achieving positive outcomes? Given these outcomes, why are these programs still in use?

8. Discuss the importance of individual accountability and community responsibility in the community / restorative justice framework. Explain why both are important to the promotion of positive youth development for all children.

9. If research helps us to know what works with youth, why is this knowledge not always used to shape our policies and programs?

10. In your opinion, what areas need further research in order to understand how best to provide effective intervention and prevention?

CHECK IT OUT

Watch

The original Scared Straight video:
www.youtube.com/watch?v=gXRIR_Svgq4
Interview with Dwayne Betts:
www.youtube.com/watch?v=SD_iLRYYOfE

Listen

http://freshairnpr.npr.libsynfusion.com/
    size/25/?search=dwayne+betts

Websites

Blueprints for Healthy Youth Development website:
www.blueprintsprograms.com/
Models for Change website:
www.modelsforchange.net/index.html

NOTES

[1] Weisburd, D., and Eck, J. E. (2004). What Can Police Do to Reduce Crime, Disorder, and Fear? *Annals, AAPS, 593*, 42–65.

[2] See Wolfgang, M. E., Figlio, R. M., and Sellin, T. (1972). *Delinquency in a Birth Cohort*. Chicago: University of Chicago; Racine, WI, and London.

3 Guerra, N. G., Boxer, P., and Cook, C. R. (2006). What Works (and What Does Not) in Youth Violence Prevention: Rethinking the Questions and Finding New Answers. *New Directions for Evaluation, 110,* 59–71.

4 Lowenkamp, C. T., Latessa, E. J., and Smith, P. (2006). Does Correctional Program Quality Really Matter? The Impact of Adhering to the Principles of Effective Intervention. *Criminology, 5,* 575–94.

5 Lipsey, M. W., Howell, J. C., Kelly, M. K., Chapman, G., and Carver, D. (2010). *Improving the Effectiveness of Juvenile Justice Programs.* Washington, DC: Georgetown University, Center for Juvenile Justice Reform.

6 Ibid.

7 For example, see Keller, T. E. (2007). *Program Staff in Youth Mentoring Programs: Qualifications, Training, and Retention.* Research in Action Series. Alexandria, VA: MENTOR/National Mentoring Partnership.

8 Ibid.

9 Lowenkamp, C. T., Latessa, E. J., and Hoslinger, A. M. (2006). What Have We Learned from 13,676 Offenders and 97 Correctional Programs? *Crime & Delinquency, 52,* 77–93.

10 Rubak, S., Sandbaek, A., Lauritzen, T., and Christensen, B. (2005). Motivational Interviewing: A Systematic Review and Meta-Analysis. *British Journal of General Practice, 55,* 305–12.

11 Lipsey et al., *Improving the Effectiveness of Juvenile Justice Programs.*

12 Lipsey, M. W. (2009). The Primary Factors that Characterize Effective Interventions with Juvenile Offenders: A Meta-Analytic Overview. *Victims & Offenders, 4,* 124–47.

13 Evans-Chase, M., and Zhou, H. (2014). A Systematic Review of the Juvenile Justice Intervention Literature; What It Can (and Cannot) Tell Us about What Works with Delinquent Youth. *Crime & Delinquency, 60,* 451–70.

14 Turrini, A., Cristofoli, D., Frosini, F., and Nasi, G. (2010). Networking Literature about Determinants of Network Effectiveness. *Public Administration, 88,* 528–50.

15 See www.modelsforchange.net/index.html.

16 See www.americanprogress.org/issues/economy/news/2012/11/05/43834/new-york-city-and-massachusetts-to-launch-the-first-social-impact-bond-programs-in-the-united-states/.

17 See, for example, the Campbell Collaboration Systematic Review Guidelines, www.campbellcollaboration.org/artman2/uploads/1/C2_Reviews_policy__guidelines_draft_5-1-13.pdf.

18 Lipsey et al., *Improving the Effectiveness of Juvenile Justice Programs.*

19 Taken from www.blueprintsprograms.com/factSheet.php?pid=ac3478d69a3c81fa62e60f5c3696165a4e5e6ac4.

20 Klietz, S. J., Borduin, C. M., and Schaeffer, C. M. (2010). Cost-Benefit Analysis of Multisystemic Therapy with Serious and Violent Juvenile Offenders. *Journal of Family Psychology, 24,* 657–66.

21 Welsh, B. C., Braga, A. A., and Sullivan, C. J. (2014). Serious Youth Violence and Innovative Prevention: On the Emerging Link between Public Health and Criminology. *Justice Quarterly, 31,* 500–23.

22 Morenoff, J. D., Sampson, R. J., and Raudenbush, S. W. (2001). Neighborhood Inequality, Collective Efficacy, and the Spatial Dynamics of Urban Violence. *Criminology, 39,* 517–39.

23 Gebo, E., Boyes-Watson, C., and Pinto-Wilson, S. (2010). Reconceptualizing Organizational Change in the Comprehensive Gang Model. *Journal of Criminal Justice, 38,* 166–73.

24 Office of Juvenile Justice and Delinquency Prevention Model Programs Guide. Available at www.ojjdp.gov/mpg/; Gebo, E., Bond, B. J., and Campos, K. (2015). The Office of Juvenile Justice and Delinquency Prevention Model: The Comprehensive Gang Model. In S. H. Decker and D. C. Pyrooz (eds.)., *The Handbook of Gangs,* 392–405. New York: Wiley.

25 Petrosino, A., Turpin-Petrosino, C., Hollis-Peel, M. E., and Lavenberg, J. (2013). *Scared Straight and Other Juvenile Awareness Programs for Preventing Juvenile Delinquency: A Systematic Review.* Campbell Systematic Reviews, 5. Available at file:///C:/Users/CAS/Downloads/Petrosino_Scared_Straight_Update.pdf.

26 Dodge, K. (2006). Professionalizing the Practice of Public Policy in Prevention of Violence. *Journal of Abnormal Child Psychology, 34,* 475–79.

27 Petrosino, A., Turpin-Petrosino, C., and Guckenburg, S. (2010). *Formal System Processing of Juveniles: Effects on Delinquency.* Campbell Systematic Reviews. Available at www.campbellcollaboration.org/library/formal-system-processing-of-juveniles-effects-on-delinquency.html.

28 Steiner, B., and Wright, E. (2006). Assessing the Relative Effects of State Direct File Waiver on Violent Juvenile Crime: Deterrence or Irrelevance? *Journal of Criminal Law & Criminology, 96,* 1451–77.

29 Moon, M., Sundt, J., Cullen, F. T., and Wright, J. P. (2000). Is Child Saving Dead? Public Support for Juvenile Rehabilitation. *Crime & Delinquency, 46,* 38–60.

30 American Psychological Association, Zero Tolerance Task Force. (2006). Are Zero Tolerance Policies Effective in the Schools? *American Psychologist Association, 63,* 852–62.

31 Kozol, J. (2005). *The Shame of the Nation.* New York: Random House.

32 Catalano, R. F., Berglund, M. L., Ryan, J. A., Lonczak, H. S., and Hawkins, J. D. (2004). Research Findings on Evaluations of Positive Youth Development Programs. *Annals, AAPSS, 591,* 98–124.

[33] Hawkins, J. D., Catalano, R. F., Morrison, D. M., O'Donnell, J., Abbott, R. D., and Day, L. E. (1992). The Seattle Social Development Project. Effects of the First Four Years on Protective Factors and Problem Behaviors. In J. McCord and R. E. Tremblay (eds.), *Preventing Antisocial Behavior: Interventions from Birth through Adolescence,* 139–61. New York: Guilford.

[34] Adapted from Communities That Care Survey, Louisiana, http://icare.ebrschools.org/eduWEB2/1000011/docs/risk_and_protective_factors.pdf.

[35] Hawkins et al., The Seattle Social Development Project. Effects of the First Four Years on Protective Factors and Problem Behaviors, 139–61.

[36] Lerner, R. M. (2005). *Promoting Positive Youth Development: Theoretical and Empirical Bases.* Prepared for the Workshop on the Science of Adolescent Health and Development. Washington, DC: National Research Council.

[37] Catalano, R. F., Berglund, M. L., Ryan, J. A., Lonczak, H. S., and Hawkins, J. D. (2002). Positive Youth Development in the United States: Research Findings on Positive Youth Development Programs. *Prevention & Treatment, 5,* Article 15.

[38] Sampson, R. J., Winship, C., and Knight, C. (2013). Translating Causal Claims. *Criminology & Public Policy, 12,* 587–616.

[39] Federal Interagency Forum on Child and Family Statistics. (2015). *America's Children: Key National Indicators of Well-Being, 2015.* Washington, DC: US Government Printing Office.

GLOSSARY

A

adjudicated delinquent Label for youth on a petition that has been found true.

adolescent-limited offenders Individuals who engage in delinquent activity during peak crime-prone years and desist in adulthood.

adversarial system System of justice where two parties argue their sides in front of an impartial judge who makes a decision on which side wins the case.

adverse childhood experiences (ACEs) A specific set of risk factors that make individuals vulnerable to poor well-being.

aftercare Community correctional intervention after incarceration; also called juvenile parole.

age segregation Separation of individuals based on age.

amenability to treatment Ability of offender to respond to actions taken to improve his/her behavior.

androcentric bias Male-centered view of society.

anomie A state of normlessness where people experience confusion, anxiety, conflict, and alienation.

arraignment Court stage where the youth must respond to a delinquency petition.

arrest Taking someone into custody by legal authority.

B

bail The release of accused juvenile prior to the next court date in exchange for money, or other assurance, of court appearance.

blended sentencing Juvenile and adult court jurisdiction over a case at disposition.

boot camp Short-term correctional placement in military-like setting typically with education and treatment components; also called shock intervention / shock incarceration.

broken windows theory Proposition that reducing all forms of disorder in a neighborhood, including fixing broken windows and removing abandoned cars, will reduce crime.

bullying Abuse that is physical, verbal, and/or emotional that is repeated and causes someone physical or psychological discomfort.

bystanders Those present at an event who do not take part in it.

C

cafeteria-style offending Engaging in a variety of delinquent or criminal offenses.

case management Planning, supervising, and supporting clients to meet individual and community safety needs.

child savers Privileged individuals who sought to protect children from the ills of society, often by removing lower-class and immigrant youth from their environments.

chivalry hypothesis Belief that girls are in need of protection influencing the way agents of the justice system handle girls' cases.

chronic offenders Individuals who have committed five or more offenses.

classical juvenile justice paradigm Initial period of juvenile justice that removed youthful offenders from community settings to treat them in residential facilities.

code of the street Thesis that under conditions of concentrated disadvantage, inner-city neighborhoods produce a violent subculture.

cognitive behavioral training (CBT) A best practice technique that assists youth in understanding the connection between thinking and actions.

collective efficacy The capacity of the community to work together on a shared set of tasks.

community policing Police partner with the community to reduce crime and problems within the community.

comprehensive community initiatives (CCIs) Community-level initiatives that address large-scale social problems from multiple angles.

Comprehensive Gang Model (CGM) A multi-stakeholder approach to addressing gangs utilizing coordinated strategies.

concentrated disadvantage Areas that have a combination of heterogeneous population, high population mobility, and high poverty.

conditions of probation Stipulations of behavior placed on probationers by the court.

contraband Any item that is illegal to be possessed or sold.

co-offending Youth who commit crimes in concert with other youth.

courtroom workgroup Court actors who work together to develop a routine to manage their caseloads.

crackdowns Sudden increases in police presence and sanctions for specific offenses or in specific areas.

criminal liability The age at which a person is held responsible for illegal acts or omissions in adult court.

crystallized gangs Local gangs with more structure, organization, and involvement in criminal activity than emergent gangs.

cultural competence Incorporating cultural heritage and diversity within the curriculum and school environment to create welcoming school communities for students of all backgrounds.

cumulative disadvantage Indirect factors of race, ethnicity, and class are compounded throughout the juvenile justice process, resulting in more-disproportionate involvement in the system at each stage.

cyberbullying Electronic media posting of derogatory remarks and pictures, or hurtful texts, instant, or e-mail messages.

cycle of reform Pendulum of rehabilitation and punishment for juvenile offenders that swings back and forth across juvenile justice eras.

D

dark figure of crime The number of unreported crimes.

day reporting center (DRC) Facility that houses daily supervision and programming for offenders, but does not include overnight accommodations.

decriminalization Removing behaviors from the juvenile (or adult criminal) justice legal code.

deinstitutionalization Removing individuals from residential or locked facilities.

delinquency Illegal acts committed by legal minors.

delinquent offense An act committed by a juvenile that is considered a crime.

demeanor Attitude, manner, and body language of youth during interaction with police which influences police discretionary decision-making.

dependent youth Youth who are orphaned, who are deemed to be inadequately cared for, or who are harmed by parents are placed under state control.

desistance Stopping delinquent/criminal activity.

detention Keeping someone temporarily in official custody.

developmental competence Ability to navigate social, emotional, cognitive, and behavioral tasks at different developmental stages of maturity.

developmental institutions Organizations and systems beyond the family that nurture, care for, and socialize youth.

deviance Any conduct which is contrary to the norms of a group.

differential association Criminal behavior is learned through interaction with deviant peers.

differential involvement hypothesis Explanation for DMC is that youth of color are disproportionately involved in serious crime.

differential opportunity structure Subculture that offers alternative means to earn status, respect, and other social rewards.

differential socialization Pattern of treatment that is different for girls and boys.

differential treatment hypothesis Explanation for DMC is that youth of color are given more punitive treatment in all stages of juvenile justice processing.

disposition Juvenile court sentence.

disproportionate minority contact (DMC) Overrepresentation of black and brown youth in the justice system compared with the general population of black and brown youth in society.

diversion Keeping individuals out of the juvenile justice system, or juvenile placements through alternative programs.

divest Removing interest in specific behaviors (such as status offenses) from the purview of the juvenile justice system.

dosage The intensity, frequency, and duration of an intervention.

double jeopardy Being tried twice for the same crime.

double standard Unequal application of a rule or principle to different peoples/groups.

dual-system youth Youth who are, or who have been, involved in both delinquency and the child welfare systems; also called multi-system youth.

due process rights Protect individual's rights to fair and constitutional judicial proceedings.

E

ecological context An individual's behavior is affected by relationships, the community, and the society; also called socio-ecological context.

electronic monitoring Technological device connected to offender that records offender's location at various times throughout the day and night.

emergent gangs Most common gang structure, with informal leadership and organization.

emerging adulthood Youth in their early to mid-twenties who have not fully taken on adult responsibilities independent of relatives, especially parents.

evidence-based Practices, programs, and policies that have been shown through scientific evaluation to work to prevent and intervene with juvenile justice system youth.

extralegal factors Factors other than present offense and offense history that play a role in decision-making.

F

fees Court-imposed payment for criminal justice–related services.

feminist pathway theory Exploitation of females leads to delinquency that is reacted to paternalistically by the juvenile justice system.

fidelity The degree to which a program is implemented according to protocol.

fines Court-imposed monetary sanction on the offender.

folkways Group expectations about everyday behaviors of its members.

formalized gangs Highly structured national and sometimes transnational gang organizations that function as criminal enterprises.

foster care Out-of-home placement for youth in a family setting.

G

gender-specific programming Interventions which are tailored to meet the specific developmental needs of girls.

general strain theory Stress due to the inability to achieve positive goals, the removal of positive stimuli, or the introduction of negative stimuli that can lead to delinquency.

get tough paradigm Punitive policies that increased the penalties for juvenile offenses and facilitated the transfer and waiver of juvenile cases into adult courts.

graduated sanctions Increased system of penalties for continued delinquent or criminal behavior.

group home Congregate living out-of-home placement supervised by a house parent.

H

halfway house Temporary community placement for youth transitioning from training school to home.

hate crime A crime motivated by prejudice that involves violence.

hegemonic masculinity Practices that promote the domination of men over women.

horizontal violence Violence directed toward one's peers.

hot-spot policing Assignment of police resources to areas where crime is concentrated.

house arrest Court mandate to remain in house with few exceptions.

hybrid gang A gang that may span ethnic and geographic boundaries with no gang loyalty.

I

indeterminate placement Juvenile facility stay for an unspecified amount of time determined by the judge, or until legal age of majority.

index crimes More-serious crimes, including murder, non-negligent manslaughter, forcible rape, robbery, aggravated assault, burglary, larceny, arson, and motor vehicle theft.

indigent person Person deemed poor and eligible for a court-appointed attorney.

informal adjustment Discretionary decision by police to not refer youth to further juvenile justice processing.

institutionalized racism Organizational practices and policies that systematically discriminate against certain races.

intake screening Review of juvenile case to determine next steps in court process.

intensive supervision probation (ISP) Probation with a high degree of surveillance.

intermediate sanctions Penalties between probation and incarceration.

intersectionality The study of how social statuses associated with gender, class, race, and ethnicity influence the opportunities, privileges, choices, and discrimination within the society.

intervention Stop any further delinquency after it has occurred.

J

judicial waiver Judge has discretion to transfer a juvenile case to adult court.

juvenile drug courts Problem-solving courts to redress substance abuse problems through in-depth knowledge of addiction.

Juvenile Justice and Delinquency Prevention Act (JJDPA) Act that decriminalized status offenses, promoted diversion of minor offenders, and deinstitutionalized most juvenile offenders.

juvenile rights paradigm Era that provided increased procedural safeguards to juveniles involved in the juvenile justice system.

L

labeling theory Delinquency is in part the product of the activities of institutions and individuals that respond to youth behavior.

latent trait theories Define some conditions present at birth or occurring early in life as accounting for the onset of criminality.

law Written norm enforced through state authority.

life course–persistent offenders Individuals who begin offending in adolescence and continue into adulthood.

life course perspective View of individuals that takes into account experiences over time that influence individual development and action.

life course theories The factors influencing behaviors change over time, as does propensity to commit.

M

matching Ensuring the right youth is placed in the right program for the purposes of optimal delinquency prevention.

medical model Addressing troublesome youth as sick and in need of medical treatment to be cured.

Miranda rights Legal safeguards of the right to remain silent and the right to an attorney that must be provided by police to a suspect before questioning.

moral crusades Actions taken by those who seek to impose a particular view of morality on others within a group.

moral entrepreneurs Individuals who attempt to change behavior by mobilizing the group against the behavior or for making sure that a law is written against a behavior.

moral panic Imposition of fear about the threat of a behavior to the well-being of the group.

mores Norms of great importance to the group.

N

National Crime Victimization Survey (NCVS) Official survey that asks people about their own criminal victimization.

National Incident-Based Reporting System (NIBRS) Official reporting that provides arrest details.

net-widening Increasing the number of persons involved in the justice process.

norms Societal or group expectations of how people must, should, may, or may not, behave under specific circumstances.

O

Once an Adult, Always an Adult statute Law stipulating that once a youth has been processed in adult court, all subsequent court cases will be processed in adult court.

overpolicing-underpolicing paradox Policing practices that are heavy-handed for minor transgressions (overpolicing) and lack of prompt response to resident calls for service (underpolicing).

P

paradigm A cognitive framework containing basic assumptions, ways of thinking, and methodologies that are commonly accepted by members of a discipline or group.

parens patriae Doctrine that allows the juvenile court to act as a father figure to all children.

patriarchy Social or family system in which the male is the head and governs all within the society or the household.

peer group A group of individuals who spend time together.

placed out Youth sent to relatives to serve as household servants or hired out as apprentices for a fee.

plea bargain An agreement offered by the prosecutor to the defendant that allows the youth to plead "true" to lesser offenses in exchange for a lighter penalty.

policies Management of actions/plan to address delinquency.

positive youth development (PYD) Focuses on youth strengths and abilities, rather than deficits, that lead to healthy development.

positive youth development and community / restorative justice paradigm Emerging era focusing on using prosocial, community-based treatment for justice-involved youth.

positivism Broad philosophical approach that relies on science to understand the social world.

predisposition investigation (PDI) Report detailing a youth's social history by a probation officer that makes sentencing recommendations to the judge.

primary deviance Youth commit acts of delinquency but are not treated or categorized as "delinquents" by others.

primary prevention Stop delinquency from occurring in the general population of youth.

probable cause More likely than not that a law has been violated.

probation officer Person who investigates, reports on, and supervises youth while under court control.

problem-solving courts Courts that focus solely on a specific problem; also known as specialty courts.

procedural justice The perception of fairness and respect in the process, not the outcome, of a situation.

programs Courses of action to address delinquency.

Project Safe Neighborhoods (PSN) A comprehensive community-based approach that prosecutes gun offenders while providing prevention programming for youth in the neighborhoods most exposed to gun crime.

promotive factor Something that increases the chances of positive well-being.

prosecutor State's attorney; often a district attorney.

prosecutorial waiver Prosecutor has discretion to transfer a juvenile case to adult court; also known as direct file.

protective factor Something that buffers against the chances of a negative well-being outcome.

public defender Attorney provided to the defendant free of charge.

Pulling Levers Approach that provides both severe penalties and prosocial opportunities to offenders.

R

radical nonintervention Policy that ignores minor youthful misbehavior and allows youth to age out of delinquency.

randomized control trial (RCT) Research design that randomly assigns participants to treatment and control groups; considered the "gold standard" to understand effects of programs; also called true or classical experiment.

rational choice theory (RCT) Individuals will engage in crime if the benefits outweigh the costs.

reasonable suspicion Specific facts/circumstances that allow police to stop and frisk that does not rise to the level of probable cause.

recidivate To reoffend.

reentry An offender's return to society after being institutionalized.

referees Individuals appointed by the court to hold hearings and make recommendations to the judge on juvenile justice matters.

resiliency The ability to recover from / withstand adversity.

restitution Refers to the offender "giving back" to the community and/or the victim.

restorative circles A restorative practice to establish positive norms and develop a sense of belonging and connection, resolve conflict, and provide alternatives to exclusionary discipline.

restorative justice Addressing the needs of the offender, victim, and community when an offense has been committed.

reverse waiver Mechanism to move a juvenile case from adult court to juvenile court.

review hearing Post-disposition review of a case.

revocation hearing A court hearing occurring when court orders have not been obeyed.

risk factor Something that increases the chances of a negative well-being outcome.

risk-need-responsivity instruments Structured decision-making tools that are used when making supervision and treatment decisions for offenders.

risk principle Risk of recidivism taken into account in determining appropriate level of supervision and programming.

rough justice Unfair treatment of a suspect by police to teach a "lesson."

S

Safe Harbor laws Laws that protect and assist children that have been exploited for labor or sex.

school climate The quality and character of school life based on perceptions of students, school personnel, and parents.

school connectedness Belief by students that adults at school care about students' learning and well-being.

school resource officers (SROs) Police officers who are assigned to work in schools.

school-to-prison pipeline Concept wherein youth are pushed out of school and into the justice system through harsh school policies.

search incident to arrest Physical examination of a suspect and the area under a suspect's control prior to an arrest.

search warrant Search order issued by the court allowing police to search particular areas for specific property and to bring that property to court.

secondary deviance Youth are labeled delinquents and develop an identity around that label.

secondary prevention Stop delinquency from occurring among those at a heightened risk for delinquency.

self-report surveys Surveys that allow individuals to reveal information about their own law violations without legal repercussions.

serious, violent, chronic (SVC) offenders Term used to describe the small por-

tion of youth who repetitively engage in crime, and serious and violent crime in particular.

shelter care Staff-secure, short-term community facility housing youth awaiting court or placement.

social construction Created ideas about individuals and ideas based on a shared sense of reality.

social control theory Those who maintain strong bonds to conventional society are less likely to be delinquent.

social disorganization theory Delinquency is the result of community instability and the inability of social institutions to transmit proper values to youth.

social impact bonds (SIB) Contract between an agency and the government to pay for services only if the program is successful.

socialization The process by which we are taught to conform to the code of our particular group.

social learning theory Behavior is learned from those with whom we are in contact most frequently.

stake in conformity The result of investment and commitment to conventional activities that buffers against delinquent activity.

stationhouse adjustment Discretionary decision by police to detain a youth at the police station and call a parent or guardian without further juvenile processing.

status offenses Actions that are deemed illegal only for youth.

statutory exclusion State law exempting certain crime(s) and/or juvenile(s) from juvenile court; also known as legislative exclusion.

streetworkers Community workers who engage gang members to help them find a way out of the gang lifestyle and who mediate gang disputes.

subcultural theory A shared set of alternative values and norms distinct from the dominant culture developed by a subgroup.

survival sex Selling sex in exchange for money, food, or shelter.

T

technical violation Noncriminal offense for which probation can be revoked.

techniques of neutralization Rationalization of antisocial behavior that is contrary to individual values.

Terry stop A brief detention of a person by police on reasonable suspicion of involvement in criminal activity allowing for stop, frisk, and questioning.

tertiary prevention Stop further recidivism after delinquency has occurred.

training school Incarceration for sentenced youth; also called reform school.

trauma-informed care Addressing trauma within the context of treatment.

two-track system Differential treatment by class wherein those with financial means avoid the system, while those without do not.

U

Uniform Crime Reporting (UCR) Arrest report compiled yearly by the Federal Bureau of Investigation from information provided by US law enforcement agencies across the country; supplanted by NIBRS.

W

writ of habeas corpus A legal claim to the court arguing that a person is imprisoned or detained illegally.

Y

youth courts Alternative to juvenile court, where trained youth volunteers hear their peers' cases as judges, attorneys, and jury members; also called teen courts.

Youth Level of Service / Case Management Inventory (YLS/CMI) A structured decision-making tool that assesses risk, and identifies needs and responsiveness to treatment.

Z

zero-tolerance policies Strict enforcement of severe consequences, such as suspension and expulsion, for prohibited behavior regardless of circumstances.

zero-tolerance policing Policing strategy that involves a crackdown on all offenses, including public order disturbances, in an effort to show that even petty crime will not be tolerated.

PHOTO CREDITS

INDEX

Page references for figures are italicized.

ERIKA GEBO is a professor of sociology at Suffolk University in Boston, Massachusetts. Her teaching and research interests are in the areas of youth crime and justice and violence prevention. She often collaborates directly with communities, assisting in youth and gang violence reduction efforts. She has published more than twenty essays related to youth, crime, and justice. Her 2012 co-edited book, available from Lexington Books, is titled *Looking Beyond Suppression: Community Strategies to Reduce Gang Violence*. When she isn't in the classroom or working in the community, she enjoys spending time outside with her family and their occasionally well-behaved dog.

CAROLYN BOYES-WATSON is a professor of sociology at Suffolk University, where she serves as founding director of the Center for Restorative Justice (CRJ).

She is the primary author of the textbook *Crime and Justice: Learning through Cases* (with Susan Krumholtz), and co-editor of the Learning through Cases series with Susan Krumholtz. She has published extensively in the field of restorative justice, including two manuals, *Circle Forward: Building a Restorative School* and *Heart of Hope*, with Kay Pranis. In the sociology department Dr. Boyes-Watson has taught a range of undergraduate and graduate courses about the criminal, juvenile justice, and restorative justice systems, and now directs the work of the CRJ in developing the capacity of schools, juvenile justice, and criminal justice organizations to effectively implement restorative justice practices. She received her PhD in sociology from Harvard University, and lives in Cambridge with her husband and two adult children, eagerly awaiting the arrival of the next generation.